NO constructive enterprise of the postwar era has enlisted greater worldwide interest and participation than the Marshall Plan operation. Yet there are many views as to its significance. Some look upon it as a vast giveaway program. Others see in it the finest international achievement of our time.

What are the facts?

What, exactly, was the Marshall Plan? How did it originate? Was it primarily an American or a cooperative venture? What were its aims? Who were the men most responsible for its conduct? How did it function? What were the sources of its vitality? What did it really accomplish? Or fail to accomplish? Against a background of Communist conspiracy, did it or did it not recover the initiative for the free world in the contest for men's loyalties? Did its successes and shortcomings provide new insights into continuing problems in the search for international prosperity, fair play, security, and peace?

The Governmental Affairs Institute—as a professional, nonpartisan research organization deeply concerned with the answers to these questions—invited Harry Bayard Price to undertake a complete examination of the Marshall Plan operation. Mr. Price had had experience in the Far East and in Europe with UNRRA and ECA and, in addition, had academic qualifications that particularly

(continued on back flap)

fitted him for such a task of research and evaluation.

Mr. Price began by conferring with hundreds of actual participants and observers of the Marshall Plan. Those interviewed, in thirteen European countries as well as in the United States, included cabinet ministers, civil servants, economists, political scientists, bankers, industrialists, leaders in trade unions and farmers' organizations, newspaper editors, and writers. Many direct quotations from the interviews appear in this work. The author was given, too, full access to pertinent documents in Washington and overseas.

This independent, comprehensive record and evaluation of the Marshall Plan experience—the first of its kind—is the result.

Part I sketches briefly the twentieth-century crisis from which the Marshall Plan emerged. Part II covers, in narrative form, the high lights of the European Recovery Program. Part III deals with associated programs in Asia. The insights and lessons to be gained from these unprecedented operations are probed in Part IV, which comprises half of the study.

This forthright, keenly reasoned volume is addressed not only to policy-makers and scholars, but also to responsible citizens everywhere who are genuinely concerned with the perils and dilemmas of international life today.

The Marshall Plan and Its Meaning

The Marshall Plan
and Its Meaning

HARRY BAYARD PRICE

PUBLISHED UNDER THE AUSPICES OF THE

Governmental Affairs Institute

WASHINGTON, D.C.

Cornell University Press

ITHACA, NEW YORK

PRINTED IN THE UNITED STATES OF AMERICA BY THE

VAIL-BALLOU PRESS, INC., BINGHAMTON, NEW YORK

23556

Foreword

THIS volume has been prepared under unusual circumstances. In January 1951 the President of the United States directed all federal agencies engaged in emergency activities to prepare histories of their programs. Most organizations responded by detailing members of their own staffs to prepare these historical analyses. Recognizing that the Marshall Plan had attracted wide public interest, the Economic Cooperation Administration decided upon a different approach. It invited a private research organization, the Governmental Affairs Institute, to prepare an independent, objective history and evaluation of the ECA and the Marshall Plan.

Subsequent arrangements with the ECA's successor organizations, the Mutual Security Agency and the Foreign Operations Administration, have resulted in the preparation of this volume. Although sponsored and financed by these federal agencies during both Democratic and Republican administrations, this Institute study has been conducted with complete professional freedom. We have had access to all pertinent records, and no censoring has been exercised over the critical conclusions set forth in this study.

Two primary considerations have determined the character of this volume. In the first place, it was intended as not only a history, but also an analysis of practical lessons in the administration of foreign aid programs. Were it no more than a history, considerable additional data would have been included. On the other hand, since it is an evaluation, emphases have necessarily been placed on subjects which would have been more briefly treated had this been no more than a chronology of development.

A second consideration has been equally significant. From the beginning it has been intended that this should be a volume addressed to the informed layman who concerns himself with foreign policy questions. Its style, its ordering of data, and much of its basic structure have been calculated to provide information for serious students of international affairs. We have not been primarily concerned that this should become a research undertaking designed in style and format to satisfy the needs of the more academic readers, though much of the material has been collected here for the first time and will therefore assist future scholarship in this field.

Several considerations have determined the manner in which our materials have been collected and analyzed. It is too early to attempt a comprehensive historical appraisal of the role of the Marshall Plan and of its administering sponsor, the Economic Cooperation Administration. This must remain for scholars who come to this subject with the benefit of the passage of time and the accumulation of records not today available. We have rather sought to utilize such data as are currently accessible and the informed opinions of those who in one way or another were active participants in the program. These we have supplemented with the views of others who had the opportunity to observe closely the impact of the Marshall Plan.

Like so many aspects of American foreign policy, the Marshall Plan has been viewed from quite different vantage points, and often contrary conclusions have been reached. We have, therefore, systematically attempted to profit from the views of those who were outside the organization as well as those who were within it. We have been assisted by Republicans and Democrats alike and have consulted as many in one administration as in another. Furthermore, we have been to some pains to incorporate the informed judgment of European observers and officials to quite the same extent as we have incorporated American views.

As in the case of all publications of the Governmental Affairs Institute, this manuscript, while prepared by Mr. Price, has been carefully reviewed by a committee of the Institute's Board of Directors. As submitted, it is an Institute project, representing the best judgment of this organization, as well as of its author. It does not purport to represent the views of the United States government or any of its branches.

EDWARD H. LITCHFIELD, *President*
Governmental Affairs Institute

Washington, D.C.
April 1955

Preface

WHEN the writer, in a rash moment, accepted the responsibility of developing within two years a condensed history and critical evaluation of the Marshall Plan and associated programs in Asia, as actually administered, he was at least dimly conscious of the formidable problems that such a task would entail.

Thoughtful friends did little to relieve his discomfiture. One, undoubtedly visualizing hundreds—perhaps thousands—of bulging file cabinets, recalled in innocent tones a comment by George Bernard Shaw that a historian relying upon one document was safe, but if he needed to consult two he was in difficulty, and if three were available his position was hopeless. Another, who had himself been immersed in the daily hurly-burly of the European Recovery Program, recited with evident relish Rudyard Kipling's quip:

> Ah, What avails the classic bent,
> And what the cultured word
> Against the undoctored incident
> That actually occurred? [1]

A third remembered a consoling remark by Lytton Strachey that "ignorance is the first requisite of the historian—ignorance which sim-

[1] From "The Benefactors," from *The Years Between*, by Rudyard Kipling. Copyright 1912 by Rudyard Kipling, reprinted by permission of Mrs. George Bambridge, Messrs. Methuen & Co. Ltd., Doubleday & Company, Inc., and the Macmillan Company of Canada.

plifies and clarifies, which selects and omits with a placid perfection unattainable in the highest art." Justice would have been served—and the reader as well—if the work of composing this book had been transferred at once to these erudite counselors!

To present in compressed and readable form an authentic record of the Marshall Plan, with its many facets and ramifications, is difficult enough. Even more so, however, is the attempt to appraise its effectiveness and significance. How does one evaluate, so short a time after the event, an undertaking of such dimensions and impact? During a particularly intensive phase of the enterprise—the "heat" was always on, but at some times more than others—an American participant was heard to say: "We need about five years in which to reach intelligently the decisions that will have to be made in the next three weeks." If five years were needed to reach one set of decisions, perhaps fifty would be an appropriate period in which to develop adequate judgments on the import of the Marshall Plan.

In any case, the present volume lays no claim to either comprehensiveness or finality. If it conveys a reasonably clear and dependable account of major developments within its purview and if the tentative conclusions which it reaches are on the whole sensible and thought-provoking, it will have accomplished a part of its purpose. If, in addition, it helps to stimulate further thinking on the unsolved problems which were faced in the course of the Marshall Plan operation and further inquiry into the insights and lessons to be derived from that unique experience, it will justify the generous cooperation that has been given during the course of its preparation.

A word should be said about the organization of this work. Part I consists of an introductory chapter which sketches, in broad-brush fashion, some of the salient features of the historic setting from which the Marshall Plan emerged. Part II contains a narrative account of the actual development and effects of the European Recovery Program, from its inception until the time when it was superseded by the Mutual Security Program. Operations in Asia are treated separately, in Part III, since they differed quite widely from those in Europe in their background, aims, and conduct. These three parts contain the bulk of the factual information required to make comprehensible the evaluation attempted in Part IV, which comprises roughly half of the volume. In this final portion of the work attention is directed principally to the conduct of operations in Europe; Chapter 18, however, deals with the question of assistance to economically retarded areas in Asia and elsewhere.

Fortunately, many facts about the Marshall Plan are widely known, and extensive information on it is readily available in both official reports and the writings of independent scholars. There is no need to repeat at length here what has been adequately covered elsewhere. Parts II and III are, therefore, highly condensed and addressed more to the general reader than to the specialist.

Throughout Part IV an effort is made not only to assess the immediate effectiveness of the operation but also to see its bearing upon a range of continuing problems. The precise conditions which prevailed from 1948 to 1952 cannot be expected to recur, of course, even in proximate form, and the perplexities of those years are assuming new shapes with the passage of time. Yet there was a core of basic problems which persist and will persist for many years to come. It is in relation to these problems, or problem areas, that the Marshall Plan experience has continuing relevance, and it is around them that the chapters of Part IV are built, with an attempt to glean from successes and failures of the 1948–1952 period insights and lessons that will be useful in the future.

It is not easy to derive from recent and current experiences valid guidelines for future conduct. But the complexity of the issues confronting the free world and the immense weight of the United States in international affairs today render it imperative that continuing efforts be made to do so. Events are forcing the pace. Against the risk that we may not learn well enough must be set the greater danger that we may not learn fast enough. In any event, it would be hard to find in recent history a more instructive chapter than the Marshall Plan experience. This modest analysis of it needs soon to be followed by others of more ample scope and depth.

In considering the question of evaluation, one fact seemed obvious: it would be folly not to consult, as fully as time allowed and while memories were still fresh, knowledgeable persons who had either participated in, or observed closely, the Marshall Plan in action. Roughly three months, therefore, were spent in an intensive round of interviews —more than three hundred in all, nearly two hundred of them being in thirteen of the European countries which took part in the joint recovery program. But for limits in time and opportunity many more persons would have been consulted. A special effort was made to elicit candid reactions from nationals of each of the countries visited.

The majority of these talks were with government personnel at the "working level" who had been actively affiliated with the European Recovery Program. But the individuals, here and abroad, who also gave freely of their time for interviews included high officials, economists, political scientists, bankers, industrialists, leaders of trade unions and farmers' organizations, newspaper editors, and writers. Those consulted were invariably well informed and many were highly articulate. My indebtedness to them and to all who facilitated the necessary contacts is incalculable. The reader will find, sprinkled throughout this work, frequent references to the interviews and many direct quotations from them. The conversations have clarified and made more vivid many aspects of the operation. They have also made possible something approaching a synthesis of opinion on a number of questions.

In addition, access has been provided to documentary materials of all types in the files of the Economic Cooperation Administration and its successor organizations—the Mutual Security Agency and the Foreign Operations Administration. The amount of these materials at home and overseas is staggering, and it has been possible in the time available to tap only a small part of this abundant resource. The assistance and advice furnished by persons associated with the agencies mentioned above and others in Europe have been more than liberal. Some have read parts or all of the preliminary manuscript of this work and offered many discriminating suggestions and criticisms.

The wise, independent counsel and guidance provided by members of the Governmental Affairs Institute's Board of Directors is deeply appreciated. Those who have undertaken work similar to this will understand the wholeheartedness with which acknowledgment is also made of the loyal assistance of a small staff in the tasks of research, editing, and typing. Thanks are extended to the Foreign Operations Administration for the pictures in this volume and for aid in preparing the charts.

Numerous individuals who took part in the program are mentioned by name, many for illustrative purposes. But it has not been found feasible to attempt to present a full and balanced roster of all who made significant contributions to the Marshall Plan enterprise. Reprehensible omissions in this respect must be laid to limitations in the author's knowledge and in the scope of this work.

While the writer must assume major responsibility for the critical views and conclusions expressed in this book, whatever merit they may contain is attributable in large measure to the richness of the vein that he has been privileged to work and to the unstinting quality of the help that has been given him.

HARRY B. PRICE

Washington, D.C.
January 1955

Contents

Part III. Associated Programs in Asia

Part IV. Evaluation

List of Illustrations

PART I

Introduction

CHAPTER 1

Perspectives

IT MAY surprise the present rulers of the Soviet world—and others—that the train of thought given historic expression in Secretary of State George C. Marshall's Harvard University speech on June 5, 1947, and embodied in the Marshall Plan, was generated nearly two months earlier in the most unlikely of places, the Kremlin.

Impasse and an Idea

In March 1947 the Big Four foreign ministers met in Moscow for another of the series of postwar conferences hopefully designed to relieve world tensions. The outlook was not promising. Previous meetings had not resolved any of the basic issues. In the Four-Power Control Council in Berlin, Western representatives had been continually rebuffed by Russian negotiators and the atmosphere had become increasingly bitter.

Two weeks before the Moscow sessions opened, the British had announced that they could no longer underwrite the security of the eastern Mediterranean region. The United States had promptly stepped in. Aid to Greece and Turkey was the first move toward putting into effect the Truman Doctrine for the containment of aggressive communism.

These developments did not prevent representatives of the Western

powers from going to the Moscow conference with substantial delegations, determined to find if possible an honorable *modus vivendi* with
the USSR. Advisors to Marshall, in the American delegation, were John
Foster Dulles, Benjamin V. Cohen, and Ambassador Walter Bedell
Smith. Early progress on the agenda and procedural matters raised
cautious hopes, but the talks began to bog down when they reached
substantive issues.

The conference had been in session for more than a month when
Secretary Marshall was invited to confer privately, on April 15, with
Prime Minister Joseph Stalin. Foreign Minister Vyacheslav Molotov
was present and a stormy session ensued. Marshall became convinced
that the Soviet government was stalling for time, that it was far from
being ready to cooperate in any reasonable scheme for lessening distress
and tension in Europe, and that it was in fact doing all it could to make
the existing situation worse.[1] He also recognized that time was running
against the forces of reconstruction in western Europe and that if anything effective was going to be done there it would have to be started—
and started soon—by the Western powers. The forward thinking and
recommendations which had been developing in the Department of
State and elsewhere were soon brought into a new focus. Out of it
developed the proposal for a European recovery program.

Many Things to Many Men

Conceived in 1947 and launched in 1948, the Marshall Plan evolved
swiftly into a vast, spirited international venture. As the enterprise unfolded, it became many things to many men.

To millions impoverished by World War II it meant food, tools, a
chance to work, a source of new hope. Worried leaders in western
Europe saw in it an assurance of help on a scale that might enable them
to cope with their most urgent recovery problems. To the governments
of a number of war-torn nations outside Europe it meant assistance toward economic stability and new development.

Among the peoples who ultimately received Marshall aid, however,
fears and hopes were mingled. Some were uncertain of American intentions. Some feared that by accepting new help they might jeopardize
their freedom of action and, possibly, be drawn into another world war.
Others welcomed the prospect of American aid as a potential factor in
world politics and as an acceptance of responsibility by the nation whose
resources and strength had figured so prominently in the victory of the

[1] Interview, Washington, October 30, 1952.

Grand Alliance. Here was an assertion of leadership, an affirmative, unwarlike answer to the new totalitarian threat from the Soviet Union.

To some Europeans—a growing number as the recovery program developed—another fundamental issue was involved. Confidence in the capacity of small nations to safeguard the liberties and opportunities of their citizens had been rudely shaken by the disasters of the past thirty-five years, especially in countries which had suffered the horrors and humiliations of defeat and occupation. The Marshall Plan emphasized European initiative in developing a collective appraisal of economic problems and collective proposals for dealing with them. This suggested—vaguely at first—a joint approach which could be the harbinger of a new solidarity within western Europe.

The violence of the Kremlin's propaganda assaults showed that Moscow looked upon the Marshall Plan as an obstacle to Soviet hegemony in Europe.

In the United States early thinking about the Plan reflected a wide disparity in attitudes and interests. Among those who tended to regard all foreign aid as philanthropic, some favored liberal assistance in response to demonstrated need, while others deplored the prospect of further "handouts." Some, fortified by reports of maladministration of funds liberally appropriated after the war, were aggressively opposed to further levies for foreign assistance. A number, on the other hand, were interested in markets abroad or in the orders for industrial and agricultural products that any large aid operation would bring. Many saw Communist expansion and its threat to liberty everywhere as the overriding issue of the day. To these, the recovery program was important chiefly as a means of bolstering the economic strength of free peoples and their will and capacity to resist subversion.

In addition, a slowly growing body of persons sensed greater implications in the Marshall Plan. The scope of thinking which evolved in responsible quarters at an early stage was reflected in the Foreign Assistance Act of 1948,[2] by which the United States Congress first authorized the recovery aid program. This act and its successive amendments, while exhibiting many familiar features of previous aid legislation, contained the elements of a new departure in American foreign

[2] Public Law 472, 80th Congress, 2d Session, approved April 3, 1948. Title I of this law was called the Economic Cooperation Act of 1948 and dealt with the proposed European Recovery Program (ERP). Title IV, the China Aid Act of 1948, was expanded by subsequent legislation to cover assistance to other countries in the Far East. The law established the Economic Cooperation Administration (ECA) to administer these programs.

policy: the interest of the United States was to be linked to an unprecedented degree with economic and political concerns in other parts of the world.

For the first time in history, resources from one continent were to be channeled, deliberately and on a huge scale, into rebuilding production, trade, and stability in another. An effort was to be made to reverse a trend of decades by breaking down European economic barriers and extending healthy cooperation. In parts of Asia outside Communist control, and indirectly in European dependencies comprising three-fourths of Africa, economic advancement was to be promoted. The preamble to the act showed moreover that its framers were concerned not only with providing economic aid, but also with preserving and strengthening individual liberties and democratic institutions among the free peoples of the world.

The Marshall Plan as approved by Congress was more, then, than a reaction to an immediate crisis. It reflected more than a desire to alleviate distress, or to restore a prewar level of economic activity, or to check Communist expansion. It revealed also the beginning of a recognition that these goals could no longer be effectively pursued in isolation.

When the operation was ended, ahead of schedule, there were many opinions, informed and otherwise, about what had been achieved. Many saw only a large-scale relief task. Many, on the other hand, attached great significance to the Marshall Plan for its contribution toward an unprecedented revival of economic life in free Europe, or to the way it brought leaders and technicians of many countries together as never before in time of peace for joint work on common problems, or to its staying effect on Communist expansion, or to its demonstration that the democracies could seize the initiative and carry out a vast international undertaking cooperatively in time of peace, or to its pioneering work in underdeveloped areas.

Widespread satisfaction with the result, however conceived, was offset in some quarters by impatience that economic assistance was still needed. Complaints or criticisms were heard on many different grounds: that the recipient countries were insufficiently aware of, and grateful for, generous American aid; that certain European countries had not done all they could for themselves; that the benefits of the assistance had not in some nations reached the neediest people; that progress toward European integration was slower than it might have been;

that development in retarded areas had only scratched the surface; that the initial concept of the Marshall Plan had been too limited; that the expectation of full European recovery in four years had been unrealistic; that the United States had failed to evolve a stable foreign economic policy for the long run.

The diversity of these viewpoints makes it clear that to understand the Marshall Plan, and to gain such insight into its meaning as may be possible so soon after the event, it is necessary to look at the background from which it emerged, a background of mounting tensions, conflicts, and problems.

Setting: An Era of Crisis

In contrast with our own times, the ninety-nine years between Waterloo in 1815 and Sarajevo in 1914, though marked by constant change, appear to have been strangely stable and full of progress. From England the tide of the industrial revolution was moving eastward through Europe and westward across America, and was beginning to lap on distant shores. Western Europe, including Great Britain, was becoming the world's workshop; from about 1830 onward, economic improvement was almost unbroken. Production and commerce expanded. Savings accumulated. Private enterprise took hold. Advances in science, technology, capital formation, and economic organization gave industrial societies a vigor unmatched in history.

Britain, successor to France as the predominant world power, led in industry and trade, steadied international finances, and guarded the peace. Across the Atlantic, Americans were busy with an ever-extending frontier. Eastern Europe was climbing out of the Middle Ages. Colonial empires were being consolidated. Other areas, however populous, seemed remote and somnolent. Wars there were on every continent, but they were local and relatively few; they failed to halt the onward march of modern man or to uproot his growing belief in spontaneous and unending progress.

This belief was a dream and dreams die hard. It did not end with the flaming destruction of World War I, or with the failure afterward to build a durable League of Nations. It revived during the booming, deceptive twenties; was pushed back but not destroyed by the great depression. It lasted through the assault on Manchuria, the rise of Hitler, the attack on Ethiopia, civil war in Spain, the invasion of China, the Nazi occupation of Czechoslovakia. Even after the second and more terrible world holocaust, the awesome portent of Hiroshima, and the unmasking of Communist Russia as a vast new totalitarian threat, the dream lingered on.

Each crisis, like a storm, had first filled the horizon, then passed over and beyond—a seemingly transient phenomenon, however earth-shaking. Each was followed by the thought of returning, as quickly as possible, to a more "normal" state of affairs in which men and nations could again pursue their private interests in a world of assured security and progress. Few, it seemed, entertained the thought that the emergencies crowding upon each other during these tempestuous years were not merely separate events but interrelated manifestations of an era of crisis, and of a transition in history from which there could be no turning back.

The Communists, of course, thought they understood the trend of events. Stalin elaborated and amended the revolutionary theories of his intellectual forebears who had sought to found a "science" of human society that would enable men not only to predict but, within limits, to engineer the course of history.

The strength of Marxist-Leninist theory [he wrote] consists in the fact that it enables the Party to orient itself in a situation, to grasp the internal connection of surrounding events, to foresee the course of events and to discern not only how and when events are developing in the present but also how and when they must develop in the future.[3]

Western scholars, by and large, rejected the dogmatic premises on which Stalinist theory was built, and they found it full of errors when checked in the laboratory of contemporary history. But the Communists retained an important advantage: they possessed a long-range concept of the nature of crisis in the modern world, a concept which, though distorted, provided an expectation of recurrent upheaval and a broad frame of reference to which developing events and policies could be related. Backed by long and cool calculation, world communism, despite expedient shifts, acquired a relentless forward motion.

In contrast, the policies of the democratic powers, responsive to the will of their peoples, oscillated widely. Periods of intensive activity, if successful, tended to be followed by phases of exhilaration and of relaxation in vigilance and effort. For example, Sir Winston Churchill

[3] Historicus, "Stalin on Revolution," *Foreign Affairs,* January 1949, p. 177, citing *Voprosy Leninizma* (11th ed.; 1945), p. 598.

wrote in his memoirs of the reactions of cheering crowds in London to the final defeat of the Nazi forces in 1945:

The Hitler Peril, with its ordeals and privations, seemed to most of them to have vanished in a blaze of glory. The tremendous foe they had fought for more than five years had surrendered unconditionally. All that remained for the three victorious Powers was to make a just and durable peace, guarded by a World Instrument, to bring the soldiers home to their longing loved ones, and to enter upon a Golden Age of prosperity and progress.[4]

Yet before two years had passed, grave new problems had arisen. When asked recently to discuss his recollections of the circumstances which gave rise to the Marshall Plan, former Secretary of State Dean Acheson[5] started his reply by saying: "The whole matter begins with the misconception which everybody had regarding the nature and depth of the problem after the Second World War. No one had a picture of the completeness of the disruption that had occurred. This was true of both European and Asiatic countries. We had operated on a theory of dealing with hunger, disease, and unrest until one or two good crops could come in. But the problems were more far-reaching, and it grew upon us toward the end of 1946 that we were heading for very bad trouble."

The Twentieth-Century Crisis in Europe

How did it happen that in the thirty-three years since 1913 western Europe had changed from the world's most dynamic and prosperous region into an area of distress and confusion? Although so large a question cannot be answered in a few paragraphs, it is possible to cite briefly a number of major factors.

To begin with, the revolutions in science and technology, taking hold wherever conditions were ripe, had begun to alter the complexion of the world economy. The most notable example was in the United States, with its rapidly growing population and seemingly boundless resources. Sparked by immigrants, ideas, and investments from the Old World, the New had acquired its own momentum. At the turn of the century America was becoming an economic giant capable of exporting, year after year, food, raw materials, and fabricated goods in a total volume greater than its imports. As productivity and exports continued to mount, the United States shifted from a debtor to a creditor

[4] *Triumph and Tragedy* (Vol. VI of *The Second World War;* Houghton Mifflin, Boston, 1953), bk. II, p. 569.

[5] Undersecretary in 1946–1947. Interview, Washington, October 20, 1953.

position and Europe began to have payments difficulties which turned eventually into a chronic "dollar problem."

Meanwhile, Germany emerged as the leading industrial power on the continent and as a growing competitor in international trade. The lonely pre-eminence of the United Kingdom in the economic sphere was disappearing and, with it, the capacity of the British to keep the peace unaided. The weakening of Britain's position in the world meant the beginning of the end of *Pax Britannica,* at a time when no other power or group of powers was capable of preventing economic competition from mushrooming into dangerous rivalries or of restraining any one strong country from attempting by force to impose its will on others.

The First World War brought not only staggering losses but a precipitous drop in western Europe's international position. As the continent was bled white, other regions—notably the United States, Canada, Argentina, Japan, and India—became economically stronger and more diversified. Some of the underdeveloped areas began to compete with Europe in the processing of raw materials and showed less interest in working their basic resources for export alone.

During World War I, when international exchange was disrupted, a strong trend away from free trade and toward economic nationalism began, a trend destined to stifle and enervate Europe's economy. Country after country, while increasing military production, tried simultaneously to develop greater economic self-sufficiency.

These policies were not reversed when World War I ended. Instead, a thickening network of internal controls, stringent quotas for imports and exports, bilateral trade agreements, tariffs, and exchange restrictions developed. Multilateral commerce, which up to 1913 had been vital to the health of the European economy, declined. Countries which had relied heavily on foreign trade began to suffer chronic unemployment. The situation was aggravated by rising tariffs in the New World. Thus, during the interwar years, commercial policy on both sides of the Atlantic took a wrong turn. The effect upon the United States, with its vast internal resources and free market area, was not too serious, but for western Europe it was disastrous.

The great depression which began in 1929 greatly accentuated these difficulties. The intricate structure of the world economy was gravely impaired. Intercontinental trade plummeted. Vast colonial areas, relying on western Europe for products and markets, suffered severe dislocations. Restlessness and resentments mounted, especially in Asia.

Crisis in Asia

The drama which unfolded in Asia during the first half of this century was of a different kind. Yet the crisis there was no less profound than in Europe. What were the more prevalent among the historic influences making for upheaval?

To start with, there has been throughout modern times a steady thickening of population on the Asiatic continent and its neighboring islands, which together support roughly half the world's people. The pressure of men against resources has surpassed any ever known in the West.

Maps of the Far East do not ordinarily show the severe limits of arable soil. Nor do the histories of that part of the world always record the divisions, redivisions, and re-redivisions of farmland which occurred generation after generation as fathers passed on to their sons fragmented holdings of ever-diminishing size. But no traveler across the countryside today can fail to note the intensity with which every available patch of earth is tilled and dressed, or the terraced gardens climbing incredibly high on mountain slopes, or the grinding poverty of peasants engaged in a relentless struggle for existence on tiny farms —many of which are not more than one or two acres in size.

The rural people of much of Asia—an overwhelming majority of the populace and its most rapidly increasing segment—are so close to the margin of subsistence that undernourishment is commonplace and a drought, a flood, a blight, or a plague of pests may bring death to thousands or even millions. Famine, as R. H. Tawney noted, is "the last stage of a disease which, though not always conspicuous, is always present." [6] The farmer, as another writer has put it, is like a person standing up to his neck in water: a ripple may drown him. And the lot of the coolie laborer in most areas is even harder than that of the peasant.

A second and related influence, dating also from a long past, was social inertia. While Europe was experiencing its unprecedented release of dynamic energies during the nineteenth century, the habits and customs of the East were becoming more deeply imbedded. Market-town and village communities, in relative isolation, lived culturally upon the past—having experienced no counterpart of the Renaissance and Reformation movements, no commercial, agricultural, industrial, or social revolutions to disturb their medieval tranquility.

[6] *Land and Labour in China* (Allen & Unwin, London, 1932), p. 77.

The build-up for future eruption, heralded now and again by spontaneous hunger riots, occurred in ways more consonant with static societies. As poverty deepened, the burdens of the common people multiplied. Land tenancy spread and there was rising underemployment. The more favored sought economic betterment not through expanding production, but by bargaining and by manipulating existing wealth. Merchants became more monopolistic and calculating, buying when prices were low and selling when they were high. Guildsmen grew more restrictive. Landlords, moneylenders, and tax collectors tended to grasp what they could; their servants resorted to "squeeze." With individual dignity ever in jeopardy, the customs and amenities which protected personal honor, or "face," became exceedingly precious. Government and education were largely tradition-bound, neither coming to grips with the real problems of the people.

Seeds of change were implanted by a third, more modern influence often referred to as the "impact of the West." The word "impact" is scarcely adequate, however, to denote the complex, diffused process that was involved. A fancier term, "cultural penetration," is not much better. Neither expression conveys sufficiently a sense of stimulus and response, or of yeast and ferment.

Although trade between Europe and Asia had already commenced when Marco Polo began his tours in the service of Kublai Khan, centuries were to elapse before the flow of visitors from Europe, and subsequently North America, reached sizable proportions. Those who came—commercial adventurers, diplomats, missionaries, sailors and soldiers, colonizers, doctors, teachers, businessmen—represented widely differing outlooks and aims.

Some were emissaries of the industrial revolution, bringing manufactured goods with them. The commerce that developed gave impetus to local production of tea, silk, rubber, and other commodities. In due course, small industrial plants began to spring up in coastal and river ports. But as transport to the hinterlands gradually improved, both imported and indigenous manufactures began to undercut a variety of village and cottage industries important to the livelihood of country folk.

With the growth of commercial and industrial centers, the evils which had attended rapid urbanization in the West were repeated and multiplied. Migrants from the depressed countryside, in search of a livelihood, threw around the cities broad fringes of mud huts beside which our slums would seem a paradise.

As contacts with the outside world were extended by students and travelers returning from abroad, intellectuals in Asia began to desire to catch up with the West by rapid industrialization. But many obstructions stood in the way, including the low productivity and purchasing power of the agrarian populace, lack of developed resources and power, lack of skilled management and labor, inexperience in large-scale organization, and a tendency to hoard savings, let them out at high interest, or use them for speculative buying rather than for investment in productive enterprise.

A widening distribution of industrial products, commonplace in the West but beyond the means of most Asians, produced a growing awareness of poverty and degradation. Discontent spread. The responsibility had to lie somewhere—and where more obviously than among the "foreigners" with their strange languages and manners and ideas, their affluence and, too frequently, their overbearing conduct and disregard of "face"?

Antiforeignism developed long before the advent of communism in Asia. This was true in the countries that had come under colonial rule: India, Burma, Ceylon, Malaya, Indochina, the East Indies, and the Philippines. It was true too in China, which had been reduced by "unequal treaties" to a semicolonial status; witness the rebellion engineered there in 1900 by the Righteous Harmony Band, better known as the Boxers. And it was true in Japan, which, after initial resistance to alien influence, had borrowed heavily from the Occident. In the 1930's, when Western colonialism had begun to recede, the Japanese used "Asia for the Asiatics" as a passionate slogan in support of their own expansionist designs.

As ancient beliefs and values were shaken by the thinking which emanated from more dynamic cultures, new conceptions of the value and rights of the individual began to take root, as did ideas about science, technology, economic and social development, freedom, democracy, and equality among nations. But the ferment was accompanied by frustrations and bewilderment. It did not bring answers to the immense problems of huge, depressed populations. Nor did it offset the animosities that had developed or the feeling, among many of the politically conscious, that somehow "foreign imperialism" was at the root of their troubles.

This feeling underlay, in country after country, the rise of nationalism, strongly tinged with anticolonialism, which has been so prominent a factor in the recent history of Asia. This fourth influence has sometimes been described as a revolt against the West, as an understandable assertion of independence, as a necessary stage in each country's development. In any event, it was not to be stopped. Repressive efforts in the colonial countries only added to its intensity, and enlightened measures did not prevent its growth.

Nationalism was a factor in Asia's deepening crisis not only because of the conflicts it engendered, but also because it directed attention away from internal problems. Leaders and potential leaders, especially students, became more ardently engrossed in eliminating all vestiges of foreign domination than in understanding and tackling the even more deeprooted causes of their countries' woes.

Only in Japan, however, among the nations of the East, did nationalism become aggressive before 1950. With a utilitarian outlook and a *samurai* or warrior tradition, the Japanese were the quickest to adopt industrial and military techniques acquired from the West. But politically Japan remained under a tight dictatorship. Formosa was annexed in 1895, Korea in 1910. During the twenties, Japan was the leading commercial and military power in the Orient. Its bid for the conquest of all east Asia and the Pacific islands between 1931 and 1945 left a frightful trail of havoc, dislodged the colonial powers in many areas, and fanned the flames of nationalism.

While often tempered by friendly intercourse and good will, antiforeignism and nationalism were widespread when the aid programs of the postwar period were launched. Amid poverty and inertia, they paved the way for the rapid extension of a fifth influence emanating, ironically, from Japan's traditional enemy, Russia.

Communism had appeared, as a hand on the horizon, during the early twenties, when Mikhail Borodin was in Canton. After Chiang Kai-shek broke with the emergent Chinese Communist faction in 1927, Mao Tse-tung and his disciplined band of followers were pursued but never destroyed. In mountain fastnesses far to the north they developed their adaptation of Marxian doctrine to conditions in China, and also the propaganda techniques and military skills which were to prove so effective after World War II. They exhibited an active interest in the oppressed peasants whose support they sought, and many were led to believe that a benign agrarian reform movement, basically different from communism in Russia, was in the making.

During the war against Japan, a "united front" was uneasily maintained between China's Nationalists and Communists. But all the while, under the nose of the invader, Mao's guerrillas and political cadres were gaining a strong foothold in the rural areas of northern China and Manchuria. When the war ended, negotiations were undertaken with American support to prolong the united front and prevent civil war. But in 1946, when the East-West rift in Europe was becoming more apparent, local clashes widened into a full-blown conflict.

Amid the chaos and distraction of this period, communism exerted a potent appeal. To land-hungry farmers and destitute laborers, it was a call to unite in a struggle for emancipation from all their oppressions. To students and intellectuals it proffered, in place of hopelessness and confusion, opportunities for leadership and a positive doctrine of national "liberation." The fallacies in these claims were yet to become evident. Ably led and thoroughly organized, communism was making its play for the control of China. And peoples throughout the rest of Asia watched, awaiting the outcome.

The threat to American security if China should go Communist was becoming increasingly apparent. There was danger that Korea, Japan, the Philippines, and all of southern Asia might ultimately follow suit. Should this occur, the relative strength of the free and Communist worlds would be radically altered.

Some observers in the West found consolation in the thought that China's Communists, with the help of their Russian mentors, were not so much generating a revolution as "capturing" one long overdue. But how did they accomplish it? Why were they, with a disguised and deceptive program, succeeding? Did any other group have a genuine and hopeful alternative to offer? These questions—especially the last—had to be faced when the ECA took up the task of trying to develop more effective aid programs—first in China and then in other parts of Asia.

Unrest in the Near East and Africa

In the Near East and Africa the stresses were somewhat different and, during the earlier part of this century, generally less acute than those in Europe and much of Asia. But here, as in the Far East, widespread poverty and social inertia prevailed. Here too, contact with Europe had resulted in extensive colonization, much social and political ferment, and, somewhat later than in the Far East, the stirrings of intense nationalism. This was especially true in southwestern Asia and northern Africa.

The policies of the European colonial powers in these regions exhibited remarkable divergencies, even among territories governed by the same country. Some colonial economies, being important sources of basic materials, were subordinated to public and private interests in the parent countries; in others, more active concern was shown for internal development designed to benefit the local peoples. In either case, tribal customs and patterns were often uprooted, and the people were exposed to the effects of severe fluctuations in world prices for raw materials. At the end of World War II the colonies showed wide variations in political status, ranging from complete subjugation to near independence. In a few, where substantial numbers of Europeans had settled permanently, racial tensions were becoming acute.

As communism began to gain footholds here and there, the Western nations were divided in their outlook on colonial questions. They were not a little suspicious of one another. Each European colonial power, with its own interests, difficulties, and apprehensions, and its special knowledge of the territories it administered, was prepared to use economic assistance for colonial development so long as its own control and freedom of decision were not impaired. There was no common approach to the problem of bringing the colonial areas more rapidly into the community of free peoples, with a larger stake in continued association with the democracies of the West. Cooperation in respect to these areas did not seem as important or as urgent as cooperation within continental Europe.

Problem Posed for the United States and the Free World

This review of longer-range influences in the crisis of our time, though sketchy and inadequate, indicates the magnitude of the problem confronting the United States and the rest of the free world in 1946. It was clearly a question of how to deal with troubled areas around the earth where dangerous emergencies had arisen. But it was also, and not so clearly, a problem of how to cope with the underlying tensions that would assuredly outlast each current emergency. More specifically, it was a question of how to develop a secure and workable free world system in which hope, opportunity, and confidence in democratic ways of life could be safeguarded and strengthened on every continent.

PART II

The European

Recovery Program

CHAPTER 2

Emergence of the Marshall Plan

THE Moscow conference adjourned without notable accomplishment. It was clear to Marshall and his aides, conferring on the return trip, that the situation in western Europe should not be allowed to go on festering. It was also evident that a broad and dramatic effort involving United States support, but relying heavily on European initiative, would be necessary to build up in western Europe the confidence and the economic health that the Soviet leaders were trying to tear down. There would have to be a search for answers and methods—one of the most critical questions relating to any proposal for action being "how to put it across." Obviously the American people would not support a program which did not promise significant results.[1]

The Search for Answers

In Washington the Secretary outlined the problem to George F. Kennan, head of the State Department's newly established Policy Planning Staff, indicating that he was deeply perturbed and that he wanted to take the initiative without waiting for Congress "to beat me over the head." He called for a plan of action and, in closing, proffered this laconic advice: "Avoid trivia."

[1] Interviews, Marshall, Washington, October 30, 1952, and February 18, 1953.

The Policy Planning Staff's memorandum, which drew upon analytical studies and recommendations previously developed in the State Department and on a disturbing firsthand report on the European outlook prepared by Assistant Secretary Will Clayton,[2] was presented to Secretary Marshall on May 23, 1947. Secret at the time, it was later declassified. Brief excerpts, indicating the general position taken on key questions, follow:

The "root" of Europe's difficulties, to which American concern should be directed—

The Policy Planning Staff does not see communist activities as the root of the present difficulties in western Europe. It believes that the present crisis results in large part from the disruptive effect of the war on the economic, political, and social structure of Europe and from a profound exhaustion of physical plant and of spiritual vigor. . . . The Planning Staff recognizes that the communists are exploiting the European crisis and that further communist successes would create serious danger to American security. It considers, however, that American effort in aid to Europe should be directed not to the combatting of communism as such but to the restoration of the economic health and vigor of European society. It should aim, in other words, not to combat communism, but the economic maladjustment which makes European society vulnerable to exploitation by any and all totalitarian movements and which Russian communism is now exploiting.

A distinction in the roles which should be ascribed to Europe and to the United States in developing a program for the revitalization of Europe—

It is necessary to distinguish clearly between a program for the revitalization of Europe on the one hand, and a program of American support of such revitalization on the other. It would be neither fitting nor efficacious for this Government to undertake to draw up unilaterally . . . a program designed to place Europe on its feet economically. . . . The formal initiative must come from Europe; the program must be evolved in Europe; and the Europeans must bear the basic responsibility for it. . . . The role of this country should consist of friendly aid in the drafting of a European program and of the later support of such a program.

The desirability of a joint European program and a joint request for American support—

The program which this country is asked to support must be a joint one, agreed to by several European nations. . . . The request for our support

[2] Interview, Kennan, Washington, February 19, 1953.

must come as a joint request from a group of friendly nations, not as a series of isolated and individual appeals.

The need for envisaging a "whole job"—

This European program must envisage bringing western Europe to a point where it will be able to maintain a tolerable standard of living on a financially self-supporting basis. It must give promise of doing the whole job. This program must give reasonable assurance that if we support it, this will be the last such program we shall be asked to support in the foreseeable future.[3]

The desirability of private consultations with the British over the course to be adopted—

The Planning Staff proposes the despatch of instructions to certain European missions designed to obtain a uniform digest of the views of the respective chiefs. It is also proposed that secret discussions with the British be undertaken at once with respect to the general approach to this problem.

The need to remove two principal misconceptions in respect to the "Truman Doctrine," these being—

(a) that the United States approach to world problems is a defensive reaction to communist pressure and that the effort to restore sound economic conditions in other countries is only a by-product of this reaction and not something we would be interested in doing if there were no communist menace;

(b) that the Truman Doctrine is a blank check to give economic and military aid to any area in the world where the communists show signs of being successful.

Copies of the memorandum were delivered for review to selected officials in the State Department, including Dean Acheson, Will Clayton, Charles E. ("Chip") Bohlen, and Benjamin V. Cohen, after which members of this group and Kennan met with the Secretary.

"Mr. Marshall's way of handling that meeting," said Kennan nearly six years later, "made a great impression on me. After summarizing the main issues, he went around the table, asking each one in turn to ex-

[3] It may be noted that while the Policy Planning Staff rejected the thesis that communism was the main "root" of Europe's difficulties, emphasizing instead the broad political, economic, and social maladjustments which made European society vulnerable to totalitarian exploitation, it attributed those maladjustments principally to the disruptive and exhausting effects of the war. This conclusion lent support to the idea that a vigorous but relatively short-term cooperative effort could do the "whole job" of placing Europe on its feet economically and could be the "last such program" in the foreseeable future. It will be seen that as the European situation came to be more fully understood, this premise was increasingly open to question.

press his views. A number of problems and some objections were raised. When all had spoken, the Secretary only asked: 'Are we safe in directing such a proposal to all of Europe? What will be the effect if the Soviets decide to come in?'

"My reply was, in effect, that we had said nothing here to indicate which countries should be contributors and which, recipients. The tenor of the approach was one which emphasized not American bounty, but the difficulties of European countries—especially those which produced for export and had to depend heavily on raw materials and trade outside their own borders—and called upon the European countries to work out a plan for overcoming these difficulties. My feeling was that if Russia accepted, we should welcome it on a basis of full participation in bearing the burdens of the plan. Our position would be: You, like ourselves, produce raw materials which western Europe needs, and we shall be glad to examine together what contributions you as well as we could make. This would mean that Russia would either have to decline or else agree to make a real contribution, herself, to the revival of the western European economy." [4]

In further discussions on the problem, Marshall was unresponsive to the view that, since the Russians could "move in at any time" to block the success of such a plan, it would be too risky an undertaking. He was convinced that it would be folly simply to "sit back and do nothing." [5]

But the timing of a public statement, he felt, required careful consideration.[6] The moment, in relation to the situation abroad—and at home, where apprehension over the European situation was mount-

---

[4] Interview cited.   [5] Interview, Marshall, cited.

[6] An address scheduled for May in the midwest was called off as being premature. Another, planned for late June in Massachusetts, was canceled because the situation in Europe was deteriorating too rapidly. Statements by departmental officials before June 5, including an address by Under-Secretary Acheson (substituting for President Truman) at Cleveland, Mississippi, on May 8 preceded the deliberations described above and were not intended as "trial balloons." The Acheson address was, nevertheless, indicative of a definite trend in Administration thinking. In an informal reminiscent comment, on October 20, 1953, Acheson said: "Before talking about solutions, we had to bring out the problem. The Cleveland speech gave an opportunity to do this before a good forum. I started in by considering the starkness of the situation—pointing to the dollar balance and the fact that Europeans had no means of dealing with it. The skiff was approaching the waterfall. What I did was to state the problem and indicate that, in some extraordinary way, there would have to be grant aid. I remember General Marshall and Senator [Arthur H.] Vandenberg discussing this at Blair House. The Senator was upset by the magnitude of the figures, but was reassured when General Marshall made clear that there was no immediate request for funds in the offing and that the whole vastly complicated problem would have to be studied thoroughly by public bodies both in Europe and here."

ing but isolationist opposition could be expected—must be such that the proposal would break with "explosive force." "The feeling seemed to be," he wrote later, "that any new proposal for more funds to be appropriated would be ruthlessly repulsed. Therefore, the manner of statement, the first approach, and similar factors had to be most seriously considered. It is easy to propose a great plan, but exceedingly difficult to manage the form and procedure so that it has a fair chance of political survival." [7] Lest premature leakage expose the proposal to harmful criticism before it could be properly presented, consultation within the government was held to a minimum and no information regarding the statement or its time of utterance was sent to friendly governments in Europe.

Marshall believed that it was of prime importance to put the emphasis on what the Europeans themselves would do, rather than on a projected outpouring of American aid. "I thought it imperative," he recalled, "that the European countries 'come clean'—that is, that they come up with a workable plan based on actual requirements beyond the existing resources at their command, not on what they thought the United States would give." [8]

The Marshall Speech of June 5, 1947

Revisions of the now-famous speech in Cambridge, Massachusetts, continued until the eve of its delivery. After describing the current outlook in Europe, Secretary Marshall said:

The truth of the matter is that Europe's requirements for the next three or four years . . . are so much greater than her present ability to pay that she must have substantial additional help or face economic, social, and political deterioration of a very grave character. . . .

Aside from the demoralizing effect on the world at large and the possibilities of disturbances arising as a result of the desperation of the people concerned, the consequences to the economy of the United States should be apparent to all. It is logical that the United States should do whatever it is able to do to assist in the return of normal economic health in the world, without which there can be no political stability and no assured peace. Our policy is directed not against any country or doctrine but against hunger, poverty, desperation, and chaos. Its purpose should be the revival of a working economy in the world so as to permit the emergence of political and social

---

[7] Memorandum to the writer, September 10, 1954. Marshall was less troubled over prospective reactions in European countries. They would be "getting something" and the responsibility for framing the initial program would be theirs. Interview, October 12, 1954.

[8] Interview cited.

conditions in which free institutions can exist. Such assistance, I am convinced, must not be on a piecemeal basis as various crises develop. Any assistance that this Government may render in the future should provide a cure rather than a mere palliative. Any government that is willing to assist in the task of recovery will find full cooperation, I am sure, on the part of the United States Government. Any government which maneuvers to block the recovery of other countries cannot expect help from us. Furthermore, governments, political parties, or groups which seek to perpetuate human misery in order to profit therefrom politically or otherwise will encounter the opposition of the United States.

The Secretary emphasized that before the United States government could proceed much further in its efforts to alleviate the situation and help start the European world on its way to recovery

there must be some agreement among the countries of Europe as to the requirements of the situation and the part these countries themselves would take in order to give proper effect to whatever action might be undertaken by this Government. . . . It would be neither fitting nor efficacious for this Government to undertake to draw up unilaterally a program designed to place Europe on its feet economically. This is the business of the Europeans. The initiative, I think, must come from Europe. The role of this country should consist of friendly aid in the drafting of a European program and of later support of such a program so far as it may be practical for us to do so. The program should be a joint one, agreed to by a number, if not all, European nations.

An essential part of any successful action on the part of the United States is an understanding on the part of the people of America of the character of the problem and the remedies to be applied. Political passion and prejudice should have no part. With foresight, and a willingness on the part of our people to face up to the vast responsibility which history has clearly placed upon our country, the difficulties I have outlined can and will be overcome.

Thus the Marshall Plan was, at its inception, a statement of policy and an idea. On June 11 President Harry S. Truman reiterated its essential doctrine in an address at Ottawa, emphasizing again the importance of European action.

The idea that Europe should take the initiative in designing a concerted plan of action was one the potency of which could be only dimly foreseen. To put it forth was a calculated risk.

Response in Europe

But the venture paid off. The response in Europe was prompt and positive, especially—at first—in the United Kingdom, France, and Italy.

The comments of two British officials, made later, are revealing. "I have always wondered," remarked one, "if Mr. Marshall expected the reaction that his speech received. Bevin heard of it in bed and got in touch with the Foreign Office immediately. It was astonishing the way in which he, with his elephantine frame, sprang into action. It is most important that Mr. Marshall's speech envisaged a self-help approach —not aid to down-and-out nations." [9] "We now realize more clearly than then," stated another, "that the United States was going to have to get the economies of the free world going before we could stand up to Russia. This was a great political judgment. Mr. Bevin was very quick off the mark in appreciating its significance. The joint result was really a turning point in the context of what came afterward." [10]

French Foreign Minister Georges Bidault also reacted decisively. On June 13 he invited Bevin to discuss the proposal in Paris. The talks were soon suspended in order that Molotov might be invited to attend. On June 23 this invitation was accepted, and four days afterward a Big Three conference opened in Paris.

During the period of this session and other negotiations which followed, American representatives—including Under-Secretary Clayton, Ambassador Jefferson Caffery and Henry Labouisse in Paris and Ambassador Lewis Douglas in London—kept in close touch with the European ministers and special delegates concerned and with the State Department in Washington.

The deliberations with Molotov did not last long. The British and French proposed a steering committee, composed of representatives of the Big Three and other states, to coordinate the work of subcommittees appointed to survey resources and develop the outlines of a European recovery program. The Soviets contended that such a committee would meddle in the internal affairs of sovereign nations; they presented a counterproposal that the United States be asked to specify the exact amount of help it was prepared to grant and that each country make its own surveys and estimates. The British and French governments adhered to their insistence upon a cooperative approach. When it became clear that they could not be pried from this position, the Soviet delegation withdrew.

The turning point in the conference was described later to Acheson.

[9] "I heard later," said Acheson, "that Bevin was advised to make an inquiry to the State Department to find out whether Marshall really meant what had been said in the Harvard speech, but that Bevin, who was very shrewd, didn't want to take the chance and preferred to go on the assumption that the statement, as made, was fully intended." Interview cited.

[10] Sir Robert L. Hall, director, Economic Section, Cabinet Planning Office. Interview, London, November 12, 1952.

"It seems," he said, "that Molotov has a bump on his forehead which swells when he is under emotional strain. The matter was being debated, and Molotov had raised relatively minor questions or objections at various points, when a telegram was handed to him. He turned pale and the bump on his forehead swelled. After that, his attitude suddenly changed and he became much more harsh. I suspect that Molotov must have thought that the instruction sent to him from Moscow was stupid; in any case, the withdrawal of the Russians made operations much more simple." [11]

Even before the withdrawal, evidences of Soviet opposition had begun to appear. *Pravda,* on June 25, alleged that the Marshall Plan was designed to prolong the postwar boom in the United States. Poland, which had signified its intention of participating in the Plan, later recanted. On June 29 *Tass* charged that the proposed American aid program was another instance of American "imperialism."

To discount these moves and the fears they played on would be to ignore the facts. Active Russian opposition might wreck the Plan. Moreover, many Europeans, keenly alive to their countries' needs and to the encroachments of aggressive communism, accepted the Marshall proposal in principle but with genuine misgivings, fearing that American aid on a large scale might indeed carry with it "conditions" committing their governments to the support of unpredictable American policies. To such persons, the acceptance of American leadership and help was a gamble—or perhaps an act of faith—which only time and events could justify.

On July 3, the day after the breakdown of the Big Three conference, Foreign Ministers Ernest Bevin and Georges Bidault issued a joint communiqué inviting twenty-two other European nations to send representatives to Paris to consider a recovery plan. Czechoslovakia, among the nations which at first agreed to attend, withdrew its acceptance after a visit to Moscow by Premier Klement Gottwald and Foreign Secretary Jan Masaryk.

The quickening drumbeat of Communist propaganda against the Plan was accompanied by other actions. On July 6 *Pravda* announced the establishment of a new organization, the Cominform, with headquarters in Belgrade, representing Communists of nine countries: Russia, Yugoslavia, France, Italy, Poland, Bulgaria, Czechoslovakia, Hungary, and Rumania. On July 12 the Soviet government negotiated trade agreements with the satellite states of eastern Europe, involving grain

[11] Interview cited.

aid and barter arrangements. These agreements, which came to be called the "Molotov Plan," diverted to the East a large volume of trade that had previously flowed to western Europe or other areas outside the Soviet orbit. On October 22 Andrei Zhdanov, speaking for the Cominform, called upon Communists everywhere to defeat the Marshall Plan, which he characterized as an instrument for "world domination by American imperialism."

The Sixteen-Power Conference

Unintimidated by this barrage, the representatives of sixteen nations, responding to the invitation from Bevin and Bidault, convened in Paris on July 12. The participant countries were Austria, Belgium, Denmark, France, Greece, Iceland, Ireland, Italy, Luxemburg, the Netherlands, Norway, Portugal, Sweden, Switzerland, Turkey, and the United Kingdom. The task confronting the conference was no less than that of conceiving and developing, in a year of acute difficulties, a concrete plan for European recovery. It may be useful to recall briefly some of the background against which the work of the conference was conducted.

Problems of Economic Crisis

In a secret memorandum of July 23, 1947, since declassified, the Policy Planning Staff of the Department of State epitomized in two sentences the economic plight of Europe in that year:

We face a situation today in which important industrial and population centers of the continent are unable to recover by dint of their own efforts the living standards which their people enjoyed prior to the war. In many instances, they are not even in a position to prevent, unaided, a further deterioration of the conditions in which their peoples are obliged to live.

Among the elements in the continent's economic crisis of 1947, three were particularly important: low production, inflation, and inability to pay for urgently needed imports from other parts of the world, especially the United States.

In early 1947 industrial output in Germany was only 27 percent of the prewar volume. It had not yet reached two-thirds of the 1938 level in Austria, Italy, and Greece, and was still below prewar planes in France and the Netherlands.[12] Agricultural yields in most areas were

[12] ECA, *Third Report to Congress* (Washington, 1949), p. 126. From 1938 to 1947 industrial output in the U.S. had more than doubled. *Federal Reserve Bulletin* (Washington, Nov. 1954), p. 1193.

not yet up to 80 percent of the prewar volume. But requirements had increased. Population had grown by approximately 8 percent between 1937 and 1947 [13] and was continuing to mount. Productivity—or output per man-hour—remained far below prewar levels. Increases in production after the war had been achieved, in some countries, only by increasing the size of the labor force and the number of hours worked.

Undernourishment was a significant cause of low productivity. In 1947 the consumption of foodstuffs in western Europe was only about 80 percent of prewar, and roughly two-thirds of the average for the United States. In some countries the level was even lower.[14]

Another factor in reduced productivity was the long interruption in the training of skilled workers for peacetime industry. Furthermore, much of Europe's labor force had been dislocated by the war; many workers had been killed or disabled; others had been unable to re-establish themselves in their former work. Few areas had been able to keep up with technological advances in agriculture and industry.

Destruction and obsolescence of equipment was yet another cause of low productivity. Replacement and proper maintenance, impossible from 1940 to 1945, had been only partially provided since the war through UNRRA and other aid. Almost every country of western Europe stood in urgent need of a large-scale investment program well beyond its capacity, unaided, to initiate or sustain.

Scarcity of basic materials, due partly to the loss of eastern Europe as a source of supply, presented a further difficulty. Coal and steel shortages, which were particularly acute, were traceable in some measure to a prolonged delay in the conversion of the German economy to peacetime production. The lack of coal was accentuated during the severe winter of 1946–1947; many nonessential activities, and some which were essential, had to be curtailed as fuel stocks declined. The coal shortage continued through 1947; thawing snows flooded the mines, and a prolonged summer drought decreased the supply of hydroelectric power, placing additional demands on alternative sources of energy. The drought had a particularly serious effect upon food production. Bread grain yields in France fell by 30 percent in the worst

[13] U.N., *World Economic Report* (New York, 1948), p. 220.

[14] The official ration in western Germany, for example, was only about 1,500 calories per day during a large part of 1947—approximately 30 percent under the western European average. Although this ration was frequently supplemented by food produced individually or purchased on black markets, the time involved in obtaining additional nutrition in these ways cut down on other productive effort.

crop year on record, and output in several other countries dropped substantially below the plane of the previous year.

Inflation, the second major problem, created social problems and added to the difficulty of increasing agricultural and industrial production. The situation in France, which was particularly serious, illustrates the problem. Wholesale prices had risen 80 percent during 1946. In early 1947 the government took urgent measures to arrest the upward spiral; prices began to level off and there was hope that stability could be achieved. This hope vanished with the drought, and agricultural prices began to rise again. Workers promptly demanded higher wages and the spiral began again, leading to a further increase of roughly 50 percent in wholesale prices during the last half of the year. The bread ration was cut to 200 grams per day, as low as during the worst war years. Continuing price rises led to a succession of strikes for higher wages. Stoppages in coal mining and other basic industries lowered production at a time when increased output was imperative.

The third problem was that of payments. Food, raw materials, and equipment to help restore productive capacity could be obtained from the New World—if they could be paid for. But Europe's foreign exchange reserves were nearly exhausted, and it could not acquire new balances by increasing exports. The prewar pattern of international payments had vanished.[15] Savings, including substantial backlogs of earnings from investments abroad, had been largely wiped out by the war. Conditions already described limited the ability to produce what was needed for home consumption and for exports which could earn foreign exchange. Exports were further curtailed by the multiplication of trade barriers within Europe, by tariff walls in other parts of the world, and by competition from countries outside Europe—especially the United States.

During 1946 and 1947 western Europe financed dollar-cost imports valued at approximately 14 billion dollars from loans and grants and by the use of its own dwindling foreign exchange reserves.[16] But with

[15] In this pattern the sterling area was in surplus with the dollar area and in deficit with continental western Europe. Western Europe was thereby enabled to use sterling surpluses to cover dollar deficits. The pattern was dependent upon a low level of European capital exports, highly favorable terms of trade, and a low level of economic activity in Europe which kept down the demand for dollar goods.

[16] Western Europe's "dollar deficit" in 1947 totaled more than 8 billion dollars (*Second Report of the OEEC* [Paris, 1950], p. 21). During the period between the end of the war and the beginning of the Marshall Plan, the U.S. supplied the rest of

UNRRA scheduled to end in mid-1947, post-UNRRA aid running out, and the proceeds of loans already largely consumed, Europe had to find additional large sources of dollar exchange or reduce imports to the trickle which could be paid for.

Payments problems were not limited to the need for dollars. Intra-European trade, though largely constricted to bilateral channels, was still important. Without stable exchange rates or any general mechanism for multilateral clearances, each country as a rule could buy only from others in which it could earn foreign exchange.[17] This stifled the triangular trade essential to healthy production and commerce.

Theoretically the countries of western Europe might have balanced accounts by wholesale curtailment of imports. But the social and political consequences of such action were utterly forbidding. Economic distress even greater than that of the war years would have swept the continent, with living standards falling to new lows, bringing starvation in many areas.[18] Such conditions would have invited a rise of new dictatorships and an accelerated expansion of Communist control, jeopardizing the entire free world.

Political Instability and Communist Expansion

Many of these economic difficulties could only be dealt with by governmental action. Where governments were secure, more effective fiscal and trade policies were possible. Conversely, the more precarious a government's position, the less it was able or disposed to adopt unpopular measures that might be necessary to economic recovery.

In some respects, postwar political developments had been reassuring. With victory, the United States had not gone "isolationist," as after World War I. Britain, with a change in political leadership, remained

the world with nearly 16 billion dollars in aid. Of this total, roughly 11.3 billion dollars went to western and southern Europe, about 4.5 billion of this amount being grant aid (including allotments to UNRRA, post-UNRRA and "interim" aid programs) and 6.8 billion in the form of credits. (See U.S. Department of Commerce, *Foreign Aid by the United States Government, 1940–1951,* issued as a suppl. to *Survey of Current Business* [Washington, 1952], p. 10.)

[17] For example, there was idle capacity in 1947 for the production of ball bearings in both France and Italy. But before output could be increased, chrome steel had to be imported from Sweden, with payment in kronor. Or again, a shortage of insulators in the U.K., for which raw materials were available, could have been alleviated by processing with existing facilities in France or Italy if the U.K. had been able to pay for this service with earnings in francs and lire.

[18] Although adverse effects in the U.S. would have been much less serious, substantial losses would have occurred for producers and exporters of wheat, cotton, tobacco, and various manufactured goods.

a democratic bastion. In other countries of northern Europe, German occupation had interrupted but had not undermined the processes of democratic government. Communist efforts to gain strong footholds in these areas were being thwarted.

But in much of the continent the great political fact of the postwar years was the rise of Communist power and influence. This was most marked, of course, in eastern Europe, where Soviet Russia had acquired a dominant position. In other areas—notably France, Italy, Greece, and Czechoslovakia—Communist parties had succeeded, during and after the war, in building up their strength. The outlook in western Germany, presenting a gamut of sensitive and difficult issues, was peculiarly baffling. Austria was vulnerable. Let us recall for a moment the position in each of these countries in 1947.

France was highly unstable. Political institutions, undermined before the defeat, had been all but destroyed during the Nazi occupation. After liberation, the country, with its fragmentation of political parties, had had to erect a wholly new government. In this setting communism could not be easily contained. In the first general election after the war, held in October 1945, the Communist party polled five million votes, the largest number received by any single party. This success confirmed the aptness of Communist tactics in building mass support, principally among industrial workers and peasants. During the next two years there was no appreciable change in the political strength of communism in France, and other parties regained only gradually a measure of stability.

In Italy the difficulties involved in establishing a new representative government after the war were even more serious. The country had just emerged from twenty years of Fascist rule. The new regime, like the government of France, was seriously weakened by the presence of a strong Communist party dedicated to the destruction of free institutions and by the ineffectiveness of some other political groups. The situation was particularly ominous in economically undeveloped and chronically depressed regions in southern Italy and among labor groups in the industrial north.[19] Persistent unemployment made it easier to recruit party members. In the June 1946 election the Communists polled 19 percent of the total vote, to which could be added that of one

[19] The Catholic Popolari had been greatly weakened in southern Italy, leaving poverty-stricken peasant masses ready prey to any political leadership promising them help. In the north the once-influential Socialist party had, with others, been disbanded as Mussolini consolidated his position.

closely collaborating "Socialist" party, raising the total Communist-dominated vote to roughly 40 percent. In May 1947, having partici-pated in each regime since the war, the Communists—followed by the Nenni Socialists—were forced out of the De Gasperi government, but their mass following was still strong.

Control of the labor movements of both France and Italy had fallen into Communist hands toward the end of the war and immediately after. The trade unions were used to foment economic chaos through disruptive, politically motivated strikes. In addition, the Communists endeavored to undermine existing political structures by intransigent opposition and to weaken the social fabric by propaganda campaigns exploiting every element of discontent.

In Greece the Communists had gained a large measure of control over the resistance movement during the war; they used this advantage to recruit followers and to consolidate their political and even military organization within the country. When a new, politically inexperienced Greek government was established, they initiated guerrilla activities which expanded in 1944 into a full-scale rebellion, with thinly veiled Russian support. Early in 1947, with American aid assured but not de-livered, the government started an abortive campaign against the in-surgents. During the remainder of the year the Communists maintained the offensive and, in December, they proclaimed a new "government" under Markos Vaphiadis. To this military rebellion was added a vigor-ous propaganda drive for a "strong, united, popular-democratic Greece."

In Czechoslovakia, before 1939 the most democratic of eastern Eu-ropean nations, political organization and leadership were decimated. The Communist party however, with Russian connivance, was greatly strengthened. The country in 1948 was almost surrounded by Soviet satellite states. Elections in 1946 had given the Communists just under 40 percent of the total vote and had resulted in a popular-front govern-ment. From the vantage point of key government posts, the party con-solidated its control over important areas of Czechoslovakian affairs. By astutely combining infiltration, internal terror, exploitation of fear of the USSR, and other more orthodox political methods, the Com-munists were able to undercut the strength and confidence of the other parties. Thus the groundwork was laid for the coup of February 1948.

In Germany political and social stability were of immediate concern at the end of the war, when both national and local governments col-lapsed. Soon after the country was divided into four occupational zones, intercourse between West and East was severely curtailed. Economic problems arising from the devastation and dislocation of the war years were compounded by reparations obligations, occupation costs, the cutoff of markets and sources of supply, the disruption of economic activity attending denazification and, in western Germany, by a huge influx of refugees. To the occupying powers fell the task not only of uprooting the remnants of Nazi power, but also of laying the foundations for an enduring democratic government. But Germany's previous experience with democratic processes was severely limited. How could the occupying powers, while carrying out essential control measures, foster a popular government which would command the loyalty of the German people? How could administrative authority be progressively, and safely, transferred to German shoulders?

Throughout 1947 Germany was the focus of deepening division and hostility between the USSR and the Western powers. Attempts to reach agreement on the German problem were made at four-power conferences in Moscow during March and April, and in London during November and December. But these sessions were of little avail. As Secretary of State Marshall remarked, the patient was sinking while the doctors deliberated.

In Austria, where East-West relations under four-power occupation were less abrasive than in Germany, early efforts to agree on a peace treaty were unsuccessful. And Communist maneuvers—including disruption of trade with countries to the east, extensive expropriation of industries and products in the Soviet zone, and attempts to build up a hard-core following in the Allied zones—brought new forebodings.

For months the attitude of the West toward the USSR had been stiffening. As early as September 1946 Secretary of State James F. Byrnes had served notice that the United States would no longer tolerate Soviet hindrance to reconstruction in western Europe and Germany. On March 12, 1947, the President asked Congress to appropriate 400 million dollars for military and advisory aid to Greece and Turkey and proclaimed what came to be known as the Truman Doctrine: a policy of active support to free peoples resisting subjugation by armed minorities or by outside aggression. The *détente* of the period was coming to an end and the lines were being drawn in a struggle which, like Communist ambitions, was world-wide. The "cold war" had begun.

It had begun at a time when morale throughout a considerable part of western Europe was at a low ebb. For many, two years of peace had not yet brought release from fatigue, anxiety, and a consuming struggle for the necessities of life. Discouragement and defeatism aggravated economic difficulties and fostered political extremism. It was evident that if recovery should be too long delayed, communism, in one country after another, would win by default.

Committee of European Economic Cooperation (CEEC)

Preparations for the sixteen-power conference were made almost literally overnight. A member of the British delegation,[20] which under the leadership of Sir Oliver Franks played a leading role, described some years later the initial phase of the effort: "The Paris meeting was set for a Wednesday. On Monday we began work. We saw Bevin that evening. He simply said, 'You go to Paris and do your best.' It was clear that we believed in the general idea of European cooperation, but if you had asked Franks or the rest of us what we were going to do in Paris, we couldn't have said.

"But when, previously, the exiled governments were in London, we had worked together. Wartime and postwar collaboration in Washington and London was also important—through a lot of joint agencies. There were people who, through this kind of effort, had known each other well and worked together for over five years. That made a tremendous difference in Paris, since the exercise called for dealing with intimate data in an infinitesimal period of time—and with confidence. Even though we had to guess at many of the figures, it was intelligent guesswork based on a lot of experience with our own and others' economies. The members of one group, which put in obviously inflated estimates, were brought up short. It was a period of great certainty in a governmental operation, with a sure touch. The British took the lead, provided the mechanics, and drove everybody mad. We had to. Franks was amazingly good where fairness and integrity were essential. Monnet [Jean Monnet of France] also made an enormous contribution, not only formally, but also in resolving matters behind the scenes." [21]

The conference began by setting up an interim Committee of Euro-

[20] Unnamed by request. Interview, London, November 11, 1952.

[21] Looking back upon this formative enterprise, Paul G. Hoffman said: "The work of Oliver Franks at that time has never been adequately recognized. He was the man of all people who laid down the principles that should guide European cooperation. The preparatory work of the American agencies and committees was monumental. But it would have had no effect unless addressed to a program. The framework for such a program was set by Franks and the CEEC." Interview, New York, January 28, 1953.

pean Economic Cooperation (CEEC) to analyze the economic resources and capabilities of the sixteen nations, to develop the principles for a European recovery program, and to agree in a preliminary way upon what each country should be expected to accomplish and what external aid it might require. Four technical subcommittees were set up to deal with food and agriculture, iron and steel, fuel and power, and transport. Staff work was directed by Robert Marjolin of France. Friendly aid and counsel were provided by American personnel—including Will Clayton, Henry Labouisse and C. H. Bonesteel. But the analyses and formulations developed were those of the European participating countries.

Four-Year Program

On September 22 the CEEC presented to the American government a report [22] outlining a four-year program for economic recovery in the participating countries and western Germany, based upon four main lines of action:

1. a strong production effort designed, broadly, to restore agricultural output to prewar levels and to raise industrial produce to a point somewhat higher than 1938 levels;

2. the creation and maintenance of internal financial stability;

3. the establishment of a continuing organization and the achievement of increasing economic cooperation among the participating countries in the fields of production, development of resources, trade, transport, and the movement of persons;

4. an attempt to solve the dollar deficit of each participating country, principally through an expansion of exports.

The calculations in the report were based on several assumptions, among which the following were particularly noteworthy: that consumption standards would not be higher at the end of the program than the respective countries expected to be able to maintain; that production and consumption would be brought to levels consistent with "high and stable employment"; that the estimate of import requirements would be consistent with the aim of reducing dollar deficits to levels manageable without external assistance; and that foreign

[22] *Committee of European Economic Cooperation,* Vol. I, "General Report" (Paris, 1947); reproduced as U.S. Department of State Publ. 2390. See also Vol. II, "Technical Reports" (Paris, 1947). It may be noted that the first cooperative step toward bringing about a close association of western Germany with the economies of western Europe was taken during the planning of the European Recovery Program.

exchange essential for financing such imports would be available. It was not assumed that midway in the program a military crisis in Korea would involve the free world in a vast new rearmament effort.

The report estimated import requirements from non-European sources and net balances of payments during the projected four-year period. In order of magnitude, the largest import requirements were food, feedstuffs and fertilizers; industrial, power, and transport equipment; petroleum products and coal; and iron and steel. The estimated balance of payments of the participating countries, their dependent territories, and western Germany showed net deficits with the United States and other Western Hemisphere countries totaling 8.0 billion dollars in 1948, 6.35 billion in 1949, 4.65 billion in 1950, and 3.3 billion in 1951.[23]

Pledge to Action

In evidence of good faith, the participating countries embodied in the first volume of the CEEC report a series of pledges:

In order to ensure that the recovery programme is carried out, the 16 participating countries pledge themselves to join together, and invite other European countries to join with them, in working to this end. . . . In particular, each country undertakes to use all its efforts:—

to develop its production . . . [making] the fullest and most effective use of its existing productive capacity and all available manpower;

to modernize its equipment and transport, so that labour becomes more productive, conditions of work are improved, and standards of living of all peoples of Europe are raised;

to apply all necessary measures leading to the rapid achievement of internal financial monetary and economic stability while maintaining in each country a high level of employment;

to co-operate with one another and with like-minded countries in all possible steps to reduce the tariffs and other barriers to the expansion of trade both between themselves and with the rest of the world . . . ;

to remove progressively the obstacles to the free movement of persons within Europe;

[23] Total imports from outside Europe for the same four-year period (not counting imports from overseas dependencies) were estimated at a total value (in round figures) of 57.4 billion dollars, of which 20.4 billion dollars' worth would be required from the U.S. and 14.8 billion from other American countries. Imports from the U.S. were calculated at 6 billion dollars in 1948, 5.3 billion in 1949, 4.8 billion in 1950, and 4.3 billion in 1951. Initial estimates of American aid required were cut back when it became apparent that they were substantially above what the U.S. Congress would probably be prepared to support.

to organize together the means by which common resources can be developed in partnership . . . [p. 13].

The countries represented on the CEEC also pledged themselves that, when stabilization had been fully achieved and could be successfully maintained, they would make their currencies convertible. To achieve the freer movement of goods, they further resolved to abolish as soon as possible the abnormal restrictions hampering their mutual trade; and to aim, as between themselves and the rest of the world, at a sound and balanced multilateral trading system.[24] Furthermore, stated the CEEC:

The participating countries will do all that lies in their power to promote the development of production in their overseas territories, and . . . to develop and make more efficient their production of exportable goods [thus providing] so far as they are concerned, for a rapid expansion of their exports to the American continent . . . [pp. 117–118].

Groundwork in the United States

While the work of the CEEC was in progress in Europe, a complementary chapter was unfolding in the United States.

The positive British and French response to the Marshall speech produced in many quarters here a hope that European initiative might lead to a well-conceived recovery effort, in conjunction with which American aid could be more than a temporary palliative. But questionings arose about the amount of aid the American economy could safely provide, and there were early rumblings of discontent over the prospect of continuing taxes to "bail out Europe."

On June 22, the day before arrangements were completed for the Big Three conference in Paris, President Truman appointed two committees to make studies needed in drawing up a program for Congressional approval, and he directed the recently established Council of Economic Advisors to develop a complementary analysis.

The most important of these three studies was conducted by the President's Committee on Foreign Aid, consisting of eminent private citizens and chaired by W. Averell Harriman, then Secretary of Commerce. This body analyzed the principles and policies which should guide the conduct of an aid program, the needs and capacities of the European countries, the volume of assistance required, its relation to

[24] *Committee of European Economic Cooperation*, I, 29, 31.

the American domestic economy, and problems of finance and administration. The second committee, under the chairmanship of Secretary of the Interior Julius A. Krug, investigated United States resources and physical capabilities in relation to a large new aid program. The Council of Economic Advisors, headed by Edwin G. Nourse, studied the probable effect of anticipated exports, financed in part with government funds, upon domestic production, consumption, and prices.

Although the conclusions reached by the two committees and the Economic Council were at variance in minor respects, the consensus was that to avoid economic collapse, western Europe must have long-range assistance on a comprehensive scale; that with such aid the countries of western Europe could achieve recovery; that with skillful management the resources and productive capacity of the United States were equal to the extraordinary task contemplated; and that if assistance should not be extended, free institutions everywhere, including those in the United States, would be in jeopardy.[25]

More specifically, the "Krug committee," in a report issued on October 19, 1947, under the title *National Resources and Foreign Aid*, declared that while preserving national security and standards of living, the American economy could provide the resources for a considerable program of foreign aid. This conclusion was based on detailed studies of commodities deemed most likely to be required for the program—wheat, nitrogen fertilizers, coal, steel, industrial equipment, farm machinery, nonfarm tractors, petroleum, and petroleum products.

A summary of the "Nourse report" was released on November 1.[26] It predicted that without a new aid program there would be a sharp drop in American exports. While such a rapid reduction, in the opinion of the Council,

would probably not inflict serious short-run damage on our own economy, substantial problems of adjustment would be generated. Moreover, the industrial paralysis which could be expected to result in some other countries would have repercussions of major proportions upon our own economy and upon world stability. . . . In the longer run, the economic restoration of Europe will benefit our own economy by enabling us to obtain more goods by advantageous trade [pp. 74f.].

[25] Cf. *First Report to Congress of the Economic Cooperation Administration* (Washington, 1948), p. vi.

[26] *The Impact of Foreign Aid upon the Domestic Economy: A Report to the President by the Council of Economic Advisors* (Washington, 1947), submitted October 28, 1947.

Indicating that a larger annual impact than that anticipated had been sustained in the past, the report concluded that the aid program could be supported. But it stressed that "problems raised by specific commodities in relatively short supply could distort or overturn this generally optimistic picture if not dealt with effectively." And the Council cautioned that the "general inflationary threat resulting from the combined impacts of foreign and domestic demand requires the continuance of tax revenues at present levels, maximum economy in government expenditures, stimulation of saving, and the enlargement and aggressive use of measures to control dangerous expansion of credit."

The "Harriman Committee"

The President's Committee on Foreign Aid, known as the "Harriman committee," carried the major responsibility for anticipating the problems that would arise, and for laying a groundwork of analysis essential to wise policies and a sound program. The committee was a nineteen-member advisory group composed of "distinguished citizens" representing major sectors of American life. The caliber of the group and its nonpartisan character were attested by its membership.[27]

The idea of such an advisory council seems to have originated with a recommendation by Senator Arthur H. Vandenberg during a bipartisan consultation at the White House shortly after the Marshall speech.[28]

[27] Hiland Batcheller, president, Allegheny-Ludlum Steel Corp., Pittsburgh; Robert Earl Buchanan, dean, Graduate College, Iowa State College; W. Randolph Burgess, vice-chairman, National City Bank of N.Y.; James B. Carey, secretary-treasurer, CIO; John L. Collyer, president, B. F. Goodrich Co., Akron; Granville Conway, president, Cosmopolitan Shipping Co., Inc., New York; Melville F. Coolbaugh, Colorado School of Mines; Chester C. Davis, president, Federal Reserve Bank, St. Louis; R. R. Deupree, president, Proctor & Gamble Co., Cincinnati; Paul G. Hoffman, president, Studebaker Corp.; Calvin B. Hoover, dean, Graduate School, Duke University; Robert Koenig, president, Ayrshire Collieries Corp., Indianapolis; former Senator Robert M. La Follette, Jr.; Edward S. Mason, dean, Graduate School of Public Administration, Harvard University; George Meany, secretary-treasurer, AFL; Harold G. Moulton, president, The Brookings Institution, Washington, D.C.; William I. Myers, dean, New York State College of Agriculture, Cornell University; Robert Gordon Sproul, president, University of California; and Owen D. Young, honorary chairman, board of directors, General Electric Co. Named as executive secretary heading an executive staff of nine, was Richard M. Bissell, Jr., professor of economics at the Massachusetts Institute of Technology and former member of the War Shipping Administration. Although the group was chaired by the Secretary of Commerce and had the full cooperation of government agencies, it was itself only in a limited sense a governmental organization.

[28] Interview, Marshall, October 30, 1952. See *The Private Papers of Senator*

William C. Foster, then Under-Secretary of Commerce, took a leading part in the nomination of members.

"The initiative in actually setting up the committee," said Harriman later, "was taken by Acheson; Marshall had a hand in it. As the plan progressed, Vandenberg was consulted and approved; he suggested Bob La Follette to help in the work. A number of the members made important contributions. The section on America's interest in Europe was done largely by La Follette. Disagreements in the committee, which were not too serious, were mainly over what our economy could afford." [29]

If not "too serious" in retrospect, vigorous debate developed on a number of issues. The problems and the data confronting the group were of an enormous range and complexity. The committee and its staff worked at full speed throughout the summer and into the autumn, and its report, entitled *European Recovery and American Aid*, was transmitted to the President on November 7, 1947.

The committee agreed that the United States had a vital interest—humanitarian, economic, strategic, and political—in helping Europe achieve economic recovery, declaring:

Our position in the world has been based for at least a century on the existence in Europe of a number of strong states committed by tradition and inclination to the democratic concept. The formulation of the Paris [CEEC] report is the most recent demonstration that these nations desire to maintain this concept. But desire is not enough. The democratic system must provide the bare necessities of life now and quickly rekindle the hope that by hard work a higher standard of living is attainable. If these countries by democratic means do not attain an improvement in their affairs, they may be driven to turn in the opposite direction. Therein lies the strength of the communist tactic; it wins by default when misery and chaos are great enough. Therefore the countries of western Europe must be restored to a position where they may retain full faith in the validity of their traditional approaches to world affairs and again exert their full influence and authority in international life [p. 4].

At the beginning there was some disagreement in the committee whether the program should be envisaged as essentially a charity or as a cooperative effort to bring about economic recovery. But as discussion progressed, thinking crystallized in favor of the latter approach.

Vandenberg, ed. by Arthur H. Vandenberg, Jr. (Houghton Mifflin, Boston, 1952), p. 376.

[29] Interview, Washington, October 1, 1952.

The report stressed the importance of a great upswing in production. But the committee, foreshadowing a future issue in several European countries, expressed concern lest the Paris group might have put a disproportionate emphasis on capital expansion.[30]

The advisory group recognized a basic imbalance between the European and American economies. "Our goal," it asserted, "should be to bring about a condition where exports from this country are more nearly balanced by a return flow from abroad of services and materials essential to our own economy." It believed "that the European nations desired to achieve such equilibrium in the interests of their self-respect and prosperity," and that "to make this equilibrium possible should be a major objective of any program of aid."

A particularly difficult question was the amount of assistance needed. In considering this problem, the committee had to take into account the uncertainties of the situation in Europe and the extent to which the American Congress and people would support a massive aid effort. The conclusion reached was that "because of the inherent impossibility of narrowing the margin of error to a tolerable size, no honest man will try to decide at this time how much aid Europe will need and how much it would be wise for the United States to give for a period as long as four years." Grave consequences would follow from any attempt to achieve a finality for which there is no basis. "A rigid ceiling set too low would provoke another crisis; one set too high would encourage waste." However, since the American people had a right to know what was likely to be the ultimate cost of any commitment upon which they entered, upper and lower limits were estimated, supplemented by more precise figures covering the first year.

With these qualifications, the report indicated that the dollar financing required over a four-year period might range from 12.5 to 17.2 billion dollars (in round figures) in grants and loans from the United

---

[30] "It is obvious," stated the committee's report, "that if Europe is to be revived and made self-supporting—if our aid program is not to degenerate into just another relief program—the European nations will have to rehabilitate their capital plant. But it cannot be too strongly stated that the process of investment and capital formation imposes a severe strain on the country undertaking it. . . . At the present time, gross investment in the United States is running at about 17 percent of total national product at the height of a boom. Some of the European nations have attempted to exceed this rate. It seems unlikely that European nations can prudently afford to sustain capital formation on as large a scale as they have planned. What this means, in effect, is that housing programs and capital development may have to be slowed down until European recovery is much more advanced than at the present" [pp. 6–7].

States Treasury, and roughly 5.8 billion dollars from the World Bank
and other sources. To cover the calendar year 1948, it was believed,
appropriations—past and future—of the order of 5.75 billion dollars
would be necessary. The amount of American aid required, the report
stated, could be estimated only by calculating the foreign exchange deficit of the participating countries. This broad approach—an innovation
in aid programing—obviously reflected a determination to see the problem of European recovery in more than piecemeal terms. The report
found "little evidence that the goals set at Paris to restore standards of
living were excessive in terms of basic requirements."

On the thesis that "the hope of western Europe depends primarily on
the industry and straight thinking of its own people," the committee
underscored Secretary Marshall's original emphasis on European initiative. Aid was to be viewed not as a means of supporting Europe, but as
a "spark which can fire the engine."

The Harriman committee went more deeply than the CEEC into the
need for reducing economic barriers within Europe. Scaling down tariff
restrictions, it held, was of little moment if exchange and other controls
were to be maintained. It asserted that whatever one's attitude toward
free enterprise might be, "there is all but universal agreement" that
true economic recovery depended on releasing the energies of individuals and cutting down on time-consuming regulation of production and
distribution.

Disagreement arose in the committee over using the aid program to
foster expansion of free enterprise in countries with socialist governments. Certain members argued in favor of this course, convinced that
it would speed recovery and help counter disparagement of the program on the ground that it tended to "coddle" socialism. Others, including the chairman, were opposed. Paul G. Hoffman became, in effect,
the mediator on this issue. The position finally agreed upon was embodied in a temperate statement:

Aid from this country should not be conditioned on the methods used to
reach these [agreed] goals, so long as they are consistent with basic democratic principles. Continued adherence to such principles is an essential
condition to continued aid but this condition should not require adherence
to any form of economic organization or the abandonment of plans adopted
and carried out in a free and democratic way. While this committee firmly
believes that the American system of free enterprise is the best method
of obtaining high productivity, it does not believe that any foreign-aid program should be used as a means of requiring other countries to adopt it.

The imposition of any such conditions would constitute an unwarranted interference with the internal affairs of friendly nations [pp. 4–5].

Sharp differences also arose over the question whether the American economy could support, without serious damage, an aid program of the size proposed. The "hottest fight," recalled a member of the committee's staff, was touched off by a discussion of crude steel resources. After a detailed canvassing of American supply availabilities the cautiously optimistic conclusion was reached that, if funds were available and European requirements known in detail, exports could be maintained, and in many cases stepped up. The committee emphasized, at the same time, that "supply will be a limiting factor in many cases" and that "the aid which the United States gives will impose definite sacrifice on this country."

The report took direct issue with the Communist propaganda line that Marshall Plan aid would be merely a device for dumping American surpluses abroad, and also with a widely held view on the desirability of subsidizing exports:

The Committee regards as nonsense the idea which prevails to a considerable degree in this country and abroad that we need to export our goods and services as free gifts, to insure our own prosperity. On the contrary, we are convinced that the immediate economic danger to the United States is inflation, which means, among other things, a shortage of goods in relation to demand [p. 3].

With support from Senator Vandenberg and others, the committee considered the moot question of organization and recommended that, to insure unity of administration, a new independent agency be set up in the federal government.

As a "final word," the committee expressed the view that

success depends on giving way neither to over-optimism or undue pessimism. It is one thing to propose a program, it is another to see it through. The immediate months and indeed years ahead are not apt to be easy either for this country or for the European nations. It is not wise to underestimate the steepness of the climb. . . . At no time in history has there been more need for western Europe and the United States to stand firmly together. And who will say that, if we will apply to the making of the peace the same spirit which triumphed in war, we may not see an equally dramatic vindication of the ideals and principles of free men everywhere? [31] [Pp. 11–12.]

---

[31] "The quality of the committee's report," commented Hoffman more than four years afterward, "was due largely to the tireless work of Dick Bissell; he was 'it'—

Many of the questions dealt with by the Harriman committee were later analyzed much more fully. But, like the CEEC, it broke new ground, providing a considered rationale for the program and an indispensable basis for the work that was to follow.

Labors in the Executive Branch

Extensive groundwork was also being laid, concurrently, by the executive agencies of the government, under the general direction of Under-Secretary of State Robert A. Lovett. Part of this consisted in support given to the Harriman, Krug, and Nourse committees. Part was in further converting the Marshall Plan from a broad, general conception into a specific program which could be presented to Congress. Participants in this intensive effort, to name but a few, included Willard Thorp, C. Tyler Wood, Paul Nitze who provided much of the intellectual and organizing drive, Lincoln Gordon, Colonel C. H. Bonesteel, III, Charles Kindleberger, Ernest Gross, and Ambassador Lewis Douglas who was called back from London repeatedly to give political guidance and to conduct key consultations with members of Congress. Cooperating extensively with these members of the State Department were high-level personnel in other agencies—for example, Frank Southard in the Treasury Department and Frederick Northrup in the Department of Agriculture.

Those named above, and many others with them, fed to the Harriman committee much of the substance of its report, developed in large part the detailed case to be presented to Congress, and set up a temporary unit for the handling of initial planning and shipments which made it possible, after the Marshall Plan was approved, for the operation to be launched promptly with a quick flow of aid to countries nearing bankruptcy. This work did not proceed without problems. An interdepartmental committee employed was not a wholly satisfactory instrument. Part of the voluminous technical data prepared under pressure was unwieldy. Certain of the recommendations readied for Congressional consideration were not politically feasible—e.g., a proposal for a general four-year authorization of about 17 billion dollars. But these were marginal aspects of a body of solid preparatory work without

---

pulling together a vast amount of material, selecting what was important, and preparing an effective presentation for the committee and for Congress. From a public relations standpoint," he continued, "I think the work of the Harriman committee was crucial. It was an appraisal with the participation of representatives of business, labor, agriculture, and the public generally. It was well conceived and was taken seriously." Interview cited.

which the Marshall Plan could not have been launched as a sound undertaking.

Emergence of the Marshall Plan

The CEEC report, the findings of the Harriman, Krug, and Nourse committees, and preparatory work done within the executive branch of the government laid the foundation for consideration by Congress. Thus by early November 1947 the idea put forward by Secretary Marshall on June 5 had grown into the outlines of a plan. Five months had elapsed since the Harvard speech; two more were to come and go before Congress, in regular session, could begin the task of systematic examination of specific bills.

In anticipation of such activity in January, President Truman on December 19 sent to the Congress—then in special session—a message on "A Program for United States Support to European Recovery." [32] "Our deepest concern with the European recovery," he stated, "is that it is essential to the maintenance of the civilization in which the American way of life is rooted."

Interim Aid

Events in Europe did not wait upon planning and lawmaking in the United States. The winter of 1946–1947, the severest in living memory, had been followed by a summer of drought. On September 3 Under-Secretary of State Lovett stated that the economic plight of western Europe was becoming worse faster than expected. Secretary Marshall told a news conference that Europe faced "intolerable hunger and cold" during the coming winter unless food and fuel were provided. On September 25 the President, making public a report from a special cabinet committee on world food problems,[33] declared that any significant cut in the already low rations of some of the European countries would have "most serious consequences for their rehabilitation." The situation was particularly acute in France and Italy.

Four days later, after a meeting with Congressional leaders, the President stated that the longer-range Marshall Plan could not be realized unless the United States provided food and fuel to help France and Italy "survive this critical winter as free and independent nations." On October 23 he issued a call for a special session of Congress, for "two compelling reasons"—the "continued rise in prices" in the United States and

[32] Reproduced in House Doc. 478, 80th Congress, 1st Session (1947).
[33] Headed by Secretary of Agriculture Clinton P. Anderson.

the "crisis in Western Europe." The session opened on November 17, and a month later Congress approved as a stopgap measure an Interim Aid Program providing for a grant of 522 million dollars to France, Italy, and Austria.[34] Thus time was gained for searching public and Congressional consideration of the longer-term European Recovery Program.

[34] Foreign Aid Act of 1947 (Public Law 389) and a supplemental appropriations act (Public Law 393), 80th Congress, 1st Session. An additional 55 million dollars was appropriated on March 31, 1948, raising the total Interim Aid figure to 577 million dollars. Public Law 470, 80th Congress, 2d Session.

1. The British build a giant surface condenser for a new power station.

2. Power development was a major emphasis. Here, Limberg Dam is under construction as part of Austria's Glockner-Kaprun project.

3. This "dam above the clouds" holds back the waters of melting glaciers.

CHAPTER 3

Debate and Decision

THE drama that precedes a momentous legislative decision is only faintly reflected in the enactment which finally emerges. This is particularly true of the Foreign Assistance Act of 1948 authorizing the Marshall Plan operation.

Emergency in a Political Year

What was the outlook when Congress convened in January 1948? Abroad, only two and a half years after victory in the costliest of wars, the situation was still deteriorating. Great-power negotiations on Germany and Austria had broken down, deepening the European crisis already described.[1] In China the Communist tide was still rising.

Only the United States possessed the economic strength needed to help restore the vitality of western Europe and instill new hope in non-Communist Asia. If that resource was not used, advocates of the Marshall Plan believed, widening chaos would gravely imperil the free world. The American people were becoming aware that they must face alternative risks and reach a decision.

The people of Europe outside the Soviet sphere, lacking resources

[1] The Council of Foreign Ministers meeting in London had adjourned *sine die* on December 15, 1947.

for rapid reconstruction when speed was imperative, were much closer to the dangers that threatened. Britain's Chancellor of the Exchequer, Sir Stafford Cripps, saw United States aid as Britain's main hope. To Premier Robert Schuman of France it was essential to his government's urgent economic plans. Italian statesmen saw the recovery program as their salvation from communism. Czechoslovakia, Greece, and Turkey were in immediate peril, although aid to the latter two countries was beginning to strengthen their position. The western zones of Germany and Austria were haunted by uncertainties.

Events were forcing a decision, however, at a most inauspicious moment in the United States. Nineteen forty-eight was a "political year." The Democratic party was in power, but the Eightieth Congress, convening in January for its second regular session, was Republican-controlled. Elections were only ten months away. The legislative record of that year turned out to be one of the most controversial in recent American history, not only on domestic issues but also on foreign policy, especially in relation to China. Favorable action on a question of major importance was most unlikely without strong bipartisan support. Moreover, the events leading up to the Marshall Plan proposal had occurred since the last election, and there was no clear mandate from the people for dealing with them.

This in brief was the outlook when the Foreign Relations and Foreign Affairs Committees of the Senate and House began formal consideration of the aid program.

Advance Preparation

These committees came to their work well prepared. For months Congress, on its own initiative, had been preparing the way for a decision. Shortly after the Harvard speech and President Truman's unqualified endorsement of the Marshall proposal, leaders from both parties conferred with the President and the Secretary of State. This conference was followed by a long series of intimate discussions between Senator Vandenberg, chairman of the Foreign Relations Committee, and Secretary Marshall. When preparation of the project was at its height, these talks were held twice a week at Blair House. Because it was deemed wise not to publicize them, Marshall was at times accused of not following a bipartisan approach to the European recovery program. But the conversations were, in fact, exceedingly fruitful.[2]

[2] Interview, Marshall, Washington, October 30, 1952.

Herter Committee

On July 29 the House of Representatives created a select committee of nineteen members to study the Marshall proposal.[3] Speaker Joseph W. Martin named Representative Charles A. Eaton, who presided over the Foreign Affairs Committee, as chairman. Congressman Christian A. Herter was appointed vice-chairman and designated to head the group when it went overseas for firsthand observation and study. The primary objective of this body, generally referred to as the "Herter committee," was self-education. Its membership, drawn only in part from the Foreign Affairs Committee, included a geographically and politically representative cross section of the House. The group sailed for Europe with a small staff on August 28, armed with questionnaires prepared with State Department assistance. Intensive briefing began during the crossing. Dividing into subcommittees which included some senators, the members visited every nation in Europe except Russia, Yugoslavia, and Albania. Each subcommittee traveled widely: one, on finance, went to twenty-two countries.[4] In addition, Representatives Frances P. Bolton of Ohio and Chester E. Merrow of New Hampshire visited the Near East, and Congressman Walter H. Judd of Minnesota went to China, Japan, and Korea.

The subcommittees interviewed private citizens as well as government officials. "We talked," said Congressman Donald L. Jackson, "to members of the Greek press, American and foreign correspondents, magazine writers, officers and men of the Greek Army and Air Force, priests, villagers, businessmen and captured bandits."[5] Such conversations were no less important than the information on the European economy compiled by the committee and its staff.

The Herter committee's success in its aim of self-education was attested not so much by bulging portfolios brought back as by the deep personal interest developed among individual members and by their own store of newly acquired knowledge. After wide discussion with other members of Congress and with people in their own constituencies, the group became one of the wellsprings of the ensuing legislation.

Soon after their return, the members reported to the Foreign Affairs Committee. Although these hearings, in November 1947, bore directly

[3] House Res. 296, 80th Congress, 1st Session (1947).

[4] *Emergency Foreign Aid,* Hearings before the Committee on Foreign Affairs, 80th Congress, 1st Session (1947), p. 181.

[5] *Ibid.,* p. 211.

on interim aid, much of the testimony and discussion dealt with longer-range problems involved in the Marshall Plan.[6] The reports were discursive, touching many questions and reverting to certain problems repeatedly. No major disagreements materialized. The few differences that arose—in interpreting the situation in one country or another, for example—appear inconsequential, even on a close reading of the record. Commenting on the subcommittee of ten members which he headed, Representative Karl E. Mundt stated:

They were a most congenial group. They were tough-minded and approached the problems objectively. I was not only amazed but gratified by the fact that the Members from the two Houses of Congress, from every section of the country, equally divided between the two parties, should arrive at such a widespread area of agreement as we wrestled with the prodigious problems overseas.

Firsthand study—focused on realities abroad rather than on divisions at home—resulted not in confusion but in greater harmony of outlook and a release of constructive thought and energy. This was true among those who had been regarded as "isolationists" as well as among those looked upon as "internationalists." Lawrence H. Smith of Wisconsin, for instance, speaking of United States information programs overseas, said:

I want to state, Mr. Chairman, without any equivocation that I join with the other members of the committee who were abroad in stating that I believe it is absolutely necessary to augment the so-called information program. You may recall my own reservation in this matter. I become a convert on this trip and I want to state that for the record.

Unanimity was especially evident on one subject, the peril of Communist expansion. Mundt spoke of Communist "overlords" deliberately slowing down economic activity "so as to produce chaos and put an end to freedom." Herter cited the danger of disruption to production by Communist-controlled labor unions. Bolton of Ohio linked the cold war in Europe to America's future security, and John Davis Lodge of Connecticut saw in it a challenge to the democratic system and its moral and spiritual values. Pete Jarman of Alabama, who visited Soviet

[6] *Ibid.*, pp. 136–326. In the order of their appearance, the witnesses were Representatives Christian A. Herter, Karl E. Mundt, Pete Jarman, Frances P. Bolton, John Davis Lodge, Donald L. Jackson, James P. Richards, Lawrence H. Smith, Chester E. Merrow, Walter H. Judd, Everett M. Dirksen, August H. Andresen, Jacob K. Javits, Ellsworth B. Buck, John M. Vorys, Francis Case, E. E. Cox, and Charles W. Vursell.

satellite states, declared: "I am impressed that it is necessary actually to experience that feeling of pressure, that feeling of strangulation that one has behind the iron curtain, in order to appreciate the situation that exists there and the absolute necessity of our doing whatever is necessary to prevent its spread." Some members felt that recent assistance to Greece and Turkey and the Interim Aid Program had deterred communism in Europe. Yet witness after witness stressed the interdependence of the countries they had visited and the danger of a chain reaction if one or another should fall under Communist domination.

Many members returned more deeply convinced of the necessity for American leadership and aid. "Whether we like it or not," said Jarman,

this great country of ours . . . has grown . . . into a position of leadership and power in the world which places on the shoulders of our country a responsibility which heretofore had not rested there. . . . Practically all of Europe is in danger of losing its way of life. . . . [Our] position of leadership demands action on our part. . . . Somebody, some member of Congress very aptly described the situation upon returning from Europe when he asked the question: "What would it cost us not to aid Europe?"

Everett M. Dirksen of Illinois saw three choices before the American people. One was to withdraw from Europe and be prepared to let the Kremlin take over. Another was to give "niggardly aid." He continued:

There is a third choice, and that is the choice that we must make. I want to make it. I have been back home. People have talked to me about giving away my country, and I have talked to them. . . . And I have said, "Look, let us examine this whole picture." And it is amazing to me to see how the people back home have changed their minds on the basis of such facts as you disclose them. I am not afraid of the reaction in this country. I am confident that in proportion as we do our jobs as representatives to bring them the story—that they will go along with the third choice, and the third choice in my book is immediate—adequate—aggressive aid. My formula, Mr. Chairman, is very, very brief. Do it—do it now—and do it right.

Some misgivings were voiced. Smith said, for example: "We ought to do all we possibly can. But I raise the question—and it is a sincere one—can we expect from these nations any more in the future than we have in the past so long as we give and give and give?" Such doubts were partly offset by the belief shared by many of the committee that the people of Europe, by and large, were struggling to find a way through their problems.

The Congressmen recognized that miracles could not be expected and that a very short-term aid program would not put Europe on its feet. Herter said: "I do not want to get into a situation where Congress takes an interim bite and thinks that everything is settled." Jacob K. Javits of New York referred to the need for giving "political assurance that we will stay in Europe." John M. Vorys of Ohio asserted that "unless this present interim aid is part of a cure, an installment on a long-term program, it is unjustified." Mundt expressed the view that "this emergency program, on which we are now working, can provide some experience tables which will be of value to us in considering a more comprehensive program, running over a longer period of time." On the other hand, the Congressmen repeatedly stressed the necessity for maximum self-help by European countries and maximum aid to their neighbors.

The committeemen gave special attention to American information programs abroad. Judd of Minnesota discussed at length the skill with which Communist propaganda played upon nationalistic and other sentiments, the danger that it would undercut American prestige, and the need for a more resourceful information program addressed to the real interests of peoples abroad. Lodge reported that few Italians were aware of what we were doing in providing aid. Bolton, Lodge, Smith, and E. E. Cox, among others, deplored the weakness of United States information programs overseas and urged vigorous expansion. Mundt underscored the obligation to keep the American people informed and to answer, through a permanent program, vicious misrepresentation abroad.

Some of the suggestions made by the committee in its 883-page report [7]—especially those on administration and distribution of aid— were not adopted. But on many subjects the committee and its staff made significant contributions to Congressional thinking and to the legislation which finally emerged. These included production and production management, utilization of resources, local currency "counterpart" funds, the relationship of Germany to European recovery, American participation, and acquisition of strategic and other materials by the United States. The breadth and responsibility of Congressional

[7] *Final Report on Foreign Aid of the House Select Committee on Foreign Aid,* House Report 1845, 80th Congress, 2d Session (1948). The small staff which assisted the committee to coordinate its findings and prepare its reports and recommendations was headed by Professor William Yandell Elliott of Harvard University, who as "agent general" also participated actively in the committee's discussions.

interest in the European recovery program were nowhere more convincingly demonstrated than in the work of the Herter committee. Through its firsthand reports and the influence of its individual members, its impact was unique in United States legislative history; it fixed attention upon realities in Europe and set the tone for the deliberations that followed. "Without it," asserted Paul G. Hoffman some years later, "the program couldn't have gotten Congressional approval. It was a bipartisan approach." [8]

Public Opinion and Pressures

Meanwhile, a growing number of citizens were becoming aware that without prompt and widespread support the proposal for a large new aid program would encounter heavy opposition in Congress and that failure might be disastrous. Private organizations, in increasing number, became actively interested, and Secretary Marshall and other Administration leaders accepted invitations to meet with groups in different parts of the country while Lovett and others had many talks with Congressional leaders.

In late 1947 a special citizens' Committee for the Marshall Plan was organized to inform the American people of the facts and issues and to enlist their support for the program. Impetus for this organization was given by former Secretary of War and Secretary of State Henry L. Stimson, through an article in the October 1947 issue of *Foreign Affairs*.[9] In this article the elder statesman discussed in realistic terms the role of the United States in the postwar world:

We Americans today face a challenging opportunity, perhaps the greatest ever offered to a single nation. It is nothing less than a chance to use our full strength for the peace and freedom of the world. This opportunity comes when many of us are confused and unready. . . . We are having our first experience of constant, full-scale activity in world politics. . . . We require a skillful foreign policy, of course, but . . . farsighted and experienced men . . . can develop [such a] policy with success only if they have the understanding support, on basic principles, of the American people.

First, and most important, Americans must now understand that the United States has become, for better or worse, a wholly committed member of the world community. . . . Time after time in other years we have tried to solve our foreign problems with half-way measures, acting under the illusion that we could be partly in the world and partly irresponsible. . . .

[8] Interview, New York, January 28, 1953.
[9] "The Challenge to Americans," pp. 5–14. Quoted by permission.

It should by now be wholly clear that only failure, and its follower, war, can result from such efforts at a cheap solution. . . .

A second principle . . . is that we are forced to act in the world as it is, and not in the world as we wish it were or as we would like it to become. . . . The world's affairs cannot be simplified by eager words. We cannot take refuge from reality in the folly of black-and-white solutions. . . .

The reconstruction of western Europe is a task from which Americans can decide to stand apart only if they wish to desert every principle by which they claim to live. And, as a decision of policy, it would be the most tragic mistake in our history.

When the Committee for the Marshall Plan was formed, Stimson agreed to serve as national chairman. Former Secretary of War Robert P. Patterson became chairman of an executive committee, Mrs. Wendell L. Willkie headed a women's division, and John H. Ferguson was appointed executive director. The executive committee included Dean Acheson (then in private life), Winthrop W. Aldrich, James B. Carey, David Dubinsky, Herbert H. Lehman, Philip Reed, and Herbert Bayard Swope. Its membership consisted of more than three hundred prominent citizens in different parts of the country. Advertisement of the committee's organization in leading newspapers, with an appeal for funds, was followed by generous contributions from nearly every state. Regional committees were promptly organized, the cooperation of scores of national organizations enlisted, and relevant publications given wide circulation.[10] The committee promoted broad news and editorial coverage in metropolitan newspapers, set up a speakers' bureau, and employed a news agency which arranged for press releases, a special mat service for small town and country newspapers, and national and local radio broadcasts.

Since its avowed purpose was the enactment of legislation, the committee and its principal staff members registered under the Regulation of Lobbying Act. Petitions were circulated in nearly every Congressional district throughout the country and forwarded to members of

[10] These included a reprint of Stimson's article, a full-scale supplement to the *Washington Post*, leaflets, pamphlets, and a weekly "fact sheet." An illustrated pamphlet by Munro Leaf called "Who Is the Man Against the Marshall Plan?" attracted particularly wide notice. Current opposition to the Marshall Plan stemmed in part from a book by Henry Hazlitt entitled *Will Dollars Save the World?* (Foundation for Economic Education, Irvington on Hudson, N.Y., 1947.) An answer by John P. Simpson in the *Commercial and Financial Chronicle* was reprinted and widely distributed. These and other facts cited above are contained in a published "Report on the Activities of the Committee for the Marshall Plan to Aid European Recovery," April 5, 1948, 8 West 40th Street, New York.

Congress. Through a Washington office directed by Harold Stein, active contact was maintained with executive departments and Congressional committees. Materials were prepared for use by supporting witnesses in Congressional hearings. Analyses of various legislative proposals were issued and found considerable demand not only from the public but among legislators as well. Special effort was directed against the inclusion of "harmful" restrictions and amendments. When the committee issued its final report in April 1948, it had raised and expended, from private contributions only, more than $150,000, and felt a pride in the part it had played in securing "so overwhelming an endorsement of the promising program now enacted into law."

Meanwhile, other nonpolitical bodies were at work analyzing economic, political, and administrative questions which the American people and Congress would have to face in reaching decisions about the Marshall Plan. Among the more influential were the National Planning Association, the Committee for Economic Development, and the Brookings Institution.

The National Planning Association (NPA)—an independent nonprofit organization composed of representatives from agriculture, business, government, labor, and the professions—had gained wide prestige by its previous cooperative work for common objectives. The NPA produced a study of "the general principles and administration of the Marshall Plan." Prepared by a subcommittee which included Luther H. Gulick and Wayne Chatfield Taylor, this analysis foreshadowed closely the form of the organization that emerged to administer the recovery program.

So did the recommendations for "effective administration" contained in a policy statement issued by the Committee for Economic Development (CED), an organization of public-spirited businessmen headed by Paul G. Hoffman. The similarity between these two administrative patterns recommended was not altogether coincidental, for Taylor chaired the CED's subcommittee on European economic cooperation.

These and other organizational proposals by private groups—including the National Association of Manufacturers, the National Foreign Trade Council, and the Congress of Industrial Organizations— were available to the Brookings Institution when, in response to a request from the Senate Foreign Relations Committee, it undertook to prepare a report on the administration of United States aid for a European recovery program. Its recommendation of an organizational structure parallel in many respects to that proposed in the NPA and

CED studies was well received by the Foreign Relations Committee. Broadly speaking, it set the pattern of administration later approved by Congress.

Doubts and reservations about the Marshall Plan were also voiced. "At every stage of this complicated operation," said Felix Morley, "Russia is in a position to block progress. . . . The breadbasket of Europe is in those countries now under complete Russian control." [11] Former President Herbert Hoover, in contrast to his own former Secretary of State (Stimson), who urged that "we must be sure we do enough," called for "more safeguards" and a limitation of aid during the first fifteen months to a total of around 3 billion dollars.[12]

Senator Robert A. Taft declared:

Aid to Europe at the rate proposed by the European nations means $8,000-000,000 of taxes in 1948 on the American people over and above what they would otherwise pay. . . . The adoption of the Marshall Plan has a direct tendency to inflate prices further in the United States. . . . The Marshall Plan, unless very carefully administered, can easily be an encouragement to the continuation of unsound policies by European governments. I feel very strongly that we overestimate the effect of our dollars in foreign countries. [But he added] I am prepared to support in some reasonable amount the general principle of aid to European countries to enable them to help themselves. . . . We must do what we can to prevent the spread of Communism.[13]

Skepticism was registered more strongly in some quarters—for example, in the McCormick newspapers. Writing for the *New York Times* of November 2, 1947, William S. White reported: "Latent hostility to the Marshall Plan is a very real fact out over the country even though as a general policy the Plan is strongly favored in all public forums." Organized opposition came from the American Labor Party, the National Economic Council, the American Coalition (composed of patriotic, fraternal, and civic societies), and the Illinois Manufacturers Association, among others. Individual opposition witnesses at the Congressional hearings included Henry Hazlitt, author; Henry J. Taylor,

[11] *Pathfinder*, July 30, 1947, p. 3, quoted in Robert E. Summers, *Economic Aid to Europe* (H. W. Wilson Co., New York, 1948), p. 111.

[12] Letter to Vandenberg, dated January 18, 1948, reproduced in Hearings before the Committee on Foreign Relations, on United States Assistance to European Economic Recovery, Senate, 80th Congress, 2d Session (1948), pp. 707–712.

[13] Address before Ohio Society of New York, November 10, 1947, reproduced in *Congressional Record* (1947), pp. A4250–A4253.

radio commentator; and former Vice-President Henry A. Wallace, who proposed a larger, longer-range program to be administered by the United Nations.

But the advocates of the Marshall Plan were more organized and active than the opponents. As more people became familiar with the Plan, resistance slackened. The list of organizations supporting the proposal (some with qualifications) expanded until it included the American Farm Bureau Federation, the American Federation of Labor, the American Legion, Americans for Democratic Action, the Chamber of Commerce of the United States, the Congress of Industrial Organizations, the Federal Council of Churches, the General Federation of Women's Clubs, the National Association of Manufacturers, the National Catholic Welfare Conference, the National Farmers Union, the National Grange, the National League of Women Voters, and the Veterans of Foreign Wars. Scores of other nation-wide and local organizations might be added, including business and industrial groups, labor unions, farmers' associations, educational councils, and religious and racial bodies.

Economic interests were generally favorable. Few opposed the Plan on principle, but some wished to insure that their own position would be strengthened or safeguarded. Shipping companies, backed by the CIO maritime committee, opposed leasing idle American vessels to European countries to transport aid supplies; they sent Congress a list of influential organizations which supported their stand.[14] Agricultural groups wanted surplus commodities to be drawn upon and commodities in short or potentially short supply conserved. Tobacco-growing sections presented a case for including tobacco among "incentive goods" furnished under the program.[15] Flour dealers wanted a substantial share in the provision of food. Oil companies called attention to the world shortage of petroleum and opposed increases of petroleum-consuming equipment under the program when alternative fuels or sources of power could be found. In these and similar cases there was a mixture—and sometimes a conflict—of private interests and the public interest.

The trend of opinion during the latter part of 1947 was reflected in a Gallup poll released on December 7. In four and a half months the

[14] Hearings before the Committee on Foreign Affairs on United States Foreign Policy for a Postwar Recovery Program, House, 80th Congress, 2d Session (1948), pp. 1391–1409.

[15] Senate Hearings, cited, pp. 1465–1466.

proportion of the population which had not "heard or read" about the Marshall Plan had dropped from 51 to 36 percent. During the last five weeks of the period, those with "no opinion" on the proposal had dropped from 38 to 27 percent, whereas those favorably disposed toward it had risen from 47 to 56 percent, leaving 17 percent opposed.[16]

Effects of Soviet Opposition

Public opinion was shaped by another dynamic influence of enormous impact—Communist action. The Soviets had quickly recognized the Marshall Plan as a potential obstacle to the realization of their objectives in Europe. During the ten months from its inception to its endorsement by Congress the European Recovery Program became the "top target" on the Kremlin's list.[17] All the weapons, short of war, in the well-stocked arsenal of the Soviet government and the Cominform were directed against it. The Marshall Plan, so went the Soviet cry, aimed at the subjugation of Europe.

In the latter half of 1947 strikes and riots were fomented in France and Italy as "spontaneous protests" against American capitalism. Waters already troubled were further muddied in Greece and Turkey. In Austria propaganda played on the fear of permanent partition. Socialist governments wondered if they would be caught between conflicting pressures from the United States and the USSR. As the food situation in Europe grew worse, the Russians increased obstacles to East-West trade. The Russians hardened their rule in east Germany, attempted to create a Balkan federation, and strengthened their strategic positions near the perimeter of the Mediterranean.

These maneuvers boomeranged in the United States. As early as January 18, 1948, for example, the *New York Times* ran a feature article entitled, "Kremlin, as Usual, Comes to the Rescue of ERP." [18] The recent Russian moves, said the article, were expected to convince Congress that the program was essential.

The Soviet action which, above all others, contributed to the authori-

---

[16] *Public Opinion Quarterly*, Winter 1947–1948, pp. 674–676. A summation of the views of 430 community leaders—businessmen, educators, lawyers, editors, and others—in 21 cities was published on March 4, 1948, by the Council on Foreign Relations (New York) in a pamphlet entitled *The Marshall Plan as American Policy*. A substantial majority of those polled supported the objectives of the Marshall Plan, felt that arbitrary conditions attached to aid should be minimal, believed that aid recipients should trade where they could to best advantage, and held that western Germany should be included in the recovery program.

[17] *New York Times*, March 28, 1948, IV, p. 3.   [18] IV, p. 3.

zation of the European Recovery Program was the coup in Czechoslovakia, in mid-February 1948. By this aggressive move, long in the making, the Soviet rulers showed their hand. The nations of western Europe, in spite of their exposed position, sped their plans for defensive alliance and recovery. In the United States, Congress intensified its work on the economic cooperation bill.

Committee Hearings

The Foreign Relations Committee of the Senate and the Foreign Affairs Committee of the House opened public hearings on the same day, January 8, 1948. As a starting point for their deliberations, both committees had the proposal for a European Recovery Program sent to Congress by President Truman on December 19, 1947. Initial witnesses for the Administration included Secretary of State Marshall, Ambassador Douglas, Secretary of Commerce Harriman, Secretary of Agriculture Anderson, Secretary of Interior Julius A. Krug, Secretary of the Treasury John W. Snyder, Secretary of the Army Kenneth C. Royall and Secretary of Defense James Forrestal.

The published hearings present an absorbing and voluminous record. Those before the Senate committee fill three volumes totaling 1,466 pages; [19] those before the House committee, two thicker tomes of 2,269 pages.[20] The Foreign Relations Committee heard 9 governmental and 86 other witnesses and recorded 76 additional written statements and communications. The Foreign Affairs Committee heard 25 spokesmen for the Administration and received testimony, most of it oral, from about 150 nongovernmental persons.

"Somebody remarked," said the Senate committee's chief of staff Francis O. Wilcox, "that the chairman, Senator Vandenberg, killed the opposition by kindness—and this is what happened. He was patient and thorough throughout, and showed great statesmanship and skill in the conduct of the hearings." [21] "The House committee," stated that body's administrative officer, Boyd Crawford, "took its work extremely seriously and worked very hard. It was willing to hear all who wanted to be heard." [22]

Space precludes a detailed analysis, but the scope of the hearings can be suggested by listing some of the questions raised. What should be the amount of aid? On what basis had the estimates been made?

[19] Senate Hearings cited.   [20] House Hearings (1948) cited.
[21] Interview, Washington, August 8, 1952.
[22] Interview, Washington, August 12, 1952.

Were they reliable? Should American assistance be in the form of grants or loans or both? How would it be determined whether a grant or a loan should be provided? Should conditions or "strings" be attached? If so, what strings and how should they be applied?

How could aid be used most effectively to promote a rapid upswing in European production? to check inflation and stabilize currencies? to induce increases in intra-European trade and in the continent's capacity to earn dollars? to foster European cooperation and unity? Should Germany be brought into the program? If so, what should be done about reparations? Should military assistance be considered in conjunction with economic aid?

In supporting a recovery effort of such dimensions, what safeguards should be provided for the American economy? What kinds of commodities and equipment would be required from the United States and how would their availabilities be determined? What would be the place of private channels of trade—including "small business"—in the conduct of the program? What use would be made of existing financial institutions, public and private?

Should a separate organization be established to administer the operation, or should it be conducted by an existing agency? If the former, what would be its relation to the Department of State? Should it be directed by a board or by one man? If by a single administrator, what should be the scope of his authority and responsibilities? Should a coordinating office be set up in Europe? Should special missions be established in each participating country? If so, what would be their relationship to the American embassies there? What administrative provisions needed to be incorporated in the law to govern the conduct of the operation and at the same time allow it needed flexibility? How would Congress maintain close contact with the new organization?

The deliberations thus brought into focus a wide range of issues on which decisions were needed. Some of these are cited below. Two questions prominent later did not enter significantly into the discussions. One was the kind of long-term development needed before Europe could achieve a strong, self-reliant economy. The other was the extent to which changes in American policy, especially tariff reductions, might reduce the need for aid and help Europe pay its own way.

After the hearings the committees spent several weeks "marking up" the bills under consideration. "I remember especially one night session," said Boyd Crawford, "in which all of the House committee participated in the writing."[23] In due course the bills were ready for presentation to Congress.

The Role of Vandenberg

On March 1, 1948, Senator Vandenberg, a one-time "isolationist," rose before a packed Senate to deliver his major address in support of the Marshall Plan.[24] The writer was in the gallery, where standing room was filled. House members lined the walls of the Senate Chamber. A hush fell over the entire assembly as the white-haired Senator began:

Mr. President, with the unanimous approval of the Senate Foreign Relations Committee, I report the Economic Cooperation Act of 1948 in its perfected text. In the name of peace, stability and freedom, it deserves prompt passage. In the name of intelligent American self-interest it envisions a mighty undertaking worthy of our faith. . . .

The act asserts sound doctrine when it says that it is "the policy of the people of the United States to sustain and strengthen principles of individual liberty, free institutions and genuine independence through assistance to those countries of Europe which participate in a joint recovery program based upon self-help and mutual cooperation." Mr. President, this act may well become a welcome beacon in the world's dark night, but if a beacon is to be lighted at all it had better be lighted before it is too late.

Nevertheless, Mr. President, the decision which here concerns the Senate is the kind that tries men's souls. I understand and share the anxieties involved. It would be a far happier circumstance if we could close our eyes to reality, comfortably retire within our bastions, and dream of an isolated and prosperous peace. But that which was once our luxury would now become our folly. This is too plain to be persuasively denied in a foreshortened, atomic world. We must take things as they are.

. . . There are no blueprints to guarantee results. We are entirely surrounded by calculated risks. I profoundly believe that the pending program is the best of these risks. . . .

This legislation, Mr. President, seeks peace and stability for free men in a free world. It seeks them by economic rather than by military means. It proposes to help our friends to help themselves in the pursuit of sound and successful liberty in the democratic pattern. The quest can mean as much to us as it does to them. It aims to preserve the victory against aggression and dictatorship which we thought we won in World War II. It strives to help stop World War III before it starts. It fights the economic chaos which would precipitate far-flung disintegration. It sustains western civilization. It means to take western Europe completely off the American dole at

[23] Interview cited.

[24] *Congressional Record* (March 1, 1948), pp. 1981–1986.

the end of the adventure. It recognizes the grim truth—whether we like it or not—that American self-interest, national economy, and national security are inseverably linked with these objectives.

Within the purview of this plan are 270,000,000 people of the stock which has largely made America. These are 26 percent of all the literates of the earth. Before the war they operated 68 percent of all ships that sailed the sea. They grew 27 percent of all the world's cereals. They produced 37 percent of the world's steel. They sold 24 percent of the world's exports and bought 39 percent of the world's imports. They are struggling, against great and ominous odds, to regain their feet. They must not be allowed to fail. The world—America emphatically included—needs them as both producers and consumers. Peace needs their healthy restoration to the continuing defense of those ideals by which free men live. This vast friendly segment of the earth must not collapse. The iron curtain must not come to the rims of the Atlantic either by aggression or by default.

The Senator then sketched the "chain reaction of events responsible for the issue we here confront"—the "electric effect" in Europe of "a few sentences in a quiet sequence" spoken by Secretary Marshall at Harvard; the way in which, in the days that followed, "history wrote with a rushing pen"; and the painstaking care with which the Foreign Relations Committee had analyzed the major problems to be faced. In closing, he said:

There is only one voice left in the world, Mr. President, which is competent to hearten the determination of the other nations and other peoples in western Europe to survive in their own choice of their own way of life. It is our voice. It is in part the Senate's voice. Surely we can all agree, whatever our shades of opinion, that the hour has struck for this voice to speak as soon as possible. I pray it speaks for weal and not for woe.

The committee has rewritten the bill to consolidate the wisdom shed upon the problem from many sources. It is the final product of 8 months of more intensive study by more devoted minds than I have ever known to concentrate upon any one objective in all my 20 years in Congress. It has its foes—some of whom compliment it by their transparent hatreds. But it has its friends—countless, prayerful friends not only at the hearthstones of America, but under many other flags. It is a plan for peace, stability and freedom. As such, it involves the clear self-interest of the United States. It can be the turning point in history for 100 years to come. If it fails, we will have done our final best. If it succeeds, our children and our children's children will call us blessed. May God grant His benediction upon the ultimate event.

Senate and visitors rose in applause. When asked, years later, whether Senator Vandenberg had received much assistance in preparing this speech, Francis Wilcox replied: "No. He typed it himself, and re-worked it seven times." [25] "Vandenberg," remarked Hoffman more than four years later, "was the giant on the Congressional side. It was his leadership, both intellectually and legislatively, that led to the almost unanimous agreement given to the ECA program." [26]

Secretary Marshall spoke warmly of Senator Vandenberg as "a full partner in the adventure. At times," he said, "I was his right-hand man, and at times he was mine. I worked closely with him on the Reso-lution which he presented to Congress. In fact, the first draft was pre-pared in the State Department at my request. Senator Vandenberg took this draft and improved it enormously on his own typewriter. He made it a practical proposition, and, but for his leadership and coordination in the Senate, the plan would not have succeeded. I feel that he has never received full credit for his monumental efforts on behalf of the European Recovery Program, and that his name should have been as-sociated with it." [27]

Floor Debates

Time was uppermost in the minds of Administration officials as the Congressional floor debates opened. Nine months had elapsed since the Harvard speech, five since the CEEC report, and three since the completion of preparatory work in the special committees and the ex-ecutive agencies. The Czech coup had added to the sense of urgency. But the relatively few who actively opposed the bill and those who wanted qualifying amendments had full opportunity to express their views.

Majority support in both houses was soon certain, but some sharp exchanges took place. When Senator James P. Kem asked whether the Marshall Plan would have prevented Russian infiltration into Czecho-slovakia, Vandenberg replied, "I do not know how we can apply the Marshall Plan retroactively for purposes of speculation." [28] When, after holding the floor for nearly two days in opposition, Senator George W. Malone approached the end of his speech, Senator Scott W. Lucas was moved to comment that not more than eight senators were in the Cham-ber listening.[29] By and large, however, the discussion in both houses was free from acrimony as members sought to understand the proposed act more fully and to assess its far-reaching implications.

[25] Interview cited. See Vandenberg, *op. cit.*, p. 389.   [26] Interview cited.
[27] Interviews, October 30, 1952, and October 12, 1954.
[28] *Congressional Record* (March 2, 1948), pp. 1981–1982.
[29] *Ibid.* (March 5, 1948), p. 2217.

Special mention ought to be made of the energetic participation of the House of Representatives in the deliberations, by virtue of its predominant voice in appropriations. Each chamber was jealous of its prerogatives. The exceptionally active role of the lower house was an innovation in the conduct of American foreign relations.

Issues

Not all of the issues introduced during committee hearings and floor debates were settled. The committee memberships had been well aware that "when witnesses had convinced them, the job was only about one-fourth done." [30] The legislation had to go to the Rules Committees and then to both Houses where, to pass, it had to have public support. Efforts were therefore made to exclude provisions that might impede or wreck the legislation. But many basic issues were resolved.

It became clear that American economic assistance had to be viewed in relation to American foreign policy as a whole. And it was agreed that aid had to be based on a plan for European recovery that included a "strong production effort, the expansion of foreign trade, the creation and maintenance of internal financial stability, and the development of economic cooperation. . . ." Such a plan was seen not only as an economic necessity, but as vital also to "the establishment of a lasting peace, the general welfare and national interest of the United States, and the attainment of the objectives of the United Nations." These purposes were regarded as closely linked with the restoration or maintenance in European countries of "principles of individual liberty, free institutions and genuine independence"—principles which were found to rest largely upon "the establishment of sound economic conditions, stable international economic relationships, and the achievement by the countries of Europe of a healthy economy independent of extraordinary outside assistance." [31]

Secretary Marshall's original emphasis on European initiative and joint endeavor in evolving a program was amplified. Congress emphasized the importance of using the breathing spell afforded by American aid to devise measures to facilitate "mutual assistance and cooperation." [32]

[30] Interview, Crawford, cited.   [31] Foreign Assistance Act of 1948, Sec. 102.
[32] "Mindful of the advantages which the United States has enjoyed through the existence of a large domestic market with no internal trade barriers, and believing that similar advantages can accrue to the countries of Europe, it is declared to be the policy of the people of the United States to encourage these countries through a joint organization to exert sustained common efforts as set forth in the report of the Committee of European Economic Cooperation signed at Paris on Sep-

The question of eligibility of individual countries to participate in the program arose particularly in connection with Spain, on account of conflicting attitudes toward the Franco regime. Congress finally decided that any country (together with its dependent areas) would be eligible if it signed the initial CEEC report or adhered to a joint program of European recovery designed to accomplish the purposes set forth in the legislation. There was agreement that participation by western Germany was important, economically and politically, and should be welcomed.

The law provided for bilateral agreements under which each participating country would undertake to increase its own production, take measures for achieving financial stability, and cooperate in mutual efforts to reduce trade barriers. Each government was to deposit local currency "counterpart" funds equivalent to the amounts received in grants. Ninety-five percent of such funds was to be used, with the concurrence of the United States government, for domestic recovery; the remaining 5 percent was to be reserved to help meet American administrative and procurement costs. Each country was expected, furthermore, to assist in the accumulation of strategic materials required by the United States.

An appropriation not to exceed 4.3 billion dollars was authorized for the first twelve months, to which was added up to one billion dollars for assistance on flexible credit terms.[33]

General provisions required that procurement in the United States be so conducted as to minimize the drain on goods in short supply and to encourage the use of commodities in surplus, and that petroleum products be obtained as far as practicable from sources outside the United States. Only two "protective clauses" could be construed as concessions to "special interests." One stipulated that 50 percent of all assistance goods be transported in American ships; and the other, that not less than 25 percent of all wheat shipments from the United States be in the form of flour. The danger of such clauses, even when advocated on grounds of national interest, was recognized. "I don't believe," commented Francis Wilcox later, "that Congress was swayed too much by the demands of particular pressure groups. In general the action that was taken was in the national interest." [34]

---

tember 22, 1947, which will speedily achieve that economic cooperation in Europe which is essential for lasting peace and prosperity." Foreign Assistance Act, Sec. 102.

[33] Secs. 114(c) and 111(c) (2). Pending actual appropriation, the Reconstruction Finance Corporation was instructed to make advances up to one billion dollars.

[34] Interview cited.

The question whether a separate United States government agency should be created to administer the program, or whether the responsibility should be given to a permanent department never developed into a real contest. Sentiment in Congress—especially Republican sentiment—clearly favored a new "businesslike" organization designed to accomplish an emergency operation with maximum efficiency. Key officers in the executive branch, including Marshall and Harriman,[35] personally favored the establishment of a separate agency, and the President so recommended.[36]

Three related questions, however, were actively debated: the character of the new organization; its scope of authority; and its relationship to the permanent agencies, especially the Department of State.

Mention has been made of various proposals on the type of agency to be established. The decision reached, to create a new administrative organ to be known as the Economic Cooperation Administration (ECA), followed lengthy discussion. The law directed the establishment of a headquarters for the new agency in Washington, a coordinating office in Europe, and a special mission in each participating country.[37]

The Administrator was to review and appraise the requirements of participating countries, formulate programs for United States assistance, and provide for their efficient execution. On financial questions the Administrator was directed to consult the National Advisory Council on International Monetary and Financial Problems (NAC).[38] Provision was made for a twelve-member Public Advisory Board (in lieu of a supervisory council) of citizens "of broad and varied experience in matters affecting the public interest." And a joint Congressional com-

[35] Interviews cited.

[36] There had been a contest on this issue within the executive branch, where Bureau of the Budget personnel and many in the Department of State advocated an organization directly subordinate to the State Department, as the Interim and Greek-Turkish aid programs had been. The printed record does not indicate the extent to which political conditions in the U.S. as well as more objective considerations affected the Congressional decision to establish a relatively autonomous new agency. According to many witnesses, however, they were important. With control of Congress, a record of recent differences with the State Department over China policy, and a widespread expectation of victory at the polls in November, the Republicans assumed a large role in determining the character of the new agency and in according it an independent status.

[37] The ECA was empowered (Sec. 104(d)) to create a subsidiary corporation if deemed necessary or appropriate, but this authority was never used.

[38] A coordinating body established by Congress under the Bretton Woods Agreement Act.

mittee was set up to review all foreign assistance programs, reporting to both houses from time to time and making such recommendations as it deemed desirable; it became known as the "watchdog committee."

Unusual administrative flexibility contributed to the later effectiveness of the new agency. To clear the way for recruiting top-flight executives, Congress allowed fifty "excepted" positions for which normal government grades and pay could be exceeded.[39] Personnel could be borrowed from other parts of the government without loss in status. Authorization was given for special delegations of administrative authority from the State Department to the ECA. Sufficient administrative funds were authorized and missions abroad were empowered to pay local employees out of the 5 percent of "counterpart" funds to be made available by the recipient countries. Leeway was afforded for extensive decentralization of administrative responsibilities.

Relations between the ECA and the Department of State presented a knotty question. Secretary Marshall insisted that his department should direct the agency on questions involving foreign policy. Some leading members of Congress, at the same time, were opposed to a dominant role for the State Department in administration. The problem was to devise a formula which, without impairing the authority of the Secretary of State, would give the agency enough latitude to carry out its wide operational functions. Congress resolved the issue by specifying that the new Administrator, appointed by and responsible to the President, should have equal status with the heads of executive departments. He and the Secretary of State were each to keep the other "fully and currently informed on matters, including prospective action . . . pertinent to the duties of the other." Any difference which could not be adjusted by consultation was to be referred to the President for final decision.[40]

Innovations

Many of the provisions of the new law were adapted from previous aid legislation. Earlier enactments had called for the negotiation of agreements with recipient countries, stipulated methods of furnishing financial assistance, provided—although in more rudimentary fashion—for the deposit of "counterpart" funds, and embodied regula-

[39] Congressional leaders subsequently agreed on arrangements to speed up employment by quick preliminary security checks for new personnel, subject to more thorough investigation after employment.

[40] Sec. 105(b).

tions governing procurement, price control, and other activities including the termination of aid.

But the new law contained significant innovations.[41] These included the establishment of a new agency; a joint approach and a joint organization within Europe; strong emphasis upon self-help and mutual assistance; the provision for advisory groups; the establishment of a high-level regional office in Europe; procurement procedures which stressed the use of private channels of trade; provisions governing the transportation of aid supplies; authorization of guarantees to safeguard American investments abroad; measures to facilitate acquisition by "sale, barter, or otherwise" of scarce basic materials; [42] instruction to the new agency to encourage travel abroad by United States citizens as a means of enabling the participating countries to acquire needed dollars; and the establishment of a joint Congressional committee to review and report to Congress on all foreign assistance programs.

Decision

When the votes were finally taken, the count in favor of adoption was 69 to 17 in the Senate and 329 to 74 in the House of Representatives. The Republican vote in support of the Marshall Plan was 31 to 13 in the Senate, 171 to 63 in the House. The Democratic count was 38 to 4 in the Senate and 158 to 11 in the House. After differences between the Senate and House bills were resolved in conference, the act was promptly approved by both houses and became law on April 3, 1948.

The months of deliberation were ended. A decision had been reached, and the time had come to take the program "off the books" and translate it into action.

[41] For a detailed analysis, see David M. Crawford, "United States Foreign Assistance Legislation, 1947–1948," *Yale Law Journal,* May 1949, pp. 877–921.

[42] Sec. 115(b).

CHAPTER 4

Launching the European

Recovery Program (ERP)

THE first step, in accordance with the new enactment, was the choice of a man to direct the gigantic enterprise. The law had provided his title, Administrator for Economic Cooperation; his salary, $20,000 per year; his rank, comparable to that of the head of an executive department; and the means of his appointment, by the President, with the advice and consent of the Senate. It remained for the President to provide his name.

Choice of Hoffman as Administrator

This he did on April 6, when he appointed Paul G. Hoffman to be the Administrator of the new foreign aid program.

President Truman's initial choice for the post was former Under-Secretary of State Acheson. But when he consulted Senator Vandenberg, it became clear that the Republican majority in Congress wanted a man of broad business, rather than governmental, experience, preferably a Republican. Vandenberg pointed out that Hoffman's name was at or near the top of every list of possibilities proposed, and expressed confidence that his appointment would be promptly and cordially endorsed by the Senate. Hoffman had played a leading role in the earlier work of the President's Committee on Foreign Aid, and Truman, after a slight hesitation, warmed to the suggestion. "It seems," said Hoffman later, smiling, "that I was the least obnoxious of the Republicans." [1]

But for personal reasons he did not want the job. After an urgent summons to Washington, he indicated to Vandenberg his intention of declining the offer. But the Senator replied: "You can't do that. You've got to take it!" And he persuaded Hoffman to keep an open mind until he conferred with Truman.

Hoffman described later the course of that interview and what followed. "When I saw the President," he said, "I told him that I had never succeeded by employing anyone who didn't want a job, and said that I didn't want this one. But he answered that it was different in government—that here the best men are often those who don't want a job. He talked about a difference in motives, and of course there is something in that. After the conversation Truman pulled a trick on me, a good trick that I have used myself when a man is 90 percent committed. Someone brought into a press conference, where I was reporting on a trip to Korea, a notice that I had accepted the appointment. This left me way out on a limb where I couldn't withdraw without a public repudiation." [2]

A Running Start

On April 9, six days after the Economic Cooperation Act became law, Hoffman was sworn into office. He had just learned that no appropriation had yet been voted. But by prior arrangement, he was able to announce that 21 million dollars (transferred from interim aid funds) had been allocated for the recovery program.[3] The announcement

---

[1] Interview, New York, January 28, 1953. Acheson's own informal account of this development follows: "When the Marshall Plan was about to be passed, President Truman called for me and wanted me to head the new administration. I strongly advised against it, saying that I thought that it would lead to resentment on the Hill. I urged consultation with Vandenberg, real consultation; I thought that he would suggest Paul Hoffman and urged that if he did so, the President agree. That's what happened. Mr. Hoffman's appointment worked out well." Interview, October 20, 1953.

[2] Interview cited.

[3] Such use of unexpended balances had been approved under Sec. 114(b) of the Foreign Assistance Act. Congress had also authorized, under Sec. 114(a), advances by the Reconstruction Finance Corporation up to one billion dollars without interest for initial operations, pending necessary appropriations. Three months had been allowed for the conclusion of bilateral agreements with the participating countries; during this period aid could be extended in the absence of such agreements.

dramatized the fact that the urgency of the situation in Europe was to be met by speedy action.

Conception of the Task

The Administrator's essential job, as he saw it, was to help the Europeans formulate and carry out a program that would lead to genuine recovery. It was not to be a relief operation, and Hoffman, who regarded production as the crucial element in Europe's economic salvation, resisted at first the idea of extensive food shipments. "I had not myself been up against the kind of situation in which chronic undernourishment cut down people's working energy," he confessed later, "and had to see for myself how imperative food was as a tool for building up their production." [4]

The objective was not to promote American economic expansion, nor was it to develop economic warfare against Russia. "We saw," he recalled, "that Russia was going to oppose us. Some thought we should fight fire with fire: if the Soviets were going to prevent recovery in western Europe, we should prevent recovery on their side. I was opposed to this on the ground that our means should be adapted to the end we had in view—recovery. I believed that in fighting communism in Europe, we would not be justified in using amoral or immoral means. We would lose all our moorings if we adopted the Machiavellian philosophy that the ends justify the means. Therefore I insisted on confining ourselves to the recovery field."

Hoffman was faced with the dual task of constructing an organization to administer the four-year, multi-billion-dollar aid program and of providing immediate support to shaky European economies. The depressed level of intra-European trade during the first quarter of 1948 had aggravated existing shortages; the process of deterioration had to be checked before real recovery could begin. But planning for recovery had to go forward as emergency shipments were arranged.

The planning had to be done by the Europeans. "I had a strong belief," declared Hoffman,[5] "that no pattern imposed by a group of planners in Washington could possibly be effective. Among our policy and administrative group at the highest level, I tried to inculcate the idea that the responsibility must be given to the Europeans themselves. Coming into this with a business background, I thought that if we in

---

[4] Interview cited.   [5] *Ibid.*

the ECA adopted a new role—as a kind of investment banker—that would be the right approach. In order to get an effective program, each country would need to bring in its own plan, and the OEEC [Organization for European Economic Cooperation] would have to bring in a plan for coordination, with us not imposing a proposition on either. I had learned from experience that if you want enthusiastic cooperation, you have to get those concerned to do the planning, or at least to participate in it.

"Of course I was appalled by the job. No one had a blueprint. I decided first to get a group of people I could talk to—who had done some thinking. Among the number were Dick Bissell, who was very sophisticated about the problems we were facing, Tex Moore,[6] to help with personnel and organization, Ed Mason,[7] and Calvin Hoover.[8] Then I concentrated on key people for the agency. Although the White House staff had ideas, I felt that I had to pick my own people. We got hold of Bissell, Alex Henderson [9] as general counsel, and to handle the question of loans, Wayne Taylor.[10] After some inquiry, we learned that 'Fitz' [11] was at the top in agriculture and I secured him. We needed a Deputy Administrator who would know his business and who knew Washington. After careful inquiry, I chose Howard Bruce." [12]

Selection of Harriman and Foster

"For Special Representative in Europe," Hoffman continued, "I wanted either Lew Douglas [13] or Averell Harriman. I was flying high. I had to. The President wanted to appoint a Democrat, and I wanted someone in whom he had confidence. There were probably not more than five men in America equipped for that job.[14] I put the two names

---

[6] Maurice T. Moore, New York attorney, president of Time Magazine, Inc.

[7] Dean, School of Public Administration, Harvard University; former member of Harriman committee.

[8] Chairman of the Department of Economics, Duke University; former member of Harriman committee.

[9] New York attorney.

[10] Onetime president, Export-Import Bank.

[11] D. A. Fitzgerald, head of the Office of Foreign Agricultural Relations, Department of Agriculture.

[12] Baltimore industrialist and financier; onetime Director of Material, Army Service Forces. The initial group also included Donald C. Stone, experienced government administrator; Samuel Anderson, industrial expert; C. P. Fahnestock, information specialist; and Eric Kohler, auditor.

[13] Lewis W. Douglas, U.S. Ambassador to the U.K.

[14] The law had stipulated that the Special Representative in Europe, with the rank of Ambassador Extraordinary and Plenipotentiary, should serve as the repre-

to the President in alphabetical order." [15] Harriman was chosen. He was trusted by the President and well known to Hoffman as a man with whom he could work. After some persuasion, Harriman agreed to accept the appointment.

Named as Deputy Special Representative in Europe was William C. Foster, who, as Under-Secretary of Commerce, had achieved an outstanding reputation as an administrator.

Organization and Staffing of the ECA

In hotel suites and hurriedly arranged temporary offices, Hoffman and his associates tackled the job of constructing the new agency. While the broad functions and responsibilities of the ECA—to be conducted through a Washington headquarters, a regional office, and country missions—had been defined in the law, the detailed administrative structure had not been stipulated. A special "task force" under Donald C. Stone [16] was set up to work on the organizational pattern.

Early thinking envisaged a small agency dealing primarily with procurement—first of food and raw materials, then of "recovery goods" to hasten the expansion of European production. It was thought that the job could be accomplished largely by two sets of commodity specialists, industrial and agricultural, and that these groups, assisted by a fiscal and trade division, would constitute the operational core of the agency.[17]

But the emphasis soon began to fall on the analysis of economic conditions and needs, area by area, and on efforts to relate economic assistance to recovery policies in each country. Procurement and production, it was found, could not be isolated and dealt with apart from other basic elements in recovery. The task was not simply "increasing production," but increasing production in France or Italy or Greece, and it became clear that the ECA staff must concern itself with the intensive study and coordination of individual country programs as well as with procurement and planning on a "functional" basis.

---

sentative of the Administrator in Europe and also as the chief representative of the U.S. government to "any organization of participating countries which may be established by such countries to further a joint program for economic recovery." To him was to be given the responsibility of coordinating the activities of the chiefs of all the country missions.

[15] Interview cited.

[16] Subsequently appointed ECA director of administration.

[17] Interview, Samuel Van Hyning (then special assistant to Bissell), Washington, March 23, 1953.

Other aspects of the organization were developed in a similar *ad hoc* fashion. For example, when Harriman agreed to head the Office of the Special Representative (OSR) in Europe, it was with the understanding that he would have broad scope for action and decision. Before he and Foster took up their duties in Paris, the original conception of the Special Representative as a roving ambassador with a small staff of key officials had already been discarded. For it was substituted the idea of a strong European headquarters with organization and functions comparable, in its regional sphere, to those of the central headquarters in Washington. Foster assumed major responsibility for the operation of the European headquarters—leaving Harriman free to deal with broad policy and relationships.

Never before had an overseas regional office been set up to play so large a part in a peacetime operation of the United States government. Two factors appear to have been chiefly responsible. One was the need for a high-level branch of the ECA to deal with the OEEC—the joint European organization (see p. 80). The other was the necessity for an arrangement acceptable to both the Republican-controlled Congress and the Democratic Administration, giving exceptionally capable individuals from the two parties top posts of nearly equal status.

In Washington, under an assistant deputy administrator for programs (Bissell), divisions were established to deal with food, industry, fiscal and trade policy, procurement, strategic materials, transportation, statistics and reports, and (in early July) program coordination.[18] Essential staff units were created, according to accepted practice, for legal,

[18] The Program Coordination Division, composed chiefly of "country specialists," was created to help correlate the activities of the other divisions, to analyze conditions and needs in the individual participating countries, and to review economic and financial projections, formulate recommendations on dollar allocations, and participate with the "functional" divisions in the breakdown of country aid into commodity categories. The Fiscal and Trade Policy Division was responsible for defining and recommending ECA policy and action relative to the stimulation of trade (within Europe and between Europe and other parts of the world) and to the domestic fiscal and monetary policies of the participating countries as they bore upon recovery programs. A separate unit was created to handle the programing of aid to China. The "functional" divisions—one for food and agriculture and one for industry—were concerned mainly with procurement planning, efficient utilization of equipment and commodities provided by the ECA, fostering productive efficiency, and furnishing technical advice and assistance as needed. They screened aid allotments and procurement authorizations in their respective fields. These two divisions were subsequently grouped, under a director of operations, with other "functional" divisions concerned with procurement transactions, the transportation of supplies, the administration of technical assistance, and the extraction and purchase of strategic materials for the U.S.

personnel, security, and other functions. One, however, was an innovation: the Office of Labor Advisors, whose function was to stimulate manpower utilization, to present the democratic viewpoint of American labor to European trade union organizations, and to interpret the views of both American and European labor on the recovery program.

The organizational structure of the OSR followed broadly that of the Washington headquarters. The country missions approximated the same pattern on a smaller scale, with variations according to the size of the mission and the conditions faced in individual countries. In Greece, for example, emergency conditions required a mission larger than those in France, the United Kingdom, or Italy.

The difficult task of staffing called for highly skilled matching of jobs and men. The idea of incorporating a whole contingent from any other branch of the government was never adopted, and Hoffman, cautioned by Foster, was wary about accepting well-recommended castoffs from other departments.[19] It was agreed that the organization would not be "frozen" for two weeks, and that during this interval appointments would be on an "acting" basis, subject to change. Statements of the functions of key officers were developed in consultation with the intended incumbents; in a number of instances these statements were tested and refined in group conferences.[20] To ensure a "businesslike" approach, selected posts were at the outset filled with businessmen, preferably with previous governmental experience.

Lists of men with relevant experience and proven capacity had been compiled in the State Department; many names were added through consultation with business and other groups. Of some seven hundred government administrators, businessmen, economists, commodity specialists, area experts, and others on the final lists, about four hundred eventually entered the organization.[21] The higher administrative and technical positions were, by and large, filled by deciding on qualified individuals and then inducing them to serve. Most of the key posts in the agency were filled in this way rather than by relying on selections from among many thousands of applicants.

The selection of chiefs of mission in the participating countries was

[19] Interview, Hoffman, New York, October 20, 1954.

[20] Interview, Stone, Washington, September 21, 1954.

[21] Samuel Board, a senior personnel officer, was impressed by Hoffman's approach to prospective key personnel. "The way in which he could pick up the telephone and persuade outstanding people to serve was wonderful." Interview, Washington, August 6, 1952.

particularly important. These men, who ranked second only to ambassadors, were responsible for American participation in the recovery program in each country. Besides directing the economic and technical work of their respective staffs and reviewing the use and effects of American aid, they had the quasi-ambassadorial functions of day-to-day negotiations and consultations with the participating governments. The first group of appointments included Thomas K. Finletter [22] for the United Kingdom, David Bruce [23] for France, J. D. Zellerbach [24] for Italy, and Roger Lapham [25] for China.

Procurement System

The ECA did not engage directly in the purchase of aid supplies. Procurement was handled instead by recipient governments and, with their concurrence, by private firms and nationals of the participating countries. This delegation of purchasing was a major innovation and had two distinct advantages. It obviated the need for a large, expensive procurement organization such as had been established in the Lend-Lease and UNRRA Administrations. And it made maximum use of private trade channels abroad as well as in the United States.

This procedure enabled the ECA to control the planning, approval, and financing of commodities to be procured without actually purchasing them. It was based on the screening and approval of procurement authorization (PA) requests submitted by the governments or nationals of the participating countries, and the issuance of letters of commitment underwriting transfers of aid funds through existing financial channels. The procedure became known as the "PA system." Each application for a commodity was submitted by country representatives in Washington and reviewed by the ECA to ascertain whether it fell within the country's allotment, whether it conformed to established criteria, whether substitutions could be made, and what the effect of the proposed procurement would be on the United States economy. When the application was approved, a letter of commitment was issued to a cooperating bank guaranteeing ECA reimbursement of the credit extended.[26]

[22] Former government and business executive; subsequently Secretary, U.S. Air Force.

[23] Assistant Secretary of Commerce, 1947–1948.

[24] President, Crown Zellerbach Corporation, San Francisco.

[25] Former mayor of San Francisco.

[26] An alternative means of financing grant aid, especially during the first quarter of operations, was by direct ECA reimbursement to the foreign government for

As will be seen, emphasis on detailed review of procurement schedules declined relatively as attention was directed increasingly to other factors in Europe's economy. But important advantages remained. The ECA was able to give Congress a precise picture of American aid, to show that aid dollars were being used for essential purposes, and to evolve cost-control and accounting procedures ensuring a provident use of funds. Despite the opposition of a few private interests, the agency's insistence on economical procurement and its recovery of funds obligated for overpriced commodities saved tens of millions of dollars.

Operating Principles and Procedures

In April 1948 the ECA issued its first order on operating policies and procedures. It shows how the agency went into high gear on an initial "crash program" for emergency aid. The following directives were included:

Out of 1.3 billion dollars scheduled to be programed in the first three months, about one-third should be allotted in the first four weeks.

Initial procurement should be concentrated on food, fuel and fertilizer, both because of their urgency and availability and because of the relative speed of documentation on a limited number of large-scale purchases.

The bulk of procurement for this period should be done on a reimbursable basis. Participating countries should be encouraged to emphasize, as soon as possible, the procurement of "recovery" rather than relief-type commodities. The utilization of existing procurement, supply, and banking channels and practices should continue; any change should be toward greater use of private as opposed to governmental channels.

Fiscal controls should be maintained at the highest executive level to assure coordination and integration. Documentation for accounting purposes should conform to standard government accounting procedure for domestic procurement.

Only those arrangements between the ECA and the other United States government agencies found essential to initiate operations should be formalized at the outset, without prejudice to any long-range interagency agreements to be negotiated later.

---

purchases already made. In some cases, under special circumstances, the ECA made direct payments to suppliers. Loan aid was negotiated on a government-to-government basis, with the Export-Import Bank serving as the ECA's fiscal agent and disbursing funds against procurement authorizations.

Establishment of the OEEC

Meanwhile, European leaders were at work on a complementary task —creating an organization to carry out their undertaking to work jointly for recovery. Delegates to the CEEC conference of July–September 1947 had agreed that further work should be done on certain of the problems they had encountered. Accordingly, several conferences of experts were held during the winter of 1947–1948 to consider aid requirements, intra-European payments, tariff reductions, and manpower utilization.

The CEEC met again on March 15, 1948, to plan a permanent Organization for European Economic Cooperation (OEEC). The delegates were well aware that success depended on a nice balance among national points of view.

On the first day a working party was named, under the chairmanship of Britain's Sir Oliver Franks, to develop proposals for a permanent body. This group, representing sixteen participating countries and the zones of western Germany,[27] set up three committees: one to draft an agreement defining the general obligations of the participating countries; another to study the legal, financial, and administrative problems involved in the creation of a permanent body; and the third to consider the structure and functions of the projected organization. A small American group [28] was on hand for consultation, advice, and assistance.

Differences soon developed over the type of organization to be established and the nature of the cooperation that should be envisaged. The British, traditionally reluctant to identify themselves closely with Europe, conceived of an organization that would function as a continuous international conference, not as a supranational body. Among the French there was a growing belief that a stage in history had arrived when the individual nations of Europe could not alone solve their problems—either economic or political. The French delegation, therefore, favored an organization with some degree of autonomy and with functions of its own. On this issue, the British view prevailed.

Another question concerned the role of the greater and smaller na-

[27] Until October 31, 1949, officials of the occupying powers represented the three western zones of Germany. On that date, western Germany became a full member of the OEEC, as delegates of the Federal Republic took their places. The Anglo-American Zone of the Free Territory of Trieste was admitted on October 14, 1949. These additions raised to eighteen the number of full participants. In June 1950, the U.S. and Canada became "associates," but not members.

[28] Including Labouisse and Bonesteel.

4. In Norway, an electric steel-refining plant opens an industrial frontier at Mo-i-Rana, north of the Arctic Circle.

5. In Italy, automobile tops are moved from a powered stamping press.

6. At Bedford Mill, England, synthetic yarn is woven into rayon fabrics. This is the spooling room.

7. Microscope and lens manufacture in Germany is given fresh impetus with Marshall aid counterpart funds.

tions in the organizational structure. For centuries the smaller countries of western Europe had struggled against domination by the larger continental powers. Now, with Netherlands representatives taking the lead, they were determined that in the proposed new European agency France and Britain should not make all the important decisions. Their stand on this issue, against initial British and French opposition, had two consequences: a rule requiring unanimous consent, in reaching decisions, of the member governments concerned; and the appointment of a Benelux representative to one of three major positions in the organization.[29] The initial appointees to these positions were Paul-Henri Spaak of Belgium as chairman of the agency's top Council, Sir Edmund Hall-Patch of the United Kingdom as chairman of the Executive Committee, and Robert Marjolin of France as Secretary-General.

Despite these and other more technical problems, the working party succeeded in devising a preliminary draft constitution or "convention" which was formally submitted to the Council and adopted on April 16.

Through the OEEC convention, member countries assumed certain general obligations. Individually, they agreed to increase production, making fullest use of available manpower resources, and to achieve internal financial stability. Cooperatively, they agreed to elaborate and execute a joint recovery program, to reduce economic barriers and promote maximum increases in production and trade, to achieve as soon as possible a multilateral system of payments, and to correct or avoid excessive disequilibrium in their financial and economic relations. This last provision implied in essence that each country, when faced with an important economic or financial decision, would consider what effect it might have on the economies of the others and, if desirable, consult them before taking action.

To implement these pledges, an organization was established which provided for:

A Council, responsible for general or administrative decisions. This body, to be composed of representatives of all member countries, would meet at irregular intervals to direct and supervise the administration and operation of the entire organization, to reach decisions on questions of policy, and to consider preparatory studies submitted by other parts of the organization. Questions of budget, staff rules, and staff appointments were subject to the Council's jurisdiction, and all decisions had to be unanimous.[30]

[29] Interview, H. M. Hirschfeld, The Hague, November 21, 1952.

[30] There were two qualifications to this "rule of unanimity": (1) The Council could itself decide to adopt a different procedure in certain special cases. (2) A

An Executive Committee, to consist of representatives of seven member countries, to be elected annually by the Council.

Technical committees, to be composed of representatives of member countries. Six were initially created to study such broad questions as the general economic position of member countries, trade, payments, and the development of dependent overseas territories. Fourteen others were subsequently appointed to deal with food, agriculture, coal, oil, and other commodities.

An Executive Secretariat, to be staffed by international civil servants responsible solely to the Organization. This group, under the direction of a Secretary-General, would have responsibility for preparing meetings of the Council and Executive Committee, submitting proposals to them, insuring the execution of their decisions, maintaining relations with international organizations, and furnishing information to the press. The Secretariat, with appropriate staff offices, was to consist mainly of directorates dealing with general economic problems and country studies, trade and finance, and technical and commodity problems.

No time was lost in naming delegates and selecting staff members for the new European agency. By early May the OEEC was a going concern.

Would It Work?

The OEEC's first test came quickly. Late one night word was received that the American government desired the OEEC to take responsibility for recommending the division of aid for the fiscal year 1948–1949. To most delegates this news came as a shock, since it had been generally assumed that representatives of the participating countries would go to Washington with their programs and handle their aid negotiations bilaterally, as they had during the war. Commenting four years later on this development, Baron Charles J. Snoy of Belgium[31] stated: "The most important episode in the early history of the OEEC came when the Americans said: 'You recommend the division of aid.' We feared it would wreck the Organization. Yet it was possible. We had to learn cooperation. No one could take the responsibility for jeopardizing the whole plan, even if dissatisfied with any particular decision. It

---

member country could abstain if it did not wish to take part in a decision or was not directly interested in it.

[31] Second chairman of the OEEC Council at the "official level." Interview, Brussels, November 19, 1952.

was a great lesson for us. We knew intellectually that this was necessary. But here was a practical road."

The First Ninety Days

ECA operations began on the day Hoffman assumed office. Two weeks later the freighter *John H. Quick* sailed from Galveston, Texas, for Bordeaux carrying 9,000 long tons of wheat—the first shipment of goods to leave under the new program. Within another week six more ships sailed for France, the Netherlands, and Italy, carrying food and fuel.

By June 30, goods and services costing more than 738 million dollars had been authorized on a grant basis, and an additional 291 million had been programed. Negotiations were under way or completed for 289 million in loans, raising the total for the quarter to a little more than 1.3 billion dollars obligated or nearly obligated—an extraordinary volume of business transacted within the first ninety days.

Goods authorized during this initial period were almost entirely bulk commodities; only about 9.6 million dollars' worth of machinery and equipment was included.[32] About 84 percent was from the Western Hemisphere, 57 percent from the United States. In accordance with a statutory provision, the prices paid were not more than those prevailing in the United States, which in some cases were below world market prices.

The first ninety days witnessed also the negotiation, by the Department of State, of the bilateral agreements upon which continuing aid depended. Under these agreements, substantially alike in their basic provisions, the conditions of aid specified by Congress were formalized and the obligations of the recipient countries established. The key negotiation was with the British; other countries waited to make certain that the terms of their agreements were no less favorable than those acceded to by the United Kingdom.

Aid and Cooperation

On May 7 the OEEC Council requested all participating countries to prepare materials for the formulation of joint estimates of requirements for the next quarter, beginning July 1. Each country was asked for data on its import program and estimated balance of payments,

---

[32] Bread grains were sent chiefly to the U.K., the Netherlands, and France; meat to the U.K. and Germany; cotton to France and Italy. A variety of foodstuffs and other basic commodities was programed for each participating country.

and for details on its production, consumption, imports, exports, and reserves of selected items. This information, when integrated, showed that the total dollar requirements for the July–September quarter would be approximately 2.9 billion dollars, of which one billion would be obtained from current receipts and 200 million from existing credits and appropriations; the remaining 1.7 billion dollars, it was hoped, would be provided by the ECA.

These data, together with balance-of-payments estimates for 1948–1949, were available when the OEEC undertook the first division-of-aid exercise referred to above. The task proved too complex and thorny for initial handling by the entire membership, and a special committee of "four wise men" was created to study the problem and make recommendations.[33] This group's proposals became the basis for eventual agreement and decision in the OEEC Council.

The picture which emerged from the committee's work was not bright. There were drastic shortages of food, raw materials, and capital equipment, and even if the committee's recommendations were followed, Belgium, Luxemburg, Denmark, the Netherlands, Norway, Portugal, Turkey, and western Germany could not expect aid equal to their anticipated dollar deficits.

Although the committee's recommendations were based on estimates submitted by the participating countries, questions arose before agreement was reached. Perhaps the most serious was one government's declared intention to negotiate directly with Washington as it had done in the past. This problem, which afforded a test of American intentions, was resolved by a message from Washington making unequivocal the United States position that aid to all member countries was contingent upon their cooperation with the OEEC.

Other problems were ironed out one by one, paving the way for unanimous approval of the division of aid to be recommended. Aside from the creation of the OEEC, this was the most far-reaching joint accomplishment of the opening phase of the European Recovery Program. It was the first positive, successful step on the road of practical cooperation. And it led to a growth of mutual assistance within Europe. Investigation of resources had revealed that a sizable portion of each country's needs could be provided from within Europe, if only the channels of trade were unclogged. Since external aid could not fill all urgent requirements, countries with surpluses were persuaded to

[33] The committee members were Giovanni Malagodi (Italy), Robert Marjolin (OEEC Secretariat), Eric Roll (U.K.), and Charles J. Snoy (Belgium).

make them more readily accessible to other countries. This cooperative effort threw a spotlight on intra-European trade and led to the establishment of a committee to study more deeply the problems of commerce within western Europe, and between OEEC countries and eastern Europe.[34]

Concurrent with the division of aid, intensive work was proceeding in the OEEC on a whole set of formidable tasks—a detailed program for the first quarter, another for the first year, intricate arrangements for the first intra-European payments agreement, and first steps in preparing a four-year or "long-term" program.

The Cominform at Work

While these events were taking place, the disruptive counterforce of communism was still operative. In France, Italy, and elsewhere Communist party leaders were at first reluctant to pronounce against the Marshall Plan. This fact and the rising popularity of the Plan in western and southern Europe had precipitated, in the summer of 1947, the establishment of the Cominform,[35] aligning the Communist parties of France and Italy with those of eastern Europe. Soon the entire Moscow-directed propaganda machine was mobilized against the Marshall Plan, which it described as "an instrument of preparation for war," "a means for the economic and political enslavement of Europe," and a measure for saving the American economy from the crisis that it faced if "captive markets" could not be found. Ironically, this campaign was based on the "principle" of protecting national sovereignty.

It was not without effect. For example, the French Institute of Public Opinion reported in September 1947 the results of a poll indicating that only 18 percent of the people believed that Secretary Marshall's proposal was dictated by a sincere wish to aid Europe's recovery; 17 percent attributed it to America's desire to intervene in Europe's affairs, and 47 percent, to a need for external markets to avoid an economic crisis in the United States; 18 percent had no opinion.

In France and Italy the most powerful labor unions were drawn into the struggle. In the Communist press the recovery program was made

---

[34] Congress had proscribed the shipment of ECA-financed goods going into the production of commodities for eastern Europe if, for reasons of national security, such commodities would be refused export licenses from the U.S. to eastern Europe. Foreign Assistance Act, Sec. 117(d).

[35] See Chapter 2.

the scapegoat for the political and economic difficulties faced by the participating nations. Explanations were simple and slogans were palatable to national prejudices. When wine sales slumped, it was because of Coca-Cola. When a motion picture industry faced bankruptcy, the reason lay in the "invasion of Hollywood films," which were not only displacing local productions but also undermining the national culture and contributing to moral decay. Even when enthusiasm for the recovery program mounted, the Communists were assiduously at work, planting suspicions of American motives and seeking to discredit those who came out in favor of policies espoused by the United States.

To counteract this campaign, the ECA and the governments of the participating countries began to build up their own informational activities. The energy and resourcefulness shown in this effort varied considerably from area to area. In some countries, notably France and Italy, the task was handicapped by the promptness with which the Communists had seized the propaganda initiative, thereby erecting immense difficulties for those who attempted to counteract misinformation, suspicion, and prejudice after they had been widely sown.

Two events which occurred before the end of June 1948, however, offset the initial propaganda advantage gained by the Communists. One was the Berlin blockade—imposed by the Soviets partly to counteract a highly successful currency reform in western Germany—followed by the dramatic airlift which demonstrated the firmness of American support. The second event was the break between Yugoslavia and the other Communist-bloc countries, focusing attention on the completeness of Russian domination over the satellite nations.

CHAPTER 5

First Year (1948-1949):

Food and Tools

THIS chapter and the next three present a year-by-year account of high lights in the European Recovery Program after the formative period discussed in the foregoing pages.[1] Many of the essential facts about the operation have been adequately summarized elsewhere.[2] The treatment here, therefore, is compressed, with emphasis upon major problems and how they were met, the evolution of policies and techniques, and the objective data needed as background for the evaluation offered in the latter half of this volume.

The Committee of European Economic Cooperation (CEEC), after slashing its first estimates, had presented in September 1947 a tentative figure of 19.6 billion dollars required for aid during the next four years, and the Harriman committee had estimated the four-year cost to the United States Treasury at something between 12.5 billion and 17.2

[1] The coverage of one year of the operation in each of these chronological chapters is not wholly arbitrary. The aims, rationale, scope, and emphasis of the Marshall Plan undertaking were reviewed and modified annually through the process of Congressional hearings and legislation. As a result, the "ground rules" for the ECA and the funds for major phases of the operation were established largely on a fiscal-year basis which extended, for the U.S. government, from July 1 of one year to June 30 of the next.

[2] Apart from official reports, the most comprehensive factual analysis to date appears in William Adams Brown and Redvers Opie, *American Foreign Assistance* (Brookings Institution, Washington, 1953).

billion dollars, depending upon whether more or less favorable assumptions were adopted. The President proposed an authorization of 17 billion dollars for the full four years and 6.8 billion dollars for the first fifteen months. But Congress, as we have seen, was unwilling to make specific financial commitments for more than one year at a time.

Total funds made available by Congress for the European Recovery Program during the four-year period came to about 13.15 billion dollars; 4.97 billion dollars were finally appropriated for 1948–1949, 3.78 billion for 1949–1950, 2.31 billion for 1950–1951, and 1.02 billion in economic aid (under the Mutual Security Program) for 1951–1952; in addition, 1.15 billion was made available early for assistance on credit terms, and, in 1951–1952, a transfer of 478 million dollars from military to economic aid was effected. During the same four-year period appropriations for economic assistance in east and southeast Asia raised the total dollar aid for economic purposes administered by the ECA (and by its successor, the MSA, during the latter half of 1951–1952) to roughly 14.2 billion dollars.[3]

A Four-Year Look Ahead

In the summer of 1948 the OEEC invited each participating country to submit a plan of action for reaching a position, by 1952–1953, from which it could maintain its own economy without extraordinary external aid. They were also asked to indicate how they expected their economies to fit into the economy of a Europe living without such assistance.

As submitted, each country program consisted of a survey of the national economy, a plan of action according to main segments of the economy, anticipated results for 1952, and the "conditions of success." At the end of 1948 the OEEC forwarded to the ECA a report dealing with the first stages of the European program, accompanied by a full statement of the "programs" of all member countries as envisaged up to the middle of 1952.[4]

Some of the hypotheses underlying the national programs applied

[3] Department of Commerce, *Foreign Aid by the United States Government, 1940–1951*, pp. 110–115, and FOA, administrative records.

[4] *Interim Report on the European Recovery Programme* (Paris, 1948). Vol. I, "Report of the Council of the Organization for European Economic Co-operation to the United States Economic Co-operation Administration, on the First Stages of the European Recovery Programme," 195 p.; Vol. II, "National Programmes of Members for the Recovery Period Ending 30th June, 1952, Submitted to the Organization for European Economic Co-operation," 1112 p.

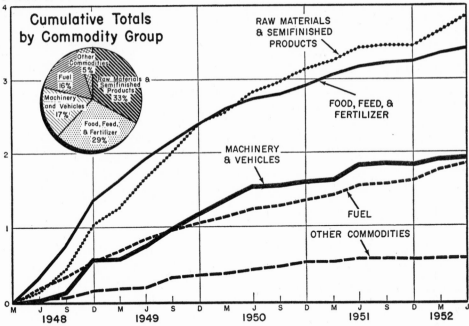

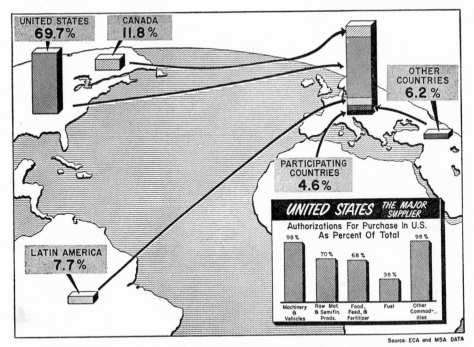

1. Aid to Europe through the Marshall Plan, cumulative April 3, 1948–June 30, 1952. *Upper:* Procurement authorizations by commodity categories. *Lower:* Sources of goods supplied.

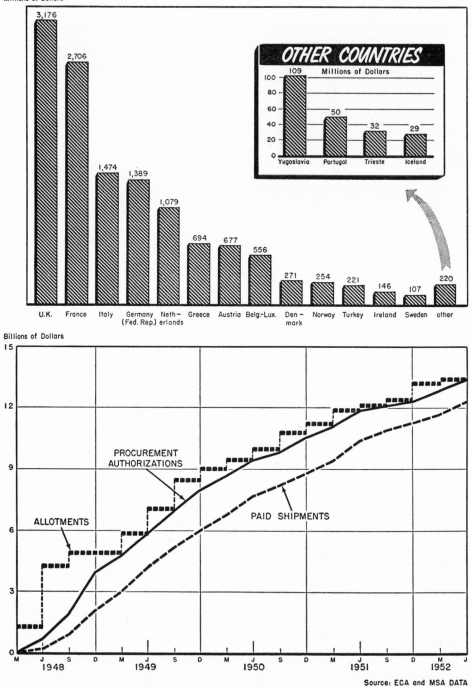

2. Aid to Europe through the Marshall Plan, cumulative April 3, 1948–June 30, 1952. *Upper:* Procurement authorized by country of destination. *Lower:* Total program allotments, procurement authorizations, and paid shipments.

only to particular countries, but many were common to all. The most important were that there would be peace throughout the four-year period; that a high level of employment would continue throughout the world and particularly in the United States; that a high level of world trade would be maintained (some countries postulating also a recovery of their trade with western Germany or with eastern Europe); that inflationary pressures would be brought under control and finances stabilized throughout western Europe; that plans of action would include those of special strategic importance; that cooperation in solving common problems would be maintained throughout the period and continued after 1952; that the "generous assistance" being provided by the United States to assist European recovery would be continued throughout the period.[5]

The OEEC recognized that the national programs, taken together, did not provide an adequate basis for a solution of the problem of western Europe as a whole. But detailed examination of the programs enabled the OEEC to push its analysis further than the CEEC had done in drawing up its 1947 report. Out of this study developed a fuller understanding of the ways in which Europe's position in the world economy had weakened. Some problems were found to be more deep-rooted than they had appeared to be in 1947.

The *Interim Report* did not claim to present a "joint" European recovery program. But, said the OEEC, "there lies behind it a period of co-operative activity unlike anything hitherto known in the economic relations between any group of independent states."

Both national effort and international cooperation were stressed. "If the objectives [set] . . . are pursued in isolation," the report continued, "grave difficulties may follow for the participating countries, both individually and collectively." Each country would need to make an "immense national effort," "to take account of the consequences of their individual programmes on all the other participating countries . . . [and] to secure the co-operative action which is indispensable."[6]

European recovery, as the OEEC saw it, was partly a European internal problem and partly a question of Europe's relations with the outside world. As to the former, the organization reached a conclusion which was to affect the entire course of the recovery program. Much more was required, it asserted, than statistical revisions in individual country programs. Statistics were valuable only as indications of existing national policies and of the size of the problem. "The modifications

[5] *Interim Report*, I, 11–12. [6] *Ibid.*, p. 14.

needed," declared the OEEC, "are changes of policy, import and export policy, investment and production policy, financial and commercial policy, in order to make possible the construction of a joint European recovery programme." [7]

Among the tasks to be faced in a combined recovery effort, high priority was given to the control of inflation, a great increase in production,[8] development of new sources of raw materials—especially in the overseas territories—and a steady growth of intra-European trade.

Europe's ability to pay its own way by 1952–1953 would depend largely on its ability to earn foreign exchange by selling goods abroad. A rise in the continent's export trade of 65 to 70 percent above existing levels was proposed as a 1952 target. Even with the most vigorous measures, the OEEC anticipated that western Europe, to break even, would still have to curtail its imports from the outside world, in 1952–1953, by some 10 to 15 percent.

After analyzing these problems, the OEEC concluded that some of the targets presented in the individual country programs probably could not be realized by the middle of 1952 and that a more realistic estimate would assume a somewhat slower but nonetheless significant recovery. The year 1952–1953 was not looked toward as "the end of the story" but as "a point on an upward curve." The effort called for, said the report, "is a severe challenge, but a challenge to which the peoples of Western Europe must respond." [9]

This first comprehensive attempt to analyze cooperatively the nature of Europe's economic crisis and to develop jointly a plan of action gave rise to a concept of recovery quite different from that which had dominated the thinking and planning of the participating countries during the previous year. No longer was the problem seen as primarily one of restoration after World War II. The war was viewed, not as the origin of Europe's economic problems, but as an occurrence which accelerated a process of deterioration that had begun much earlier with the decline, after 1913, of Europe's position in the world economy.

The ECA laid greater emphasis than did the OEEC on a rapid upswing in production. True, higher production required expanding markets in Europe and abroad. But the size of each European market was determined not only by its breadth—in terms of population and

[7] *Ibid.*, p. 123.

[8] A rise in total output of the order of 25 to 30 percent was envisaged for the four-year period.

[9] *Interim Report*, I, 121, 128.

accessibility—but also by its depth—in terms of productivity per man-day, exportable surpluses, and capacity to pay for imports. A massive rise in output was needed, moreover, before the economies of free Europe could begin to keep pace with those of the United States, Canada, and Soviet Russia. These rudimentary considerations lay behind a continuing emphasis by the ECA upon investments and productivity. "Our aid to Europe," wrote a knowledgeable commentator, "is primarily an investment operation." [10]

The case for a relatively high rate of investment throughout western Europe rested on political as well as economic grounds.[11] Without it, American aid would raise living standards temporarily and might relieve internal political stresses. But it would accomplish little toward enabling the continent to stand on its own feet. If, with the ending of aid, living standards should decline steeply, political dangers, including the risk of Communist subversion, would be aggravated.

During the interwar years, the growth of Europe's capital plant had lagged behind that of the United States and of Soviet Russia. Expansion was now urgently needed to help make good the deficit, to utilize an extensive reservoir of trained and skilled labor, to meet the needs of a growing population, and, as already noted, to make possible purchase of the goods, including food and raw materials, which western Europe could not itself produce and must obtain from abroad. Finally, capital plant expansion was fundamental to the development of military strength and security.

The relationship between European effort and American aid was nowhere more clearly apparent than in the field of investment. As Glenn Craig[12] noted later: "European industry was caught in a circle that had to be broken. There was a great need for capital accumulation. Nineteen forty-eight was about the time when it was possible to develop internally some capital accumulation if aid could be provided at critical points. For example, 300 million dollars from the ECA made possible investment on the continent of some 6 billion dollars, or twenty times as much, in thermo-generating power, over a period of five or six years; the aid was mostly in the form of thermo-equipment which Europe could not then produce. Again, in the case of rolling mill capacity, what

[10] Howard S. Ellis, *The Economics of Freedom* (Harper & Bros., for Council on Foreign Relations, New York, 1950), p. 34.

[11] See *ibid.*, pp. 32–34.

[12] Formerly director, ECA Industry Division. Interview, Washington, August 20, 1952.

was provided from the United States was only a fraction of what was needed, yet it made an enormous difference. A major theme in the industrial field was the extent to which marginal aid made possible large European internal investments."

Such considerations prompted the ECA, looking ahead from 1948, to put its main emphasis on expanding production. "For every dollar of our aid to Europe," said Hoffman later in testimony before Congress, "Europe puts six dollars into capital formation." When the program was over he recalled: "I felt that if Europe could, during the period of the Marshall Plan, go up by about one-third in its gross output, it would become a going concern. And I put this forward as an objective." [13]

The 1948–1949 Program

While looking ahead to the entire four-year period, the participating countries and the OEEC were also developing intensively their detailed plans for the first full year of operations. The year as a whole was marked by a transition in emphasis from food and raw materials to tools and machinery, and from economic stabilization to economic growth.

In preparing the 1948–1949 program, OEEC countries had to decide whether the plan should be limited to imports financed with American aid, or whether it should encompass a complete import program for western Europe. The latter and bolder course was chosen, since the role of United States-financed imports could be intelligently assessed only in the light of total anticipated imports, and since the ECA required a knowledge of prospective European resources as a whole before it could justify the American aid needed.

The year's program was presented in three parts, each of which, in the view of the OEEC, represented "a major achievement in economic cooperation." First came an internationally correlated and screened recovery program envisaging the allocation and use of nearly 4.9 billion dollars in American aid. The second involved the introduction of an embryonic system of intra-European payments linked to American aid but dependent also on assistance furnished by European countries to each other. The third grew out of the adoption of a set of rules of commercial policy to guide the future relations of the member countries.

The gains achievable with the backing of dollar aid were estimated, with production as the "touchstone of economic recovery." Agricultural

[13] Interview, New York, January 28, 1952.

output—with better weather conditions, extra effort, a larger consumption of fertilizers and a wider use of farm machinery—was expected to rise substantially over the low levels of the previous year—bread grains by some 45 percent, coarse grains by 12 percent, beet sugar by 26 percent, oil cake and meal by 45 percent. Coal production was expected to climb 13 percent, pig iron 68 percent, crude steel approximately 50 percent, and nonferrous metals (aluminum, copper, lead, zinc, tin) by ratios ranging from 16 to 78 percent. Substantial improvements over 1947 were anticipated also in maritime tonnage (17 percent) and in the output of nitrogenous fertilizers (27 percent), potash (29 percent), and wood pulp (23 percent).

The volume of trade between member countries was expected to rise from 5.8 billion dollars in 1947 to more than 8 billion dollars in 1948–1949—an increase of about one-fourth after discounting for price changes.

Projections of imports from outside Europe showed food and other agricultural items accounting for 39 percent of the total, raw materials for 25 percent, and capital equipment for 15 percent—payment to be made in considerable part out of aid funds. Agreement was reached on the distribution of aid to be recommended—with the largest shares going to the United Kingdom, France, Italy, western Germany, and the Netherlands. The dollar deficit of the participating countries was expected to decline from more than 8 billion dollars to less than 6 billion dollars, chiefly by a decrease in dollar-cost imports, although some expansion in exports was anticipated.

When the first annual program had been drawn up, the OEEC was able to say:

There exists in the Organization a means, unprecedented in the scope and continuity of its work, for the members to grapple internationally and co-operatively with the practical problems of the European economy. . . . The delegates are empowered by their Governments to conduct business of the greatest economic importance to their countries.[14]

Members felt that the program developed was "alive and practical and new." They were "encouraged that this venture in co-operation" had gone "so far forward in unanimity and friendship, and that a degree of co-operation which was yesterday an experiment" had already become a "habit and a state of mind." The extraordinarily hopeful spirit

[14] OEEC, *Report to the Economic Cooperation Administration on the First Annual Programme* (Paris, 1948), p. 15.

which animated the OEEC at the time found expression in the statement:

It is this growing sense of accomplishment, springing from the certainty that the well-being of each country can best be achieved by the proper and most efficient use of the talents and resources of all, which heartens the members of the Organization when they are confronted with the difficulties and uncertainties of these present times. As progress is made towards a greater cooperation and a growing prosperity, it is a great inspiration to the members to know that they have the good will and support of the people of the United States of America. The first steps along the common road to peace and prosperity have been taken. This programme is forwarded in the faith that what has been done will be lasting and that there will be greater successes to come.[15]

The Flow of Aid

By June 30, 1949, after fifteen months of operations, the ECA had allotted to the participating countries, for the procurement of goods and services, a total of 5,953 billion dollars [16] and nearly all of this amount had been obligated. About two-thirds of the commodities authorized for purchase were designated for procurement in the United States.[17] Raw materials and semifinished products comprised some 31 percent of commodity authorizations, as compared with 36 percent for food, feed, and fertilizer, 16 percent for fuel, and 14 percent for machinery and vehicles. Raw materials, semifinished products, and machinery and vehicles—which had accounted for slightly more than 20 percent of all shipments during the spring of 1948—rose to roughly 49 percent during the April–June quarter of 1949, while food, feed, and fertilizer dropped from nearly 50 percent to about 27 percent.[18]

Although procurement agents stationed in the United States and elsewhere were able to do most of the purchasing through commercial channels, the ECA had a staff of approximately 150 commodity specialists to counsel with them and to ensure a balanced distribution of procurement in the United States, geographically and within each industry.

[15] *Ibid.*, p. 16.

[16] Including nearly a billion dollars on credit terms.

[17] Authorizations for "offshore procurement" from sources outside the U.S., made partly to minimize the initial drain on the domestic economy, declined greatly after the first year. Some observers felt that since there was considerable procurement of supplies in Latin America, an opportunity was being missed to link that area more closely with the mutually beneficial objectives of the Marshall Plan.

[18] ECA, *Fifth Report to Congress* (Washington, 1949), pp. 106–109.

The ECA spot-checked the use, in Europe, of imports financed out of aid funds.[19] As time went on, mission chiefs and the ECA controller's office, which supervised this activity, came to view such "end-use" checking increasingly as an effort to cooperate with the governments and business establishments of the receiving countries to ensure, for the benefit of the economy, efficient use of imported aid supplies and equipment.

Production

The gains in European production achieved during 1948–1949 can be summarized quickly. During the first half of 1948 there had been relatively little increase; the industrial output of OEEC countries in mid-1948 below the prewar level, with per capita production still lower, taking into account the rise in population. New momentum was acquired during the latter part of the year and the first half of 1949. For the April–June quarter of 1949 the index reached a level substantially above the 1938 average.[20] The most notable advances were registered in western Germany, Austria, France, the Netherlands, Sweden, and Greece. Expansion was marked in crude steel, cement, engineering and metal products, motor vehicles, textiles, chemicals, electric power, and hard coal. Agricultural yields showed significant gains over 1947–1948 in nearly every category, the most conspicuous being bread grains, potatoes, oil cake, and sugar. In overseas territories there were modest increases in a number of exports, including copper, lead, zinc, tin, bauxite, copra, palm oil, and cocoa.

Efforts to increase production were, naturally, concentrated within the individual countries. The OEEC commodity experts disseminated information about marketing factors and technological developments, but there was not during this period any concerted regional drive for increased productivity.

In agriculture it was necessary for the ECA to concentrate at first on urgently needed foodstuffs, fertilizers, and seeds. Concurrently, however, a program was devised with the participating countries look-

[19] It was thought at first that cooperative arrangements for end-use checking might be worked out through the OEEC, but representatives of the OEEC were reluctant to undertake the responsibility of setting up a system of their own. Nor were they enthusiastic about exercising their influence in support of a system of ECA design.

[20] The data on production in this section are taken from the OEEC's *Second Report*, pp. 30–42 and 267–269; and from the ECA's *Fifth Report to Congress*, pp. 18–27. See chart, p. 118.

ing toward the introduction of several varieties of high-yield crops, more
effective control of plant and animal diseases and of insects, an increase
in the amount of land under cultivation through reclamation and irrigation projects,[21] a more efficient pooling of scientific knowledge, and
the stimulation of better organization and practices on individual farms.

Investment

In Europe, as in America, the Marshall Plan was viewed as primarily
an investment operation. The desire for expansion in productive equipment was strong everywhere. This was emphasized in varying degree
by governmental and business leaders interviewed in each of thirteen
participating countries visited by the writer.[22]

It was evident that the investments made during the recovery period
would affect the kind of industrial structure each country would develop.
Private savings were at a low level, and much depended upon the
discrimination shown in the planning and conduct of publicly fostered
investment programs. Even with American aid—amounting in 1948–
1949 to about 4 percent of western Europe's gross national product [23] —
the margin for error was small. Limited resources had to be apportioned
carefully to cover consumption, government services, military outlays,
and foreign exchange deficits, as well as new investments. Unwise allocations could cause serious waste and inflationary pressures without
helping to solve fundamental economic problems. Welfare needs—in
residential housing, schools, and hospitals—though pressing, were
widely deferred in favor of more strictly productive investments in
which priority was generally given to power and transport, basic to
other development, and to the industrial and agricultural facilities considered most crucial for early expansion in production and foreign exchange earnings. Much of the investment planning which ensued was
concerned with specific projects—some of them large and impressive,[24]
many small but significant.

[21] One of the major projects launched during the first year was the reclamation
or improvement, by irrigation, of 2.5 million acres of land in Italy.

[22] "In Norway," said one, "our idea was that the main emphasis should be on
investments." "An increase in investment—a heavy increase," asserted another,
"was most important for the Netherlands." "Investment," declared a third, "was
necessary to the survival of industry in Germany." Many similar statements might
be cited.

[23] Ellis, *op. cit.*, p. 38.

[24] In Italy, for instance, plans were approved for the expansion of a thermo-
electric plant in Naples and for the development of five related projects designed
to modernize the Italian iron and steel industries.

A few countries, notably France and the United Kingdom, had already developed mature investment plans before the advent of Marshall aid. In France, for example, the "Monnet Plan" had been well worked out, providing chiefly for expansion and rationalization of the coal and steel industries and the repair and re-equipment of railroads.

An attempt was made, through the OEEC, to explore the possibilities of a coordination of investments in Europe which might eliminate needless duplication and facilitate a more rational employment of capital resources. But this effort, broadly speaking, was unsuccessful. To be sure, some unpromising ventures were discouraged and a few adjustments in specific projects were effected by bargaining. Exchanges of information which occurred as resources and markets were analyzed undoubtedly influenced the thinking of delegates and their home governments in connection with investment prospects then under consideration. But there were many hurdles to a frontal attack on the problem of coordination. The participating countries were not prepared to commit themselves to such coordination without prior examination in terms of national interests and of apparent implications for particular industries. Nor were they disposed to accept in advance the restrictions upon their investment activities—public or private—that might flow from attempts to extend and integrate governmental planning. Future demands, moreover, were difficult to assess. And there was some fear that, in the absence of any controlling political organization, attempts to coordinate investments might prove conducive to the formation of cartels, which would be contrary to the spirit and intent of the recovery program.

In a number of countries, local currency "counterpart" funds played a useful part in the development of investment projects.[25] Up to June 30, 1949, counterpart deposits reached the equivalent of nearly 2.7 billion dollars. Almost 90 percent of this amount was earmarked for capital outlays or to maintain monetary and financial stability where further expansion in investment programs might result in inflation. Whether counterpart or other indigenous resources were used for investment purposes was, from an accounting standpoint, inconsequential. The use of counterpart did reduce, to some extent, the temptation to employ this particular resource generated by grant aid for other purposes less important to recovery. It also provided a means for the exerting of some degree of American influence in the formulation of investment programs.

[25] For illustration, see p. 105.

Attack on Inflation

The severity of inflation and the length of time necessary to bring it under control varied widely from country to country. Wholesale prices in France, for example, soared by more than 120 percent between the middle of 1947 and the end of 1948, when the rise was checked. In Greece they mounted about 70 percent between July 1947 and June 1949. In the United Kingdom they climbed during 1947 and the first half of 1948. Inflation was acute in Italy in 1947, in Germany during the last half of 1948, and in Austria during late 1948 and 1949.[26] Price rises do not, of course, tell the whole story. In some countries, rationing and other physical controls suppressed inflationary pressures which were nevertheless real.

Inflation was attacked in two ways. Through the supply program, critical shortages in producer and consumer goods were eliminated. And governments were encouraged to promote savings, thereby reducing effective demand for goods in short supply.[27] For most of western Europe, during the spring of 1949, inflationary pressures were being brought under control. (See chart, p. 153.)

Trade within Europe

Cooperative action to reduce trade barriers made little real headway during the first year of the recovery program. The OEEC proposed that member countries report on the measures they were prepared to take. A trade committee was formed to study the problem. A proposal for a European customs union was studied, but enthusiasm was lacking. Protectionism had become rooted; the tariff problem was intricate; and negotiations on this question were already under way in Geneva as an outgrowth of the General Agreement on Trade and Tariffs (GATT) concluded in early 1948. Although pledged in the OEEC convention, a broader assault on trade restrictions did not develop until the autumn of 1949.

First Agreement on Payments

A limited first step was taken, however, toward developing a multilateral system for the clearance of international payments within Europe. Though only a beginning, it was important for trade.

[26] See OEEC, *Second Report*, p. 271.

[27] For discussions of the problem of inflationary controls in Europe during this period, see Ellis, *op. cit.*, pp. 36–41; and J. H. Williams, *Economic Stability in a Changing World* (Oxford Univ. Press, New York, 1953), pp. 97–99. Steps taken to check the inflationary crisis in France are mentioned later in this chapter.

The need for action was acute. Such commerce as survived between OEEC countries was being conducted mainly through a network of bilateral agreements. Since currencies were not freely convertible, foreign exchange acquired by sales in one country could not be used to settle debts with another. To have changed this system suddenly and radically by removing all exchange restrictions would have led to severe monetary dislocations.

A scheme was developed, therefore, whereby each country's credits with other countries might be used to offset its debits with third countries—through a system of periodic clearances of outstanding balances. The Bank for International Settlements in Basel, Switzerland, was designated to serve as the clearing agency. The plan was embodied in a first Agreement for Intra-European Payments and Compensations, signed by OEEC countries in October 1948.

ECA support for this plan was developed through an arrangement whereby dollars received from the United States might be used to eliminate, among OEEC countries, the net creditor or debtor relationship remaining after each clearance. A part of each creditor country's dollar aid was made "conditional" upon its proffering an equivalent amount in its own currency, in the form of "drawing rights," to other participating countries which were in a net debtor position within Europe.

Although the plan, admittedly, did not go far toward restoring multilateral trade within Europe, it was an initial breakaway from the tight constrictions of a system dependent almost entirely upon bilateral agreements. How far it was responsible for the sizable increase in intra-European trade which followed is debatable. The concurrent rise in production undoubtedly accounted for part of the increase. However, drawing rights were used for the settlement of nearly two-fifths of the gross deficits and surpluses incurred by the participating countries during the agreement's operation, and it may be assumed that at least a substantial part of this represented a net increase in trade.

Despite its significance in breaching the vicious circle of bilateralism in Europe, the drawing-rights device, linked with "conditional" United States aid, was regarded in the ECA and in many European circles as far from adequate. It was subject to severe criticism on three main counts: first, that although it expanded considerably the scope of multilateral settlements, it still rested procedurally to a large extent upon bilateral negotiations; second, that it depended on American aid in the form of conditional grants and made little contribution to the development of a basis for intra-European settlements which would out-live the recovery program; and third, that it provided little incentive for creditors to increase their export surpluses or for debtors to reduce their deficits. A durable and satisfactory payments system for all of free Europe had still to be devised.[28]

External Trade and Payments

During 1948–1949 western Europe was less successful in increasing its exports, especially to the Western Hemisphere, than in increasing its production. One reason was a slight recession in the United States. Exports to the rest of the world, during the year, rose somewhat less than 2 billion dollars in value. But those to the United States, after reaching an early postwar peak of 280 million dollars in the last quarter of 1948, dropped to 230 million in the first quarter of 1949 and 160 million in the second. Sales in other Western Hemisphere countries followed a similar pattern.[29] Although imports from the United States gained only slightly and there was a decline in imports from other Western Hemisphere countries, the excess of imports over exports re-mained high. The deficit was met in large part by American aid but some countries, notably the United Kingdom, experienced a heavy drain on their dollar reserves. For western Europe as a whole, lower levels of imports as compared with the previous year, and moderate increases in invisible earnings (principally from shipping services and tourist trade), led to a modest improvement in the continent's gold and dollar balance-of-payments position.

The doctrine underlying the recovery program was that, with Amer-ican aid, production, exports, and earnings from other sources (in-cluding invisibles and exports from the overseas territories) could be increased enough to make Europe's external payments position man-ageable as aid from the United States declined.

In addition to a broad increase in internal production, two groups of measures were contemplated. The first, designed to increase the con-tinent's exports and foreign exchange (especially dollar) earnings, consisted of export drives in each participating country, cooperative action to help each country determine the most effective means for ex-

[28] For a full discussion of this question, see William Diebold, *Trade and Pay-ments in Western Europe* (Harper & Bros., for the Council on Foreign Relations, New York, 1952).

[29] ECA, *Recovery Guides*, No. 11 (Washington, 1949), p. 8; *Fifth Report to Congress*, pp. 5–7.

panding its sales abroad, analysis of methods for increasing the competitive advantage of European exports, encouragement of tourism, and attempts to maximize earnings from shipping. The second group was aimed at reducing import demand by eliminating as far as possible items not essential to the recovery program and by developing alternative sources of supply within Europe and the overseas territories.

Organization within Participating Countries

The European governments organized their recovery efforts and their use of American aid in widely different ways.

In the United Kingdom a central economic planning staff had been formed in 1947 and eventually placed in the Treasury, traditionally a coordinating department in the British government. There was also an advisory economic section attached to the Cabinet. Both groups advised the government and especially the Chancellor of the Exchequer on broad economic problems. Together they came near to being a general staff on economic matters. By preparatory work in 1947–1948, they gave the United Kingdom a head start in recovery planning. In addition, a special London committee supervised the government's relations with the OEEC.

Germany established a Marshall Plan Ministry to coordinate internal operations and external relations. The organization provided for "opposite numbers" to the principal officers in the local ECA mission and in the OEEC.

In the Netherlands and Belgium, too, new agencies were created, closely linked with the Foreign Office. "At first," said a Netherlands official later, "the special agency here experienced no difficulties. It was a new thing, having to do with the division of aid within the country. As time passed, some of the older agencies wanted more responsibilities. But the interconnections were so close, and the negotiations so complex, that we kept the coordination." Austria adopted the same general pattern in late 1949. In Sweden, where direct aid was relatively small, activities were successfully coordinated through the Foreign Ministry.

In Greece, where the government had been all but wiped out by war and occupation, personnel from friendly powers during the periods of UNRRA and interim aid had had a large hand in public administration. The conduct of the recovery program during the ECA period involved a strengthening of indigenous governmental institutions and a progressive transfer of operational responsibilities to Greek shoulders.

Relations of the participating governments with the ECA were channeled principally through ECA missions.

Country representatives in Washington facilitated contacts with the United States government and American suppliers, care being taken not to duplicate the main lines of communication through the missions.

Role of the ECA

The role of the ECA was without precedent in the peacetime conduct of American foreign relations. Contacts developed within each of the participating countries were far wider than the traditional communications between embassies and foreign offices. ECA missions were in constant contact with several governmental departments—such as ministries of finance, economics, agriculture, and industry—and with a wide range of private financial, industrial, agricultural, and labor interests. Each aspect of American aid was a subject of frequent consultation with responsible officials and nationals most directly concerned. What developed was, in effect, a new and greatly broadened pattern of diplomacy linked with a massive economic program.

With it came new responsibility. For the ECA was in a position to influence policies and operations in the participating countries. Congress expected such influence to be exerted as a means of ensuring the success of the recovery efforts to which the United States was making a large contribution. The question was not whether such influence should be exercised, but how, to what extent, and with what degree of discrimination and tact.

The ECA's most obvious "leverage" was its power to determine the size of aid allotments and to approve authorizations for specific commodities.

Another means of affecting recovery efforts in some countries was through the control which the ECA shared over the release of counterpart funds. During the summer of 1948 a general policy for counterpart releases was formulated. It stipulated that in countries beset by inflation the use of counterpart for productive purposes had to be accompanied by governmental measures for achieving and maintaining internal financial stability.

The most interesting outgrowth of this policy occurred in France when, in 1948, that country was in the midst of a financial crisis. A substantial budget deficit and the absence of a firm policy on bank credit, which during the third quarter of the year were reflected in an expansion of the money supply, threatened to wipe out the progress which had been made in stabilizing prices. Confidence in the franc was deteriorating rapidly; the black market quotation for the dollar rose by about 50 percent in the latter half of 1948. Political instability had made it impossible to apply rigorous anti-inflation remedies. Social disorders were erupting in the form of serious strikes. The government, caught in a cycle of deficit financing that meant printing-press money, had not been able to remove the state from its role as the chief creator of new inflation. The situation presented a major road block to economic recovery, which depended upon expanding production.

The broad investment plan developed under the leadership of Jean Monnet had aroused widespread interest, but it required substantial financing. The necessary funds, unless some other source became available, could only be secured from the central bank, but this would entail more deficit financing and would require parliamentary approval which the government was loath to request.

By working closely with Prime Minister Henri Queuille and Finance Minister Maurice Petsche, David Bruce, chief of the ECA mission to France, was able to exert a significant influence in this situation. An understanding was reached whereby the ECA concurred in the use of substantial counterpart funds for the investment program, while the French government, on its part, agreed to adopt decisive measures essential to fiscal stability. These measures, requiring political courage and foresight on the part of the French authorities, included additional taxes, an undertaking not to increase the ceiling of indebtedness to the Banque de France, and quantitative controls over private credit. Further counterpart releases were made conditional upon evidence that the stabilization program was being carried out successfully.

The ECA, by its stand, had given needed support to a realistic group within the French government who themselves wished to carry out the formidable measures essential to bringing the crisis under control. In effect, the ECA helped to take the "heat" off those leaders at a time of great political difficulty. The attitude of ECA officials, throughout this episode, was that the responsibility for effective action rested with the French government.

In Germany, where Allied occupation controls were extensive, counterpart releases under joint ECA-government auspices contributed to an extraordinary recovery of productive capacity beginning in 1948–1949. Commenting on this later, Vice-Chancellor Franz Blücher said: "One reason for the recovery which we experienced is that there were such strict controls over counterpart that the economy had been like a regi-

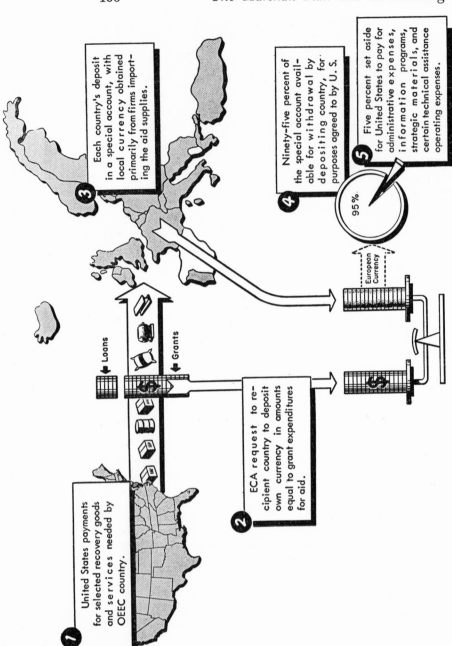

The mechanism of European counterpart funds.

1   United States payments for selected recovery goods and services needed by OEEC country.

2   ECA request to recipient country to deposit own currency in amounts equal to grant expenditures for aid.

3   Each country's deposit in a special account, with local currency obtained primarily from firms importing the aid supplies.

4   Ninety-five percent of the special account available for withdrawal by depositing country, for purposes agreed to by U. S.

5   Five percent set aside for United States to pay for administrative expenses, information programs, strategic materials, and certain technical assistance operating expenses.

Loans

Grants

European Currency

95%

3. The mechanism of European counterpart funds.

ment drilling under its colonel. Due to this strict control, counterpart was spent almost entirely for investment and increase of productivity. This was not always morally pleasant, but it contributed to the great effort." [30]

During the second quarter of 1949 the ECA concurred in the earmarking of counterpart funds in the United Kingdom for the retirement of short-term debts, in Italy for investments primarily in shipping, in Greece for refugee rehabilitation and other emergency purposes, and in other countries for an expanding range of agricultural and industrial projects.

To encourage private investment in Europe and the overseas territories by stimulating American investment in development projects abroad, Congress had authorized guaranties covering the conversion into dollars of income from new foreign investments by American firms. Opportunities at home were extensive, however, and few availed themselves of this provision. During the first fifteen months of the program, about 4.6 million dollars in guaranties were actually issued, some 1.9 million being for informational media.

More significant was the technical assistance provided by the ECA in the installation and use of equipment furnished under the aid programs, the training of personnel in special skills and techniques, and the planning and carrying out of specific development projects. Arrangements were made for European technicians to observe recent developments in the United States. This type of activity gained headway only gradually during the first year.

The United Kingdom was a notable exception. The way in which a program of technical cooperation between the United States and the United Kingdom was initiated is described by Hoffman in his book, *Peace Can Be Won*. After explaining the origin of his own "burning conviction" that American labor and management practices could be a great boon to European labor, management, and consumers, he states:

My chance to do something about it came one warm summer day in Paris in 1948. Sir Stafford Cripps, Britain's ascetic Chancellor of the Exchequer, and I were talking over the economic recovery obstacles that lay ahead.[31] "If we are to raise the standard of living in Great Britain," he said, "we must have greater productivity." My heart quickened; this was the kind of talk

[30] Interview, Bonn, December 3, 1952.

[31] A few informal conversations on productivity between Britishers and ECA officials in London had preceded this discussion. Interview, Finletter, New York, November 11, 1954. William L. Batt, second ECA Chief of Mission in London, supported vigorously the work of the Anglo-American Council of Productivity.

I wanted to hear from a European. Then he continued. "Great Britain has much to learn about that from the United States and"—he paused—"I think we have a few manufacturing secrets we've been concealing for a generation or so that you might like to learn. Why don't we interchange this information?" Naturally, I jumped at the idea. "Let's set up a system of transatlantic visits," I replied. "We can take British management and labor on tours of American factories and send Americans to Britain for a look at your shops." Sir Stafford made the deal right there and within weeks he had thrown his amazing vegetarian energy into the creation of an Anglo-American Council of Productivity.[32]

Top figures, including Philip Reed of General Electric and Victor Reuther of the CIO, were enlisted to represent American management and labor. The late Sir Frederick Bain, deputy chairman of the Board of Imperial Chemical Industries, and Lincoln Evans, general secretary of the Iron and Steel Trades Confederation, were among those brought in by the British. Together they settled upon the industries which would benefit most from an exchange of ideas and soon laid out plans and schedules. The first British team to arrive in the United States represented labor and management in the steel industry. Said Hoffman:

This group spent six weeks over here, taking notes by day and chewing over them in the evenings. These were no junketeers; they came with a determination to learn. When they returned to England they sat down and wrote a report so much of an eye-opener that it sold twenty-five thousand copies in a fortnight and went into three extra printings. Its gist: productivity per man in American foundries was from 50 to 90 percent higher than in British foundries; the latter must mechanize and raise output or national living standards could not rise as they should.[33]

With this auspicious start, Hoffman had high hopes that the technical assistance idea would be embraced with similar enthusiasm in other countries. But it was not, during the first year. Various reasons might be given: the novelty of the effort, early weaknesses in the ECA's technical assistance administration, language barriers, local inertias. As Hoffman often said, "Technical assistance cannot be exported; it can only be imported." Whatever the explanation, awareness of what technical assistance could do to help modernize the industrial process was much slower in developing in most of the continental countries. Even in Britain

[32] From *Peace Can Be Won*, by Paul G. Hoffman, pp. 101–102. Copyright 1951 by the Great Books Foundation, reprinted by permission of Doubleday & Company, Inc.

[33] *Ibid.*, p. 102.

the response was uneven. But an important beginning had been made.

Perhaps the most fundamental evolution in ECA activities during the first year occurred in the handling of its central responsibility: the programing of aid. The change, in essence, was from an emphasis on the physical programing of commodities to a concept of economic programing in which attention was directed more predominantly to the impact of aid upon the economic processes and policies of the recipient countries. While the techniques of procurement, end-use checking, project analysis, and technical assistance continued to play an important part, the central direction of aid planning fell increasingly into the hands of those whose primary concern was with total impact. The new approach entailed greater reliance on country studies, increased emphasis on balance-of-payments and internal-accounts analyses, and a more realistic concern with national economic policies.

In some countries the ECA helped develop more up-to-date methods of analyzing the interrelationships among major components in the economy as a background for recovery operations. In late 1948 OEEC and ECA officials discussed the problem of making the national income data of the various participating countries more comparable. As an outgrowth of this discussion, a National Accounts Research Unit headed by British economist J. R. N. Stone was established in Cambridge, England, in the summer of 1949 to prepare a general system of national accounting and accompanying data for the individual participating countries.[34]

To develop a fuller awareness abroad of the purposes and accomplishments of the recovery program and to counter the highly organized propaganda of the Communists, particularly among labor groups, the ECA, with Congressional backing, began toward the end of the year to step up its information program in western Europe. Special efforts were made to acquaint workers with the program and to secure organized labor a position of full partnership in the effort. Labor advisory posts in ECA headquarters, in the OSR, and in the country missions were filled by experienced trade union leaders drawn almost equally from the CIO and the AFL. They consulted local leaders and counseled the

[34] This type of analysis was still relatively new in the U.S. and the U.K. In early 1947 the Statistical Office of the U.N. studied the problem of establishing comparable systems of national accounting, and a committee headed by Mr. Stone prepared a system to be used in reporting to the U.N.; this differed only in relatively minor respects from the "standardized system" developed subsequently at Cambridge. Two American experts, Richard and Nancy Ruggles, participated in the planning of the Cambridge Unit.

ECA on such problems as the resettlement of workers, vocational training, labor productivity, and the growth of free labor movements in countries where such movements were weak. They sought to help secure active support of the recovery program by labor groups in the participating countries, an exceptionally difficult task, of course, in countries where trade unions were predominantly under Communist influence.

While the ECA in all of these ways was expanding its activities abroad, it had to give continuous attention to the home front. The effects of aid procurement on the domestic economy needed watching; fortunately, the heavy inflationary impact which had been feared by Senator Taft and others did not materialize. Constant vigilance was required to hold the agency's administrative costs to a minimum. Contact had to be maintained with key members of Congress and with executive agencies of the government. Complying with a legislative amendment adopted in April 1949, an Office of Small Business was established in the ECA and steps were taken to assist smaller establishments in the United States to participate equitably in the supply program. An energetic information program was essential to keep the American public informed about the European Recovery Program and to ensure uninterrupted support for what the Administration believed to be an undertaking of vital concern to the United States. The results of a Gallup poll, released in late 1948, showed that nearly two-thirds of those who knew about the Marshall Plan believed that Congress should continue to support it, whereas 13 percent were opposed and 22 percent had no opinion.[35]

East-West Relations

Those who grappled day after day with the problems of the recovery program were constantly reminded, through morning and evening headlines, of the tension between East and West. Their own constructive efforts, being less sensational, were usually reported if at all on the inside pages of the newspapers. Thinking, consulting, and building went forward in an environment rarely free from a din of international controversy. On the whole, however, 1948–1949 was not a good year for the Communists.

Their deranging efforts were most strikingly displayed in a continuation of the Berlin blockade, which had begun at midnight on June 18, 1948; in frequent attempts to disorganize economic and political life, especially in countries where they had strong trade union follow-

[35] *Public Opinion Quarterly,* Winter 1947–1948.

ings; [36] and in ceaseless propaganda activity. In April 1949 they organized, in opposition to the Atlantic Pact, a "peace front" of "all who reject the policy of military alliances."

But Western reactions were vigorous. On September 9, 1948, a quarter of a million citizens of Berlin rallied to protest the blockade. The Allied airlift was so effective that on May 12, 1949, the blockade was lifted. Nine days later, railway workers in eastern Berlin went on strike, demanding payment in western marks; this strike embarrassed the Communists by demonstrating the inferiority of the currency of the Soviet Zone. During the blockade, the three Western occupying powers made plans for the establishment of a new German government. A basic law for the western states was adopted, and on May 23 inauguration of the Federal Republic of Germany was announced.

Almost simultaneously the People's Congress of the Soviet Union adopted a constitution for a "democratic" republic in East Germany, and in October the establishment of that regime was proclaimed. Elsewhere in Europe, efforts to foment strikes and other disturbances had met with some success. But the repercussions of these activities were such that the Communists resorted increasingly to "pin prick'" strikes which had nuisance value but did not provoke reactions which might endanger their party organizations. Propaganda attacks against the United States had diminishing effect as the recovery program took shape and Europeans saw for themselves that no attempts were being made to "subjugate" their economies.

[36] An oustanding example was a strike among French coal miners which lasted from October 4 to November 27, 1948, at a time when coal was a critical factor in the French economy.

CHAPTER 6

Second Year (1949-1950): Toward

Economic Growth and Integration

THE second year of the European Recovery Program was in many ways its most interesting. It was marked by a further tapering off of relief-type assistance, new orientations in thinking and planning, extraordinary gains in economic health and political confidence, greater financial stability, less dependence upon external aid, and a series of pioneering steps toward economic integration in Europe. The end of the year did not bring assurance that OEEC countries would be able to attain full economic self-reliance by 1952, but the changes needed in order to accomplish this objective were better understood. It was, of course, the year preceding the outbreak of war in Korea.

June 1950 had been looked toward as the halfway point—or a little beyond—in the recovery program. It marked, instead, the end of an exclusively economic program. The assault on Korea in that month radically changed the political situation; thereafter, military preparedness occupied an increasingly important position. In retrospect, 1949–1950 takes on a special significance among the four years of the recovery effort because it was the most indicative of what could be accomplished in the absence of an overriding military danger.

Redirection in Thinking

Planning for the year was begun months in advance. The OEEC's *Interim Report* issued in late December 1948 was an important first step.

8. With new units, Italy's wartorn Po Valley rehabilitates its oil refinery potential.

9. At a metallurgical plant in France, a seventeen-year-old girl operates a machine producing fine brass and copper wire.

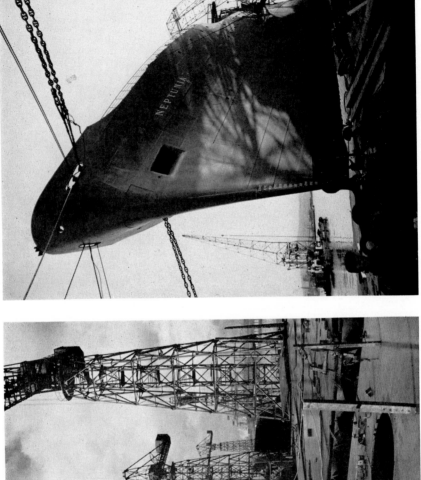

11. The *Neptunia* was one of three 13,000-ton liners being constructed at the Trieste shipyards, with American aid.

10. First plates of an oil tanker are welded on the bank of the Clyde, as Britain regains her shipbuilding strength.

During the following quarter the OEEC and the ECA turned their attention to the problems revealed in this report and to plans of action for dealing with them. On March 26, 1949, the OEEC Council approved a plan of which the basic aims and principles were:

On the national level, 1949 must be a year of financial and monetary stabilization in Europe.

A rapid increase in exports is an essential condition for the success of the European Recovery Program. Of equal importance . . . is the increase of invisible earnings . . . [especially] from tourism and shipping.

The danger . . . from a drastic and sudden reduction of imports when the European Recovery Program ends must be forestalled by a continual re-examination of current import programs, particularly so as to curtail dollar imports not vitally needed. . . .

Steps must be taken towards the elimination of internal disequilibrium in Europe, this process to be assisted by an adequate system of intra-European payments leading to a healthy expansion of trade between the participating countries.

Investment and modernization projects should be developed rationally and in concert.

The ECA undertook to rethink its position in the light of changing conditions, which included an interruption of economic progress during the summer. A cable sent in early October to the European Regional Office emphasized the importance of increasing dollar earnings in the participating countries, of more active interest by the ECA in the fiscal policies of those countries, of much more interest in capital formation and the channeling of aid and counterpart funds into "critical sectors" of each country's investment program, and of further efforts to foster competitive conditions and more liberal commercial policies.

The message reported that conviction was growing in Congress that American aid should be used to build up western European organizations, and not indefinitely to prop up separate national economies. This, it went on, coincided with "our own belief" that, in the long run, economic health as well as political and military security required a western European union or unions. Greater coordination was also felt to be of immediate importance, for as ECA aid declined, the shocks of integration would be more difficult to cushion.

Time was running out. The ECA felt it imperative, therefore, to bring home to the mission chiefs the urgency of the situation and the need to "overcome customary inhibitions" in pressing Europeans "actually to do those things which both we and they know must be undertaken sooner or later."

Aid and Influence

This accent on efforts to influence European governments to adopt policies needed for recovery became increasingly noticeable during late 1949 in the ECA's internal communications and external actions.

A letter of October 21 from Bissell to Milton Katz, Deputy Special Representative in Europe, discussed the way in which the ECA should review the OEEC's second annual program:

The review process should be designed to reveal to the Europeans and to us the problems on which we, the OEEC, and the countries individually must take action during the coming year, and the nature and timing of the actions themselves. . . . A major part of ECA's appraisal and review of the program should be undertaken by the ECA country missions. The mission reports should not be encomiums on recovery progress or persuasive briefs arguing the need for this or that list of imports. Nor should they describe once again geography, natural resources, population and war damage of the country concerned. They should be considered as internal ECA documents. . . . If they are to meet the purposes I have in mind, they must be independent and objective appraisals of the countries' programs. . . .

It would be very helpful if OSR were to undertake the preparation of a report on the participating countries as a group. I believe that ECA-Washington should [then prepare] . . . a series of statements or papers which would propose specific recommendations to be made to the OEEC and to the countries in the course of negotiations, and might also propose other types of action to be taken by ECA. These papers would then be sent in draft form to the OSR and the individual country missions for their comments and suggestions and, after the necessary revision, would constitute a part of the ECA's plan of action with respect to the Second Annual Program.

This letter is quoted at some length not because the procedure which it outlines was adhered to in detail, but because it is indicative of the thinking, at the time, of the principal architect of the ECA's economic policies.[1]

ECA interest in the character of internal recovery efforts was again reflected in a letter of August 31, 1949, from Katz to Robert Marjolin,

---

[1] "One of Bissell's great contributions," said Harlan Cleveland later, "was the concept that the important thing is not the volume of our aid, but the effects in Europe and our influence in Europe upon national economic and financial policies." Interview, Washington, September 29, 1952. Cleveland was for a time deputy to Bissell and, subsequently, was in charge of the agency's European programing.

Secretary General of the OEEC, which noted that the ECA "proposes to reserve a general fund of $150,000,000 which is not to be initially allocated among the participating countries as part of the general division of aid for the Second Annual Program." The broad objective of the general reserve fund, the letter went on,

is to permit the financing of activities which are expected to make an exceptionally significant contribution towards European economic recovery but which cannot be incorporated at this stage into the various national programs toward which the bulk of ERP aid is being allocated. . . . Three such uses are presently envisaged, namely, (a) to encourage the further development of the overseas territories, (b) to finance development projects of special international significance, and (c) to promote the most rapid possible liberalization of intra-European trade and payments by providing safeguards against unforeseeable risks involved in measures of liberalization.

The ECA's principal method of influencing the OEEC and the participating governments was continuous consultation.

The objectives of both the OEEC and the ECA during this period may be grouped under four main headings: first, economic growth in all of the participating countries; second, a real acceleration of progress toward European economic integration; third, the fostering of national economic policies conducive to genuine recovery; and fourth, a rapid increase in western Europe's dollar earnings and savings.

Toward Economic Growth

In a circular dispatch to all missions, dated November 29, 1949, the ECA's Paris office called attention to the divergent rates of economic growth in the United States and Europe. The United States, it pointed out, had the highest productivity in the world principally because of its wide, competitive internal market and its unusually rich endowment of natural resources in relation to population. The slower growth of European productivity, in the face of a rapid rise in consumer expectations, tended to keep the continent's export cost and prices high and to exaggerate its import demand. Competitive ability was thereby impaired and payments could not be kept in balance without large American aid. To meet this problem, two main lines of effort were required: more efficient use of resources through well-directed investments; and an attempt to develop in western Europe a single large market area, freed from stifling restrictions upon trade and payments.

ECA policy on investment as a key to economic growth had already been a subject of repeated exchanges. In a summarizing cable to the

OSR, ECA-Washington had laid down several guiding principles. Effort was to be concentrated on "critical" sectors of each economy in which possibilities of accomplishment were substantial—in which something both needed to be done and could be done.[2] Local currency counterpart releases for investment were to be maximized; for general financial purposes, minimized. Analysis of critical sectors—agricultural and industrial—would provide a more rational basis for the review of projects. The review of a particular steel project involving both dollar-aid and counterpart components, for example, might be used as a basis for getting a rational program developed for the steel industry in a particular country, as had been done in Italy. Increasing attention was to be given to overseas development as a part of the investment programs.

As already noted, economists have repeatedly emphasized that the European Recovery Program was primarily a program of investment.[3] By 1949–1950 the participating countries had made good to a substantial degree, though by no means completely, the immense destruction of the war and the large arrears of maintenance and replacement. A total industrial production gain of about 10 percent in 1949–1950 over the previous fiscal year was slightly less than the gain of the year before, but the rate of economic expansion during the two-year period was unprecedented in Europe. An exceptionally high proportion of resources—considerably more than the prewar ratio—was being devoted to investment. Unemployment was generally low, being serious only in Italy, Germany, and Belgium; in the latter two it was substantially reduced. The United Kingdom, Norway, and Sweden enjoyed full employment. Days lost through industrial disputes were only a fraction of what they had been after World War I. For western Europe as a whole, recovery was proceeding much faster than in the previous postwar period.[4]

During the second quarter of 1950 industrial production in ERP countries was about 18 percent higher than in 1938, and 28 percent above the first quarter of 1948. Thus it had risen more than one-fourth during the first two and a quarter years of the Marshall Plan. The most dramatic part of this gain was registered in Germany, where total industrial output more than doubled, rising from about 41 to 90 percent

[2] This emphasis proved, in practice, to be largely a reinforcement of what the countries themselves were already doing.

[3] See, for example, John H. Williams, "The Task of Economic Recovery," *Foreign Affairs*, July 1948, p. 629.

[4] Data cited in this section are drawn largely from OEEC, *Second Report*, pp. 48–78, and ECA, *Ninth Report to Congress* (Washington, 1950), pp. 4–10.

of the prewar level. The largest increases over prewar levels occurred in Norway (47 percent), Sweden and Denmark (each 69 percent), and the United Kingdom (49 percent).

Coal production was approaching the 1938 volume again; output of electric energy climbed to 80 percent above prewar.[5] In general, increases were more striking in manufacturing—such as textiles and vehicles—than in the output of basic materials. Transport facilities were brought back to 1938 levels or better in most countries. Shortages of food and raw materials became much less critical.

Agricultural products, usually slow gainers, showed some remarkable increases. After two years of recovery effort, grain, meat, eggs, and dairy products were up by roughly a third over the relatively low 1947 level, potatoes by a fourth, and sugar by nearly half. With favorable weather and better supplies of fertilizers, seed, and equipment, farm production was expected to go up by another 7 percent in 1950—reaching prewar levels in total yield, though not in per capita supply owing to a 10 percent population expansion.

Production and exports of the overseas territories regained their 1938 volume for most commodities, and were substantially higher for non-ferrous metals, rubber, and phosphates. Potentialities for further expansion of output in these areas were great.

The rapid gains in European production during the first two years of the recovery effort reflected the fact that it is easier, in some respects, to restore output from an abnormally low level than to maintain a given rate of growth after the earlier levels have been achieved. Further progress then depends not only on the rate of new investments, but also on improvements in productivity and on the size and competitiveness of assured markets.

The measurement of productivity (as distinct from total production) presents theoretical and practical difficulties, but the OEEC, using available statistics and the 1938 level as a base of 100, estimated that industrial output *per man-year* in all OEEC countries could be given rough indices of 75 in 1946, 80 in 1947, 90 in 1948, and 100 in 1949.[6]

---

[5] As industrial production increased, the expansion of power sources in western Europe became a major problem. Plans called for continuing heavy reliance on coal (which in 1938 had supplied 85 percent of requirements), but also for increasing outlays in petroleum refining and hydroelectric power until, by 1952, they could supply about 12 and 10 percent, respectively, of western Europe's energy needs. See ECA, *A Report on Recovery Progress and United States Aid* (Washington, 1949), pp. 77ff.

[6] OEEC, *Second Report*, p. 35.

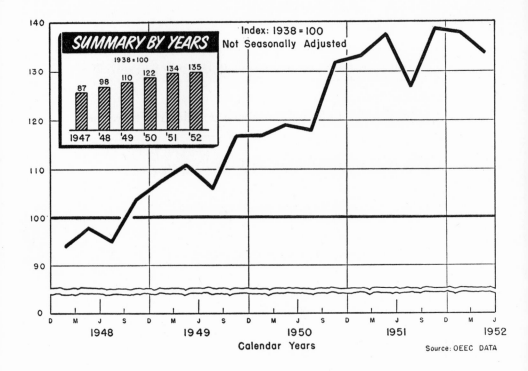

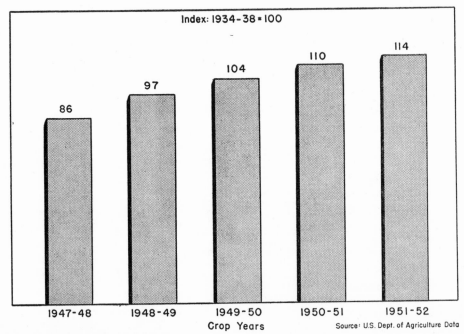

4. Production in OEEC countries. *Upper:* Industrial production. *Lower:* Gross agricultural production.

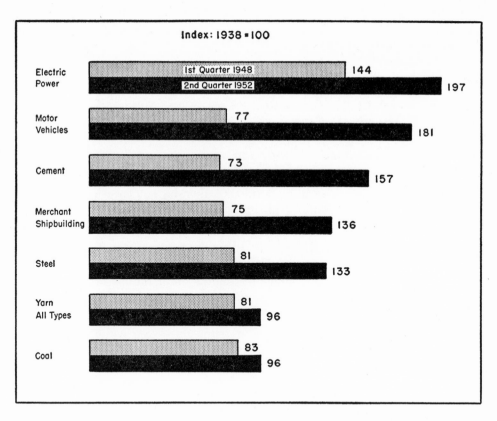

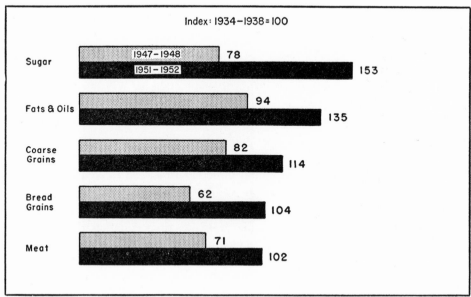

Source: OEEC DATA

5. Production of selected commodities in OEEC countries. *Upper:* Industrial commodities. *Lower:* Agricultural commodities.

Germany, Italy, Austria, and probably the Netherlands had not yet attained, in 1949, their prewar standards of productivity. Belgium, Denmark, Greece, and Norway were at about their 1938 levels, while these levels had been exceeded in France, Ireland, Sweden, Switzerland, Turkey, and the United Kingdom.

Toward Economic Integration

American interest in greater integration of the European economy was first reflected, it will be recalled, in the Marshall speech of June 5, 1947, and subsequently in the Economic Cooperation Act, which referred to the "economic cooperation in Europe which is essential for lasting peace and prosperity." In 1949 this statement was strengthened by addition of the sentence: "It is further declared to be the policy of the United States to encourage the unification of Europe." No attempt was made, however, to define "unification" or to indicate how it might be achieved.

A ferment of thinking on this question developed within the ECA and other United States agencies. As intermediate goals were considered, differences in views and emphases became increasingly evident. The spectrum of opinions ranged from opposition to any overt American support for definite steps toward economic coordination in Europe, at one extreme, to conviction, at the other, that every legitimate means should be employed to foster unification in the interest of economic health and political strength in Europe and the free world. Some favored a gradual lowering of trade and payments barriers as part of a world-wide effort in behalf of these aims; others believed that progress could be made more rapidly on a regional basis. Among the latter, some were concerned with exclusively economic aims; others viewed economic integration in Europe as one main avenue toward greater political unification. The forms which United States policy actually took in 1949–1950 reflected the fact that during this period the ECA had the initiative in formulating and directing American foreign economic policies and programs.

For some members of the ECA's programing divisions, the question of economic integration became a major preoccupation during the summer and autumn of 1949. In October a memorandum indicating one main line of thought was prepared by H. van Buren Cleveland and Theodore Geiger and circulated within the ECA for study and comments. Salient excerpts from it may be quoted to illustrate the manner in which "think pieces" by staff members played their part in the formation of ECA policies.

It is now generally accepted that most of the individual countries of Western Europe will not achieve or maintain a status of self-support until their economies can be grouped into one, or perhaps more than one, free trade and payments area, within which currencies are convertible and quantitative restrictions, exchange controls and tariffs have been eliminated. This conclusion rests on an analysis of the economic decline of Western Europe over the last generation relative to the rest of the world.

Western Europe's ability to maintain its export prices at competitive levels despite the continued growth of American productivity, and thereby to earn a larger share of the world's supply of dollars, will depend directly on the degree of success in establishing for European industry and agriculture the necessary basis in a wide competitive market. . . .

What solution is there to the German problem outside of membership in a Western European union? . . . Membership in a union might well be the one method for making Europeans out of the Germans and for harnessing their talents for management and production in a better cause than German nationalism. . . .

There is now no [other] living and dynamic challenge which can inspire self-confidence and a sense of security in Western Europe. . . . This, then, is the crucial and compelling reason for Western European union. It provides the main hope for a regeneration of Western European civilization and for a new period of stability and growth. . . .

The historical moment . . . is now. The participating countries possess their greatest postwar ability to withstand the necessary economic adjustment and ECA is now best equipped to assist them. Promised improvements in general conditions have appeared. . . . Most countries thus find themselves in a condition of rapidly increasing welfare. At the same time, ECA still disposes of sufficient funds to assist in overcoming dislocations which may arise from the elimination of barriers to trade. After 1952, however, and progressively until then, these factors will be dissipated. The sharp decline in U.S. aid in the last two ERP years will greatly reduce ECA's ability to cushion the shocks of union. The decline in the present and unusual and temporary rate of productivity increase will wipe out whatever resilience the European countries now possess for economic adjustment. . . .

Persons most familiar with attitudes in Congress are afraid that a continuation of ERP at the minimum necessary level of aid cannot be expected unless Western European countries have clearly embarked on the course of economic unity.

It was not to be supposed that a working paper of such amplitude would meet with full acceptance or that it could forecast the actual course of negotiations and actions. In the weeks that followed several important developments took place.

On October 31, 1949, as we have seen, western Germany became a full member of the OEEC, being represented thereafter not by officials of the occupying powers but by delegates of the Federal Republic. The significance of this first instance of German participation, on a basis of equality, in a joint postwar western European effort was not lost upon the other delegates. British, French, and American spokesmen for the western zones had already brought German problems, and their relation to European problems, into OEEC deliberations. The facts of economic interdependence had not removed misgivings about Germany, but they had offset them to a remarkable degree.

On the same date Hoffman delivered to the OEEC Council a major address in which he maintained that to hold the ground already gained and to assure further progress, Europe would have to balance its dollar accounts, which meant increased exports and control of inflation. But the accomplishment of this task, he said,

will not be meaningful unless we have come to grips with our second task— the building of an expanding economy in Western Europe through economic integration.[7] The substance of such integration would be the formation of a single large market within which quantitative restrictions upon the movement of goods, monetary barriers and the flow of payments and, eventually, all tariffs are permanently swept away.

Recognizing that it would take time to change the physical structure of European industry, Hoffman held that "the massive change in the economic environment" resulting from the first steps in integration would "set in motion a rapid growth in productivity."

Integration, Hoffman said, was not just an ideal, it was a practical necessity. A permanent single market of 270 million consumers, in which European manufacturers and farmers could sell freely, would accelerate the development of large-scale, low-cost industries; make easier the effective use of both material and human resources; stimulate the growth of healthy competition; and facilitate a rapid increase in productivity. These developments, in turn, would improve Europe's competitive position in the world and would satisfy more of the expectations and needs of its people. The alternative was "disaster for nations and poverty for peoples."

[7] The term "integration" came into general ECA usage at about this time, reflecting an adaptation to diverse currents of thought on both sides of the Atlantic. The word, though never precisely defined, connoted more than casual cooperation but less than full unification. Marjolin of the OEEC later spoke of integration as embracing all the steps taken toward unification, even though they might fall far short of that ideal. See his *Europe and the United States in the World Economy* (Duke University Press, Durham, N.C., 1953), p. 41.

The ECA Administrator then gave notice, in diplomatic terms, that the American Congress and people regarded European economic integration as essential and would be more apt to continue substantial Marshall Plan aid if they saw real progress toward it. If economic integration continued to lag in 1952, with Europe's economy still in precarious balance with the dollar area, there would be a new cycle of nationalism as one country after another sought to protect its reserves. "For all of these reasons," Hoffman said, "but particularly because of the urgency of the need—I do make this considered request: That you have ready early in 1950 a record of accomplishment and a program, which together will take Europe well along the road toward economic integration." [8]

Hoffman called for intensified efforts to remove restrictions on trade and for elimination of double pricing, whereby scarce commodities were priced higher in export trade than in domestic markets. A "realistic plan" for further action, he believed, should provide for substantial coordination of national fiscal and monetary policies, exchange rate adjustments when prices and costs in different countries were too far out of line, means to cushion the shock of integration, and some reconciliation of national trade policies to avoid excessive strains. The steps needed, he concluded, would require concerted action by all OEEC countries, and he urged that no path toward integration be left unexplored.

The statement was well timed. Despite increases in production, the total volume of trade between OEEC countries had shown only a slight gain during the preceding twelve months.[9] Commerce was still choked by a network of import quotas, high tariffs, discriminatory trade practices, and currency restrictions.

The first solid blow was struck against import quotas when, on November 2, the OEEC requested each member country to eliminate, by December 15, quantitative restrictions on at least 50 percent of its imports on private account from other member countries. On January 31, 1950, the OEEC decided that the ratio should be lifted to 60 percent, upon approval of the European Payments Union (discussed below), and that an increase to 75 percent by the end of 1950 should be considered.[10]

[8] *New York Times,* November 1, 1949. [9] OEEC, *Second Report,* p. 67.

[10] On the initiative of the French, the Council subsequently decided to draw up a "common list" of agricultural and industrial products to serve as a guide in liberalization negotiations, special attention being given to products for which the creation of a single European market would produce significant gains in productive efficiency.

Although some countries could not meet the liberalization ratios in full, the partial abolition of import quotas was one cause of a new upswing in intra-European trade. The total volume rose from a little over 90 percent of the prewar level during the first half of 1949 to 115 percent in the first half of 1950.[11] Another important factor was Germany's resumption of her traditional position as a supplier of manufactured goods to other parts of Europe.

A second and even more important assault was begun against the chaotic currency situation. The problem was intricate. Little real progress had been made toward genuine convertibility of currencies. The first intra-European payments plan, referred to in the previous chapter, expired at the end of June 1949. It was followed by a second plan which incorporated a number of modifications. The most notable of these placed 25 percent of the "drawing rights" established under the previous plan on a multilateral basis, so that they could be used freely against any participating country when bilateral rights or other resources were not available. Although several advantages were claimed for this change, it was recognized that both payments plans fell far short of the requirements of a really effective intra-European system.

The subject increasingly engaged the attention of financial technicians in the OEEC and the ECA, and it was primarily they who conceived new plans which culminated in the European Payments Union (EPU)—one of the most significant developments of the postwar era. "There were in fact," said Frank Figgures [12] of the United Kingdom, "about six main proposals in the general EPU direction, all maturing in November and December 1949."

Within the ECA, thinking "in the general EPU direction" had begun during the previous summer. Several economists on the staff—and in other United States agencies—had been exploring the advantages of a clearing union in international trade over the limited mechanism of the International Monetary Fund.[13] "Working under forced draft," said a member of the working committee which studied the problem,[14] "we

[11] OEEC, *Second Report,* p. 71; ECA, *Ninth Report to Congress,* p. 18.

[12] Head of the OEEC Trade and Finance Directorate, 1948–1950. Interview, November 11, 1952.

[13] More broadly, the thinking which led up to the EPU represented an alternative to the "universalist" approach to currency convertibility and trade liberalization reflected in the Bretton Woods and GATT agreements, an approach which had strong advocates within the Treasury and State Departments, and among central bankers in Europe as well as directors of the International Monetary Fund.

[14] Included were John Hulley, H. van Buren Cleveland, Theodore Geiger, and Walter Stettner of the ECA and Albert Hirschman of the Federal Reserve Board.

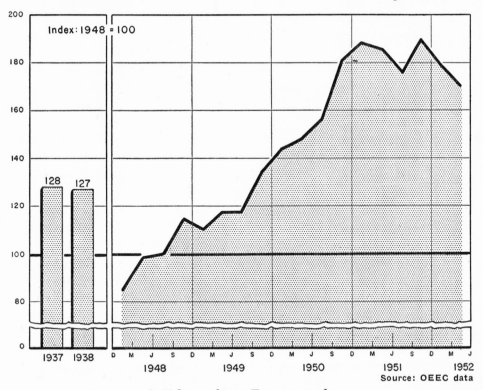

6. Volume of intra-European trade.

considered, reviewed, and revised until we had a fair proposal for a logical successor to the then existing payments agreement." A clearing union was envisaged, with machinery for fully multilateral payments that would obviate the need for bilateral balancing between countries. The union, it was tentatively suggested, might be based on a new European settlements currency fully backed by gold but convertible into gold only in case of large multilateral imbalances. Incentives were to be provided for both creditors and debtors to balance.

The proposal was summarized in a cable to Bissell, then in Paris, who discussed it with Harriman and with specialists in the ECA regional office who had been thinking along somewhat similar lines. On November 11, after Bissell's return to Washington, a more formal message was sent to the OSR, amending and elaborating the proposal for presentation to OEEC governments. The message was written with a view to the establishment, not later than July 1, 1950, of a European Clearing

---

Other active contributors, as thinking matured, included James McCullough, Arthur Smithies, and Edward Tenenbaum.

Union which could (1) provide a mechanism for full multilateral clearance and settlement of all bilateral payments and imbalances among the participating countries; and (2) provide temporary cushions for debtors and creditors, in addition to an equivalent of drawing rights and conditional aid, which would make exact, short-term balancing less urgent and would thus allow more time to redress imbalances by nonrestrictive methods. The message made it clear that, for any such arrangement to become permanent, "really effective" machinery would be necessary for the coordination of national policies, either by agreement or by some international control over governments and central banks.

Meanwhile, a similar ferment had been taking place on a wider scale in European capitals. Comparable proposals were being developed by both OEEC and member-country experts; these have been described in detail by John T. McNaughton,[15] then special assistant to Milton Katz of the OSR. The long and impressive succession of schemes presented within a few months reveals the intensity of the study given to the European payments problem—in the OEEC and in several European capitals.

Thus when Harriman conveyed to the finance minister of each country the broad terms of the ECA's proposition for a European clearing union, and when the problem was put on the OEEC agenda, the ground had already been extensively tilled.

The European Payments Union was brought into being by the OEEC, in consultation with the European Office of the ECA.[16] Contributory propositions from many sources were extensively modified as the experts sought a consensus. In top-level negotiations, where Harriman took the lead for the ECA, the most difficult question was the relation of the United Kingdom and the entire sterling area to the EPU. "There was a tough discussion with the British on this," recalled Harriman later, "but when Cripps came through, it was all the way."[17]

The OEEC countries agreed on the principles of the EPU during the second quarter of 1950. Congressional approval of the use of sup-

[15] Unpublished doctoral thesis (Harvard University) on the "Genesis of the European Payments Union" (1953).

[16] Participants for the ECA in this active phase of the development of the EPU included Milton Katz, Lincoln Gordon, Henry Tasca, Robert Triffin, Hubert Havlik, and Thomas Schelling.

[17] Interview, Washington, October 1, 1952. The problem of bringing the U.K. and the sterling area into the EPU was the subject of vigorous and almost continuous discussion and negotiation from December 1949 to May 1950, evolving

porting ECA funds was obtained, and the Union was formally launched on July 7.

During the final stages of this development, another event of great importance to European unity occurred. This was French Foreign Minister Robert Schuman's proposal, on May 9, 1950, for pooling European coal and steel industries. The French government proposed that all French and German coal and steel production be placed under a joint authority, in an organization open to other European countries. Such a pooling, Schuman held, would make another war between Germany and France not only unthinkable but impossible.

This unprecedented proposition, entailing a greater voluntary surrender of national sovereignty to a new federal authority than in any previous step toward unification in Europe, was made entirely on the initiative of European statesmen. The United States gave it immediate moral support.

National Policies

In attempting to ensure the most effective use of American aid, the ECA faced not only problems of economic expansion and economic integration common to all the participating countries, but also questions of national policy which varied greatly from one country to another. It was necessary to move from "shopping lists" of commodities required in each economy to a more rational basis of planning and evaluation. On this point, Bissell, in the aforementioned letter to Katz, said:

A certain amount of concentration on commodity problems is, of course, inevitable because we must issue procurement authorizations and prevent uneconomic use of resources. But, in our analytical work, I have tried in every way possible within the limit of Congressional expectation and good public relations to focus our attention on what is called a national accounts type of analysis—that is, upon resources availabilities and uses by major categories—in contrast to the forecasting and screening of elaborate lists of commodities. . . . Not only is it a waste of our and the OEEC's time to concentrate so much attention upon detailed commodity forecasting and screening, but it strengthens those tendencies toward restrictionism which are already becoming far too evident.

As mentioned earlier, study of the relationship of American aid to the European economies had led to special country studies and to the

---

through four major sets of proposals. The first of these contemplated a bilateral, discriminatory European trade and payments pattern; the last envisioned the multilateral, nondiscriminatory system that was actually obtained.

development of balance-of-payments analyses for each country. But there was a flaw in this approach, not fully recognized at first. As long as a country did not take the difficult and sometimes painful measures needed to improve its capacity to earn and save dollars, its dollar deficit would persist and its apparent need for assistance would remain large. On the other hand, a country which adopted such rigorous policies would stand to lose, proportionately, in the aid provided. The incentive was in the wrong direction.[18] Moreover, projections of payments deficits were bound to be somewhat arbitrary, depending on the assumptions made as to levels of imports, consumption, investments, and outlays for military expenditures and social services. These conditions were partly responsible for the attention given during the next two years to the more penetrating national-accounts type of approach.

In the spring of 1949—as planning for the 1949–1950 program developed—a new method was adopted for the division of aid which, though primarily an adjustment to a reduced volume of assistance, cut down on any incentive to retain high balance-of-payments deficits. Each country was asked to indicate the use it would make of a volume of aid 25 percent below what it was currently receiving.[19] This approach put limits on aid for each country and increased the incentive to make the adjustments required in order to get along with a lower volume of aid.

One major problem in achieving this goal was the uneven relationship of prices and exchange rates in each country to those of other OEEC countries and particularly to those of the United States. Studies had shown that if European countries were to expand their exports enough to meet the goals of the four-year program, they would have to offer them at more favorable prices in terms of non-European currencies—especially the dollar, and to discourage nonessential imports as far as possible. This problem was met in part by a succession of currency devaluations in September 1949. Although it had been realized that exchange rates would have to be readjusted, the immediate cause of the devaluations was a sharp decline in the gold and dollar reserves of the United Kingdom. These had dropped from 2.7 billion dollars at

[18] The difficulty of programing aid on the basis of "merit" rather than of "need," as pointed out by Lincoln Gordon in early 1950, was that merit in the sense of economic success in reducing exchange deficits could not be rewarded by providing unneeded aid.

[19] Devised by OEEC experts, this device became known as the "Snoy-Marjolin formula." Certain exceptions had to be made, notably in Greece.

the end of 1946 to 1.8 billion at the end of 1948, and to 1.3 billion as of September 17, 1949.

On September 19 the British government announced a 30 percent devaluation in the pound sterling. To compete with British exports and to maintain their sales in the British market, nearly all of the remaining OEEC countries devalued their currencies to some extent. The Scandinavian countries and the Netherlands, which had close commercial ties with the United Kingdom, devalued in the same proportion. Some governments, which had been pursuing deflationary policies, devalued by smaller percentages—counting upon internal pressure on domestic prices to keep their exports competitive. As a result, these countries had to continue deflationary policies to ensure that their export industries would not be placed at a disadvantage. In certain countries, for example in Italy, such policies reduced the stimulus for business expenditures and led to a slower rate of growth than might otherwise have occurred. But several governments, including the French, achieved during the months following the devaluations a much needed stabilization of their internal finances as well as increased export earnings.

Dollar Earning and Saving

Efforts to expand European exports to the United States included the appointment of a joint mission of the ECA and the Department of Commerce, under the chairmanship of Wayne C. Taylor, which published its findings in October 1949 after ten weeks of study and consultation in Europe.[20] The United States, the report said, would have to buy at least 2 billion dollars more annually from Europe if the latter was to balance its trade by the end of the recovery program. American imports from OEEC countries were currently only a little over 1 percent of the gross national product of the United States, as contrasted with approximately 2 percent before the war. The report recommended that four obstacles to the expansion of American imports from Europe be removed: first, restrictive controls imposed by the governments of the exporting countries; second, high American tariffs on a large number of products; third, needlessly complicated customs procedures in the United States; and fourth, a series of "buy American" restrictions on federal, state, and local government procurement in the United States.

Concurrently, the ECA initiated, under the direction of Herbert

[20] *Report of the ECA-Commerce Mission* (Washington).

Woolley and A. Ford Hinrichs, a study of European and American trade in relation to international trade generally. This resulted in the development of a "world trade model" involving projected increases in European exports to dollar areas to a level of 850 million dollars. Further attention was also directed to specific commodities upon which European "dollar drives" might best concentrate.

Dollar export boards or commissions were established by various participating governments, in cooperation with private enterprise, to stimulate the flow of exports to dollar areas. Efforts were also made to curtail dollar-cost imports and, by making purchases in the cheapest available markets, to ensure economical use of aid dollars and other hard currency holdings. Creditor countries in the European Payments Union, however, appeared less anxious than others to restrict their dollar imports. Some wanted to use their credit balances in Europe to meet their dollar deficits; this was a basic point of disagreement within the EPU.

During the second quarter of 1950 the ECA helped the participating countries to determine the articles with the greatest sales opportunity and appeal in the United States, to analyze the problems of entering the American market, to prepare for special trade fairs in the United States, and, as far as it could, to cope with American import duties and customs procedures.[21]

The adverse trade balance of the European countries (excluding overseas territories) with the United States during 1949–1950 was about 2.5 billion dollars.[22] For the last quarter it was about 100 million dollars lower than for the first quarter, but this rate of progress had to be greatly accelerated if anything approaching equilibrium was to be achieved by 1952.

The Aid Picture

At the end of June 1950 aid allotments to Europe totaled approximately 9.46 billion dollars, of which 8.8 billion had been obligated through commodity procurement authorizations.[23] The largest recipi-

[21] See ECA, *Ninth Report to Congress*, pp. 19–21.

[22] OEEC, *Economic Progress and Problems of Western Europe* (Third Report of the OEEC; Paris, 1951), p. 121.

[23] ECA, *Ninth Report to Congress*, pp. 48, 124. Some 662 million dollars had also been authorized for ocean freight. Many authorizations were approved during the final weeks of the fiscal year. Late appropriations and heavy orders for "long lead" items of equipment requiring months for manufacture resulted in a substantial lag between the issuance of procurement authorizations and paid procurement. The

ents, in order of magnitude, had been the United Kingdom, France, Italy, western Germany, and the Netherlands. Authorizations had reached totals of roughly 2.7 billion dollars for food, feed, and fertilizer, 1.2 billion for fuel, 2.8 billion for raw materials and semifinished products, 1.6 billion for machinery and vehicles, and .4 billion for other miscellaneous items, including tobacco. Authorizations for technical services were slightly in excess of 35 million dollars.

Looking Ahead

As the year 1949–1950 drew to a close, OEEC countries, while they were encouraged by the striking progress that had been made, realized that serious difficulties had still to be faced. Living standards and levels of economic activity were still dependent on American aid, which would diminish rapidly over the next two years. Rapid increases in productivity and in dollar-earning exports would not be easy to achieve. And the next stage of freeing intra-European trade and payments, it was believed, would be more difficult than the first.[24]

The planning for the final two years of the recovery program, therefore, demanded that two facts be recognized: first, there would be much less aid; second, flexibility was needed to allow individual economies to adjust to increased economic integration among OEEC countries.

Three major programing assumptions were made by the OEEC and the ECA. The first was that Marshall aid, compared to the 1949–1950 total, would be 25 percent less in 1950–1951, and 50 percent less in 1951–1952. The second was that there would be no more "special grants and credits" to help meet intra-European deficits. The third was that business activity in the United States, on which the dollar-earning capacity of the participating countries depended, would remain at the high level reached in 1949. A fourth assumption was not made—that hostilities in Korea would precipitate a huge and costly defense program.

Great stress was laid on expansion of dollar earnings by exports to the dollar area and on reduction of imports from that area, chiefly by developing alternative sources of supply. Plans called for a reduction of approximately 2 billion dollars in western Europe's "dollar gap" during the next two years—1.2 billion through cuts in imports, 650

ECA's balance sheet, as of June 30, 1950, showed unexpended appropriations and loan funds totaling nearly 2.6 billion dollars. *Ibid.*, p. 152.

[24] See OEEC, *Second Report*, pp. 78–84 and 135–136.

million through additional earnings from exports, and about 100 million through increased returns from tourism, shipping, and other invisible items.

June 25, 1950

But the outbreak of war in Korea, five days before the end of the second full year of the Marshall Plan, altered the bases on which these calculations had been made.

CHAPTER 7

Third Year (1950-1951): Economic

Progress and Military Crisis

TWO years, two months, and twenty-two days after the launching of the Marshall Plan, the Communists struck in Korea. Lashing without warning through the military barrier which they had erected along the thirty-eighth parallel, they attempted by surprise and superior numbers to achieve a swift conquest of the southern half of the peninsula. And they nearly succeeded.

The parts played by Soviet Russia, Communist China, and the North Korean puppet regime in deciding to risk this attack, the reaction which they anticipated, and the results which they hoped would follow are questions for future historians to unravel. The stake for the North Korean Communist regime was at least titular domination over the entire country. And it seems probable that the Soviet and Chinese rulers expected, by completing and consolidating their grip on northern Asia, to undermine the prestige and position of the United States in the Far East, especially in Japan; to convince the peoples of south and southeast Asia of the ascendancy of Communist power; to offset their reverses in Europe by sowing anxiety and discord in the Allied camp; and to accomplish these purposes through a use of North Korean manpower trained by Soviet officers and supplied with ordnance from Russia and China.

If these assumptions are correct, there was considerable miscalculation on every count. Two days after the assault began, the United Nations Security Council—which Russia was currently boycotting—recommended that all United Nations members assist the South Korean republic to repel the attack and to restore peace. By the end of September more than thirty nations were contributing in various ways to an unprecedented international "police action."

After reeling back with heavy losses to the tip of the peninsula, the United Nations forces rallied and, reinforced, began the counterattack that carried them near to the northern boundary of Korea. When, again by surprise, Communist China in November suddenly threw its most seasoned divisions—labeled "volunteers"—into the struggle, the grim story of retreat and resurgence was re-enacted at even heavier cost, spelling frustration once more to the Communist hope of military conquest.

Impact of the Korean War

While the conflict itself was restricted to Korea, its reverberations across the free world were immediate and profound. Like a flash of lightning it threw into bold relief the military strength and aggressive purposes of the Soviet bloc and the woeful unpreparedness of the free nations to cope with such a threat—in Europe as well as in Asia. The North Atlantic powers promptly launched an immense rearmament program.

In the two years that followed—the last two of the Marshall Plan period—defense moved to the center of the stage. The determination to build up enough combined power in the free world to deter the Communists from further aggressive action or, failing that, to be able to meet force with force, deeply affected the political and economic developments of those years. Increased effort and cooperation in the military field brought new economic stresses and political tensions.

When the Korean War began, however, the legislation governing United States support of the European Recovery Program in 1950–1951 [1] had already been passed. It followed closely, in language, the acts of the two preceding years. The most notable amendments reflected the growing emphasis on American encouragement to European integration. The Administrator was authorized "to transfer funds directly to any central institution or other organization formed to further the purposes of this Act by two or more participating countries, . . . in order to facil-

[1] Economic Cooperation Act of 1950, Title I of Public Law 535, 81st Congress, 2d Session, approved June 5, 1950.

itate the development or transferability of European currencies, or to promote the liberalization of trade." [2] It was further provided that of the 2.7 billion dollars authorized for the fiscal year ending June 30, 1951, 600 million dollars would be available "solely for the purpose of encouraging and facilitating the operation of a program of liberalized trade and payments . . . and for furnishing of assistance to those participating countries taking part in such programs." [3] Approval was given to the use of counterpart funds for the same purposes.[4]

Linked with the Economic Cooperation Act of 1950 was a new piece of legislation, the Act for International Development,[5] which brought to fruition the "Point Four" concept enunciated in President Truman's 1949 Inaugural Address. This act declared it to be the policy of the United States

to aid the efforts of the peoples of economically underdeveloped areas to develop their resources and improve their living and working conditions by encouraging the exchange of technical knowledge and skills and the flow of investment capital to countries which provide conditions under which such technical assistance and capital can effectively contribute to raising standards of living, creating new sources of wealth, increasing productivity and expanding purchasing power.[6]

Authority was given for a greatly expanded program of technical aid to economically underdeveloped areas.

The approval of these enactments, twenty days before the attack on Korea, thus gave momentum to existing aid programs and to an enlargement of American interest in the development of retarded areas.

But the Korean War led to a re-examination of all existing programs in the light of defense requirements. On July 26, 1950, Congress, amend-

---

[2] *Ibid.*, Sec. 111(d).   [3] Sec. 114(c).

[4] Other amendments (a) emphasized the use of material and financial assistance in such a manner as to aid the participating countries in promoting "increased productivity, maximum employment, and freedom from restrictive practices"; (b) expanded earlier provisions relating to guaranties in support of private investments; (c) called for a reduction in the amount of dollar purchases by the participating countries to the greatest extent practicable; (d) called upon the Administrator to "encourage emigration from participating countries having permanent surplus manpower to areas . . . where such manpower can be effectively utilized"; and (e) authorized the use of 5 percent counterpart funds "to give full and continuous publicity to . . . peoples of the participating countries regarding the assistance, including its purpose, source, and character, furnished by the American taxpayer."

[5] Title IV of Public Law 535, 81st Congress, 2d Session (1950).

[6] Sec. 403(a).

ing the Mutual Defense Assistance Act of 1949, authorized 1.25 billion dollars to continue and expand existing military programs; on September 27 supplemental funds of 4 billion dollars were appropriated.[7] Responsibility for broad coordination of all foreign aid programs— military, economic, and technical—was given to an International Security Affairs Committee, under the Secretary of State, which included representatives of the Departments of State, Defense, and Treasury, the ECA, and the Executive Office of the President. And a Committee on Foreign Supplies and Requirements was established, under the chairmanship of William C. Foster, to advise the United States defense mobilization director on economic aspects of foreign requirements.

Concurrent with these developments were changes in the ECA's high command. In July 1951 Milton Katz was appointed Special Representative in Europe, succeeding Averell Harriman. On October 1, Foster succeeded Hoffman as Administrator for Economic Cooperation.

In the ECA and other parts of the Administration there was some concern lest rearmament disrupt the European Recovery Program. As early as July 27 Foster had moved to forestall this possibility in a letter to Senator Tom Connally, chairman of the Senate Foreign Relations Committee. The letter reviewed the accomplishments of the ERP and argued that since the buildup of military strength would place a greater load on the European economy, it was essential to continue efforts to strengthen Europe economically. It pointed to the multiplier effect of dollar aid and to its contribution to the strengthening of western Europe's military defenses. And it contended that, as a symbol of American partnership, recovery aid should not be seriously curtailed.

Momentum of the Recovery Program

Although the psychological, political, and military impact of the Korean War was prompt and profound, its full economic impact was delayed. There was, to be sure, a rapid growth in the demand for, and prices of, raw materials, resulting in adverse terms of trade for industrialized countries and a beginning of new inflationary pressures. But in general the momentum of the recovery program continued for several months, with gains on nearly all fronts.

[7] Public Law 843, 81st Congress, 1st Session (1950). Military assistance funds ultimately appropriated for 1950–1951, on a grant basis, came to about 4,959 million dollars for North Atlantic Pact countries; 325 million for Greece, Turkey, and Iran; and 394 million for Korea, the Philippines, and China—a total of 5,678 million dollars.

This led, for a time, to a mood of overoptimism in both Europe and the United States. The third OEEC report, dealing with developments to the end of 1950, stated:

Whatever new problems the future may hold, there can be no question that a comparison between the economic position of Member countries in 1947 and that in 1950 shows a remarkable and most encouraging contrast, almost whatever aspect is considered. . . . Marshall Aid was the blood transfusion which sustained the weakening European economies and gave them the strength to work their own recovery. . . . [The 10.8 billion dollars allotted up to the end of the first quarter of 1951 was] substantially less than the sum which was originally thought to be necessary to reach the present stage of the Recovery Programme.[8]

In a similar vein, the ECA declared:

The two and one-half years since the start of the European Recovery Program has witnessed a profound change in Western Europe—from an area disorganized by war, occupation and isolation, and dominated by a mood of helplessness, into a reasonably smoothly functioning economic and political community. Although it cannot be said that Western Europe's economic and social problems have been completely resolved and that it has fully recovered from the most devastating war in history, it can be truthfully asserted that much of the heritage of destruction left by World War II has been overcome and the most difficult part of the reconstruction task has been accomplished.[9]

There was ground for encouragement. The rise in production during 1950 was comparable to that achieved in 1949. Available statistics indicated an aggregate increase for OEEC countries of about 25 percent, to a level one-seventh higher than that of 1938.[10] A little more than two years of recovery effort, during which the United States had furnished 4 to 5 billion dollars of aid each year, had seen a rise of about 30 billion dollars in the annual value of western European production.

The United Kingdom had fought its way up to a point where it was able to have aid suspended as of January 1, 1951; Ireland followed suit in May. French industrial production reached in 1950 a volume 20 percent above that of 1938, while agricultural output approximated the prewar level. In 1950 alone, Germany expanded its industrial output by about 27 percent and virtually doubled its export sales to the United

[8] *Economic Progress and Problems*, pp. 10–11.

[9] *Tenth Report to Congress* (Washington, 1951), p. 6.

[10] Since the population had increased by about one-tenth, the average level of output of goods and services per head was slightly higher in 1950 than in 1938.

States. In Italy, although farm yields were only a little above those of 1948, industrial production was up by more than 25 percent. Norway showed a 15 percent increase in exports over the previous year. The volume of industrial output in Sweden and Denmark stood at 65 and 55 percent, respectively, above prewar levels. Recovery in Greece was much slower, but gains were being registered along many lines. With the opening up of hitherto inaccessible cultivable areas, Turkey was entering upon a period of extraordinary new agricultural expansion.[11]

For OEEC countries as a whole, industrial yield during the second half of 1950 was some 25 percent above the 1938 level, thus nearing the target that was originally set for 1952. The only serious lag was in coal: western Europe's production of less than 450 million metric tons in 1950 was only slightly above that of 1949 and still below 1937 and 1938 totals of roughly 480 million metric tons.[12] The lag was partially offset by improved efficiency in the use of fuels and by a greater use of petroleum, natural gas, and hydroelectric power. Production of refined oil products in 1950 was 200 percent above prewar, while electric power generated was up by more than 75 percent.

Steel products were more than 65 percent above the 1947 level, climbing to 13.6 million metric tons in the last quarter of 1950; this was 18 percent higher than in the comparable 1949 period and the largest volume on record. Other industrial items—including textiles, chemicals, cement, motor vehicles, and merchant vessels—showed comparable rises, especially during the latter half of 1950.

Increases in agricultural production were less spectacular but continuous. Total net output in 1950–1951 was approximately 33 percent above the depressed 1947–1948 level and 14 percent higher than the prewar average, compensating for a population increase which reached 11 percent over the 1938 total. An estimated average of 2,825 calories per day approximated the prewar average, and the quality of the diet was improved.

Much of the effort being devoted to the increase of production looked toward further expansion in the future. From 1947 to 1950 OEEC countries devoted about 20 percent of their available resources to investment, substantially more than in the interwar years. Although much of this had gone to make good war losses and to reduce the backlog of projects delayed by the war, and although the need for investment of

[11] Data from OEEC, Monthly *Statistical Bulletin*, Paris, November 1954.
[12] *Thirtieth ECA Report for the Public Advisory Board* (Washington, 1950), inside cover.

all kinds—particularly in housing—remained high, the OEEC could say that "there have been few periods in history when so high a proportion of resources has been freely devoted to investment under such unpromising conditions and with such impressive results." [13]

Technical assistance was rapidly gaining pace. The 5 million dollars authorized for this purpose in 1949 had been increased by the end of 1950 by 19.4 million dollars. As of December 31, funds had been committed to 625 technical assistance projects in the Marshall Plan countries and their overseas territories. During the last quarter of the year, 124 technical groups from Europe concluded visits to the United States. And the program was being broadened. The number of joint management-labor survey teams was increased. Management seminars or clinics were conducted in Europe. Engineers and plant foremen visiting the United States were given opportunities for both in-plant and academic training.

The gains registered in industrial and agricultural production were accompanied by an extraordinary rise in European trade. The volume of commerce between OEEC countries reached in 1950 a level more than 69 percent above that of 1948, while exports to non-Marshall Plan countries were more than a fourth above the prewar level and some 41 percent higher than in 1948.

Spurred in part by a "dollar drive" conducted in the participating countries with ECA help, western Europe's export trade during the last quarter of 1950 was 48 percent higher in volume than that of 1938, with an average monthly value above the 2-billion-dollar mark for the first time on record. This increase, combined with a reduction in dollar imports, reduced Europe's adverse trade balance with the United States and Canada. For 1947, 1948, 1949, and 1950 the adverse balance amounted to 6.1, 4.5, 3.8, and 1.75 billions.

When exports from overseas territories and invisible earnings were counted, improvement in Europe's dollar position was even more impressive. In 1947 the dollar gap was a staggering 8.5 billion; in 1949 it was still as high as 5 billion. But in 1950 it was lowered to approximately one billion. Gold and dollar holdings of OEEC countries increased by about 2.4 billion dollars during the fifteen-month period from September 1949, when devaluation occurred,[14] to the end of 1950.

[13] *Economic Progress and Problems*, p. 60.

[14] See Chapter 6. The devaluations increased the relative attractiveness in Europe of commodities from nondollar areas, which were becoming available in increasing quantities.

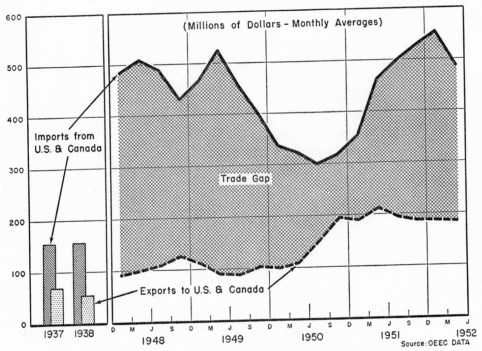

600

500

400

300

200

100

0

(Millions of Dollars - Monthly Averages)

Imports from
U.S. & Canada

Trade Gap

Exports to U.S. & Canada

1937 1938

D M J S | D M J S | D M J S | D M J S | D M J
1948 | 1949 | 1950 | 1951 | 1952

Source: OEEC DATA

7. Western Europe's trade with the United States and Canada.

During the last quarter of 1950 alone, these holdings mounted by more than 500 million dollars.[15]

Western Europe was beginning to hit its stride. Sales in the United States market and the dollar earnings which could reduce further the need for external aid might have expanded even more rapidly than they did but for a number of influences: the preference of many European merchants for smaller turnovers at higher profits per item; leanings toward non-American markets when United States customers were considered too demanding in specification and price; lack of knowledge of the United States market; and the fear that gains there might be temporary due to internal competition and to the harassing effect of uncertain tariffs and customs administration.[16]

The problem of internal financial stability was more complex. Production within Europe had increased and the payments imbalance with dollar areas had decreased. On the other hand, the terms of trade

[15] Foregoing data are from OEEC, *Economic Progress and Problems*, pp. 12–15, and ECA, *Eleventh Report to Congress* (Washington, 1951), pp. 6–19 and 50.

[16] These factors were cited in a special report by Edwin J. Marks of R. H. Macy and Co. to Paul Hoffman, on October 2, 1950.

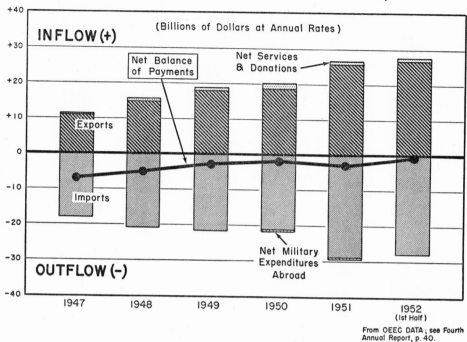

8. OEEC countries' over-all balance of payments on current account (excluding overseas territories and Switzerland).

became more adverse for several countries late in 1950, as prices of imported raw materials and other goods rose substantially more than the prices of exports. This led to increased living costs and insistent pressures for wage increases. Demand had to be cut if a new inflationary movement was to be forestalled.

At the end of 1950 workers in most western European countries were approaching their prewar levels of real earnings. Even so, their standards of living were still dangerously low, especially in France, Italy, western Germany, Austria, and Greece—countries in which the threat of internal dissension was greatest. Food distribution was uneven, being governed almost entirely by price. "Low income groups, including most industrial workers," stated the ECA in a report to Congress, "have great difficulty in providing adequate diets for their families in view of current wage-price relationships. This situation continues to be an important element in the susceptibility of urban areas to Communist propaganda." [17] It was clear that the benefits of increased economic activity did not automatically "trickle down" to wage earners and

[17] *Tenth Report*, p. 13.

farmers—especially in countries where free labor movements were weak and where economic stratification was reinforced by fiscal policies, legislation, and custom.

Although impressive advances had been made, deep structural problems in Europe's economy remained. A wistful note appeared in an OEEC comment that

the progress achieved, though necessarily uneven as between the various countries, represented on the whole a remarkably successful attack on Europe's economic problems as they had been seen in 1947, and it seemed that OEEC could turn hopefully to the task of trying to solve some of Europe's long-term structural problems. The outbreak of the Korean war, however, confronted the Western World with the new task of strengthening its defences. This gave rise to a whole new set of problems.[18]

Before examining some of these problems, let us review briefly developments during the latter half of 1950, in the field of European economic unification.

Further Efforts toward Integration

The agreement among OEEC members that 60 percent of each country's 1948 level of intra-European imports on private account would be freed from quantitative restrictions became effective on October 4, 1950. In the same month it was determined that similar restrictions on 75 percent of such imports would be removed by February 1, 1951. Agreement was also reached on a "common list," first proposed by France, of agricultural and industrial products for which efforts would be made to remove all quantitative import restrictions.

While these developments were taking place, three OEEC countries put forward proposals for the further economic integration of Europe —identified as the Stikker, Pella, and Petsche Plans, after the names of the sponsoring delegates from the Netherlands, Italy, and France. The three proposals were alike in advocating not only the removal of quantitative restrictions, but also the progressive reduction of tariffs and of dual pricing and other discriminatory practices. Each envisaged a wider European market as a means of reducing production costs in western Europe and as a step toward the achievement of other economic aims, including a return to multilateral world trade.[19]

[18] *Economic Progress and Problems*, p. 29.

[19] The Stikker Plan called for an industry-by-industry approach comparable to that of the Schuman Plan, in which liberalization measures would be applied in

First Year of the EPU

The European Payments Union Agreement, formally signed by the eighteen OEEC member countries on September 19, 1950,[20] was made retroactive to July 1 of that year. Thus 1950–1951 was the first full year of the Union's operation.

The agreement, it will be recalled, provided for a fully automatic multilateral system that would permit each participant to offset its deficit with any member against its surplus with other members, so that each country would need to be concerned only with its balance of payments with the rest of free Europe as a whole, and not its balance with any single member of the Union.

An illustration of the way in which the EPU facilitated multilateral trade was given in an ECA report to its Public Advisory Board:

Belgium traditionally has exported steel; Denmark and Norway have imported it. Yet Denmark could not sell enough dairy products and meat, nor Norway enough fish, lumber and wood pulp directly to Belgium to pay for the steel they wished to purchase. The Danes and Norwegians, consequently, tended to curtail the importation of many useful goods which they would otherwise have taken from Belgium, even though they had surpluses with other countries. The credits accumulated in these countries could not be applied to offset their payments deficits with Belgium. Under the EPU clearing arrangements the Danes and Norwegians can pay for steel and other Belgian goods with foreign currency proceeds earned from their exports to other European countries. Their ability to import from other member coun-

---

turn to one segment of the European economy after another, aided by the establishment and use of a European integration fund which would give assistance to governments for the modernization of industries adversely affected by liberalization measures or for new investments in unrestricted industries. The Pella Plan placed emphasis upon a preferential reduction of tariffs among OEEC member countries. The Petsche Plan called for the establishment of a European investment bank to finance the modernization of industries, and for investment projects involving concentration and specialization of industries under the most suitable conditions; the more general purpose of this fund would be to assist in financing projects whose production would yield a commercial return in an unrestricted European market and would become, as rapidly as possible, competitive in world markets. As a permanent institution, the bank would lend to private and state enterprises as well as to governments and would require the participation of private capital in all projects assisted.

[20] Special provision was made in the agreement for the sterling area, which included Iceland, Ireland, Iraq, India, Pakistan, Burma, Ceylon, Australia, New Zealand, and dependencies or protectorates in Africa, the Middle East, the Far East, and the Western Hemisphere, but not Canada, whose currency was more closely linked with that of the United States.

tries is limited only by their overall capacity to export to these countries, collectively.[21]

Technical aspects of the EPU's organization and operation were necessarily complex, but the essential facts can be stated briefly. A managing board was established under OEEC auspices. Each member country was assigned a "quota" equal to 15 percent of its intra-European exports, imports, and invisible transactions in 1949. The quotas totaled 3,950 million units of account (u/a)—a unit being defined as an amount of gold equal to the current gold content of the American dollar. This aggregate determined the maximum cumulative deficit or surplus which might be financed through the EPU. Six countries which were expected to run deficits in their intra-European trade that could not be covered under the system or repaid in the foreseeable future were given initial credit balances totaling 314 million units of account. Three prospective creditors—the United Kingdom, Belgium-Luxemburg, and Sweden— were assigned initial debit balances totaling 215 million units; these balances represented, in effect, transfers by the prospective surplus countries to the EPU, for which they would receive equivalent amounts of "conditional aid" as part of their ECA dollar allocations. Arrangements were made for the Bank for International Settlements to serve as agent for the EPU in calculating the net surplus or deficit position of each country.

The ECA provided 350 million dollars as an initial working capital fund,[22] since it was probable that gold payments by the Union would exceed those to the Union.

In each monthly clearing operation the relationship of each country's balance to its respective quota determined the proportion of credit and gold payment required for settlement with the EPU. For both creditors and debtors, the first 20 percent of their quotas involved no transfer of gold. For clearances exceeding this percentage, creditor countries extended to the EPU credits equaling 50 percent of the settlement and received from the Union an equivalent amount in gold. For debtors, the amount of gold required for settlement with the EPU increased on a progressive scale. These arrangements were intended to stimulate member countries to avoid excessive surpluses or deficits and to encourage them to make basic shifts in their production, trade, and invisible transactions.

[21] *Thirty-fourth ECA Report for the Public Advisory Board* (Washington, 1951), p. 3.

[22] The terms under which the 350 million dollars was obligated by the U.S. were set forth in a letter, dated September 18, 1950, from Milton Katz to Robert Marjolin. OEEC Document C(50) 271.

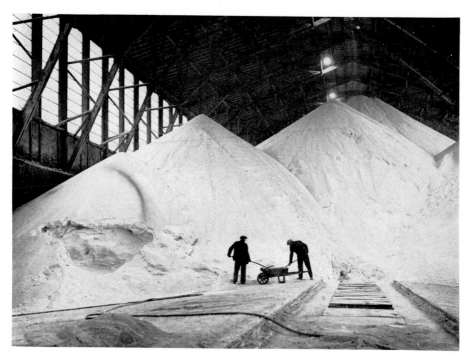

12. Agricultural development in Germany included production of chemical fertilizers.

13. Turkish farmers, using ECA-financed machinery, opened huge new areas to productive agriculture.

15. Rich crops of grain now grow on reclaimed swampland in Waidegg, Austria.

14. French Benedictine monks in the Pyrenees secure excellent results from trial plantings of hybrid corn.

Establishment of the EPU followed by only a few days the outbreak of war in Korea. Thus, on the heels of an event which was to strain the economies of the free world came the formal initiation of the most important single effort to integrate the economic life of western and southern Europe. Through it the stresses of the Korean War were more readily absorbed than they otherwise could have been. "But for EPU," declared the OEEC in 1952, "the European trade and payments system would have been dislocated by an exceptionally severe crisis." As it was, the rearmament effort gave the EPU a rigorous test, in the course of which it "proved its strength, its resilience and its efficiency." "Even so," the statement continued, "the system was not without defects" and it was apparent that "great and persistent efforts would be necessary if it was to be maintained, consolidated and enlarged." [23]

The shocks that had to be absorbed during the first year may be mentioned briefly. The defense program set off by the attack on South Korea led to competition for basic materials. A sharp change in the terms of trade ensued, to the advantage of large suppliers of raw materials such as the sterling area and the French Union, and to the disadvantage of large buyers, such as western Germany, which lacked basic resources.

By the spring of 1951 raw material prices had become more stable and some had receded. But defense costs began to climb because of the diversion of resources to military production, the flow of manpower into the armed services, higher import costs, and the monetary impact of defense spending. Germany's situation, with a notable rise in production and exports, now showed improvement, but the United Kingdom and France entered upon a period of increasing difficulties.

The aggregate surpluses and deficits between member countries came to 1.8 billion units of account during the first nine months of EPU operations. But since, for purposes of clearing operations, all European currencies were freely convertible, the gross balances were cut to a net total of 1.1 billion units, a reduction of roughly 40 percent.

The Schuman Plan

French Foreign Minister Schuman's plan for pooling European coal and steel industries under a supranational structure (the Coal and Steel Community) has been described. Unlike the OEEC and the Council of Europe, the new authority proposed in the Schuman Plan called for a substantial transfer of national sovereignty. There was favorable re-

[23] *Europe: The Way Ahead* (Fourth Annual Report of the OEEC; Paris, 1952), p. 69.

sponse from Germany, Italy, and the Benelux countries, and a more reserved reaction from the United Kingdom. The chief political objective of the Plan was to remove one of the historic causes of conflict between Germany and western Europe—especially France—by guaranteeing equal access to the coal and iron resources of the member countries. The chief economic aim was to merge the domestic markets of the European coal and steel industries into a single market area.

On August 10, 1950, the six European countries most directly concerned—France, Germany, Belgium, Luxemburg, the Netherlands, and Italy—agreed on the area to be covered and the character of the organization required. They also agreed that all tariffs, quantitative restrictions, discriminatory taxes or freight rates, and other barriers to a single market in coal and steel between the six countries should be abolished after the organization had been approved and established.

The structure proposed was fourfold. At the center was to be a High Authority, an executive body of six to nine members chosen by the governments for their economic and political competence. They were to be responsible only to the Community and not to member governments. Associated with the High Authority was to be a special Council of Ministers, one from each of the participating governments, to coordinate the economic policies of the governments with the work of the Authority; a Common Assembly, consisting of delegates from the parliaments of the participating countries, to which the High Authority would report annually; and a Court of Justice to hear appeals from member countries or firms.[24]

Growing Emphasis on Rearmament

While these developments were taking place, the war in Korea focused daily attention on the Communist military threat and the need for speeding up rearmament.

In September 1950 the North Atlantic Treaty Organization's Council of twelve foreign ministers, meeting in New York, voted to set up an

[24] The drafters of the Plan believed that temporary measures would be required to cushion the effects of dislocation which would be likely to result from the sudden removal of all domestic subsidies and external barriers to coal and steel production and trade. There was developed, therefore, a system of compensation whereby the more favored industries and governments shared the temporary negative consequences of unification with the less favored ones. This applied especially to coal, for which an equalization fund was proposed—to be raised by taxing the industries which would derive initial benefits from the abolition of trade barriers and to be used in compensating for some of the initial losses incurred as a consequence of the freeing of trade.

integrated European defense force. Three months later the creation of such a force was announced, and General Dwight D. Eisenhower was nominated for the position of Supreme Commander of the Allied Powers in Europe.

At the September meeting Secretary of State Acheson had proposed that German divisions be incorporated into the European defense system. This posed a difficult question. Caught between fear of Germany's resurgence as a military power and recognition of its potential contribution to joint defense, leaders in western Europe—particularly France—sought a means of reconciling these conflicting interests. The Pleven Plan, which contemplated the complete integration of "small" German units into a European army, slipped between the horns of this dilemma.[25]

The European Defense Community (EDC) which the Plan envisaged became a focus of increasing interest. On February 15, 1951, delegates from Belgium, France, Italy, Luxemburg, and western Germany met in Paris to discuss the creation of a European army, with representatives of Canada, Denmark, the Netherlands, Norway, Portugal, the United Kingdom, and the United States attending as observers. All agreed on the desirability of creating a unified European defense force, but there was disagreement—presaging difficulties ahead—on such specific issues as the size of the basic units, the character of the German force to be included, the incorporation of forces of the overseas territories, and the authority to be given to a European central command.

Pending creation of a European army, the question was how far the European countries could support their own rearmament. The progress achieved with ECA aid had put them in a position where they could undertake substantial defense efforts. But there were limits to what they could do.

Hence it was under conditions of partial recovery that negotiations began regarding each country's contribution to the common defense effort. These discussions centered, naturally, in NATO. On December 18, 1950, the North Atlantic Council approved a preliminary report on Germany's contribution to western defense and on the creation of an

---

[25] Under the Plan, which received an initial approval in principle by the French National Assembly by 349 to 235 votes, German rearmament—like the redevelopment of its coal and steel industries—would take place under the control of a European authority which, it was hoped, would transform an increase of Germany's military power from being a source of fear into being a source of confidence for all western Europe.

integrated force for western Europe. Holland boosted its defense budget by 25 percent from 1950 to 1951. Belgium over the same period increased its defense appropriations by two-thirds and placed restrictions on the use of certain materials in short supply in western Europe even though Belgium itself had adequate supplies of these materials. Although the political complexion of Spain was repulsive to many Americans, its political and military significance was recognized when Congress authorized loan assistance to that country up to a maximum of 62.5 million dollars.[26] On May 5, 1951, an agreement was signed between the United States government and Iceland for the use of defense facilities on the island by NATO nations.

In early April, General Eisenhower assumed command of all Allied armies in Europe and the western Mediterranean area. At the end of the month a new Financial and Economic Board (FEB) was created, under NATO. Arrangements were made for it to utilize personnel and information from the OEEC.

Raw Material Shortages

The economic problems arising from the defense program, meanwhile, were becoming more evident and pressing. The first problem to make itself felt seriously was the shortage of raw materials. Before the defense program began, world stocks of basic materials were already being consumed one and a half times faster than the prewar rate, largely because of increases in American production. By early winter of 1950–1951 scarcities in some basic items were becoming real and pressing— most importantly coal, iron ore, and certain foodstuffs. The winter was severe. Europe's coal shortage became so acute and ocean transport facilities so scarce that some five hundred vessels were broken out of the American "mothball fleet" for emergency use in transporting coal to western Europe.

The United States, as the largest producer and consumer of raw materials, instituted a control program covering domestic allocations and exports of certain scarce commodities. An International Materials Conference with recommendatory powers was organized by the United States, the United Kingdom, and France, with headquarters in Washington. At the invitation of the ECA, a delegation of the OEEC headed by Sir Edmund Hall-Patch proceeded to Washington to discuss the supply of raw materials. In January, Dirk Stikker, then chairman of the OEEC Council, was given the task of discussing with the governments

[26] Public Law 759, 81st Congress, 1st Session (1950).

of the United States and OEEC member countries the question of relationship between the OEEC and the International Materials Conference. In March the OEEC Council agreed to participate in the central group of this conference.

Development of Overseas Territories

In the overseas territories, as in other underdeveloped areas with
substantial raw material resources, economic development was gradual,
depending in part on investments in transport, port facilities, electric
power, and other basic services. Even so, the postwar colonial investment programs began to pay off.[27] The defense program gave a strong
boost to further economic development in these regions. Both Europe
and the United States had already become heavily dependent upon
them for many basic materials. More than 50 percent of Europe's copper, for example, came from the dependent overseas territories. In the
calendar year 1950 the United States obtained from them approximately 97 percent of its columbium ore, 82 percent of its bauxite, 81
percent of its palm oil, 68 percent of its cobalt (a vital item in the production of jet engines), 52 percent of its industrial diamonds, 51 percent of its tin, 48 percent of its rubber, and 23 percent of its manganese
ore, as well as large quantities of other materials.[28]

For Europe, expansion of output in the territories was the most feasible way of increasing the supply of raw materials and certain foodstuffs
on reasonable terms. And the territories were a promising long-term
market for European production.[29]

The pressures of rearmament reinforced a tendency to view the territories primarily as sources of urgently needed basic materials, not

[27] Exports from the European dependencies, in terms of actual quantity, showed
in 1950 the following indexes in relation to a prewar index of 100: bauxite—529,
zinc (ore and metal)—390, lead (ore and metal)—222, coffee—202, rubber—
181, timber—169, phosphates—163, copper (metal)—156, cotton—155, sisal—115,
and tin (metal and concentrates), cocoa and groundnuts—109 each. In terms of
value, foodstuffs (principally oilseeds, oils, and fats), beverages, and petroleum
products were the leading categories. OEEC, *Economic Progress and Problems*,
pp. 154–155.

[28] *Thirty-seventh ECA Report for the Public Advisory Board* (Washington,
1951), pp. 2–16.

[29] Total exports of equipment from the European participating countries to the
overseas territories were, in 1949 and 1950, more than three times as much as those
from the United States. Taking the 1938 level as a base of 100, France's exports
to its overseas areas increased to 254 in 1948, 333 in 1949, and 347 in 1950. British
exports to the U.K. dependencies showed increases to 132 in 1947, 208 in 1948,
and 261 in both 1949 and 1950. OEEC, *Economic Progress and Problems*, p. 156.

always with the interests of the territories in mind. A Presidential commission, commenting on underdeveloped areas generally—including the overseas territories—aptly stated:

These countries no longer accept poverty as an inevitable fact of life. The contrast between their aspirations and their present state of unrelieved poverty makes them susceptible to domestic unrest and provides fertile ground for the growth of Communist movements. . . . We must help bring about in these areas increased production and mutually beneficial exchange of material for civilian and defense use . . . [and] we must assist in bringing them increasingly into a network of international trade which will promote a more effective use of the economic resources of the free world and will enable the countries comprising it to achieve progress on a self-supporting basis.[30]

Complex problems were involved in balanced development of the overseas territories, however,[31] and this was one reason why European countries tended to move more slowly than many Americans considered desirable. Even so, investments for development in these areas reached, in 1951, annual levels estimated as equivalent in value to approximately 370 million dollars for France, 200 million dollars for the United Kingdom, and 160 million dollars for Belgium.[32]

ECA assistance, which comprised a marginal but significant part of these investment programs, was derived from four sources. The first consisted of regular program funds allocated to individual European countries. Only France made extensive use of this source, committing, up to June 30, 1951, about 287 million of its aid dollars for dollar-cost equipment and supplies needed in its overseas areas.

The second source was a special reserve fund established by the ECA for assistance to key development projects in the territories. By June 30, 1951, 63.8 million dollars had been obligated from this source. The projects were of a wide scope, with special emphasis on roads, railways, port improvements, agricultural production and reclamation work.

The third source was the ECA's technical assistance fund, which financed surveys of resources and technological improvement in agriculture, land utilization, transportation, and other fields.

[30] *Report to the President on Foreign Economic Policies* (Washington, 1950), p. 49. The Commission was headed by former Secretary of the Army Gordon Gray.

[31] See "ECA and the Dependent Territories," *Geographical Review*, January 1951, pp. 66–87, by John E. Orchard, former advisor on overseas territories in the ECA's European office.

[32] *Thirty-seventh ECA Report*, p. 11. The French investments included those in North Africa, regarded as part of the French Union. There was, at the time, much discussion of the need for greater private investment in underdeveloped areas generally, and some efforts were made to encourage it. But with some exceptions, especially in the mining of strategic minerals, the results were not impressive.

Thousands of U.S. Dollars

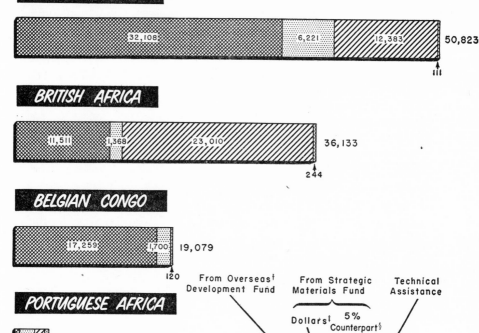

FRENCH AFRICA

32,108   6,221   12,383   **50,823**

BRITISH AFRICA

11,511   1,368   23,010   **36,133**

244

BELGIAN CONGO

17,259   1,700   **19,079**

120

From Overseas†   From Strategic   Technical
Development Fund   Materials Fund   Assistance

PORTUGUESE AFRICA

Dollars‡   5%
Counterpart§

1,118
1,804   **4,098**

663   513

Estimated European and Territorial Investment Programs for Overseas Development, Calendar Year 1951, and Obligations from ECA Overseas Development
Fund, July 1950 – June 1951

FRANCE   **UNITED KINGDOM**   **BELGIUM**

$370 MILLION   ECA 8% $200 MILLION   ECA 6% $120 MILLION   ECA 12%

Source: ECA and MSA DATA

9. Aid to European dependencies in Africa from special ECA funds,* cumulative
April 3, 1948–June 30, 1952.

* The French government used in addition $281.8 million of its regular Marshall Plan program
funds for developmental purposes in Africa.

† Used chiefly for equipment needed in developing basic economic services such as transport,
power, and irrigation.

‡ Principally advances for developmental purposes repayable in strategic materials.

§ Counterpart funds made available to U.S. and used for strategic materials procurement and
development.

The fourth source was a strategic materials fund administered by the ECA, supplemented by drawings from the 5 percent counterpart fund made available to the United States government. Up to June 30, 1951, the equivalent of 47 million dollars had been committed for strategic materials development projects with loans repayable in such materials.[33]

Inflationary Pressures

In June 1950 the OEEC was uncertain whether inflationary or deflationary forces would predominate during the remainder of the year.[34] Events soon dispelled all doubt. By the end of September the Secretary General, Marjolin, stated that the danger of inflation was the gravest of the economic problems raised by the change in the international situation.

Both reduced supply and increased demand were responsible. Resources for civilian production were curtailed by material and financial allocations to defense, and by diversion of productive facilities from civilian to military uses. On the demand side, excess purchasing power created by defense expenditures was not entirely siphoned off by increased taxation. As early as the end of 1950, credit expansion for defense was beginning to generate severe inflationary pressures in Europe; in the United States defense outlays were running at an annual rate of 14 billion dollars.[35] Rising living costs provoked pressure for higher wages, which tended to produce the familiar costs-and-incomes spiral.

Psychological factors were also important. Confidence in some currencies was low—notably the French franc, the Italian lira, and the German mark. The memory of violent inflations in the twenties and forties had drastically reduced the incentive to save in these currencies and had generated such a hypersensitivity to rising prices that mildly inflationary influences could produce explosive price increases. The problem of inflation was, of course, more acute because advances in military technology had greatly increased the cost of defense. Ordnance, planes, ships, and tanks were already more than twice as expensive as they had been during World War II.[36]

"Inflationary pressures," declared the OEEC in May 1951, "threat-

[33] *Thirty-seventh ECA Report*, pp. 2–16.

[34] OEEC, *Internal Financial Stability in Member Countries* (Paris, 1950), pp. 17–26.

[35] See R. M. Bissell, Jr., "The Impact of Rearmament on the Free World Economy," *Foreign Affairs*, April 1951, pp. 385–405.

[36] For illustrations, see Mutual Security Agency, *U.S. Defense Support in Western Europe* (Washington, 1951), p. 3 (pamphlet).

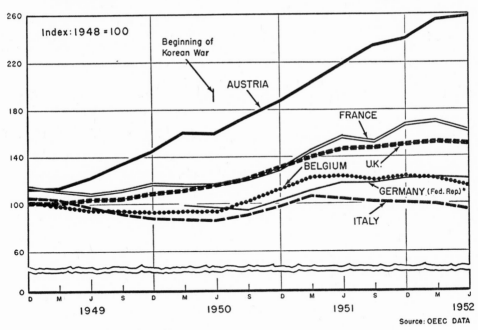

10. Wholesale prices in selected countries.

* Data for Germany not available prior to March 1950.

ened to interrupt the economic development of Europe, endangered the progress already achieved and rendered more difficult the accomplishment of the defense effort from which they had sprung." [37] They tended to throw the burden of increased defense expenditures on those least able to bear it, and to stimulate production and investment in unessential industries at a time when they should be curtailed.

As we have seen, achievement of financial stability, even before the defense program, had not been easy. A further complication was that maladjustments in income distribution had been met, in many countries, by large-scale social security programs into which between 20 and 25 percent of the national income was channeled. With such a high percentage politically pledged, it was more difficult to take another 7.7 percent (the level actually achieved in 1951–1952) for a new purpose such as rearmament.

Each government could accomplish this diversion in any of three ways, or by some combination of them.[38] It could employ fiscal or

[37] *Economic Progress and Problems*, p. 19.

[38] See Committee for Economic Development, *Economic Aspects of North Atlantic Security* (Washington, 1951), pp. 11ff. (A statement on national policy by the Research and Policy Committee of the CED.)

monetary measures (such as drastic increases in taxation, reduction in nondefense spending, and strict control over credit) while relying on military orders and selective credit controls to divert economic resources to military production. Or it could suppress inflation by the use of direct price and wage controls and consumer rationing. Or it could permit open inflation, using bank credit or the printing press to the extent necessary to outbid civilian demand for labor, production facilities, and materials.

No government could, in practice, carry the third alternative very far, since it would soon disrupt the economy, exhaust foreign exchange reserves, and raise bitter political issues. But in a number of countries—including France, western Germany, and Italy—formidable obstacles had to be met before the first two methods could be employed. The governments of these three countries, particularly, were based upon coalitions embracing divergent political and economic opinions. As a result, they had great difficulties in raising taxes, reducing less essential government expenditures, and mobilizing public opinion. Their budgets were already heavily burdened with social security charges, pensions, and other politically sensitive payments. Large public investment programs were necessitated in part by the timidity of private capital. Their tax systems were, generally speaking, antiquated and inequitable and were already drawing off a substantial percentage of the national income. Personal savings were low, and the public market for governmental and industrial securities was extremely limited.

All of this did not mean that governments were unaware of the Soviet peril or that they were less anxious than the United States or the United Kingdom to regain security through rearmament. But it meant that they had to operate within a range of policy alternatives which was narrowed considerably by the "economic vulnerability and political fragility of their societies." [39]

Resources and Productivity

Shortages, inflation, and political uncertainty made it much more difficult, of course, to divert substantial resources to defense. Would it be necessary, in order to achieve a substantial buildup in military potential, to devote to defense over the next few years the total growth in each country's output and thereby bring on economic stagnation and political instability? The answer clearly depended on the efficiency with which existing resources could be utilized or, as the Gray report

[39] *Ibid.*, p. 13.

put it, whether aggressive measures could be taken to eliminate under-employment of resources.[40] Cutting out a sizable slice of the pie for defense would not be such a difficult operation if, in each successive year, the pie could be enlarged.

But how could this be accomplished? How, amid the problems of this period, could the vitality and productiveness of the European economy be increased? In countries such as West Germany, with its technological traditions and its large accretions of manpower since the war, new investments might supply part of the answer. In countries such as Italy, with its overpopulation and limited resources, emigration of man-power to other economies where it could be more fruitfully employed seemed to hold some slight hope of beneficial result.

But the problem for western Europe, seen as a whole, was deeper. Increase in production to permit both a strong defense and an expand-ing economy called not only for technological advances. It called also for elimination of restrictionism in finance, industry and commerce; for greater incentives to owners, managers, and workers; for the re-vival of an entrepreneurial class, the growth of vigorous and free labor movements, the extension of reforms in land tenure; for greater em-phasis on high-volume, low-cost output; for the development, many Americans felt, of a more competitive system through which new vigor could be injected into European society. It called, in a word, for a peaceful revolution which could incorporate into the European eco-nomic system some of the features which had enabled American pro-duction to reach unprecedented levels.[41] Commenting on the need for such a change, Bissell wrote:

What social forces can be unleashed in Europe to achieve this result? What leverage can the United States exert to foster them? The detailed answer would require a volume. The broad answer is that the United States must exploit to the full the example of its own accomplishments and their powerful appeal to Europeans (and others) among all groups. Coca-Cola and Holly-wood movies may be regarded as two products of a shallow and crude civiliza-tion. But American machinery, American labor relations, and American management and engineering are everywhere respected. The hope is that a few European unions and entrepreneurs can be induced to try out the philos-ophy of higher productivity, higher wages and higher profits from the lower prices of lower unit cost. If they do, if restrictionism can be overcome at merely a few places, the pattern may spread. The forces making for such

[40] *Op. cit.,* p. 36.

[41] See Bissell, *op. cit.,* pp. 403–404; also *Report to the President on Foreign Economic Policies,* pp. 34–35.

changes are so powerful that, with outside help and encouragement, they may become decisive. It will not require enormous sums of money (even of European capital) to achieve vaster increases in production. But it will require a profound shift in social attitudes, attuning them to the mid-twentieth century.[42]

During the first half of 1951 a new "production assistance drive" was begun with ECA support.[43] Technical assistance activities of all sorts were stepped up. Production "teams" in increasing number were sent to the United States for intensive observation and training, many of them representing both management and labor. The results cannot be measured, but some instances may be cited to show the effects achieved in certain industries.

In France, for example, investigating groups representing the French Ministry of Commerce, the French Productivity Center, and the ECA mission visited firms chosen at random from among those which had had participants on teams sent to the United States. Sixteen surveys showed that, in all but one case, notable improvements had been realized. A manufacturer of heavy electrical equipment had upped production by 28 percent with an 8 percent rise in labor force. An increased output of 30 percent was achieved in a shoe factory without engaging extra labor, and a 16.8 percent gain was reported by a firm producing tanks for the storage and transportation of liquids.[44] In some cases the benefits of increased productivity were reflected in higher wages and bonuses for workers.

Beginning in June 1951 a new technique was employed for acquainting key industrialists with the advantages of high productivity—management seminars for European executives. The first of these, held in the Netherlands, concentrated on production engineering; standardization, simplification, and specialization; marketing and marketing research; and training.

Re-emergence of the Dollar Gap

The remarkable progress achieved during 1950 in reducing Europe's "dollar gap" was checked by the rearmament program, and in the spring of 1951 a reverse trend appeared. During the second quarter of that year the trade gap of the participating countries with the rest of the

[42] Bissell, *op. cit.*, pp. 404–405.

[43] The lead, in the ECA, was taken by William H. Joyce, Jr., assistant administrator for production.

[44] ECA, *Thirteenth Report to Congress* (Washington, 1951), pp. 50–51.

world rose to the highest level since 1947, averaging around 650 million dollars per month; the increase reflected primarily the higher cost of imported materials. While exports to America remained approximately the same, imports from the United States rose by nearly 270 million dollars over the first quarter.

It was therefore clear that American aid had to be continued on a substantial scale if OEEC countries were to step up their defense effort while maintaining their civilian economies at politically tolerable levels. The amount and duration of the aid required obviously depended on the size and period of rapid military expansion in western Europe and on the proportion of its military requirements which would be produced in the United States.

The most obvious means for limiting the dollar gap was to increase exports from the European countries and their dependencies to the United States. Otherwise, markets lost during the war and slowly and painfully regained from 1946 to 1950 might be lost again, and the prospect of a western Europe able to support itself by two-way trade in the world economy might become, once more, as remote as it seemed in 1946.

This situation underlay efforts to intensify the "dollar drive." In France, for example, the Counseil National du Patronat Français, patterned after the British Dollar Export Board, sought to expand French exports to the United States through market surveys and advertising, better merchandizing methods, and better established marketing channels.[45] Similar efforts were undertaken in other countries.

Political Problems

While the above questions were being grappled with, the cold war continued its uneasy course. Its scope and challenge were epitomized by Paul Hoffman in his book, *Peace Can Be Won:*

To wage the peace intelligently we must realize the kind of war that threatens us. The Soviet Union has been and is carrying on a completely new kind of war. . . . For the Kremlin, the military is only one of four fronts—each a battleground of implacable attack. These four fronts are the military, economic, political and psychological. . . . We must wage the peace along the same four fronts—the military, the economic, the political and the psychological.[46]

[45] See Warren Baum, "The Marshall Plan and French Foreign Trade," in *Modern France*, ed. by Edward M. Earle (Princeton University Press, 1951), pp. 397–398.
[46] *Op. cit.*, pp. 16–18.

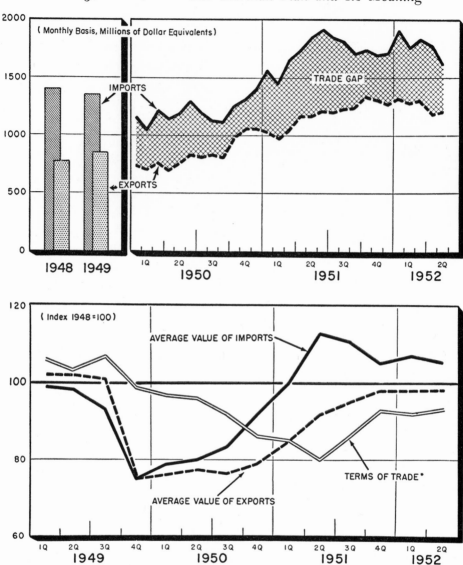

11. Western Europe's world trade, 1948–mid-1952. *Upper:* Trade of the Western European countries with the world (including overseas territories). *Lower:* Western Europe's terms of trade with the rest of the world. (Note: The devaluation of currencies in September 1949 caused a drop in monetary value but not in volume.)

* Ratio of average value—$\dfrac{\text{exports}}{\text{imports}}$.

The Communists convened, in February 1951, a "World Peace Council" in East Berlin. In March there was another of the series of meetings of the foreign ministers of the Big Four powers. The Western nations called for a German peace treaty, German unification, and an Austrian treaty. There was disagreement from the outset, and, once again, no progress was made toward the relaxation of existing tensions. Communist parties vigorously continued their subversive efforts, particularly in France and Italy.

In the United States, meanwhile, attention was shifting from the European scene to domestic issues. The shock of the Korean War had followed by less than two years the shock of the Communist conquest of China. Lack of preparedness to meet the threat which these events posed was deeply disturbing to the American people. As in the preceding "great debate" on China, the "great debate" on the Korean War —after the relief of General Douglas MacArthur from his Far East command—showed widening fissures in American public opinion. Issues arose as to the role and the burdens the United States should assume in the free world while undertaking its own vast rearmament program. How much should the United States rely upon and support the defense efforts of its NATO partners? Should cold war strategy be related to the four fronts—military, economic, political, and psychological—emphasized by Hoffman and others, with efforts to fortify Allied unity and strength on all of those fronts? Or should it focus predominantly on the military, rapidly diminishing priority for economic assistance? Should the United States be ready to "go it alone" if serious divergencies should arise within the Atlantic Community?

These questions were not resolved by clear-cut answers, but the trend of American thinking was signalized by a change in terminology when the Administration presented its European aid proposals to Congress in the spring of 1951. The term "economic cooperation" was dropped in favor of "mutual security."

With the transition, new tensions began to appear between the United States and some of its allies. The stresses were attributable not only to the new sacrifices required in a period of rapid rearmament, but also to differences in approach. On the American side, where a strong sense of urgency prevailed, there were signs of growing impatience over delays in rearmament and over the disunity which appeared in some European countries. Many Europeans, on the other hand, feared that American impetuosity in defense programing might undo economic and political gains that had been achieved with great effort. Some were worried too lest, by an extension of the Korean conflict to China, a third world war might be precipitated in which Europe would again become the major battlefield. These strains were not sufficient to undercut Allied unity, but they gave warning that unity required a continuing process of give and take.

CHAPTER 8

Fourth Year (1951-1952):

Transition to Mutual Security

BY THE summer of 1951 military security had superseded economic self-reliance as the primary objective of American policy in western Europe. The total volume of United States aid to Europe remained high, as indicated by the table on the following page of the new funds made available by Congress through appropriations and loan authorizations between April 3, 1948 (when the Marshall Plan was approved), and June 30, 1952.[1]

The transition in emphasis from recovery to defense was formalized, at the end of 1951, by the termination of the ECA and the launching of the Mutual Security Program. The funds appropriated by Congress, however, including those approved for economic and technical assistance under the terms of the previous Economic Cooperation Act, were for the entire fiscal year. The present chapter, therefore, carries the story of the recovery effort through the transition period and up to June 30, 1952.

[1] For a full recapitulation see Department of Commerce, *Foreign Aid by the United States Government, 1940–1951*, pp. 112–115. The summary table below does not cover 670 million dollars under special Greek and Turkish aid programs between 1947 and 1949, or some 2.7 billion dollars appropriated for Government and Relief in Occupied Areas (GARIOA) in both Europe and the Far East, or 207 million appropriated for the worldwide operations of the International Refugee Organization and the International Children's Emergency Fund.

	Total for ERP and NATO countries	*European Recovery Program* *(ERP)*	*Mutual Defense Assistance* *(MDAP)*	*Mutual Security Program*	
				Military assistance	Economic and technical aid
		(Billion dollars—in round numbers)			
1948–49	6.05	6.05	. . . .	. . . .	. . . .
1949–50	4.48	3.78	.7	. . . .	. . . .
1950–51	7.27	2.31	4.96	. . . .	. . . .
1951–52	5.94	(1.022) *	. . . .	4.92 †	1.022 *

* This appropriation, within the Mutual Security Program, was for assistance under the terms of the Economic Cooperation Act of 1948, as amended; 478 million dollars was also made available in 1951–1952 for economic assistance under a Congressional authorization for transfers of funds (up to 10 percent) from military to economic assistance. Thus the total funds made available for obligation under the European Recovery Program, up to June 30, 1952, came to approximately 13.6 billion dollars.

† For aid to NATO countries plus 100 million dollars for military, economic, and technical assistance to Spain.

The year 1951–1952 was marked by intensification of the cold war, with the projected European Defense Community (EDC) as the prime target of Communist attack. Many obstacles remained to be overcome prior to ratification of the proposed treaty. In June 1952 the outcome was still in doubt. But, with broad coordination through NATO, rearmament programs were carried forward vigorously.

"Defense Support"

To emphasize the importance of economic strength as a foundation of military security, the 1.5 billion dollars requested for ERP-type aid in 1951–1952 was characterized as "defense support."

The ECA and subsequently the MSA contended that by providing resources and equipment—such as cotton, foodstuffs, coal, and machinery—in which the European economies were deficient and which they could not buy with available foreign exchange resources, the United States would make possible a much larger use of European resources for defense. This type of assistance, it was claimed, would serve the same purpose as did the nonmilitary goods furnished to allies under the Lend-Lease program during World War II.[2]

This argument met a cautious response among economy-minded members of Congress, some of whom continued to regard all economic aid as a "giveaway." Many who had been impressed with Europe's

[2] See MSA, *First Report to Congress on the Mutual Security Program* (Washington, 1951), p. 15.

economic resurgence, as revealed in previous ECA reports, questioned the desirability of continuing the types of aid that had been provided under the Marshall Plan, especially when the added burdens of military defense at home and abroad were taken into account. This issue was not met head-on. The case for promoting continued economic expansion in Europe in order to support civilian *plus* military production at necessary levels was not made as forthrightly and cogently as it might have been.

The executive branch of the government did try with considerable effect, however, especially in the spring of 1952, to demonstrate how economic assistance—envisaged as "defense support"—could have a "multiplier" effect on defense production in Europe. It was shown, for example, that relatively small dollar expenditures for machinery and equipment not available in Europe could frequently bring into productive use much larger local industrial resources, leading to military output substantially above what could be directly purchased in the United States with the same dollars. The less direct connection between nonmilitary commodities such as coal and cotton, on the one hand, and the production of tanks and ammunition on the other, though valid, was more difficult to demonstrate.

The ECA emphasized that Europe's continuing foreign exchange problems were largely attributable to the defense burden. But "dollar gap" estimates did not carry as much weight as when the aims of the program were primarily economic. Even members of Congress who agreed that the economic and political health of Europe was indispensable and that the patient might suffer a relapse if all economic aid were cut off prematurely, could not easily agree to the amounts of "defense support" deemed necessary by the executive branch. Only about two-thirds of the amount requested was appropriated.

Administrative Problems

The change in emphasis raised administrative as well as financial questions. Through what channels should further assistance be provided? Should the ECA be continued? Should aid to civilian and to military production in Europe be administered by a single agency? Or should the latter be handled along with the provision of military end-items? To what extent, in planning assistance, should plans for military production in Europe be allowed to cut into the capacity of the continent to export—especially to dollar areas? To what extent should support for the OEEC and its offshoot, the EPU, be continued? Should the OEEC be subordinated to, or even become a part of, NATO? [3]

The administrative tangles which developed during the period of transition were exceedingly hard to unravel. It was easier to talk about a clear demarcation of responsibilities than to achieve it; areas of joint concern among different agencies were inescapable. In simplest terms, the question was one of fixing primary responsibility for each activity and then ensuring adequate consultation and clearance before decisions affecting other agencies were reached. Without a central authority to initiate and supervise such coordination, however, the task was all but hopeless. Each agency tended to assume all the responsibility permitted by its enabling legislation. Jurisdictional jockeying was inevitable.

During 1950–1951, it will be recalled, there had been a growth of sentiment in favor of a single agency to deal with foreign economic operations, using the ECA as a core. This view had adherents in the ECA, of course, but also in such disinterested bodies as the commission headed by Gordon Gray, appointed by the President to make recommendations in the field of foreign economic relations and policies; the International Development Advisory Board, also a Presidential commission; [4] and a number of independent organizations including the Committee for Economic Development. But in the executive branch and in Congress, there were wide differences of opinion reflecting the intricacy of interrelated political, military, and economic objectives. [5]

Mutual Security Act of 1951

Presentation to Congress of the foreign aid programs for 1951–1952 began in late June and early July 1951, three or four months later than usual. The delay was occasioned by the complexity of the problem and by the effort to put provisions for all forms of aid into one package, as desired by Congress. Estimates had to be made of the desirable size of European defense forces, the timetable for their formation, the contributions of NATO members, and the deficiencies to be made up by American assistance.

[3] For discussion of these questions, see Brookings Institution, *Current Issues in Foreign Economic Assistance* (Washington, 1951), pp. 90–91, 96–98; *Report to the President on Foreign Economic Policies* (Gray Report), pp. 39–42; CED, *Economic Aspects of North Atlantic Security*, pp. 26–28.

[4] See *Report to the President on Foreign Economic Policies* (Gray Report), p. 99; and International Development Advisory Board, *Partners in Progress* (Rockefeller Report; Washington, 1951), pp. 16–26.

[5] See Brown and Opie, *op. cit.*, pp. 501–509.

Finally, on October 10, after lengthy Congressional hearings, the Mutual Security Act of 1951 [6] was adopted. Three weeks later appropriations were approved covering 4.92 billion dollars for military assistance and 1.022 billion for "defense support"; the President was empowered to transfer, if necessary, up to 10 per cent of either one of these funds to the other.

The new legislation abolished the Economic Cooperation Administration and established in its place the Mutual Security Agency (MSA). It authorized appointment, within the Executive Office of the President, of a Director for Mutual Security, with the dual task of coordinating and supervising all foreign aid programs (military, economic, and technical) and of directing the Mutual Security Agency. W. Averell Harriman was named Director.[7] Within the new coordinating framework, the Department of Defense continued to administer direct military assistance and the State Department retained responsibility for technical aid under the Point Four Program.[8] The responsibilities of the Special Representative in Europe (to which post William H. Draper, Jr.,[9] was subsequently appointed) were broadened to cover military, economic, and technical assistance, and a deputy was named for each.

Under the new legislation, the MSA's defense support functions were widened and its relations with other agencies were extended. The relative freedom which the ECA had enjoyed was gone. In the new context of interlocked political, economic, and military goals, the problem of correlating economic and defense aid was basic and inescapable. The work of the MSA became more closely meshed with that of other agencies, particularly the Departments of State and Defense. The unifying legislation required—some thought to an extreme degree—more complicated administrative procedures. The transitional difficulties experienced by the MSA were aggravated by a reduction in administrative funds and a 10 percent cut in personnel. Although the operating funds to be administered were also reduced, the agency's workload did not decline. Indeed, the problems of meeting military

[6] Public Law 165, 82d Congress, 1st Session (1951).

[7] Harriman concentrated on the coordinating role, leaving the administration of the MSA to his deputy, W. John Kenney, former chief of the ECA mission to the U.K. and a former Under-Secretary of the Navy.

[8] This did not apply to former ECA programs in the Far East and the dependent overseas territories, which antedated Point Four; responsibility for these was retained by MSA.

[9] Investment banker; Under-Secretary of the Army, 1947–1949.

and defense support needs, with smaller funds and new areas of responsibility, were more complicated than before.

While the Mutual Security Act of 1951 achieved the desired reorientation of American aid objectives, it provided only in part the foundation needed for adequate integration of aid operations. During the ensuing months, this goal was brought somewhat nearer by efforts within the executive branch to delineate administrative responsibilities more clearly and to simplify interagency procedures.

In Europe the OEEC continued its significant functions, especially in such areas as trade liberalization and the operation of the European Payments Union. But the relative roles of the OEEC and the Financial and Economic Board of NATO remained unclear for some time. This matter was finally resolved when the FEB was abolished and it was agreed that the OEEC should have primary responsibility in the economic field. The OEEC was looked to for information and guidance on basic economic problems, but of course it did not have full knowledge of NATO plans for military force targets in each country, especially since the national membership of the two organizations was not identical. Coordination of economic and military effort in Europe, therefore, was also a knotty problem.

Defense Goals

At the Ottawa meeting of the North Atlantic Council in September 1951, attention was directed to a substantial "gap" between commitments by individual countries and the over-all targets which NATO had previously established.

A Temporary Committee of the Council (TCC) was set up to analyze the capabilities of each country. The basic work of this committee was done by an executive group consisting of W. Averell Harriman (United States), Sir Edwin Plowden (United Kingdom), and Jean Monnet (France), who were promptly dubbed the "three wise men." In December the TCC presented its findings; in many cases, they pointed to larger defense budgets. The TCC recommendations were largely approved by the North Atlantic Council at Lisbon in February 1952.

The revised military force goals included fifty combat-ready and reserve divisions in western Europe by December 31, 1952, as well as 4,000 operational aircraft and a naval force of some 1,600 vessels. NATO members undertook to meet these targets, assuming assistance expected under the Mutual Security Program.

Stretching Economic Aid

While the TCC was going through its intricate exercise, it became clear that the ECA estimates of economic assistance or defense support needed in 1951–1952 had been none too high. The smaller amount appropriated left little leeway for emergencies. Fortunately, the Congress had provided for considerable flexibility in the use of the funds. The authority given the President to transfer to defense support up to 10 percent of the amounts appropriated for direct military assistance has been mentioned. Provision was also made for a shift from one geographic area to another of up to 10 percent of funds earmarked for any one region. Other legislation authorized use of domestic defense appropriations for "offshore procurement" in Europe of military items required by the United States. Through recourse to each of these means, economic aid was stretched to meet pressing needs.

It will be recalled that in early 1951 a large expansion in the dollar reserves of the sterling area had occasioned a suspension of aid to the United Kingdom. The prediction of some economists that the improvement would be only temporary was borne out. Prices of many raw materials exported by the sterling area declined while those of essential imports rose. There were other losses, including those in income from Iranian oil. By winter a financial crisis impended, and dollar assistance was needed again. In February 1952, 300 million dollars of the amount designated for direct military assistance in Europe was transferred to the United Kingdom. A transfer of 100 million dollars was made to forestall a crisis in France. Amounts totaling 78 million dollars were made available, under the same authority, to Greece, Turkey, and Yugoslavia. The French financial situation grew more acute as a result of the heavy drain of the war in Indochina. A transfer to Indochina of military assistance financed out of funds initially earmarked for Europe averted a budgetary crisis in France. These measures augmented the total volume of direct and indirect economic assistance to Europe, thereby cushioning the impact of the defense effort.

Auxiliary Commitments in Europe

The Mutual Security Act made military and defense support assistance after January 8, 1952, conditional upon assurances by each recipient country to:

(1) join in promoting international understanding and goodwill, and maintaining world peace; (2) take such action as may be mutually agreed upon

to eliminate causes of international tension; (3) fulfill the military obligations which it has assumed under multilateral or bilateral agreements or treaties to which the United States is a party; (4) make, consistent with its political and economic stability, the full contribution permitted by its manpower, resources, facilities and general economic condition to the development and maintenance of its own defensive strength and the defensive strength of the free world; (5) take all reasonable measures' which may be needed to develop its defense capacity; and (6) take appropriate steps to ensure the effective utilization of the economic and military assistance provided by the United States.[10]

Technical assistance to non-NATO countries was similarly conditioned upon their agreement:

to join in promoting international understanding and goodwill, and in maintaining world peace, and to take such action as may be mutually agreed upon to eliminate causes of international tension.[11]

The response to these requirements was not altogether cordial—not because of their content but because they seemed redundant. The NATO countries generally felt that such assurances had already been given in the North Atlantic Treaty, the United Nations Charter, or the previous ECA and Military Defense Aid agreements. There was therefore some resentment of what seemed to be a reflection upon their good faith. Certain recipients of technical but not military aid feared that the assurances required might imply that they were abandoning, under American pressure, a neutral status in the cold war. With a few exceptions, however, the participating countries signed the new agreements.[12]

Restrictions upon East-West Trade

The Economic Cooperation Act of 1948 had encouraged western European trade with other areas as one means of reducing Europe's requirements; trade with eastern Europe was discouraged only for items of specific strategic value. Soon the question arose of how the historical trading pattern between eastern and western Europe could be modified to keep the economic benefits to the free world from being

---

10 Sec. 511(a). 11 Sec. 511(b).

12 Ireland was not prepared to accept all of the purposes expressed in the act, and the Irish aid program (principally technical assistance) was suspended. In Asia, the governments of Indonesia and Burma, after periods of negotiation, indicated their unwillingness to undertake commitments which might appear to align them militarily with the Western powers.

outweighed by military advantages to the Communist bloc. After hostilities began in Korea, the problem became more acute. It was difficult to decide what items in a long and complicated list should be embargoed as of strategic significance, and to coordinate the control policies of the Western nations.

Results were necessarily slow, and the negotiations could not be publicized in detail. Little was known of European measures in this area. Some members of Congress became increasingly concerned about the reported reluctance of some governments to take adequate measures for controlling East-West trade. The so-called "Cannon amendment" of September 1950 and its successor, the "Kem amendment" of June 1951, both enacted after somewhat hasty consideration in committee, expressed the view that American aid should be denied to countries which would not completely shut off the flow to Communist-bloc countries of potential military supplies. The Kem amendment required the Secretary of Defense to draw up a list of prohibited goods which aid recipients would have to embargo to the Soviet bloc if they were to remain eligible for American assistance. And it specified that the list should include not only arms and military materiel, but also commodities which might be used in the manufacture of military equipment or which the United States itself embargoed for shipment to the Soviet bloc. At the last minute a clause was inserted authorizing the President to make temporary exceptions while Congress and the executive branch considered alternative approaches to the problem.

From the point of view of the latter, the amendment was too sweeping. It apparently disregarded the fact that some types of East-West trade were more advantageous to the defense effort of western Europe than to the Iron Curtain countries. And in practice, the countries concerned could not comply with all the terms of the amendment in time to avoid suspension of American assistance. In signing the legislation, therefore, the President indicated that wide use would be made of the exception procedure provided.

More extensive deliberation preceded enactment of the "Battle Act" [13] in October 1951. This act strengthened the system of controls already in effect and required the termination of military as well as economic aid in the event of violations. But it provided more flexibility by permitting exceptions for strategic items other than arms or atomic energy materials "when unusual circumstances indicate that the cessation of

[13] Mutual Defense Assistance Control Act of 1951. Public Law 213, 82d Congress, 1st Session, approved Oct. 26, 1951.

aid would clearly be detrimental to the security of the United States."

Responsibility for administering the "Battle Act" was given to the Director for Mutual Security. Lists of items to be embargoed under the act became effective on January 24, 1952. The administration of this law presented intricate problems.[14] Commitments previously made to deliver to the Soviet bloc materials of some strategic worth, for example, had to be carefully weighed.[15] But no difficulty occurred over shipments of strictly military items because no cases arose. And some projected shipments of goods of potential strategic value were prevented.

Production

Increased European production in 1951 reflected returns on earlier investments and some increases in efficiency. Industrial output in OEEC countries, which in 1947 had been at about 87 percent of the prewar level, climbed in 1948 to 98 percent; in 1949 to 110 percent; in 1950 to 122 percent; and in 1951 to more than 134 percent. Steel production, which was a little less than 7,600 tons per quarter in 1947, was nearly double that amount in 1951. The output of cotton yarn rose in the same period from 245,000 metric tons quarterly to more than 380,000, while rayon yarn and fiber went up from 75,000 to 179,000 tons. Cement production more than doubled. All of the major coal-producing countries showed increases in output during 1951.[16] Petroleum refining, which in 1948 had regained the prewar level of about 250,000 barrels per day, reached approximately 1.5 million barrels in 1952, a sixfold increase.[17]

In 1952, however, most production curves leveled off. During much

[14] See Chapter 17.

[15] The case of a Danish tanker illustrated the Hobson's choice posed in dealing with certain prior commitments. Despite U.S. pressure, in the summer of 1952 the Danish government felt itself compelled by a 1948 trade agreement to turn over to the Soviet Union a tanker capable of delivering aviation gasoline to the Red Chinese forces in Korea. The probable military value of the transfer could not be denied. But the consequences of terminating aid to Denmark seemed even more dangerous in view of Denmark's strategic importance to western European defense plans, and of its contribution to NATO defense efforts. The President, in this case, decided not to prohibit further aid to Denmark, as permitted under the act, citing Danish cooperation in the development of collective programs to eliminate shipments of strategic commodities to the Soviet bloc.

[16] See OEEC, *Statistical Bulletin*, November, 1954; and ECA, *Thirteenth Report to Congress*, pp. 15–21.

[17] Interview, Oscar B. Bransky, deputy director, Industrial Resources Division, OSR, Paris, November 3, 1952.

of the year output was either not rising or was rising at a relatively modest rate.[18] Efforts in behalf of greater productivity were therefore intensified.[19]

ECA assistance to industrial projects reached a total of 338 million dollars' worth of actual shipments in early 1952, while procurement authorizations stood at 479 million dollars. Aid to 142 projects in thirteen countries had been approved in the fields of manufacturing, raw materials extraction, transportation, communications, and utilities.[20]

A concern for Europe's long-term as well as immediate needs—and for American needs as well—was evidenced in the efforts to augment the output of basic materials in the dependent overseas territories.[21] Support given through the ECA to developmental and technical-assistance programs in these areas, taking into account all sources of aid, came to more than 400 million dollars during the four years of the Marshall Plan.[22] This assistance, coupled with much larger investments by the metropolitan countries—which reached a total of some 600 million dollars in 1951 alone—helped bring exports from these areas up to a monthly value, in 1951, of more than 400 million dollars.

Competition

Some members of Congress had become convinced that the European economy could achieve the new dynamic which it required only if in-

[18] OEEC, *Europe: The Way Ahead*, p. 15.   [19] See Chapter 15.

[20] Significant steel projects developed included the Usinor mills at Denain and Montataire, the Sollac rolling mill facilities in Lorraine, and the Longwy project—all in France; the Finsider group of steel plants, the Falck steel works, and the Terni plant—in Italy; a new and important plant at Margram in the U.K., intended to increase production of flat-rolled products of improved quality and at lower cost in amounts sufficient to meet immediate demands of the U.K. and leave a substantial export surplus, as well as mills to enlarge the output of tubular products at Corby, Clydesdale, and Tolcross; and a new Donawitz blooming mill and a new slabbing and blooming mill at Linz—both in Austria. Comparable illustrations might be given for electric power installations in Italy, France, and Turkey; for petroleum-refining projects in France, Italy, and the U.K.; for raw materials extraction projects in Turkey, France, and Norway; and for transportation and communication projects in Turkey and France. See MSA, *Monthly Report for the Public Advisory Board* (Washington, January 31, 1952), pp. 3–34.

[21] Summarized in MSA, *The Overseas Territories in the Mutual Security Program* (Washington, 1952), pp. 6–16 (booklet). The rapidly growing dependence of the U.S. upon foreign sources of raw materials was revealed in a monumental world-wide survey of raw material availabilities and prospects prepared by the President's Materials Policy Commission. This report, entitled *Resources for Freedom* (5 vols., Washington, June 1952) is frequently referred to as the Paley Report.

[22] Less concern for Europe's immediate problems was evidenced by an abrupt shift in American stockpiling policy in late 1951, which aggravated payments difficulties, especially for the sterling area.

vestment, production, and trade could be further released from artificial
shackles and if the benefits of increased productivity could be spread
through lower prices and higher wages. A result of this belief in the
possibilities of greater competition and better distribution was the "Benton amendment." Under the heading, "Encouragement of Free Enterprise," this amendment stated:

It is hereby declared to be the policy of the Congress that this Act shall be
administered in such a way as (1) to eliminate the barriers to, and provide
the incentives for, a steadily increased participation of free private enterprise in developing the resources of foreign countries consistent with the
policies of this Act, (2) to the extent that it is feasible and does not interfere
with the achievement of the purposes set forth in this Act, to discourage the
cartel and monopolistic business practices prevailing in certain countries
receiving aid under this Act which result in restricting production and
increasing prices, and to encourage where suitable competition and productivity, and (3) to encourage where suitable the development and strengthening of the free labor union movements as the collective bargaining agencies
of labor within such countries.[23]

These objectives were reaffirmed in the Mutual Security Act of 1952
through the "Moody amendment," which called for a liberal use of
counterpart funds in efforts to stimulate free enterprise and economic
expansion and to promote an increasingly "equitable sharing of the
benefits of increased production and productivity between consumers,
workers and owners." [24]

Integration

Cooperative efforts through the OEEC during the final year of the
recovery program were directed less at innovation than at holding and
consolidating gains already achieved. This was done, to a large extent,
despite financial drains which caused Britain and France to recede from
the 75 percent level for trade liberalization, and despite new stresses imposed upon the European Payments Union.

There was also the beginning of one new development, in a basic
economic sector in which integration, up to this time, had not been
attempted, namely, agricultural production and marketing. The first .
significant step occurred, outside of the OEEC framework, in March
1952. With Pierre Flimlin of France [25] and S. L. Mansholt of the Nether-

[23] Mutual Security Act of 1951, Sec. 516.

[24] Public Law 400, 82d Congress, Sec. 539, approved June 20, 1952.

[25] Minister of Commerce and External Economic Affairs, former Minister of
Agriculture.

lands [26] as the prime movers, a conference for the Organization of European Agricultural Markets, attended by ministers from fifteen countries, was convened in Paris. The conference created an interim working party of experts which made a start on the collection and examination of information on agricultural production, consumption, prices, and trade; a selection of commodities for more intensive study; and preparations for the next meeting of ministers at which the scope of attainable integration was to be considered.

Here the story ends—for the period of our study—but it may be added that this activity paved the way for more ambitious efforts in 1953 and 1954 to break down agricultural trade barriers in Europe, to encourage regional specialization where this would be mutually advantageous, to exchange scientific and technical information, and to expand demonstration projects and extension services within each agricultural economy. Regional specialization appears to be especially desirable in enabling countries with natural advantages for the output of particular commodities to produce them in larger quantities at lower unit costs for wider European markets.[27] Steps toward an absorption of the "Green Pool," as the joint organization was called, into the OEEC, presaged a rounding out of the latter organization and closer contact for the agricultural ministers of the participating countries with the liberalizing influences of the OEEC.[28]

Outlook in June 1952

By the end of the fiscal year 1951–1952, it could be reported that the Mutual Security Program had shown "progress—enough to justify cautious optimism." [29] The MSA developed, as a major strand in the rationale of the 1952–1953 program, a case based more articulately than before on the "multiplier" effect of defense support. Many in Congress became convinced that money so used could provide more collective defense-per-dollar than the same amounts added to the national defense budget. A total of 1,282,433,000 dollars was authorized for defense support in the Mutual Security Act of 1952.

The European economy, as a whole, was continuing to produce at the

[26] Minister of Agriculture.

[27] For example, dairy products in the Netherlands and Denmark, or fruits and vegetables in southern France, Italy, Spain, and Greece; expansion of markets for the latter would lessen the need for high-cost production under glass in Belgium, the Netherlands, and Scandinavia.

[28] Interview, Charles M. Elkinton (agricultural officer, later director, in the OSR), Washington, November 13, 1954.

[29] MSA, *Second Report to Congress* (Washington, 1952), p. 3.

levels achieved. On the other hand, there still remained a deficit of roughly 500 million dollars monthly in the continent's external balance of trade. Gold and dollar reserves, particularly in the United Kingdom, had dropped sharply during the first quarter of 1952 and had only slowly begun to recover. But further inflation had been curbed, and investment programs and production for defense had increased.

Many problems remained. With defense, the dollar gap had widened; few of the participating countries could get along without external assistance. Some had not yet adopted policies essential to their own economic health and political stability. Important steps had been taken toward economic integration, but much remained to be done. The danger of Communist subversion had been pushed back but not eliminated. In other parts of the world where European interests were deeply involved, communism was an everpresent menace. Solidarity between the United States and western Europe had receded from the high level of the early Marshall Plan years. The problems of an era of crisis had not been removed in four short years.

Yet the situation in 1952 was vastly different from that in 1947 and 1948. The economy of Europe had been greatly strengthened. It had new vitality, an increased capacity to grapple with its problems. This great area was once more a force in the world, and its weight was overwhelmingly on the side of freedom. European civilization had been preserved, and behind the clamor of dissident voices, constructive influences promised continuing advancement.

But for the gains achieved through the recovery program, Europe would not have been able to meet as well as it did the compelling test of a huge defense effort, even with the marginal assistance which the United States continued to provide. As it was, defense expenditures by NATO countries during the first half of 1952 were about double the pre-Korea level.

Amid many uncertainties there were indications, too, that the economic health and strength of western Europe would continue to be a major concern of the United States. One piece of evidence was a statement by the eminent American who was shortly to become President of the United States. On April 2, 1952, in his first annual report as Supreme Allied Commander, Europe, General Dwight D. Eisenhower said:

Everywhere we turned we ran into political and economic factors. One thing was clear: nothing would be gained and much lost through any substantial lowering of the already low standard of living in Europe. Our central problem was one of morale—the spirit of man. . . . No man will fight unless he feels he has something worth fighting for. Next . . . is the factor of the strength of the supporting economy. Unless the economy can safely carry the military establishment, whatever force of this nature a nation might create is worse than useless in a crisis. Since behind it there is nothing, it will only disintegrate.

16. Launching a willow mattress, as part of a dike-building operation in Holland destined to convert sizable inland seas into fertile farmlands.

17. A dredger at work on a land reclamation project in Italy.

18. Irrigation channel under construction in Greece.

PART III

Associated Programs in Asia

CHAPTER 9

Aid to China and Korea

OUR story now moves to Asia and the southwestern Pacific, where, concurrent with the European Recovery Program, American aid was extended to China and Korea, to the Philippines, Indonesia, Indochina, Thailand, and Burma, and, through an emergency wheat loan, to India.

Unlike the European Recovery Program, aid to Asia between 1948 and 1952 did not develop as a unified undertaking in behalf of a whole group of countries at once. It began with an authorization of aid to China, under the legislation which launched the Marshall Plan.[1] Then, as of January 1, 1949, the President transferred from the Department of the Army to the ECA the responsibility of administering economic assistance to Korea; nearly 30 million dollars in unexpended GARIOA [2] funds were turned over to ECA for this purpose. By 1950 continental China had fallen largely under Communist sway and the Foreign Economic Assistance Act of that year, approved June 5, authorized the use of residual China aid funds totaling more than 100 million dollars

[1] As previously stated, the China Aid Act was Title IV of Public Law 472, the Foreign Assistance Act of 1948. Subsequently 275 million dollars was appropriated under Public Law 793, 80th Congress, 2d Session (1948), for technical aid to China, and an additional 125 million dollars for other (primarily military) assistance.

[2] Government and Relief in Occupied Areas.

for economic assistance "in the general area of China." Under this authority, programs were initiated in the countries of southeast Asia and, in April 1951, the Philippines.

This chapter deals briefly with the conduct and results of the economic aid programs in China (including Formosa) and Korea. The following chapter summarizes the programs in other parts of Asia. Chapter 18 undertakes to explore the insights and lessons that can be derived from ECA operations in these areas.

Origin of the China Aid Program

Less than three years after the hard-won victory of Allied forces in the Pacific and Asia, China was in imminent peril of falling under the yoke of a new conqueror. This time, however, the potential conqueror was not a foreign invader but a well-organized, highly disciplined political party and military organization within the country, aligned with a broader menace than the Japanese militarism of 1937— namely, world communism. It was clear that if China should fall, south and southeast Asia and the southwest Pacific would be placed in jeopardy; should these areas fall, the balance of power between East and West would be radically altered. Unfolding in China was an opening phase of the Leninist plan for world conquest.

This ominous outlook led the American Congress, as it considered a gigantic aid program for Europe, to give urgent attention also to the possibilities of effective assistance to the government and people of China. But the coherent view and strong bipartisan support behind the European Recovery Program were lacking. In an atmosphere of disappointment, bafflement, and uncertainty, public debate over the course of events in China and of American policy there waxed partisan and bitter.[3] There was nothing comparable to the painstaking study and analysis, or the thorough consultation between Administration and Congressional leaders that preceded approval of the Marshall Plan for Europe.

Beneath the surface of the controversy could be seen—whatever the merits of the positions taken—evidences of deep concern over developments in China, on the part of leaders in both the Republican-controlled Congress and the Democratic Administration. The latter, having failed in its attempt to promote a *modus vivendi* between China's Nationalists and Communists which would forestall another conflict in

[3] For background see Herbert Feis, *The China Tangle* (Princeton University Press, 1953).

that war-torn country, sensed grave difficulties in any course of action that might be followed. Administration leaders were concerned over the capacity of the weakening Nationalist government to make efficient use of any large amounts of military or economic assistance, and they doubted that it would or could carry out the basic reforms necessary to reinforce its waning popular support. At the same time they viewed with mounting apprehension the rapid growth of Communist power in China. Faced with this dilemma, they tended to wait and "let the dust settle."

Yet there were differences of opinion within the Administration. And there was rising pressure—especially from Republican Congressmen and from organized segments of public opinion—for more vigorous American efforts to keep China from falling under Communist domination. Accusations were made of leftist influences within the Department of State. Despite misgivings as to what could be accomplished without military intervention, the Administration did not wish to assume the responsibility of letting the rapidly deteriorating China situation go by default. Congressional approval had been secured, therefore, for limited military and economic assistance, to be administered in such a way as not to involve the United States in deep and irrevocable commitments in China.

To some influential Republican spokesmen in Congress, failure to give all possible assistance to the Chinese Nationalist government was tantamount to abandoning a wartime ally. The practical difficulties of making an aid program effective did not appear so forbidding to these critics as they did to leading Administration officials.

As the China situation worsened, demands for action, in which some Democrats participated, became more insistent. A temporary planning unit was set up in the State Department. On February 18, 1948, President Truman sent to Congress a message on economic aid to China. Two days later, the State Department presented to the House Foreign Affairs Committee a proposed program of assistance accompanied by a somber analysis of the recent and current situation in China. After six weeks of hearings and debate, Congress adopted the China Aid Act of 1948.

Conditions Faced

The situation in China was difficult indeed. The aid program was to be carried out amid civil war and progressive contraction of the area and resources under the control of the Nationalist government. Despite the assistance previously provided through UNRRA [4] and "interim aid," millions were still destitute. An eleven-year inflation—the longest on record for any major country—soared ever higher. The widening conflict with the Communists drained away 70 percent of the government's slender resources. Spreading civil disturbances reduced the flow of food from the countryside to major cities and increased their dependence upon such imports as could be obtained.

Communist agents were everywhere, subtly telling the people why they were downtrodden, whom they should blame, and what they could do to achieve "liberation." Amid desperate war-weariness, they skillfully exploited the passion for peace. Politically as well as militarily the Nationalist government was ill equipped to stem the Communist tide. More than a decade of war and upheaval had sapped its revolutionary zeal. Outstanding individuals were still to be found in its Executive Yuan, but its centers of power lay in the military and in an effete political party. It lacked the will, the organization, and the strength to carry out urgently needed economic, political, and social reforms.

By April 1948, when the China Aid Act was approved, the Communists had gained control of nearly all of Manchuria and were beginning to close in on Mukden. They had established effective control over large parts of China north of the Yellow River. Between the Yellow and Yangtze Rivers they were extending their sway across much of the countryside, and from these rural areas they were able to cut or harass communication lines between major cities. American military observers were generally less sanguine than Chiang Kai-shek and his commanding generals; neutral estimates of the military situation varied considerably. Military aid as approved by Congress was continued, but with increasing misgivings. Attempts to insure its efficient use and to prevent materiel from falling into Communist hands were only partially successful. An American military advisory group gave counsel on the use of equipment but did not assume responsibility for advising on the conduct of the war.

Revenues covered less than a third of the government's expenditures, the balance being met almost entirely by "printing press" money. The budgetary imbalance became fantastic. Expenditures in May 1948 amounted to 75 trillion Chinese dollars.

In August, prices in China reached a level three million times those

[4] See George Woodbridge *et al.*, UNRRA: *The History of the United Nations Relief and Rehabilitation Administration* (Columbia University Press, New York, 1950), vol. II, pt. vi.

of the last prewar half-year. In the first eight months of 1948 alone prices increased more than 6,000 percent, and the black market rate for United States dollar notes more than 7,000 percent.[5] As a sign of the final stage of hyperinflation when financial collapse is inevitable, the rise in prices was about three times the rise in note issue. Amid universal uncertainty, private capital flowed largely into speculation and hoarding. As a result, not only did China's productive plant fail to expand, but existing facilities deteriorated. A forlorn effort to introduce a new currency did not touch the budgetary imbalance which was the taproot of the inflation. In the end, this weak and desperate measure did more harm than good, wiping out a large part of the remaining savings of the country's middle class.

During the last few months of the year important cities in north and central China were virtually cut off, and economic activity became chaotic. Food and other commodities were increasingly exchanged through barter. As the military strength of the Communists increased, Nationalist strength was sapped by military defeats, defections, sinking morale among troops and citizenry, and a crumbling economic front.

Under such conditions, it was less and less possible to be sanguine about the results attainable through a limited aid program. Its continuation as the situation deteriorated attested to a desire to give evidence to the Chinese people of continuing friendship at a time of extreme hardship, and to indicate to other peoples of Asia that America would not desert China while any part of the country remained free. But the hope that economic assistance might help prevent Communist conquest of even the southern part of the country became increasingly tenuous.

Aims and First Steps

The aim of the China aid program from the outset was much more modest than that of ERP. The State Department, in presenting its proposal to Congress, had used guarded language, declaring that there was "immediate necessity for an economic-assistance program for China which will afford the Chinese government an opportunity to take steps which only that Government itself can take to arrest the trend of economic deterioration, and to begin effective steps toward more stable economic conditions." The purposes enunciated by Congress were less restricted but vague. The ECA, under the Congressional

[5] ECA, *Economic Aid to China under the China Aid Act of 1948* (Washington, 1949), pp. 26–27.

mandate, saw its task as one of doing all it could, with limited means, to arrest the rate of economic deterioration.[6]

On April 30, 1948, the President allotted to the ECA an initial 36.5 million dollars, under a special arrangement authorized by Congress pending an actual appropriation. On the same date the United States and Chinese governments exchanged notes setting up interim arrangements. In May, ECA established a special Office of the China Aid Program under Harlan Cleveland; Roger D. Lapham, former mayor of San Francisco, was appointed chief of the ECA mission to China; and the first supplies were procured for shipment. In June the ECA mission, with a reconstruction survey group headed by Charles L. Stillman,[7] started work in China. The Chinese government established the Council for United States Aid (CUSA). To the 275 million dollars appropriated by Congress for economic aid under the terms of the China Aid Act, 125 million dollars were added for further—principally military —assistance.[8] In July, an economic aid agreement was signed in Nanking.

The China aid program may be divided into two main phases: first, the period up to late 1949, when the major focus was on aid to the shrinking parts of the China mainland not under Communist control; second, the period 1950–1952, when attention was centered upon Formosa, where, after the attack on South Korea in mid-1950, new impetus was given to American aid.

The Mainland Operation

Economic aid provided through the ECA to the China mainland consisted of three relatively distinct parts: a commodities program, an industrial reconstruction and replacement program, and a rural reconstruction program.[9]

[6] Testifying before a subcommittee of the House Committee on Appropriations, ECA Administrator Hoffman said: "I cannot emphasize too strongly that this program, even if administered in the most effective way, cannot be expected to work any miracle in China. The program is designed to give China this further opportunity to work out for itself the means of arresting the deterioration of its economy, and of laying the groundwork for rehabilitation and recovery. In according our help, we must do the very best job we can with what we have, calling on China for a continuation and intensification of its efforts to create the necessary conditions for success."

[7] Treasurer of Time, Inc.

[8] Under Public Law 793, 80th Congress, 2d Session (1948).

[9] The factual data for this section and the next three have been derived in large part from unpublished ECA memoranda.

The commodities program involved deliveries of food required to support rationing programs in seven major cities—Peiping, Tientsin, Nanking, Tsingtao, Shanghai, Swatow, and Canton; cotton to maintain production and employment in China's chief modern industry, textile manufacturing; petroleum and small quantities of coal to operate utilities and transport; and chemical fertilizers to increase rice production in central and south China.

The industrial reconstruction and replacement program required careful planning; the special survey group headed by Stillman was sent to China for this purpose. Following the recommendations of this group, extensive engineering studies were undertaken with the assistance of American firms. By the time these surveys were completed, however, the military situation in China had so deteriorated that, in December 1948, Hoffman ordered an indefinite suspension of this line of effort. The projects envisaged, requiring from one to three years to complete, would not only be jeopardized by Communist expansion, but if taken over would also improve the Communist position.

The agrarian program grew out of a unique provision in the China Aid Act, first inserted by the House Foreign Affairs Committee after hearing several witnesses familiar with the successes of Communist "land reform" propaganda in China and with previous efforts there in the field of rural rehabilitation.[10] The provision—section 407(a) of the act—was as follows.

The Secretary of State, after consultation with the [ECA] Administrator, is hereby authorized to conclude an agreement with China establishing a Joint Commission on Rural Reconstruction in China, to be composed of two citizens of the United States appointed by the President of the United States and three citizens of China appointed by the President of China. Such Commission shall, subject to the direction and control of the Administrator, formulate and carry out a program for reconstruction in rural areas of China, which shall include such research and training activities as may be necessary or appropriate for such reconstruction.

This program, starting slowly but gaining momentum, became the most significant part of the aid effort in China; for this reason it is discussed in further detail below. It did not depend on extensive supply movements. It did not involve heavy investments, and it was financed largely from local currency generated by the sale of aid supplies. The

[10] Among the witnesses was Dr. Y. C. James Yen, well-known leader of the Chinese Mass Education Movement.

projects under this program could be terminated if and when any area fell under, or was imminently threatened by, Communist domination. They appeared to offer the best available means for improving the lot of a segment of China's huge peasant population.

In view of the chaotic situation, provision was made for closer ECA control and supervision over the program than was deemed necessary in western Europe. The disorganization of economic life and political controls created opportunities for irregularities and corruption, and the military situation had to be closely watched to minimize the amount of materiel which might fall to the advancing Communists. The ECA and the CUSA, therefore, established a tight "end-use" control system for each commodity program, the most interesting being a food rationing system in cities where rationing had never before been used extensively. More than twelve million people were served by this system—planned, developed, and executed without scandal.

The cotton aid program was directed by a joint management board whose decisions required CUSA and ECA concurrence. Petroleum was distributed by major oil companies which helped to make sure that ECA-financed oil went only to the uses for which it was allocated; a joint CUSA-ECA petroleum committee estimated requirements and supervised distribution.

The ECA could not anticipate, of course, the timing of Communist advances. Timing was particularly important in the case of Shanghai, where stocks of food, cotton, and petroleum were essential to the economy of a city of some five million people. An effort was made to keep reserves at a low level. About 110,000 metric tons of ECA-financed supplies valued at 22 million dollars were either evacuated or distributed during the weeks immediately before the Communist capture of the city. But more than 12 million dollars' worth of cotton and yarn were on hand when the Communists came in. A small contingent of ECA personnel headed by George St. Louis remained to negotiate with the Communists about the use of these supplies, but despite efforts lasting nearly a year the Communists ultimately appropriated them outright.

In May 1949, just before the fall of Shanghai, the ECA transferred its China headquarters to Canton. A part of the Nationalist government moved to Chungking. In September, as the Communists gained headway in south China, the ECA shifted its office again, to British-controlled Hongkong. In October both the government and the small ECA office were removed to Formosa. Even after this transfer, the Joint Commission for Rural Reconstruction was able to continue for a short time its efforts in parts of south and southwest China.

Toward the end of 1948 and during 1949 the rate of expenditure under the China program fell rapidly. First by administrative determination and later by legislative direction, aid was limited to the areas not under Communist domination.[11] After the fall of Nanking, Shanghai and Tsingtao in the spring and summer of 1949, the commodity program was confined to the provision of limited rice, fertilizer, and petroleum to south China and Formosa. In its final months the mainland operation was conducted on a week-to-week basis. Of the 275 million dollars which had been appropriated by Congress, a little more than 100 million dollars remained unobligated or recoverable through diversion of supplies to other programs.[12]

The Formosa Operation

Starting on a small scale, the ECA program in Formosa expanded gradually as the mainland operation shrank.

The cutoff of traditional markets through the blockading of Shanghai and other China ports was a heavy blow to the island economy. Fresh strains were imposed when the Nationalist government arrived, and in its train approximately a million soldiers and civilian refugees, suddenly increasing the island's population by one-eighth. To help meet these strains, ECA aid allotments were substantially increased. When the Communists struck in Korea eight months later, Formosa acquired a new political and strategic significance, and efforts to bolster its economic strength and military security were intensified.

In its early stages the program there followed generally the pattern developed on the mainland. Besides financing food and other commodity shipments, the ECA helped rehabilitate the island's own facilities for producing chemical fertilizers and sugar, with a view to lessening the rice-growing island's dependence upon external aid and increasing its foreign exchange earnings.[13] Beginnings were made in rural reconstruction.

As activity increased, the aim of the program was defined as that of helping the island become economically self-supporting. The early

[11] Public Law 47, 81st Congress, 1st Session (1949), stipulated that unobligated balances of funds appropriated for aid to China could be used only for areas which the President deemed to be not under Communist domination.

[12] Through two successive actions, Congress authorized the use of 10 million dollars of these unobligated funds for relief and assistance to some three thousand Chinese students in the United States whose sources of funds had been cut off.

[13] Investments were initiated in 1950 which, with subsequent U.S. aid, were expected to make Formosa nearly self-sufficient in fertilizer production by about 1956.

emphasis was predominantly upon agriculture. But the island had a rapidly growing population already dense in relation to its arable area. Existing manpower was grossly underutilized. To import essential consumer goods, it would be necessary to produce more manufactured goods for export. For economic self-reliance, industrial as well as agricultural development was a *sine qua non.*

Increasing emphasis, therefore, was given to technical assistance, to limited capital equipment for industry as well as agriculture, and, on a limited scale, to assistance as requested for improving governmental administration and services. A significant part of the technical aid provided, especially in the industrial field, was administered under an ECA-financed contract between the Nationalist government and the J. G. White engineering firm whereby American engineers were stationed in Formosa to provide assistance in the development of public utilities and local industries. Use of consulting engineers, contemplated but not carried out on the mainland, proved to be an effective innovation in the technology of assistance, and it was later adopted in other underdeveloped areas.

Through this device and a growing number of technical assistance projects, help was given in the development of food and animal-feed processing, the tapping of underground water supplies, the development of forests and fisheries, petroleum refining, and the manufacture of textiles,[14] metal products, chemicals, soap, pulp, paper, and an expanding range of other items. Special emphasis was given to electric power output, on which the industrial future of Formosa depended. The gains achieved can be seen in increases in power consumption during 1951 as compared to 1950—of 89 percent in textile industries, 48 percent in metallurgical plants, 58 percent in machine shops, 97 percent in chemical plants, and 43 percent for agriculture and irrigation.

Nearly 180 million dollars was obligated for aid to Formosa during the two years prior to June 30, 1952.[15] This was not sufficient to offset inflationary pressures created by the influx of population from the mainland and increased government outlays for both defense and civilian purposes; the military budget, already large, expanded further

[14] The local cotton-spinning industry was able in January 1951 to meet only a fifth of the island's yarn requirements; through a combination of raw cotton imports and engineeering help, the ratio was upped to 66 percent in December of the same year.

[15] See ECA, *Thirteenth Report to Congress,* p. 79, and MSA, *Second Report,* p. 32.

as United States assistance increased—to safeguard the island against invasion. The assimilation of imported military supplies and the building of necessary installations required large internal expenditures.

Stringent financial measures became necessary. Withdrawals of currency from circulation by various means [16] enabled the government to hold the note issue within a legal limit of 200 million Taiwan (Formosa) dollars, equivalent to about 20 million American dollars. And steps were taken to control domestic prices of some items. These measures tightened the money market, with consequent difficulties for businessmen, and resulted in heavier tax burdens especially for middle and lower classes. But by the autumn of 1951, with the help of a bumper crop, financial stability was at least temporarily assured. By mid-1952 open market interest rates, which had been 18 percent in early 1950, were down to 7 percent.

The actions taken by the government to set its financial house in order were greatly facilitated by the establishment, in March 1951, of an Economic Stabilization Board, ably administered by Chinese personnel. Americans participated as observers, since so large a share of the island's foreign exchange resources were derived from American aid. The linking of this institution with the aid program kept United States representatives informed on economic developments and made possible a coordinated use of foreign exchange and local currency resources.[17]

In agriculture, notable increases were registered in the production of rice, soybeans, tobacco, beans, and peas, and more modest rises in the output of sweet potatoes and cassavas. But some crops remained below prewar levels, including tea, bananas, citrus fruits, and, most important as an export, sugar. Industrial production in 1952 was more than 80 percent over 1948 levels and roughly 40 percent over those of 1937, the most important gains being in textiles and fertilizer output. Exports were almost 30 percent higher in value than those of 1950, more than half of the trade being with Japan.

Serious problems persisted. Military costs absorbed roughly half of all public expenditures.[18] Surpluses available for exports lagged far

---

[16] Among the methods used were allocations of foreign exchange and Japanese barter credits to importers; the collection of special surtaxes; sales of gold, U.S. dollar notes, patriotic bonds and lotteries; and compulsory purchase by most of the population of short-term savings coupons.

[17] Memorandum from Frank L. Turner (former member, subsequently chief, China Division) to the writer, January 29, 1954.

[18] During the two years after the invasion of South Korea, nearly 20 percent

behind import requirements, nearly half of which were still being financed by American aid.

Joint Commission for Rural Reconstruction

The work of the Joint Commission for Rural Reconstruction (JCRR) was probably more significant than any other aspect of the China aid program.[19] Its approach to rural problems in Asia went beyond anything under previous aid programs. It offered hope of maturing into a rationale and method capable of competing—in other parts of Asia if not on the China mainland—with the much-publicized but narrow "land reform" program of the Communists. The pattern of operations developed by the commission could be adopted, improved, and refined in underdeveloped countries elsewhere, as one means of coming to grips with the deep-lying problems of depressed agrarian areas threatened by communism.

The JCRR's basic objective was to provide constructive rather than destructive outlets for the energies of rural peoples during a period of general distress and revolutionary ferment, thus improving their living conditions and raising their hopes for the future. The contrast between this approach and that of the Communists in China was defined in a memorandum written in December 1950 by Dr. Chiang Mon-lin, chairman of the commission:

Land reform is an extremely complicated problem. In this part of the world the problem is one of paramount importance. Whether a country is going democratic or totalitarian depends upon, to a large extent, the way the problem is solved. The totalitarian way is drastic, accompanied with violence and liquidation of landlords and rich farmers. The aim is: state ownership of the land and the collective farm. The democratic way is gradual and humane and in accordance with the spirit of fair dealing. The aim is: the family-size farm.

Each of the five members of the commission,[20] named by Presidents Chiang and Truman, had had long experience or contact with rural

---

of the ECA/MSA commodity program consisted of defense support items and about a third of all counterpart funds withdrawn were used for local defense procurement.

[19] For extensive coverage of the JCRR program and activities, see *General Reports* published by the commission in Taipei, Taiwan (Formosa). Each report covers a year or more of operations.

[20] Chiang Mon-lin, chairman, Raymond T. Moyer, Shen Tsung-han, John Earl Baker, and Y. C. James Yen. The American members were appointed on September 19, 1948.

rehabilitation efforts in China. They needed it. Their task on the mainland was exceedingly complex, if not indeed hopeless. It was uncertain how long their operations could be continued. To make even a dent in China's vast agrarian problem, they had not only to reach agreement among themselves, but to express their aims and principles in terms simple enough for all to understand.

In a statement issued on October 15, 1948, the commissioners declared that their objectives were to improve rural living conditions; to help increase agricultural production; to help rural people reconstruct their own communities and participate in the reconstruction of national life; to help strengthen governmental services necessary to rural reconstruction; to revitalize private agencies, notably those associated before and during the war with the "rural reconstruction movement" in China; and to offer "liberals, educated youths and other constructive elements" opportunities to participate in a program of service.

Projects, the Commission stated, would be suited to the existing emergency; priority would be given those likely to contribute most directly and immediately to the economic welfare of the rural people. A literacy program with audio-visual aids would be an essential part of the effort. Simple, inexpensive projects already found successful would be expanded; financial aid to new projects would not be considered unless they could support themselves for a reasonable length of time thereafter.

The commission expressed its determination to support, as far as possible, proven, needy agencies already at work rather than to embark on hurriedly conceived new ventures. A "direct extension type of adult education" was stressed as "the most effective and quickest means of promoting the understanding, acceptance and correct use of recommended practices." Throughout the program, local initiative was to be fostered and local resources mobilized. To safeguard against political interference or lack of political support, assistance was made contingent on the cooperation of provincial and local officials. It was the commission's view that

the purpose of JCRR, being to give direct benefits to the farmers, should be pursued in the following order of importance: land reform, agricultural extension, farmers' associations and social education. . . . All agricultural and educational work . . . might be incorporated into the land reform program [thereby] helping to win the people and establish a solid democratic front. . . . It is only when farmers possess their lands or at least when they are assured of definite land tenure and are relieved of excessive rent that they can take with enthusiasm and optimism to new farm technology, rural health and education, and ideas of civil rights and democracy. The general improvement of rural living conditions can be achieved only if there has been permanent land reform.

Among the techniques adopted by the JCRR, a number are worthy of special mention. A constant attempt was made to learn from the farmers what they wanted and needed, thus making the program, as Chiang Mon-lin put it, "always dynamic." "We do not know better than they," he said, "what they themselves need. Regardless of how good our intentions may be and how sound the program, if the rural people do not want it, it cannot be imposed upon them." [21] Special emphasis was given to self-conducted farmers' organizations.

The commission tried, while striving for increases in production, to keep in mind the problem of distribution, or, as the members frequently expressed it, of "social justice." By this was meant a serious facing of intrenched, custom-bound inequities: usurial interest rates, exorbitant rentals, monopolistic marketing practices. The approach opened the door, even if only a little, to an attack upon the deep structural problems of Chinese agrarian society—problems which lay at the root of the country's weakness and instability.

The most significant advance made in three southern mainland provinces, as well as in Formosa, was in lowering exorbitant land rentals. In a few districts, progress was also made in reducing tenancy —through required sales to landless peasants on equitable terms rather than by the Communist method of liquidating landlords.

Hundreds of specific projects were approved. In Kwangsi province, for example, they included: completion, repair, or development of local irrigation systems; loans to farmers' cooperatives to buy water buffalo to replace draft animals lost in the war; assistance to an adult literacy and visual-aid education program sponsored by a provincial bureau; aid in developing industries for processing tung oil, vegetable oils, and starch; help to a sugar cooperative in buying improved animal-powered sugar mills; assistance in distributing improved varieties of rice and corn seed already developed in experiment stations; distribution of pesticides and demonstration of their use in controlling rice, vegetable, citrus fruit, and tung-tree pests; distribution of fertilizers; assistance to an antimalaria program in the worst mosquito-breeding

[21] Letter to the ECA, Washington, December 23, 1949.

areas and to a field program for vaccination of cattle against rinderpest.

In Formosa, the JCRR was able to complete many more projects than on the mainland. Rice seeds treated for protection against disease were widely distributed. Irrigation and drainage were improved and extended on nearly half a million acres of rice land. Improvements were made in the distribution and use of chemical fertilizers.[22] Health stations were increased from 60 to 370, stressing preventive as well as curative measures for tuberculosis, malaria, trachoma, hookworm, and dysentery. The commission strengthened farmers' organizations, improved the methods of bringing financial and technical assistance to bear on the needs of the rural population, and extended the use of improved agricultural techniques. Breeding and vaccination programs reduced hog cholera by more than a third in two years, with a saving of about 1 million dollars' worth of hogs.

The JCRR's most far-reaching effort in Formosa was the reduction of land rentals. For years rents had absorbed the sales proceeds of as much as two-thirds of the crops produced. The archaic land tenure system, a major basis for Communist propaganda, threatened the internal security of the island. With JCRR support, rents were reduced by law to a maximum of 37.5 percent of the value of the main crop, and tenure was assured for from three to five years. A program was designed to enable the farmers to purchase the land they cultivated at a fair price.

The effect of rent reductions on the economic condition of the farm populace and on their incentive to produce was immediate.[23] The political effect was also notable. Formosa had been ill prepared to support a refugee government and an influx of a million people. The islanders were sullen and resentful. Severe economic dislocations had followed the end of Japanese occupation in 1945. Unconscionable

[22] These activities contributed to a record rice crop of more than 1.5 million metric tons in 1951, 7 percent above the 1950 crop, which had been the best in the island's history. This harvest left an exportable surplus of more than 100,000 tons, valued at 15.4 million dollars, which was bartered to Japan for industrial items and consumer goods.

[23] Two unpublished, impartial analyses of rural conditions in Formosa and of the techniques and effectiveness of land reform and other measures discussed above were prepared, on the basis of field studies, by W. I. Ladejinsky of the U.S. Department of Agriculture ("Observations on Rural Conditions in Taiwan," June 1951) and Robert B. Moody, an economist with previous experience in the Far East and Turkey ("Land Reform in Taiwan," March 1953). A third study by Arthur F. Raper, MSA project evaluation officer (*Rural Taiwan—Problem and Promise*) was published by the JCRR in Taipei, Formosa, in July 1953.

bungling and repression by Nationalist officials first sent to occupy the land had led to public disorders and culminated in a massacre.[24] The islanders had not been given genuine representation and participation in the government.

The land reform program was the first means by which the new regime presented to the local people a better picture of its intentions. Some fourteen thousand government employees and other workers were estimated to have made about 400,000 house calls and conducted 27,000 meetings attended by more than five million people during the period when the rent reduction program was being introduced. Widely displayed posters explained to farmers their rights under the new law, and in 1952 arrangements were made for the local election of land commissions.

The various developments cited above led to substantial improvements in agricultural conditions in Formosa, but many serious problems remained. Farmers complained that a lack of balance between farm and nonfarm prices made it difficult for them to pay for such simple essentials as salted fish, soya sauce, piece goods, cloth shoes, and plows. Heavy and increasing taxes siphoned off part of the gains realized through increased output. Small agricultural loans could be obtained only at usurious rates of 10 to 15 percent per month. For lack of reserves, crops often had to be sold cheap. Proceeds from household industry remained low. And progress in the sale of land to tenants was gradual at best. The peasant population of Formosa would have remained in dire straits had it not been for increased yields— especially in rice—and the widespread benefits of the rent reduction program.

Aid to Korea

The objective of a free and independent Korea, after thirty-three years of Japanese rule, was announced in the Cairo Declaration of December 1943 and reaffirmed in the Potsdam Declaration of July 1945. At the end of the war United States forces occupied the southern half of the peninsula and Soviet forces the northern half, with the thirty-eighth parallel as the dividing line. The American government's efforts during the next two years to reach agreement with Russia on plans to unify the country came to nothing.

In the autumn of 1947 the problem was taken to the United Nations.

[24] The official primarily responsible was later tried and executed for traitorous negotiations with the Communists.

A resolution adopted by a large majority on November 14 called for an election, under a United Nations commission, to choose a representative national assembly which would draft a democratic constitution and establish a national government. The United Nations commission was barred from North Korea, but the election was conducted in the southern half of the country on May 10, 1948. The government of the Republic of Korea which emerged from the assembly's efforts was declared by the United Nations to be a lawful government based on a valid expression of the will of the electorate, and to be the only such government in Korea. The United States, China, France, Great Britain, and the Philippines promptly recognized the new republic.

On January 1, 1949, United States economic aid administration in Korea was transferred from the Department of the Army to the ECA. The United States Army, concerned principally with the prevention of disease and unrest, had helped restore the area's capacity to feed itself, and had helped reduce the proportion of tenants from roughly three out of four farmers to two out of five, mainly through subdivision of former Japanese-controlled lands.[25] But little had been done to compensate for the loss of industrial and power facilities in northern Korea.

The economic aid program was administered by the ECA without interruption for approximately a year and a half. After the invasion from the north it was conducted in a radically modified form for another eleven months, after which it was turned over to other agencies.

The problems confronting the ECA stemmed in part from the long Japanese occupation and in part from the disruption of the economy during World War II. As a part of the Japanese empire, Korea had been integrated into the Japanese economy. The exploitation of resources, the direction of trade, and the control of business were almost entirely in Japanese hands. Japanese investments entered into the balance of payments, and Japanese nationals held all key technical and managerial positions. Koreans were not given an opportunity to acquire administrative or technical skills. During World War II the Korean economy was tied even more closely to Japan's. Resources were diverted to war production and peacetime industries were converted. As the war dragged on, new investments stopped and maintenance fell off. Mining, transport, and communication facilities deteriorated. The people of the country were kept at a subsistence level in order to increase food and raw material shipments to Japan.

When hostilities ended, the economy was near collapse. There were

[25] Brown and Opie, *op. cit.*, p. 374.

critical shortages and, since all Japanese were deported, there were virtually no managers, technicians, or experienced civil servants. Refugees from North Korea and repatriates from elsewhere swelled the population by about 2,500,000 during the next three to four years, to a total of approximately twenty million. Partition of the country greatly complicated the problem of recovery because more than 75 percent of Korea's industry and 90 percent of its electric generating power were located north of the thirty-eighth parallel.

ECA operations in Korea were conducted within the framework of three primary objectives of United States policy:

(1) To establish as soon as possible a united, self-governing, and sovereign Korea, independent of foreign control and eligible for membership in the United Nations; (2) to ensure that the government so established shall be fully representative of the freely expressed will of the Korean people; and (3) to assist the Korean people in establishing a sound economy and educational system as essential bases of an independent and democratic state.[26]

The ECA maintained that a relief program, unless continued indefinitely, would not increase South Korea's capacity to survive as an independent nation. It believed that a recovery program designed to increase productive capacity could make South Korea economically self-reliant within a relatively few years. Such aid would cost more at the beginning, but in the long run it would be much less burdensome.

This hopeful view was taken in face of the fact that extensive remodeling of the economy and large increases in production and exports would be necessary before South Korea could become self-supporting. When ECA aid began, the country was unable to earn more than about 20 percent of its foreign exchange requirements. But the agency estimated that, with aid of 500 to 600 million dollars in all for the fiscal years 1949–1953, and with uninterrupted effort, the republic's balance-of-payments deficits could be progressively reduced from the existing annual level of 148 million dollars to approximately 85 million dollars in fiscal 1952 and 35 million dollars in 1953.[27] Exports, it was calculated, could be upped in four years from 17 to 61 million dollars in value, and imports lowered from 125 million to roughly 73 million dollars.

It may be observed that in Korea—where the United States had a special position and greater knowledge of the area because of post-

---

[26] As summarized in the ECA's *Fourth Report to Congress* (Washington, 1949), p. 87.

[27] *Ibid.*, p. 26.

war occupation—the ECA felt able to adopt a comprehensive balance-of-payments approach to the problem of recovery and economic self-support comparable to the approach employed for recovery planning in Europe. To develop the Korea program, experience and knowledge from many sources were tapped: the new Korean government; the Civil Affairs Section of the United States Army in Korea; private United States engineering firms whose help was secured in surveying the prospects of industrial, transport, and power development; and ECA personnel in the field and in Washington.

There was strong motivation for an effective aid operation in Korea. As declared in a general statement submitted to Congress by the Department of State and ECA:

So long as democratic ideals survive and grow among this energetic population, and so long as their democratically chosen government demonstrates its stability and independence, there will exist in the minds of the people of vast adjacent areas a continuing challenge to the Communist ideology which has been imposed upon them. . . . To the extent that the Republic of Korea succeeds and flourishes, the people in these areas will see a convincing demonstration of the practical value of democratic government. To the extent that the United States continues to support the efforts . . . to develop a self-reliant economy and a stable democratic regime, the populations of this vast area will have proof of the determination of the United States to encourage people seeking to retain or achieve independent and democratic ways of life.

The survival of democracy in Korea is of crucial importance also to the maintenance and further development of democracy in Japan.[28]

To June 30, 1950, Congress approved 110 million dollars for economic aid to Korea, in addition to the 30 million dollars transferred from the Department of the Army to the ECA. Although the ECA had issued procurement authorizations against 108.8 million dollars of this total before the Communist invasion, paid shipments had reached only 59.9 million dollars.[29]

Because the shortage of technicians and administrators was so acute in Korea, much of the ECA's energy had to be devoted to helping the government plan and direct its activities and to training the personnel required for effective operations. The other problems of greatest importance were capital investment, land tenure and utilization, foreign trade, and internal financial stability.

[28] Dept. of State and ECA, *Economic Aid to the Republic of Korea: ECA Recovery Program for Fiscal Year 1950* (Washington, 1950), p. 1 (pamphlet).
[29] ECA, *Ninth Report to Congress,* pp. 91–93.

Aside from rice output, discussed below, capital development was directed mainly to coal and other minerals, electric power, manufacturing, and fisheries.

With the loss of bituminous coal supplies formerly obtained from North Korea and Manchuria, South Korea was largely dependent on imports from Japan. The ECA helped rehabilitate South Korean mines, open new ones, and conduct surveys for new sources. Production more than doubled, to 1.1 million tons, making possible a 40 percent cut in imports.

When electric power from North Korea was severed, high priority was given to the construction of thermal generating plants.[30] A moderate increase of about 20 percent in power output was achieved before the outbreak of war interrupted work on three major projects.

Before partition, about three-fourths of the nation's industrial output came from northern Korea. Development of new industries to compensate for this loss was gradual at first, largely because of the shortage of technicians and skilled workers. New or expanded development was undertaken in textiles, paper, salt, firebricks, coal briquettes, building materials, automobile tires, pottery, and electric insulators—all chiefly for domestic use. Plans for greatly enlarged fertilizer output depended upon increased electric power and were interrupted by the outbreak of war. Industrial production during the year before the Korean war was roughly 60 percent above that of the previous year.

Improvement in the fishing industry, a main source of protein food and of items for export, lagged because materials for rehabilitating the fishing fleet were scarce. In 1949–1950 the catch rose about 15 percent, and exports totaled about 9 million dollars.

Plans were made to extend the land redistribution started under the military government. A land reform law enacted in June 1949 provided for public purchase of land owned by absentee landlords; farmers could pay in kind or in shares over a five-year period. The law envisaged a redistribution of about 1.8 million acres among approximately a million tenant farmers, reducing the ratio of tenants to about one out of ten farmers in South Korea.

President Syngman Rhee authorized an outlay for preparatory surveys, but the National Assembly, because of inflation or pressure from landlords, was slow to adopt the budget needed to execute the law.

[30] As a temporary expedient, two floating power plants were loaned by the U.S. Navy.

However, in the spring of 1950, the ECA reported that the land reform was well started.[31]

The foreign trade balance, when the ECA began in Korea, was discouraging. Imports, of which 90 per cent were being supplied by the United States, were about ten times as great as exports. The solution to this imbalance appeared to depend chiefly on increasing trade with Japan, which many Koreans resisted. But the government gradually adopted a more conciliatory attitude. Improvement in the country's trade balance was conditioned upon a substantial increase in rice production, which would permit larger exports to Japan, a heavy food importer whose supplies from southeast Asia had been curtailed. Other export items which could be increased were salted fish, dried shellfish, laver (an edible seaweed), agar-agar and other marine products, and various ores and metals, including graphite and tungsten.

From a low level in 1947 irregular gains were achieved, with a heartening spurt shortly before the Communist attack. The value of exports, by quarterly averages, approximated 2 million dollars in 1947, 4.7 million in 1948, 3.6 million in 1949, and 7.4 million during the first quarter of 1950.

With the invasion, the whole picture was altered. As the Communist armies swept southward, everything was subordinated to the demands of defense. Of 160 Americans employed by contracting firms who were participating in the ECA program in Korea when hostilities began, about 120 were reassigned either to military operations or to ECA work directly related to the new emergency situation.

On September 29, 1950, responsibility for the financing of supplies for civilian relief was transferred from the ECA to the United Nations command. On December 1 a new agency, the United Nations Korean Rehabilitation Agency (UNKRA) was established. Four months later the ECA closed its Korea mission.

The communist assault had blocked the recovery effort in Korea at the end of a year and a half. No one can say whether the goals set in early 1949 would have been realized in two more years. But the difficult formative period showed promising developments and momentum had been achieved as the operation progressed.

In May 1950 nearly every candidate for election to the National Assembly referred to American assistance and pledged that he would use his influence to support its equitable use. The people understood that the joint program was a real effort to strengthen their ability to

[31] *Ninth Report to Congress*, p. 91.

advance as an independent, democratic nation. Difficult obstacles, such as inflation, had still to be overcome, but confidence and morale, as well as faith in the integrity of the United States, had been bolstered. Without these, and the prompt support of the United Nations, it is doubtful whether the people of South Korea could have withstood for more than a few days or weeks the shock of invasion by overwhelmingly superior forces.

CHAPTER 10

Aid to Southeast Asia

IN INDONESIA, Indochina, Thailand, Burma, and the Philippines, World War II had intensified political and social unrest, aggravating the long-standing difficulties discussed in Chapter 1. All were fought over and occupied by Japanese armies. Japan had drained away local resources and tied the whole area's trade and finance into its own war economy.

Except for Thailand, all these countries had been under colonial administration.[1] Nationalism, already strong, grew more intense during the war. Japan's early military successes lowered the prestige of the colonial powers; its attempt to weld the area into a "co-prosperity sphere" strengthened the desire for independence. Japanese defeat put freedom more nearly within reach. The postwar period was one of chaos but also of rising expectations.

Common Problems

In history, language, and culture, the five countries were very different, but many of their problems were the same. All were politically shaky, with new governments that had but limited contacts with the

[1] Philippine independence had been promised in the Tydings-McDuffie Act of 1936.

people. All faced a huge neighbor under Communist control, and Communist agents within their own borders. All lacked the experience required for effective organization and survival as independent countries during the critical period following the Communist takeover of China. In all, millions of citizens looked for relief from want, malnutrition, disease, illiteracy, exploitation. The end of colonialism meant not only the death of external domination but also the loss of a scapegoat. The first surge of hope was shattered against hard realities.

The period of transition from war to peace was one of great political turbulence. To the casual observer, individuals and organizations of diverse political tendencies seemed to combine and separate like the pieces in a kaleidoscope. It was hard to draw lines of ideological distinction or group loyalty. Most of the new governments were coalitions of political leaders, occasionally including Communists. Each leader had his constituents and some had organized bands of followers which held together even after their leaders had been eliminated from government. Some unreconciled groups rebelled, harassing the government with guerrilla activities. Not all dissident groups were Communist-controlled, but all were threats to inexperienced governments and some were open to Communist manipulation. The new governments lacked effective communication with their peoples; there were gulfs between new national institutions and traditional organizations in the villages.

The Communist threat was serious everywhere. Capitalizing on colonial resentments, pointing to the misery of the people and the need for action, the Communists posed as the real champions of revolutionary improvements. Their strength lay not in their local accomplishments but in ceaseless intrigue and skill in exploiting every form of discontent.

Common economic problems were particularly prevalent in agrarian areas. Some three-fourths of the people were peasants. Poverty, deplorable health conditions, primitive tools and techniques, tenancy, high rents, high interest rates, high taxes, exploitative marketing systems, lack of consumer goods, and loss of external markets—all these were sources not only of social discontent, but of economic weakness and political vulnerability as well. Political opponents found their most potent arguments in concentrated land holdings, exorbitant rentals and interest rates, burdensome taxes, corruption, and the inability of local governments to improve the conditions of rural life.

The region depended heavily on selling abroad such basic commodities as rice, rubber, tin, and sugar. Resumption of this trade was by no means automatic.[2] During the war alternative sources of supply had been found for some of these commodities. Nevertheless, the best hope for increases in foreign exchange earnings, which were essential to industrial development, and for higher living standards lay in increased production and export of raw materials, semiprocessed goods, and foodstuffs. But nationalistic attitudes toward foreign traders and to investments from abroad were an obstacle. On what new basis, and on what terms, could trade and investment be restored and expanded?

An American Dilemma

The role which the United States should assume in southeast Asia after the defeat of Japan was far from clear. Historic interests in the area did not provide, save in the Philippines, the outlines of a consistent policy. Anticommunism alone was not enough in dealing with peoples struggling alone against grinding poverty and a host of problems with which they were ill prepared to cope. But the basic dilemma was how to advance the security and well-being of these countries and their capacity to deal with their own problems, including the threat of Communist subversion, without inviting suspicion and resistance.

Beginnings of Aid

American aid in southeast Asia, as in China, was not preceded by the kind of comprehensive analysis of problems and American interests that paved the way for the European Recovery Program. Economic assistance began as a series of responses to specific situations. After the Dutch had reoccupied Indonesia, the first ECA aid to the islands was negotiated with the Netherlands government on the same basis as assistance to other European dependencies. When difficulties developed between the Netherlands and Indonesia, American aid was suspended, to be resumed after agreement was reached on the terms of Indonesian independence. Aid to Indochina,[3] Thailand, and Burma began with an ECA suggestion to Congress that unexpended China program funds be used "in the general area of China." Aid to the Philip-

---

[2] See Claude A. Buss, "New Relationships: Economies and Diplomacy in Southeast Asia," in *Southeast Asia and the Coming World*, ed. by Philip W. Thayer (Johns Hopkins University Press, Baltimore, 1953), pp. 81–95.

[3] U.S. aid to Indochina began when that country was being reoccupied by a French colonial administration and was developed through negotiations with the French government. As greater autonomy was gradually given to the three Associated States of Indochina, American relations were broadened to include direct contacts with the emergent governments of these states.

pines, where postwar assistance had already been substantial, was a logical next step.

Shortly after economic assistance to these areas was approved, the ECA organized "special technical and economic missions"—soon referred to as the STEM missions—for the handling of contacts with the governments of the region and for the administration of American aid activities there.

Contrast with ERP

ECA operations in southeast Asia differed in several basic respects from the European Recovery Program. They were designed primarily to bring Communist brushfires under control. The economic problems confronted were radically different. The Asian economies rested mainly on rather primitive agriculture and secondarily upon the export of raw materials. Since land holdings were minute, each country had vast pools of underutilized manpower. Probably no more than 5 percent of southeast Asia's gross product was in capital goods.

There was no question, therefore, of restoring advanced industrial economies; capacity to use capital goods was severely limited. The need was for extensive technical assistance and relatively small quantities of material aid. Aside from emergency commodity shipments, the supplies sent to southeast Asia consisted mainly of such items as hand tools, light agricultural equipment, medicine, seeds, and fertilizer. Despite large populations and great poverty, therefore, economic assistance to Asia cost much less than aid to Europe, though it demanded greater resourcefulness in adjusting to unfamiliar conditions and in transmitting skills.

It was not feasible to use a regional approach based on the concept of mutual aid, like that which led to the formation of the OEEC. In southeast Asia "at this stage," the ECA reported to Congress in mid-1950, "there is relatively little provision for mutual aid; strength must be built largely country by country until there is a floor of economic and political stability." [4] Each program was, therefore, separate and distinct. [5]

---

[4] *Ninth Report*, p. 100.

[5] There was an element of a regional relationship in the U.N. Economic Commission for Asia and the Far East (under the Economic and Social Council) in which the U.S. participated; the work of the ECAFE, however, was limited to research and periodic conferences. On the initiative of India, a conference was convened in early 1949 to explore the possibility of developing closer ties in the region, but due partly to neutralism and reluctance to form a group closely identified with the Western powers, no proposal for a specific regional grouping emerged.

Aims and Methods

Through preliminary surveys, research, and early field studies, some analysis of each economy was made. More would have been desirable, but such statistical data as were available were generally unreliable; there was no basis for elaborate national-accounts and balance-of-payments computations comparable to those developed in Europe.

But obvious, pressing needs could be confirmed without refined analysis. Existing resources had to be better mobilized, critical shortages met, and transport bottlenecks reduced. Food production had to be increased. Trade between food-surplus and food-deficit countries had to be restored and expanded. Capacity to produce and export such raw materials as tin, rubber, oil, graphite, manganese, and abacá had to be increased. To help in meeting these needs, relationships of mutual confidence had to be established.

The stake was the survival of moderate democratic governments throughout the area. This depended on their ability to provide constructive leadership and resist Communist subversion among their peoples and to participate in friendly and cooperative relations with the United States and other free nations. The ECA emphasized these points on many occasions. Thus, in a report to Congress, it declared:

No modern self-governing state—and especially no state with a democratic form of government—can maintain itself and develop its potential unless it performs a minimum of public services in the fields of health, agriculture, education, transport, power and communications, industry and overall planning. The countries of southeast Asia, although richly endowed with natural resources, are acutely deficient in these public services and in the technicians, supplies and institutions for developing them. The initial step in any program designed to increase governmental strength, raise production and living standards, and lay a foundation for social-economic development in this part of the world must therefore be the organization and maintenance of adequate, self-sustaining public services.[6]

In another report, the agency spoke of assisting in the "creation of social and economic conditions and institutions under which the people

---

The Colombo Plan for Co-operative Development in South and Southeast Asia, initiated by the British in 1950, evolved into a six-year program for economic cooperation involving principally the U.K. and Commonwealth countries in the area. The U.S., while "wholly sympathetic," did not at first participate. See Brown and Opie, *op. cit.*, pp. 409–412; also U.N., *Economic Survey of Asia and the Far East* (annual), prepared by the ECAFE Secretariat; and Great Britain, H.M. Treasury, *The Colombo Plan: Second Annual Report* (London, 1953).

[6] *Thirteenth Report to Congress* (Washington, 1951), p. 72.

feel that their basic needs and aspirations are being satisfied by their own free and independent governments" and of promoting "confidence, good will, friendship for the United States among the governments concerned and among the masses of the people." [7]

A major aim was to help develop institutions and practices which would not require prolonged American support. One way of doing this was to help train local people and to make sure that projects begun under the ECA were of types that could be carried on with governmental or other local funds. Hence, efforts were made to help—to the limited extent that help was welcome—in the institutions and practices involved in taxation, budgetary planning, banking, and the management of foreign exchange. A leading example of assistance in governmental administration was the support given to the Public Administration Institute established at the University of the Philippines. [8]

Previous efforts to aid economically retarded areas had often bogged down in long advisory reports to governments. Without waiting to develop comprehensive surveys, the ECA put special effort into developing promptly a village-level or "rice-roots" approach. Thus health programs emphasized mobile units, local clinics, and health centers; agricultural assistance used a wide range of extension services; and industrial planning frequently included the development of village and cottage industries.

Counterpart funds, used effectively in Europe, were even more important in southeast Asia, where, due to greater poverty, the raising of local revenues imposes a severe strain. [9] Indonesia, the Philippines, and Formosa deposited counterpart funds commensurate with the dollar cost of the aid received, to be released for purposes agreed upon with the United States. Other countries deposited the proceeds from the sale of ECA-financed commodities and services, the ECA retaining the right to require deposits up to the value of the aid provided.

Except for the earlier but arrested beginning in Indonesia, ECA assistance to the countries of southeast Asia commenced in the latter half of 1950, after Congress had authorized for the purpose the residual funds of the China program, which came to about 100 million dollars. Before this action was taken the Department of State—following consultation with the ECA—had requested R. Allen Griffin, a Cali-

[7] *Twelfth Report to Congress* (Washington, 1951), p. 64.

[8] See MSA, *U.S. Technical and Economic Assistance to the Far East* (Washington, 1952), pp. 8–9.

[9] See ECA, *Thirteenth Report to Congress*, pp. 74–76.

fornia publisher who had served as deputy chief of the ECA mission to China, to head a small survey group of Far Eastern specialists sent to the area to assess immediate requirements for economic and technical assistance and to recommend the types of programs that should be considered. The report of the Griffin mission provided initial estimates and laid an essential foundation for the planning which ensued.

Country Programs

Let us turn now to a brief but more specific examination of the problems faced in each of the countries of southeast Asia, the nature of the programs and projects developed, and the results which appear to have been attained.[10] Since detailed treatment is not possible here, it should be said at once that ECA operation throughout the area was featured by much trial and error and by a constant striving for understanding of basic problems, for genuinely cooperative relations with local leaders, and for methods of work adapted to local conditions.[11]

In *Indonesia*—against a background of some three hundred years of Netherlands colonial administration—the desire for independence had become more organized and articulate since the early years of the twentieth century. More than three years of Japanese occupation, during which Netherlands control was suspended, gave added impetus to the independence movements. In order to pacify the country and consolidate their own control, the Japanese deliberately grounded their appeal to the Indonesians on preservation of the latter's culture. Some local units were armed in order to strengthen resistance to re-entry by Allied forces. As the Japanese came under increasing military pressure, they tried to win support of the local populace by promising them full freedom and by giving them greater participation in governmental administration.[12]

Although Indonesian leaders declared the country's independence two days after the Japanese surrendered, this status was not legally recognized by the Netherlands until four years later, in December 1949, when sovereignty, except for New Guinea, was transferred to the United

[10] The factual data in this section are derived principally from the ECA's *Ninth* to *Thirteenth Report to Congress;* its *Twenty-eighth* and *Thirty-eighth Report for the Public Advisory Board;* MSA, *U.S. Technical and Economic Assistance in the Far East;* and a number of unpublished ECA documents.

[11] See Chapter 18.

[12] See Virginia Thompson and Richard Adloff, *Empire's End in Southeast Asia* (Foreign Policy Association, New York, Headline Series No. 78, November–December 1949), pp. 12ff.

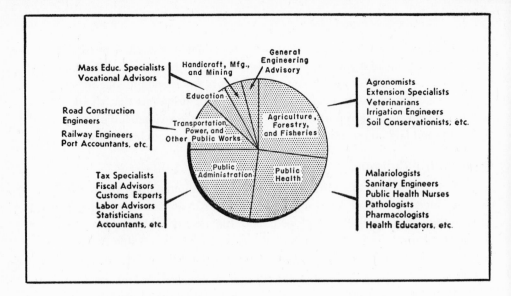

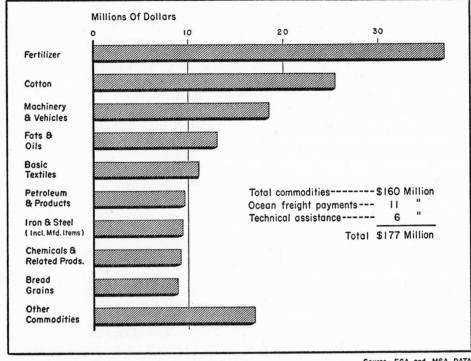

Source: ECA and MSA DATA

12. The economic program for Southeast Asia. *Upper:* Technical assistance—319 technical experts were sent to Southeast Asia by June 30, 1952.* *Lower:* Supplies—paid shipments June 5, 1950–June 30, 1952.

* Also, 315 local people were brought from countries for training, mostly in the U.S.

20. Young lumbermen in Cambodia take a lesson in filing a saw.

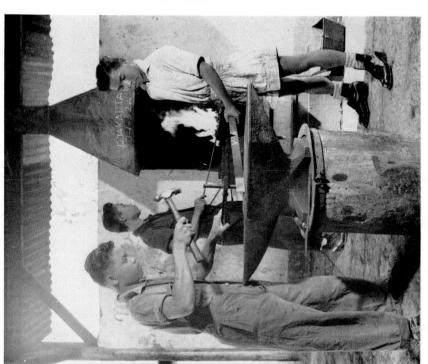

19. Indonesians learn to use machinery in a new training school.

21. Building a road with American equipment in Cameroons, Africa.

22. One of many mining developments in the Katanga region of the Belgian Congo.

States of Indonesia as an equal partner with the Netherlands under the titular sovereignty of the Dutch Crown. During those four years, Indonesia went through a long struggle. The Dutch attempted to regain control through both negotiation and the use of force, and until independence was assured strife persisted. An inevitable period of internal instability followed.

ECA-administered aid, beginning in 1948, was first channeled, it will be recalled, through the Netherlands government; about 101 million dollars was earmarked, under the European Recovery Program, for Indonesia as a dependent territory. When the program was still in an early phase, however, it was suspended as a result of strife in the islands.

United States economic assistance to Indonesia as an independent country dates formally from March 24, 1950, when an agreement was signed providing for the new government to take over all obligations pertaining to the aid which had been suspended. The Export-Import Bank also extended a line of credit of about 100 million dollars for capital development.

Special significance was attached to economic recovery in Indonesia because of its political vulnerability and pressing internal needs, and also because of its reservoir of raw materials. The strategically situated island chain, with its seventy-five million people, extended across more than three thousand miles of the Indian and southern Pacific Oceans. Its exports [13] were highly important to other economies in southeast Asia, to the United States, and to Europe.

Ten years of war and revolution had taken a heavy toll and the country faced extraordinary problems. After the exodus of the Dutch, it suffered from a lack of experienced administrators and technicians.[14] The new government leaders, reflecting popular sentiment, were apprehensive of any "strings" attached to foreign help. Although needs were pressing, time was required to negotiate the new agreement and to establish planning and administrative machinery to carry out the revived aid operation.

The ECA program, following the recommendations of the Griffin mission, placed primary emphasis on technical assistance and supplies

[13] Principally tin, rubber, petroleum, cinchona bark, pepper, kapok, copra, palm oil products, sugar, coffee, cordage fibers, nickel, bauxite, manganese, and coal.

[14] This difficulty was eased, however, by the fact that a considerable number of the Dutch remained as advisors to the Indonesian government and to government corporations.

for establishing health, agricultural and training services, and it made provision also for agricultural hand tools, fishing boats and gear, equipment for lumbering, and technical help for the management of forests.

Health programs were directed first to malaria control, nurses' training, and provision of supplies for hospitals and quarantine stations. Technical assistance projects were developed to improve and distribute rice seed, to control plant diseases, to develop disease-resistant livestock, to introduce more efficient use of fertilizers, and to improve irrigation and drainage. With the assistance of an American firm of consulting engineers, help was given in restoring and improving transport facilities and in assisting with plans for the new nation's economic development.

Each project had its problems and was packed with drama. Not all were successful. One example, among many, was the assistance given to the country's fishing industry. "There is nothing wrong with catching fish from sailing vessels," said an ECA staff member, "except that you can't go very far from shore, and, if the wind is against you, the fish you catch may spoil before you get back to port." With the help of two American experts—one from Hawaii and one from Massachusetts —Indonesian fishermen found that if their craft were equipped with small diesel motors of twenty-five to forty horsepower, they could catch and deliver to port about five times as many fish as before. Once this was demonstrated in a number of coastal villages, local fishermen everywhere started talking about motorized fishing operations. Technical training and distribution problems remained, but a start had been made in modernizing the country's fishing industry.

The MSA report of March 1952 on *U.S. Technical and Economic Assistance in the Far East* cites a list of accomplishments through the Indonesian aid program. Thirty-nine technical experts had given or were giving direct help in fields ranging from health to industrial development. Thirty-one Indonesians had been brought to the United States for training in a similarly wide variety of specialties. About 100,-000 people had been given antimalaria treatment in pilot projects in which local health teams had been trained; a project was under way to treat three million. Extensive equipment had been provided to hospitals, laboratories, clinics, nursing centers, and medical schools; to farms, agricultural experiment stations, and fisheries; to a variety of local industries and to vocational teacher training schools.

Indochina, with an area larger than Texas and a population of approximately twenty-eight million, consisted of three Associated States—

Vietnam,[15] Laos, and Cambodia—brought together under a single French colonial administration but never fully integrated. All were members of the French Union, however, and they had a common currency and customs system. When the Japanese occupied the country in 1941, they made use of the existing administration until the end of the French Vichy regime, after which they hurriedly set up local governments. But the new regimes were unable to maintain their positions after the Japanese surrender, and a long internal struggle for power began, in which Communist elements became increasingly prominent. British forces in the area took the Japanese surrender in southern Indochina, and Chinese Nationalist troops took it in the north. During 1946 authority in both areas was transferred to French forces.

In the meantime, independence movements of various kinds had gained headway in all the states. The most significant was that of the Vietminh, led by Ho Chi-minh—a veteran Comintern agent—whose objective was the "independence" of all of Indochina and its unification under Communist control. Unable to negotiate successfully with Ho or to defeat him in the fighting which broke out in December 1946, the French turned to Bao Dai, former ruler of Annam, and asked him to head up a provisional government as Emperor.

The economy of the area was severely disorganized as a result of fighting and guerrilla activity in Vietnam and, to a lesser extent, in Laos and Cambodia.[16] A rice surplus normally produced for export, chiefly to China and Hongkong, was no longer available; the same was true of other surpluses such as corn, tea, and dried fish. Mineral production—coal, tin, iron, and zinc—was partly under the control of Vietminh and had greatly declined. Some rubber plantations had been destroyed; some were being used as armed camps.

Faced with this situation, in which an important factor was the relationship between Ho and the Chinese and Russian Communists, the American government considererd carefully what action it should take. In due course it was decided to provide United States military and economic aid to the French-sponsored provisional government in an effort to prevent Ho from gaining control of the country with aid from Communist China. Under Congressional mandates economic assistance was furnished through the ECA, and military assistance—to the Associated States and to French forces there—through the Mutual Defense

[15] Vietnam formerly consisted of three provinces known as Tonkin, Annam, and Cochin-china.

[16] See ECA, *The Role of ECA* in Southeast Asia (Washington, 1951), pp. 6–7.

Assistance Program conducted by the Defense Department. Thus the objective of American aid was clearly political and military as well as economic. Economic health was a necessary basis for political stability and military strength. Political stability was essential for economic development and internal military security. Military power was essential to protect the new regime and to assure opportunity for peaceful economic development. All were given added weight because northern Vietnam, where the Vietminh were intrenched, was a gateway between Communist China and the rest of southeast Asia.

The ECA program, beginning gradually, developed a wide variety of activities, comparable to those cited in Indonesia. By 1952 results in many fields of activity were becoming evident.[17] In Vietnam, for example, more than 500 miles of badly deteriorated highways were under repair. In Tonkin, previously a rice-deficient area, 25,000 acres of land had been brought under irrigation with diesel engines and pumps, making possible two crops a year instead of one. In a fight against a million and a half cases of blinding trachoma, an estimated 200,000 cases had been cured or arrested. In Indochina as in China, however, constructive economic efforts were subject to political and military developments beyond the control of the United States.

In some respects *Thailand* presented a less critical complex of problems than the other countries of the area. Although overrun and occupied by the Japanese during the war, it had suffered less physical destruction than the rest. Agrarian conditions were generally better. Eighty percent of the farmers, for example, owned their own land, and for the 20 percent who were tenants, rentals, comparatively speaking, were not exorbitant—amounting to about a third of each crop. The country did not have the legacy of colonial occupation or the intensity of antiforeignism characteristic of much of the region. Unlike Burma and Indochina, it did not have a common boundary with China, although the distance from China's southern border was not great. The government in 1948 had itself succeeded in taking strong measures against Communists within its borders. The country had suffered a reduction in its agricultural acreages and some political upheaval. Armed bands in some localities were a threat to the peace. But rehabilitation efforts immediately following the war had restored agricultural production to the point where some surpluses were available for export, and the country was able to accumulate enough foreign exchange to meet its most urgent import requirements.

If the outlook was not as grim as in other parts of the region, Thailand

[17] See MSA, *U.S. Technical and Economic Assistance in the Far East*, p. 19.

still faced difficult problems. Living standards were low and the energies of the people were sapped by malaria and other diseases. Interest rates on farm loans were excessive. Droughts and floods were intermittent perils to agriculture, greater in their effects for want of adequate irrigation facilities. Transportation was inefficient and there was little electric power.

The ECA's primary emphasis was on technical assistance designed to help meet these problems and lay foundations for steady, if modest, economic growth. The fields in which technical aid was requested and provided included railway maintenance and operation, road construction, public health services, irrigation projects, agricultural improvement and extension, and training at many technical and administrative levels. The ECA recognized a need for, and was prepared to furnish, technical assistance in other fields as well, such as budgetary and fiscal management, but in these areas the Thai authorities did not seek external advice during the ECA period. About a hundred administrators and technicians from Thailand were afforded means for specialized study and observation in the United States.

Specific projects included setting up public health teams, a vigorous antimalaria program conducted by 1,400 trainees, the construction of earth dams for irrigation, the development of rural credit facilities, the development of agricultural extension work, experiments in plant breeding which—for rice—were expected to increase yields substantially in the next few years, demonstrations and experiments in road building and repair, and the initiation of mass education programs. Some technical assistance was given too for power expansion, mining surveys, and the development of a few small pilot plants for new industries.

Because of Thailand's strategic location and exposure to possible aggression, economic support was given also to a limited military program, through technical advice and the provision of small quantities of equipment for roads, railways, and air traffic control systems.

When the *Burma* program was initiated, that country's colonial ties with the British were being severed; its relations with the United States had never been extensive. Neutralist in sentiment, the Burmese government was at first reluctant to request American aid. Attitudes toward the West were deeply affected by anticolonial feeling. Consequently, the country was less apprehensive over the dangers of communism than it might have been had preoccupation with nationalism been less consuming. It took time, therefore, to establish a relationship of mutual confidence which would permit the successful launching of a modest aid program consisting primarily of technical assistance in the fields of health, agriculture, and industrial development.

Burma had once been the world's largest exporter of rice and a source of significant supplies of oil, minerals, and timber. Under the British it had acquired a well-developed rail and river transport system. Local training for administrative responsibility and the conduct of economic activities was more advanced than in most of the other parts of southeast Asia. But wartime hostilities and postwar rebellions had disrupted the economy and virtually halted all land and river transport. Rice production and trade were drastically reduced. The teakwood industry, previously profitable, was virtually closed down. Mining, except for small quantities of tin and tungsten, had stopped, as had the production and refining of petroleum. Foreign trade was down to a fraction of its prewar volume.

After initial efforts were under way the aid outlook in Burma, as elsewhere, was complicated with the change of emphasis from economic cooperation to mutual security. This change was not as drastic in the southeast Asia programs as it was in Europe. Nevertheless, the limited military commitments which receiving countries were asked to make raised apprehensions lest they be put into a relationship with China and Russia that would lead them into difficulties. The situation was further complicated by the presence in north Burma of Chinese Nationalist troops who had retreated from southwest China.

In spite of initial obstacles, an aid agreement was negotiated and a STEM mission established in Burma. The program developed gradually. Counsel and assistance were furnished for the improvement of public services—especially in health, primary education, agricultural training, and the promotion of low-cost housing. Joint study was given to the laying of better foundations for economic development—through greater diversification in agriculture, mining surveys, the expansion of cotton spinning, and the establishment of pilot plants for other types of production. Efforts were made to bring tangible benefits to outlying semiautonomous states through soil conservation, a variety of agricultural improvements, and projects relating to the animal industry and canning. And, of central importance, measures were taken to assist in restoring Burma's prewar economic asset, the production and export of rice. These measures included improved irrigation in the north, flood control projects in the south, the planning and construction of rice storage facilities, the rehabilitation of rice mills, and the restoration of transport and port facilities, notably the port of Rangoon. Much more was needed, however, particularly through improvements in extension services and expansion of rice processing facilities.

American administration of the *Philippine Islands,* during the decades before World War II, was accompanied by uneven efforts to develop the economy and to train local leadership for expanding political responsibility. Considerable economic and technical assistance had been provided. Independence had been promised and the first steps taken toward establishing a sovereign Philippine government. After the war a relief program costing approximately 100 million dollars was carried out under United States auspices, and a smaller program was conducted by the Foreign Economic Administration for the sale of basic civilian supplies through commercial channels. Additional relief was provided by the American Red Cross and private organizations in the United States. And there was a token UNRRA program. But the war had laid waste Manila and other major cities as well as large rural areas. In January 1950, when plans were under way to extend the ECA aid program to southeast Asia, the internal situation in the Philippines was still disorganized and, in some respects, deteriorating. The reasons, in addition to war devastation and continuing dislocation, were to be found in the activities of the Communist-inspired Huk guerrillas and in weaknesses in the local administration of aid previously provided.

After the invasion of South Korea, the United States announced that military as well as economic aid would be provided. A special mission under Daniel W. Bell [18] was sent at the request of President Quirino to survey Philippine needs, to suggest how the islanders could better help themselves, and to consider ways in which the United States could best assist. The Bell report, in October 1950, contained a number of severely critical comments on conditions in the Philippines and recommended certain positive steps which, it was believed, the Philippine government could take. Emphasis was given to more equitable tax legislation and a minimum wage law for agricultural workers. It was suggested that, conditional upon measures taken by the Philippines to carry out the reforms cited in the report, United States grants and loans on the order of 250 million dollars be provided over a period of five years.

The Philippine aid program, as administered by the ECA, began with the signing of a bilateral agreement dated April 27, 1951. Although the government had taken some of the preparatory measures needed, it

[18] President, American Security and Trust Co., Washington, D.C., and former Under-Secretary of the Treasury, named by President Truman to conduct the survey.

was necessary, if the program was to be conducted effectively, for the ECA mission to take a considerable hand in its administration. The preparation of requests for aid, procurement operations, and the development of local administration of the aid program all involved extensive American participation. The program was carried out under heavy time pressure, and there was later some Congressional criticism of certain projects considered to have been hasty or ill conceived. The program had four main objectives.

The first was to increase the production and distribution of rice, other foodstuffs, and raw materials such as copra and abacá (Manila hemp), and to develop small manufactures and mineral extraction. Projects were initiated for farm extension work, fertilizer production, irrigation, improved agricultural practices, reclamation work, cocoanut and abacá disease control, road construction and improvement, the expansion of handicrafts and cottage industries, industrial mining surveys, technical education, and the provision of limited equipment for agricultural and other vocational schools.

Second, there was an effort to launch a development program that would expand economic opportunities and promote higher living standards for the depressed sectors of the population. This part of the program included projects relating to farm credit, land tenancy, the enforcement of minimum wage laws, assistance to locally organized agricultural associations, and public health programs. To these were added, beginning in 1951, a series of housing programs.

The third aim was to build up governmental administration. American experts were brought in and assigned, for advisory work, to key departments of the government. Selected employees were given opportunities for special observation and training, in their respective specialities, in the United States. And technical assistance was provided in organizing college courses combined with in-service training in public administration.

A fourth specific objective was to promote settlement of the large, fertile island of Mindanao, where there was a substantial amount of arable but uncultivated land, as a means of releasing population pressure in other sections and, indirectly, aiding in the pacification of the Huks. Support to the settlement of homesteaders on Mindanao included material and technical assistance for road construction, the building of hospitals and schools, public health measures including an effort to eradicate malaria, the construction of wells, and the classification and supervision of land division, including the registration of titles.

By the winter of 1951–1952 considerable progress had been made, but conditions were still not satisfactory. Per capita production and income were below prewar levels, although both were higher than in most countries in Asia. Inequalities in wealth were particularly marked. The economy of the islands remained overdependent on the prices of three export commodities—sugar, copra, and abacá. Agricultural productivity was still relatively low, and inequitable land tenure was a factor in continuing economic depression among farm groups. This was an element in the discontent upon which the Huk movement capitalized, especially in the heavily populated region of central Luzon. Gradual improvement continued during the year, however, as, under the leadership of General Magsaysay, the threat from the Huk guerrillas was reduced.

Although *India* was not a regular recipient of ECA aid before 1951, a crop shortage in that year led to serious famine conditions, which prompted Congress to adopt, on June 15, the India Emergency Food Act of 1951.[19] Under the terms of this act and a special loan agreement with the Indian government, nearly 2.2 million long tons of grain costing 190 million dollars were delivered during the ensuing year, the final shipment arriving in August 1952. The food provided under this wheat loan was particularly important to the Telegu-speaking peoples around Madras, in the state of Andhra, among whom the Communists had gained a strong foothold. The American loan proved later to be a vital factor in staving off starvation in this area, in putting an end to grain hoarding—a particular grievance, and in preventing the establishment of a new Communist bridgehead in Asia.

Results

In June 1952 most of the economic aid programs in southeast Asia had been in operation for less than two years.[20] After Congressional approval in June 1950, it had taken time to get them started. Agreements had to be negotiated, staffs employed and sent to the field, procurement and shipping arranged in the face of increasing competition for supplies because of general rearmament for the Korean War. Previous United States relations with four of the countries—Indonesia, Indochina, Burma, and Thailand—had been limited; in all of them the ECA had much to learn. Field work could not really get under way before the end of

---

[19] Public Law 48, 82d Congress, 1st Session.

[20] Insights gained in the course of the ECA's Far Eastern operations are discussed in Chapter 18.

1950. Roughly a year and a half was a short time in which to achieve significant results in new development. Economic analyses and statistical data did not permit accurate assessment of changes in major economic sectors during 1951 and the first half of 1952.

To point, as we have done, to the results claimed for a large number of specific projects is likely to be misleading unless it is remembered that no estimates were made, in most instances, of the total impact of any series of projects upon the broad national problem to which they were related. A resumé of particular projects leaves out of account, moreover, problems (e.g. internal capital formation) which were not seriously attacked in most areas but which were important to the economic future of each country. Perhaps the most significant results, aside from those of a limited but important nature deriving from specific projects, can only be stated in general and somewhat qualified terms.

The governments and to some extent the peoples of southeast Asia were brought to a better understanding of United States aims and policies. At a meeting of the United Nations Economic Commission for Asia and the Far East held in 1951, the Soviet delegate made charges of United States "imperialism" in the area which had to be answered by the American delegate. When similar charges were made at the next meeting the following year, the allegations were refuted, on the basis of recent experience, not by the American delegate but by representatives of the governments in the area.[21] It would be naïve to suppose that all suspicion and distrust of the United States had been removed, but increased understanding was a by-product of economic and technical aid conducted in a spirit of friendship and mutual respect.

Probably more significant, in the long run, than the immediate effect of specific projects was the ferment of ideas and constructive efforts which they helped to generate. There were, of course, great variations in the degree to which such efforts "took hold," so that they could continue with vigorous local leadership and support. But the initiative and enthusiasm shown in many of the programs gave promise of future drive and leadership.

[21] Recalling this episode, Merrill Gay, delegate from the U.S. State Department said: "Toward the end of the conference, the Soviet delegate made a long speech attacking American technical and economic assistance programs in the Far East and charging a number of countries with granting special privileges as a price for United States assistance. The pent-up irritations of delegations with Soviet tactics burst forth as almost every Asian member replied to the Soviet charges, labeling them as false and insulting. The Burman delegate said forcefully: 'If this is American imperialism, give us more of it!'" Interview, Washington, July 18, 1954.

The new governments were helped as much as possible in developing the institutions and services needed for effective administration. The concept of government as existing only to serve the people could not be expanded suddenly by even the most contagious enthusiasm. Corruption and vested interests, from which no government is entirely free, are particularly difficult to deal with in poverty-stricken regimes. The ECA's contribution in this area was limited and cannot be segregated from local efforts. With all of these qualifications, however, it is fair to say that, with the assistance given, the governments of the area were better able to establish and maintain effective contacts with their peoples, to provide a modicum of essential services, and to increase thereby their own capacity for survival.

Finally, a survey of results in southeast Asia must take into account what would have happened without the aid programs, weighing the cost of action against the cost of inaction. The swift rise of Communist prestige in Asia following the conquest of China and during the periods of Allied retreat in the Korean War, together with the proven effectiveness of Communist propaganda techniques, leave little doubt that southeast Asia was in imminent peril. Solid American interest and support, and the measure of economic and political strengthening which American aid made possible, contributed toward checking a tide of reverses to the free world cause in Asia. They were at least an essential holding action, gaining time for further effort in a strategic and populous part of the world.

PART IV

Evaluation

CHAPTER 11

Organization

WE NOW turn from the record to the task of evaluation. To a significant degree the record speaks for itself. In 1947 the industrial output of western Europe, with seventeen million more people than before the war, was 15 to 20 percent less than in 1938, agricultural production 20 to 25 percent less. Trade was at a low ebb, dollar reserves had dwindled to the danger point, living standards in many countries were precarious, and the situation was deteriorating. We have seen the impressive economic results achieved under the European Recovery Program—through European initiative and cooperation buttressed by American aid.

Political results were no less striking. A peacetime partnership was established between the United States and western Europe. Within Europe, as Robert Marjolin has said, cooperation took "forms which would have been considered completely impossible before the war or even in the years immediately following." [1]

From a long-range viewpoint, what was accomplished through the Marshall Plan was not so much the final solution of transient problems as a series of national and international efforts—some remarkably

[1] Marjolin, *op. cit.*, p. 16.

effective, others faltering—*toward* the solution of continuing problems. This is the point of view from which our evaluation will be attempted, as we take up, one by one, some of the problems or problem areas that were confronted.

Let us begin with the question of organization within the United States government.[2] A good deal has been said in earlier chapters about the Economic Cooperation Administration. How well did this agency carry out its task? In what ways did it break new ground? What were its major strengths and weaknesses? Did its record justify the establishment of a separate agency? What are the principal administrative lessons to be gleaned from the unique experience of this organization?

ECA STRENGTHS AND WEAKNESSES

After its "shake down" period and during the first two years or more of its four-year existence, the ECA enjoyed an outstanding reputation among United States government agencies for ability to "get things done." The morale of the organization was evidenced by thousands of man-hours, week after week, of self-initiated, unrecompensed overtime work.[3] Visitors sensed an air of confidence and forward movement. Then, almost imperceptibly at first, the exceptional luster of the ECA as an administration began to dim. By the time its functions were transferred to the Mutual Security Agency, it was still vigorous, but its movements had become more ponderous and less sure; morale had receded from the high mark of the first two years.

Sense of Direction

The more important elements of strength and of weakness within the organization came from many influences, external and internal. The first in time and perhaps in significance was the constructive purpose of the enterprise which the ECA was designed to administer. Commenting on the spirit that prevailed among ECA personnel during this period, Paul Hoffman said: "It started, I think, with the Marshall speech. The concept was a noble one. The people in the organization wanted to work for something worth while and had the idea that they could

---

[2] The problem faced by Europeans in developing the institutions required for cooperative action is discussed in Chapters 14 and 17.

[3] "Perhaps it's a bit of nostalgia," said one executive later. "But in looking back, I am impressed with the characters who were in the organization, who worked twelve hours a day, seven days a week." It was a common observation that from the second to the eleventh floor of the ECA building in Washington lights were burning nearly every evening.

contribute to keeping the free world free. You couldn't want a better motive than that." [4]

In a time of bewilderment and discouragement, the basic purposes of the Marshall Plan [5] symbolized for many a new sense of direction in international life. Their potency was reflected in an upsurge of confidence in Europe even before the first shipment of supplies was made. In the words of Frank Figgures of the OEEC: "The kickoff was such that we never did quite get lost in details. It was really on the big line."

All of this had multiple effects upon the ECA administration. It gave the agency a position of high trust. It enabled the organization to attract gifted people with a strong sense of public responsibility. It provided a "philosophy" which contributed to the intense interest and durable enthusiasm that many brought to their daily tasks. ECA personnel were able to see themselves not as cogs in a bureaucratic machine, but as men and women who could find fulfillment in an enterprise in which they strongly believed and which demanded their best efforts.

For more than two years, the basic rationale of the Marshall Plan retained its essential unity and its capacity to give architectural meaning to the undertaking as a whole. It was to be expected that, as with previous new agencies, there would be a "settling down" process after which the high pitch of early enthusiasm would be difficult to sustain. But in the ECA it was sustained, to a remarkable degree, for more than two years. Why did it begin, gradually, to decline thereafter?

One factor was an unrealistic element in timing. Within the projected four-year program were purposes which could be achieved, with vigorous effort, in the period allotted, and for these the four-year limitation provided an important incentive to maximum endeavor. But there were also purposes—essential to the freeing of Europe from extraordinary outside assistance—which could not possibly be realized in a four-year period. Structural changes which required a longer period of sustained effort were necessary. The illusory hope of full economic self-reliance in Europe in four years—although it contributed to the initial morale and drive of the agency—needed therefore to be replaced by more realistic assessments of what was needed, and of what could be accomplished within the time and means allowed.

At a moment when the required revisions in thinking were beginning to take shape, a second factor came into play, namely, the shift in emphasis from economic "recovery" to military "security." This was no

[4] Interview, New York, January 28, 1953.   [5] See Chapters 2 and 3.

capricious change. Events in Korea had demonstrated forcefully the aggressive purposes of communism and the free world's previous neglect of military security while pursuing its constructive economic aims. When it became apparent that a new period of swift rearmament would be necessary, however, the objective of military strength was not simply added to other goals. Instead, the pendulum of public and Congressional opinion swung so far that international economic aims, and support for them, had to be justified largely in terms of "defense support." This made it more difficult to retain the full momentum and cooperative spirit of the recovery program in Europe. It also meant that the ECA had to change rapidly from a close-knit organization dealing with a specified range of economic goals into a more diffused administration increasingly subordinated to military and political objectives and to the organs of government primarily responsible for their pursuit.

The situation might have been different if the pendulum had not swung so far, if the bearing of economic strength and growth upon military and political strength had been seen more clearly, and if diplomatic, economic, and military aims had been regarded as coordinate, each indispensable to the health and security of the United States and the free world. In this event the identity of distinct administrations, each responsible for a coherent group of objectives, might have received greater support, with each preserving its special competence, and with coordination at the highest level. This would have meant, it may be argued, not less security but more, on the ground that military power without corresponding economic strength is no adequate long-range defense against aggressive communism.

As it was, the new complex of aims was beyond the competence of any one agency, and integration was difficult to achieve. Economic goals were obscured,[6] defense objectives were hard to define, and competing claims against the same resources were considered primarily from the standpoint of anticipated effect in the military sphere. The ECA lost not only its relative freedom of action, which was unavoidable, but also its distinctive purposes and sense of direction. Clarity in policy diminished and with it clarity in administration. As one employee expressed it, "After Korea, there was a filtering down of uncertainty from the top."

Notwithstanding these handicaps, an adjustment was made. By stages

[6] Data on over-all industrial and agricultural production in OEEC countries were omitted, for example, after the end of 1950, from the ECA's reports to its Public Advisory Board.

the ECA was transformed into the MSA, oriented primarily to military security and secondarily to economic recovery. Commenting on the transition, Paul Porter, onetime ECA Assistant Administrator for Europe, remarked: "In retrospect more than at the time it happened, I recognize how profoundly the Korean war changed goals and the character of ECA. We were like a peacetime factory converted to defense production. On the whole, we did the new job well, but not as well as if the agency had been designed, rather than converted, for the job." [7]

Preparation

A second source of the ECA's strength was the extensive preparation which preceded establishment of the agency. The recommendations on organization evolved by private agencies and by the Harriman and Herter committees, together with proposals developed in the executive departments, provided Congress ample material for consideration. The Senate Foreign Relations Committee gave painstaking attention to the steps needed to create a strong new agency with adequate resources and authority. Without strong two-party support in Congress, it might not have been possible to embody in the enabling legislation provisions which proved of immense advantage. The ECA, as a temporary agency, was given the scope and flexibility needed for a complex, hard-hitting emergency operation. Administrative limitations were held to a minimum; a number of conventional restrictions were waived.[8]

Initial Steps

The advantages of unusual freedom were partially offset by confusion and waste motion until orderly working systems could be instituted. But the formulation of preliminary operating procedures did not take long. Management specialists were brought in from government and business to advise on the organizational structure. Active relations were soon established with other United States agencies, the OEEC, and cooperating governments in Europe.

Two questions which were not fully resolved during the organizing period and which, as we shall see, remained to plague the agency, were the relationship between "economic" and "physical" programing of aid and the division of responsibilities between ECA headquarters in Washington, its European regional office, and the country missions.

[7] Letter to the writer, September 15, 1954.
[8] See Chapter 3.

Choice of Personnel

The selection as Administrator of Paul G. Hoffman, a man of extraordinary capacity, energy, and magnetism, gave the agency inspiring leadership and the ability to attract an eminently able "top team." Harriman, Foster, Katz, Finletter, Bruce, Zellerbach, and others brought to the leadership of the ECA's European regional office and missions outstanding combinations of experience and talent. The roster of the organization contained a balanced force of experienced government administrators, businessmen, economists with a practical turn of mind, and technical specialists of many types. A number of early appointees signed on for only limited periods; others found the task too burdensome. But efforts did not cease to enlist able business leaders [9] and technicians as well as seasoned government workers.

A distinct handicap in staffing was the shortage of people who had both practical experience and extensive knowledge of other countries. The lack was only partially made up by technical studies, by the assignment to missions of men with some previous experience in the kinds of economic problems to be faced, and by a standard two-week orientation program for overseas personnel. This program, though persistently supported by a few key officers, was not given a high enough priority. The content of the course gradually improved, but a wide discrepancy remained between what was needed and what could be done in a two-week period.[10] Another difficulty in recruiting, during the latter stages of the program, was referred to by J. D. Zellerbach, first chief of the ECA mission to Italy, as "the unwillingness of men of ability and standing to come into the organization after the bloom was off the rose."[11]

Caliber of personnel in large organizations is spotty, and the ECA was no exception, though there were nearly 200 applicants for each job. The consensus among the many who have been consulted has been dis-

[9] The initial emphasis on businessmen became somewhat less conspicuous as time went on. One officer in the agency expressed the view that the more valuable businessmen in the organization "rose above their backgrounds." Many felt, on the other hand, that the enterprise would never have achieved the results that it did, at a low administrative cost, without the practical skills and the driving energy injected by a substantial number of men with broad business experience.

[10] For a brief discussion of the need for more systematic orientation and improved training methods for overseas personnel generally, see Wallace S. Sayre and Clarence E. Thurber, *Training for Specialized Mission Personnel* (Public Administration Service, Chicago, 1952), pp. 64–81.

[11] Letter to the writer, November 12, 1954.

tinctly favorable. One British civil servant, for example, observed that "the quality and enthusiasm of personnel provided by the United States for this program—on a short-term basis with no career element involved—has been a most elevating spectacle." "I believe," said another, "that the Marshall Plan was exceptionally well administered, especially when one considers the difficulty of trying to influence other governments and people. The appointments in London were particularly good; great tact was shown. And my impression is that the same was true on the whole in Paris."

Such statements, heard in many of the participating countries, need to be counterbalanced by more critical remarks, such as one made within the agency: "There were not enough sufficiently trained Americans for the type of program that we undertook." Or in one of the smaller European countries: "People who first came to administer the program here ignored the economic facts of life everywhere; they did not realize that the main problem was not quantity but direction. There was the impression that the United States lacked skilled manpower."

Balancing of Functions

As in earlier organizations administering foreign aid, such as the Lend-Lease Administration and UNRRA, there were two main approaches to planning and allocation, and different groups within ECA representing them. Each group tended, to some extent, to underestimate the value of the other; each regarded its own function as logically the more important and therefore worthy of the central position in programing.

One function, which had had the predominant role in earlier agencies, involved procuring equipment and commodities and insuring their effective use. To industrial, agricultural, and commodity experts, and those who handled technical assistance projects, it was clear that the core of any realistic recovery program was increased production. From it, they believed, would naturally flow better living standards, improved trade, and lessened dependence upon external aid. American aid, they held, should be used primarily to stimulate production. Said one: "We were not chasing rabbits such as 'financial stability' and 'critical sectors.' Our approach has been to pick up the things that really affect the economy of a country and go after those."

The other function related American aid to the whole complex of economic resources, processes, policies, and relationships which determined economic health and self-reliance. To the economic, financial, and area specialists within the ECA who thought in these terms, production, though basic, was but one of several interdependent factors which included price movements, monetary and financial conditions, fiscal policies and practices, and aids or barriers to international trade and payments. This broader approach entailed, as we have seen, the use of national-accounts analyses within countries, and the balance-of-payments computations in assessing progress toward economic self-support. Advocates of this approach held that amounts and composition of aid should be determined not in relation to "pieces of the problem" but with a view to strengthening the total economy of each participating country and of western Europe as a region.

This characterization of the "physical" and the "economic" programing approaches, the first with a "commodity" emphasis and the second with an "area" emphasis, is oversimplified. Many shades of distinction have been omitted. But there was a cleavage between them that was never wholly bridged either intellectually or administratively.

In the earliest stage of organizational planning, major stress was put on the physical or commodity approach. Before many weeks had elapsed, however, economic programing was given the predominant role in a centralized handling of aid allotments and counterpart funds.[12]

This fundamental shift in emphasis might be explained in part by the influence of individuals in key offices and by a jockeying for position among units within the organization. But other causes were perhaps more important. Problems arose as "country" problems, which had to be viewed in a broad context. Another factor was the conception of the ECA as being in a banker role. As Daniel K. Hopkinson[13] said: "We were primarily in the business of providing foreign exchange to countries which did not have it. A banker may see that procurement or production operations come off satisfactorily, but he doesn't try to do the job himself."

Some tension between different groups of specialists was inevitable and, within limits, desirable. The dual approach gave scope for both

[12] The operating procedure was essentially as follows: in the Program Coordination Division (later called the European Program Division), programing covered the total amounts of aid for each country, based on comprehensive economic analyses and considerations of policy. In consultation with the Industry, Agriculture, and Transport Divisions, each country's program was then broken down by main sectors. Then, within sectors, there was more detailed programing requiring approvals, by the specialists concerned, of commodity schedules and individual projects.

[13] Director, European Program Division. Interview, Washington, February 6, 1953.

high-grade economists and experts in the procurement, output, and distribution of goods. Attention was focused simultaneously on immediate production goals and on the strengths and weaknesses of national economies as a whole. Each approach was used to advantage in explaining the recovery program and in developing indexes of progress.

But failure to achieve fuller integration of the two approaches also had harmful effects. A tendency in press releases and presentations to Congress to emphasize short-term gains in production obscured other essential elements in the recovery of individual countries. Encouraging production indexes in Italy, for example, diverted attention from other urgent needs—relaxation of monetary controls, a better tax system, domestic investment in new or expanding enterprises, a stronger free labor movement, and land reforms in the south—all essential to a healthy economy. On the other hand, preoccupation with aggregates sometimes made it difficult to concentrate effort on crucial production problems. Most important, perhaps, the dual approach slowed down the development of well-coordinated planning.[14]

In retrospect, it seems clear that according a central role to economic programing led to a better comprehension of the problems to be faced, a more discriminating use of American aid, and a more illuminating picture of progress toward recovery goals. But there were also losses in the lack of play given, at times, to industrial, agricultural, and transport specialists in planning aid. Perhaps a better integration could have been attained if the "economic" and "physical" programers had worked

[14] "The more I look back on it," said Harlan Cleveland, successor to Bissell in directing the ECA's European programing, "the more I think that much wear and tear would have been saved, and the forward motion of the program speeded up, if it had been realized earlier that the 'country program' was really the basic unit of planning and operation, and if the commodity and functional activities [in what we have called the physical approach] had been regarded more clearly as services that were centralized for convenience, but which did not as it were have a separate life of their own. The first couple of Congressional presentations were fuzzed up pretty badly by the attempt to explain what we were trying to do as if the two approaches were equally valid as bases for planning, and therefore for measurement of success in reaching objectives. If this had been realized earlier, we would have been more aware, sooner, that structural changes, requiring a longer period of sustained effort, would be required to solve the country problems with which the agency was trying to deal. As long as you measured success by industrial and agricultural indices, you could 'prove' to others, and gradually come to believe yourself, that the crucial problems were really being solved. But looking at the country problem as a whole, it was impossible to come to so easy (and erroneous) a conclusion. Thus the ideas about organization, in the early stages of ECA, limited the degree to which the agency could leave a legacy of enduring progress." Memorandum to the writer, August 14, 1953.

together to a greater extent on the fundamental problem of investment, in which both groups had a strong interest.

Management

The administration of the ECA was a Herculean task. It required all the skills and standards of good management. These might have been applied either through a highly regimented administration or one allowing greater scope for individual initiative. Hoffman's own comment on this point is interesting. "There is bound to be some confusion," he said, "if your aim is to get maximum thinking done. My concept of dealing with people in an organization is to try to get the maximum out of each. This creates an impression of some lack of order. The smoothest machine is authoritarian, but you don't get the best out of people that way. When they are expected to think, they operate not as smoothly but much better. I remember one man coming to my office with a request that I keep so-and-so out of his area. I said, 'From now on you're going to get interference; it's inevitable if we try to get every one to feel that his suggestions are wanted.' In government there's a tendency to go on the principle: you keep out of my empire and I'll keep out of yours. I don't think we broke this down wholly in ECA, but we did to a great extent." [15]

The novelty of the ECA operation made flexibility a prime requisite; resourceful thought and action were needed on problems as they arose. But to maintain such flexibility was not easy. Even with constant vigilance and high levels of ability and integrity in management and staff, the engine of a governmental agency may easily develop knocks and wheezes, especially when, as conditions change, internal adjustments have to be made without stopping the machine. Much depends upon the management methods employed.

One key technique emphasized in the ECA was extensive decentralization, combined with measures to assure an essential minimum of control and coordination. As the recovery operation grew and top officials found it necessary to spend more time on relations with the public, with Congress, and with European governments, decentralization was seen to be even more imperative.

Within the broad objectives and principles laid down by Congress, the Administrator was given wide latitude. He had to retain personal responsibility for many policy decisions; others could be delegated to only a few key officers. But the ECA personnel "down the line" were

[15] Interview, New York, October 20, 1954.

given significant roles in policy formation. Desk officers, branch and division chiefs, and special consultants, who were in daily contact with practical problems, were made to feel that they were responsible for recommending policies and procedures. As one European remarked: younger men in government can be only as good as their supervisors will allow them to be. To an extraordinary extent, policy and programing decisions ultimately adopted by the ECA originated within the ranks, instead of being promulgated as dicta from above. There was also a constant flow of important recommendations from field to headquarters; these were particularly crucial on matters requiring consultation with the OEEC or the governments of participating countries.

Decentralization also characterized the ECA's external relations. By using existing channels of trade and finance, the ECA developed a procurement procedure which made it unnecessary to establish a large purchasing wing comparable to those in earlier aid agencies.[16] Thus the ECA was able to remain modest in size while financing and overseeing a procurement operation involving many billions of dollars.

To avoid duplication of existing facilities, extensive use was made of contracts with other governmental and private agencies. In this way arrangements were developed for cable service by the State Department, library service by the State and Agriculture Departments, shipping services by the United States Dispatch Agent, and printing by commercial houses. The ECA cable load, handled by the State Department, was heavy; financial support was given to the department for staffing and re-equipping, which helped streamline the department's communications organization and speed up the delivery and decoding of messages.

Decentralization was also widely applied in operations, notably in personnel management and administrative services. Under broad directives, ECA missions in both Europe and Asia were given a relatively free hand in hiring American and local personnel [17] and in making arrangements for housing, travel, and the like.

One administrative dragon, which fed upon decentralized operations,

[16] See Chapter 4. The detailed review and clearance of requests, before procurement authorizations were issued, were sometimes justly criticized for slowness; with experience the tempo was improved, however, until emergency authorizations could be issued within a week or less.

[17] "The employment of nationals of other countries in both program and administrative activities," commented Alden Boyd, ECA deputy director of administration, "has made a new contribution to personnel lore and has been of itself, where properly exploited, a real contribution to the impact of our program objectives in the participating countries." Memorandum to the writer, November 6, 1952.

was not slain. The ECA faced the perennial question of how to maintain reasonable consistency, orderliness, and adherence to regulations without constructing a body of organizational directives so complex as to hinder rapid adjustment to new conditions. But for the early establishment of an Organization and Management Division and the coordinating efforts of the Executive Secretariat the problem might have become wholly unwieldy. As it was, the agency's *Manual of Operations* became so massive that employees were generally able to read only the parts most directly applicable to them, if that much. The problem grew more burdensome with the passage of detailed legislative amendments to an already complex law, necessitating revisions and expansion in the agency's administrative orders.

Efforts to hold down administrative costs were more successful. Hoffman tried to keep them below a level proposed by Appropriations Committee chairman John Taber. In some instances the attempt was partially self-defeating. Personnel "ceilings" which necessitated chronically excessive workloads—a phenomenon not uncommon in the ECA—led to cumulative fatigue and lowered efficiency and morale. On the other hand, there were instances of overstaffing and, as we shall see, of overlapping in the functions of headquarters and regional offices. But the general record of the agency in this respect was creditable. Administrative costs (exclusive of counterpart funds used) were held to less than half of one percent of the total funds administered.[18]

Much larger savings were made through safeguards and improvements in the administration of program funds. Price-checking alone, for example, led to the recovery of about 120 million dollars. Increasingly realistic programing lowered aid levels for certain countries without basic setbacks to their national economies.

Regional Office and Country Missions

The administrative capabilities of the ECA were also affected by its internal relations—between a headquarters organization in Washington (ECA/W), a regional Office of the Special Representative in Europe (OSR), and a sizable group of country missions. In this part of the or-

---

[18] The ECA was not immune to recurrent criticism of allegedly overliberal local allowances for American personnel stationed overseas. Without attempting to pass on the merits of such criticism, it may be said that this question, involving many points of fact and judgment, was one which had to be dealt with by the U.S. government generally, not independently by a single temporary agency. The cost of such allowances, during the period of our study, was defrayed largely from counterpart funds rather than from dollar appropriations.

ganization's administrative experience there was considerable "muddling through."

The disagreements that developed, especially between the central and regional offices, were not primarily political or bureaucratic. Paul Hoffman, a Republican, and Averell Harriman, a Democrat, serving respectively as Administrator and Special Representative in Europe, avoided party partisanship in the conduct of the program; each had staffs of high competence and integrity. The differences stemmed from another source: the view held in each office concerning its intended or appropriate responsibility and the response of each to the environment in which it functioned.

The regional office (OSR) was deliberately set up at a very high level, to give it adequate status in dealing with the OEEC and the European governments and to give it the ability to attract outstanding men for mission leaders as well as for the OSR. This placed the regional office in a position of near equality with the headquarters organization, wherein it exercised a considerable measure of independence.

Both units were much concerned with large questions of policy and programing, with the economic condition of participating countries, and with the progress of recovery efforts. The Washington office was particularly sensitive, however, to public and Congressional opinion in the United States. It was preoccupied, too, with consultations and clearances with other agencies, with problems of procurement, and with the effects of ECA operations on the domestic economy. The Paris office, on the other hand, was especially alert to European views, to cooperation with the OEEC and top officials in each country, to the problems of joint programing, and to political trends in Europe.

Each office emphasized its views and its role in the inclusive undertaking. Hoffman, as Administrator, remained above the battle on most issues and managed to retain the confidence of both groups. While insisting on his responsibility for ultimate agency decisions on policy—"in Washington, where I had to keep looking over my right shoulder to Congress"—he looked upon a strong regional office as a means of encouraging the European governments and the OEEC to take primary responsibility for operations. "Without a field general and a field headquarters, you couldn't have gotten the job done." [19]

Policy and operations were closely intertwined, however, and it was difficult to define precise areas of responsibility. Among leading executives in the headquarters organization, the regional office was sometimes

[19] Interview cited.

compared to a delegation to an international conference, with the proper tasks of maintaining contacts, conducting negotiations, sending in policy recommendations, carrying out directives received from the home government, and "clearing" with headquarters on all major decisions. The regional organization, on the other hand, looked upon itself as a "theater command" having wide latitude in the conduct of operations and, within the limits of broad directives from headquarters, making important decisions on the spot.

The center of government, regarded in Washington as the only place where diverse interests could be taken into adequate account in making policy, was sometimes looked upon by the European office as "that morass" in which the emergency abroad and the need for flexibility and speed in meeting it were not sufficiently understood, and where decisions better made in the field were at times needlessly altered or delayed. Headquarters personnel tended to the view, sometimes shared by the missions, that the regional office should limit its supervision over mission activities more than the officers in Paris deemed desirable. Each group felt at times that the other was injecting itself too much into detailed operations.

Differences on substantive issues were less marked, but there were a few. The European office, for example, favored aid scheduling which would make possible the accumulation of sizable dollar balances in Europe, as a means of building up reserve economic strength and confidence in the future. The Washington office, facing Congressional attitudes, did not concur.

Thus the ECA had not so much a typical headquarters-regional office problem as a dual-headquarters problem. What developed was characterized by Harriman as "a running battle." [20] The controversies were not marked, according to all accounts, by personal acrimony. They were not disastrous. But the issue of relative spheres of responsibility was never wholly settled. Much time and energy were spent in arriving at workable procedures and in resolving a multitude of questions, large and small. Some of this activity was doubtless unavoidable, but much of it was needless and wasteful. Each of the two units, moreover, expanded unduly certain categories of personnel. The European office, which reached a size of about six hundred Americans plus local employees, was particularly subject to criticism on this account.

It is not difficult to stir up a warm discussion among former ECA executives on the wisdom of the decision to establish a regional office

[20] Interview cited.

with such broad, though not precisely defined, responsibility. Did events justify the decision?

, Those who maintain that they did not point to evidences of inefficiency. Harlan Cleveland for example, expressing a headquarters viewpoint, maintained that the problem

> was solved in fact by having each of the three levels of administration [headquarters, regional office, and missions] participate in just about everything. This kept anybody from being too unhappy but it inflated the staff and slowed down action. But it was always an anomaly to have a second headquarters. The really distinctive function of a regional office was representation —not the making, even by delegation, of government-level decisions. In fact, it proved to be impossible to delegate substantial headquarters authority to OSR for the simple reason that the State Department—and later the Defense Department—had to be consulted daily about important matters, and they never made the slightest move toward a similar delegation of authority to Paris.[21] In practice, the view of most matters from a "regional point of view" didn't mean much. . . . While Linc Gordon was in Paris, we got excellent recommendations on things he worked on personally; this was not, however, because of a "regional point of view" but because Linc is a first-class mind.[22]

Those who defend the establishment of a strong regional office do so principally on grounds of the importance of high-level representation in dealing with the OEEC and the participating governments, the value of day-to-day consultations with top-flight European analysts, and the need for technical and high administrative people to explore problems on the ground and to plan and conduct negotiations. And it is sometimes maintained that an even stronger European office would have enabled the ECA to exert greater influence toward European economic integration.

The case from the standpoint of the regional office has been stated by Lincoln Gordon in these terms: "There was concentrated in Europe, at the OEEC headquarters, both in the national delegations and the Secretariat, a remarkable aggregation of economic policy talent. The great advantage which we in Paris had over our colleagues in Washington was intimate daily contact with these people. Tasca [23] and I used to meet informally and on a regular basis with Marjolin and a

[21] This was no less true after the launching of the Mutual Security Program, when William H. Draper, Jr., was Special Representative in Europe for the State and Defense Departments as well as the MSA.

[22] Memorandum to the writer, August 14, 1953. Lincoln Gordon directed economic programing in the OSR.

[23] Henry Tasca, director, Policy and Plans Staff, OSR.

group of eight or ten extremely intelligent and influential Europeans connected with the OEEC. This atmosphere produced a fermentation of ideas which were the subject of many exchanges between Washington and Paris and played a large part in American policy formation." [24]

The regional office contributed to a heightened awareness of political and economic realities in Europe. This was of immense value in making decisions within the ECA, in conducting consultations with the State Department, and in laying problems before Congressional committees. It was thus possible to maintain the emphasis, first given by the Marshall speech and the work of the Harriman and Herter committees, upon the actualities of the European situation.

These contributions came largely from the upper echelons in the regional organization. Such facts, however, do not support the contention that the regional office needed to be in a position to make broad operating or policy decisions without prior approval from the Washington headquarters. Nor do they appear to justify extensive ECA staff work in Europe which traversed much the same ground as that being covered more thoroughly in Washington.

The part to be played by the country missions was never completely clarified, although their general functions were reasonably definite: to learn about, analyze, and report the economic situation in each country; to take part, through recommendations and comments, in the formulation of ECA programs and policies; and to conduct negotiations about recovery operations in the country, providing technical assistance when requested. The wide differences between countries and, indeed, between the ECA missions themselves, precluded any uniform execution of these duties. Each mission faced a special set of problems.

The missions generally discounted the notion, widely accepted in Washington and Paris, that their proximity to national problems and their sympathetic relations with government officials might affect their objectivity. There were complaints from the missions about complicated directives and about delays in acting on their recommendations. Strongly led missions, as in the United Kingdom, tended at times to discount the importance of detailed instructions attributed to "some desk officer" in one of the headquarters organizations.[25] The missions complained that publicity from Washington sometimes failed to take into account reactions abroad. On the other hand, individual missions were at times criticized by Washington and Paris for exceeding their instructions, or being overresistant to modifications in policies and procedures, or for

[24] Letter to the writer, November 12, 1954.   [25] Interview, Finletter, cited.

identifying themselves too closely with the viewpoints of the governments to which they were accredited.

The foregoing statements do not emphasize the extensive teamwork which in fact prevailed among the various parts of the ECA organization. The treatment has been critical in order to bring out some of the lessons to be learned from the agency's internal administrative experience. It is easy, freed from the pressures and complications that were actually faced, to imagine ways in which the geographically separated parts of the ECA might have been more harmoniously integrated. It is also easy, with such immunity, to make unrealistic pronouncements. With recognition of these risks, a few general observations are offered.

A degree of disharmony was desirable. The appropriate concerns and inevitable biases of each part of the organization needed to be brought into balance by frank contention and the hammering out of differences. Otherwise, important viewpoints would have been suppressed and the benefits of a broader synthesis sacrificed.[26] Many of the difficulties might have been obviated by more careful analysis, at the outset, of the contributions which each part of the agency could best make [27] and by a more specific delineation of the responsibilities of each. Such an exercise undertaken by administrative analysts alone would have had little effect; what was really needed was an earlier and fuller meeting of minds at the top levels of the organization. Given the political setting, the pace of the operation, and the stature and vigor of the persons involved, this would have been difficult to achieve, but perhaps not impossible. Initial agreements could have been revised in the light of experience as the program developed. On the basis of such understandings, organizational patterns, with personnel strengths adjusted to specific duties, might have been more rationally established.

[26] "I had the fortunate experience to serve," commented Paul Porter, "in each of the three centers of responsibility—as a mission chief, as an assistant administrator, and for a time as head of the European regional office. If we had the job to do over again, I would not significantly alter the division of responsibility between the missions, Paris, and Washington. Together they created a balance in a program that had to be responsive to so many different public opinions and so many diverse economic situations and yet to lead firmly and imaginatively toward European integration." Letter cited.

[27] An analysis of this character was prepared, after the program was a year under way, by Harry H. Fite, L. W. Hoelscher, Arthur R. Mosler, and W. J. Sheppard, administrative specialists in the agency and the Bureau of the Budget. Findings were issued in a 136-page study entitled *Survey of Relationships of the Parts of ECA* (Washington 1949). This was followed by further analyses and a long succession of conferences and communications between Washington and the regional office.

For the development of such an approach, several considerations would have been pertinent: the need to avoid the ambiguities which would inevitably flow from splitting responsibility for final policy and operational decisions, and for the detailed staff work needed to prepare these decisions; the desirability of giving the regional office (as was done) a major role in high-level consultations and in proposing or evaluating actions affecting the interests of the OEEC and of Europe as a region; the advisability of giving the missions a similar role in decisions particularly affecting individual countries; and the advantages of decentralizing routine administration.

The line of command to the missions could have been determined with more specific reference to different types of activity. The regional office was well situated to supervise and coordinate personnel administration, public information activity, disbursements from the 5 percent counterpart funds, and many administrative services. On the other hand, broad policy and operating decisions, reached after due consultation, might better have been communicated from Washington directly to both regional office and missions.[28]

The frequent visits which were made to and from the field, and the occasional gatherings of mission chiefs and other responsible officers in Paris and Washington might well have been supplemented by more extensive interchange of key personnel between headquarters, regional, and missions offices, for periods of a year or more, thereby increasing the mutual comprehension of problems as seen from different vantage points. Despite obstacles such as personnel turnover and changes in staffing needs, interchanges of this character did occur to some extent during the later stages of the program.

It has been emphasized that in an operation as unprecedented as the Marshall Plan, adaptability was imperative. The situation was too fluid and complex, and the competence of individuals and organizational units too varied, to warrant any resort to needlessly arbitrary administrative practices. It was often necessary "to play by ear." But a review of the record suggests that the measures mentioned above would probably have made for a more clean-cut administration, reducing rather than increasing frictions within the agency and the necessity for internal delays and adjustments.

[28] Such direct dealings, with messages repeated to the regional office, increased speed and efficiency in handling technical questions relating to allotments, balance-of-payments estimates, and the detailed review of agricultural and industrial projects.

Relations with Congress and Citizen Groups

Although the need for comprehensive presentations to Congress should not be underestimated, it may be noted that this work, extending over several months of each year, imposed a heavy drain on the energies and time of ECA officials and staff members. Each annual program, after painstaking review by the Bureau of the Budget, had to go through Congress twice—first via the two foreign affairs committees and then, after obtaining authorizing votes in both houses, via the two appropriations committees to another Congressional decision. The man-hours needed for this procedure were excessive in relation to the man-hours available for actual operations. As one experienced ECA witness before Congressional committees remarked, "We had to justify the program so often, in such detail, and with such little relationship to other angles of foreign economic policy that Congress gradually took over a part of the process of minute program review that is really an executive function." No real solution was found for this problem, although it was ameliorated somewhat by improved techniques in presentation, and by the willingness of some of the harder-working committee members in Congress to examine carefully in advance of hearings the materials prepared for their consideration and to discuss with top ECA officials questions of special concern to them.

Many of the ECA's problems were relatively new, and their weight and complexity made continuous consultation with members of Congress highly desirable. It was the hope of Senator Vandenberg and other leaders, in both parties, that the so-called watchdog committee would facilitate such liaison. But this committee occupied itself principally with a somewhat ineffectual search for weaknesses in the ECA administration and contributed little to mutual understanding and greater cooperation.

Relations with the Congressional committees and with key members of both houses were handled principally by Hoffman, Harriman, and Foster, and their chief aides, including C. Tyler Wood,[29] R. M. Bissell, Jr., and the chiefs of mission during their visits to Washington. Dossiers were kept on the views of key Congressmen, especially a "middle group" between supporters and detractors. Special responsibility for relationships with Congress was given to C. Tyler Wood, who commanded wide respect for his integrity and judgment.

Rapprochement with Congress might have been furthered by addi-

[29] ECA director of operations.

tional contacts between interested members of both houses and well-
informed officers of the agency below the top administrative tiers.[30] In
discussing the formative period of the Marshall Plan, George Kennan
commented upon the lack of intellectual intimacy between working
members of the legislative and executive branches of the government; [31]
the observation could have been applied with some justification to the
ECA.

The value of the ECA's Public Advisory Board (PAB), established
by Congressional mandate, was at times discounted within the agency,
but in Hoffman's mind there was no question on this score after the
board was formed, although at first he had looked with some dismay
upon the idea of "another group" to which to report. The advisory board
became, in his opinion, "of inestimable value." In it were "good representatives" of business, labor, farm groups, and the professions. A real
attempt was made by ECA to keep them informed, and monthly reports
to this body were "a most valuable discipline." Its members became
"active participants in making policy," and because they understood the
program, they contributed to understanding and support among such
important bodies as the American Farm Bureau Federation, the National
Grange, the National Farmers Union, the CIO, the AFL, and important
national business organizations.

Public Information

The fortunes of the recovery program depended to a very large extent on public understanding. It will be recalled that vigorous publicizing by private agencies and government leaders was important in the
American decision to support the Marshall Plan. Hoffman reportedly
felt that to run the ECA without a strong information arm would be
as futile as trying to conduct a major business without sales, advertising,
and customer-relations departments.[32] The ECA's informational activities in the United States were designed to keep the Marshall Plan before the American people. In Europe they were aimed at making clear
to as many people as possible the fundamental purposes of the Marshall
Plan as an expression of American foreign policy and at dramatizing
the contributions being made through it to European recovery.

[30] Considerable help was given by ECA personnel to the employed staffs of
interested Congressional committees.

[31] Interview, Washington, February 19, 1953.

[32] Memorandum from Robert R. Mullen (ECA director of information) to Donald
C. Stone (director of administration), May 15, 1951.

After a somewhat uncertain beginning, the ECA's domestic information program gained momentum under the direction of Robert R. Mullen.[33] Individuals of high standing in journalistic and related professions were brought into the agency to guide its informational work. Effective contacts were established with all types of media, and the voluminous information made available through these channels added up in the end to an impressive account of work and accomplishment through the Marshall Plan Operation.

Real difficulties, however, had to be faced. To present the facts on gradual economic developments in such a manner as to attract wide attention was not easy, especially when the events did not impinge immediately and obviously upon the day-to-day concerns of large numbers of people. Another difficulty, which the ECA shared with the State Department, was the lack of a large domestic clientele.[34] The interests which it represented frequently appeared more alien to many Americans than those reflected in other government departments. This was a real handicap in meeting taxpayer resistance and the recurrent if unsubstantiated charges that "give-away" programs were impoverishing the country.[35] There was always the risk that the dissemination of factual information about the recovery effort would be interpreted as bureaucratic advertising designed to build up support for appropriations.[36]

So many influences enter into the formation of American public opinion that an evaluation of the effectiveness of ECA activities in this field is peculiarly difficult. One measure is the public opinion poll. But even if identical questions are used at stated intervals, this type of survey reflects the play of many influences, among which any public information program is but one. In the present case the results are far from conclusive.[37] One interesting fact stands out in the polls, however: midway in

[33] Previously an editorial writer for *Life* magazine.

[34] The State Department, remarked former Secretary Acheson, "has no constituency in the sense that Commerce and Agriculture do." Interview cited.

[35] From 1948 to 1952 Marshall aid to the recovery of nations upon which the U.S. was economically and strategically dependent amounted to less than 2 percent of the gross national product.

[36] The "Dworshak amendment" to the Mutual Security Act of 1952 (Public Law 400, 82d Congress, 2d Session, Sec. 537) prohibited the use of mutual security or counterpart funds for "general propaganda" in the U.S. in support of the program or for the travel or other expenses of U.S. citizens abroad for the purpose of publicizing the program.

[37] For example, a Gallup poll, reported in November 1948, indicated that 82 percent of those queried knew about the Marshall Plan, 53 percent believed that Congress should appropriate funds for the following year's operations, 11 percent believed that it should not, and 18 percent had no opinion. According to a February

the program support for it was substantially higher among those who saw it as basically a rehabilitation effort—a viewpoint which the ECA consistently fostered—than among those who looked upon it as a charity.

Were there any notable shortcoming in the ECA's domestic information program? Did the agency do as much as it could to give people a comprehensive picture of developments and to explain their significance to American interests? On both questions, wide divergences of opinion have been found. Two criticisms appear to merit mention. One is that the information work was too fragmentary, with too little broad planning and execution in relation to major objectives. "Many of our information people," said one ECA critic, "were too much newspapermen." The other stricture, on which views differed sharply, is that information officers in Washington were not brought into the top councils of the agency often enough to enable them to do an adequate job in interpreting the ECA's broader aims and impact. As one executive put it, they were not always "in on the kill" when important decisions were made.

Months after the European Recovery Program was ended, Hoffman remarked somewhat ruefully that "people still think of ECA as a great charity." [38] Somehow, the breadth of outlook with which the Marshall Plan was launched and conducted during its formative period was not adequately sustained among the American people. More was needed than a succession of spot news stories and features, however well presented—more even than ably prepared releases on European integration. What was wanting was a deeper public understanding of the way

---

1950 report, 65 percent were informed about the Plan, 31 percent believed that the 3 billion dollars requested by the President for its support (in 1950–1951) should be voted by Congress, 26 percent believed that it should not, and 8 percent had no opinion. In May of the same year 63 percent were stated to have given a "generally correct" answer to the question: "Will you tell me, offhand, what the Marshall Plan is?" When asked for opinions on the 3 billion dollars proposed for the following year, as compared to 4 billion for the current year, 28 percent thought that the amount was "about right," 4 percent considered it "too little," 22 percent regarded it as "too much" and 9 percent had no opinion—aside from the 37 percent who were uninformed. Among the informed, 46 percent of those who looked upon the program as "charity" believed the amount was about right or too little, 40 percent thought it too much, and 14 percent had no opinion; for those who looked upon it as "rehabilitation," the corresponding percentages were 61, 26, and 13. *Public Opinion Quarterly*, Spring 1949, Spring and Summer 1950. These findings did not of course show the relative importance of different influences, nor were they accurately indicative of changes in opinion, due to variations in the wording of the questions used.

[38] Interview, New York, January 28, 1953.

in which the recovery program fitted into the free world's epic task of acquiring the economic strength and dynamism essential to political cohesion and military security. Had this developed, a better balance between economic and military policy might have been achieved after the advent of the defense program, and better relations might have been maintained between the United States and the nations looking to it for leadership.

To imply that the ECA, singlehanded, should have promoted the extensive public education and debate required to produce such a result would be unfair. It had been given no such mandate. The job was one for all informed leaders of opinion. Perhaps no one could have foreseen how much thought and effort would still be needed before the free nations could develop a strong and durable international economic system. In any event, the "big story" with which the Marshall Plan started lost a part of its vitality whenever, in a changing environment, it remained static.

The overseas information program, after a modest beginning, became much bigger, more varied, and in some ways more effective than the information program in the United States. Among the reasons for this, two were particularly significant. The first was that many Congressmen who tended to look askance at conspicuous publicity within the United States by a governmental agency took a different view of ECA publicity abroad. Alarmed by the stupendous effort of the Communists to undermine American prestige in Europe, various members of Congress encouraged the ECA to intensify its informational efforts overseas. The agency's strong bipartisan support gave it freedom to respond to such urgings. The second reason for the size and vigor of the ECA's overseas information programs was that the funds available for them were far more ample than those the home office could tap. This was due to the fortuitous circumstance that the 5 percent local currency counterpart funds generated by grant aid and made freely available to the United States government could be drawn upon, in a manner never anticipated when these accounts were first established, for the conduct of informational activities. In this, and in the fact that Harriman, Roscoe Drummond,[39] and others recognized the importance of informational efforts overseas, lies the explanation for a rise in outlays for such work from about $500,000 dollars (equivalent) a year to approximately 20 million dollars.

From small beginnings in 1948, the ECA's overseas information pro-

[39] Appointed, in 1949, as information director in the ECA's European office.

gram expanded until three years later it was employing 224 Americans and 782 Europeans and using millions of dollars' worth of equipment.[40]

ECA information officers in Europe sat in on top-level policy conferences and were fully informed on policy developments. But they also faced many problems. A large proportion of them had never worked outside the United States before; few had had experience in international relations.[41] They were confronted with formidable barriers of language and culture. They faced, as we have seen, a stupendous effort by the Communists to discredit the Marshall Plan. Spending lavishly [42] and operating when they could through local party and labor organizations, the Communists worked with an intimate knowledge of local conditions and without the appearance of overt foreign intervention. "That the Communists operate as indigenous groups," commented Alfred Friendly,[43] "is the central fact with which any information program, large or small, must cope as best it can."

A striking evolution took place in the conception of the job to be done and how to do it. "Our first task in Europe," noted Friendly, "was simply to tell the Europeans what the Marshall Plan was. It was an absolutely novel venture." [44] The idea that one nation would transfer part of its current output to a group of other nations, with very few strings attached and for the benefit of all, was too paradoxical for easy acceptance. But as the operation expanded, information became the handmaiden of the recovery program in all aspects where public understanding and cooperation were vital. Paul Porter wrote:

In everything we did we sought to change or strengthen opinions—opinions about how to build free world strength, about America's role, cooperative effort by Europeans, investment, productivity, fiscal stability, trade, rearmament, industrial competition, free labor unions, etc. How else could this be done except by the democratic process which relies upon information? [45]

Nielsen, in describing the ECA information effort, declared that it

[40] Waldemar Nielsen (successor to Drummond as ECA regional director of information) in a memorandum on "The Information Program of the ECA in Europe" (1954).

[41] *Ibid.*

[42] One observer stated that in France alone the Communists spent more for printing and radio programs than the United States did for food shipments and that their propaganda staffs outmanned that of the ECA by fifty to one.

[43] First ECA information chief in Europe (later assistant managing editor of the *Washington Post*), in letter to Thomas K. Ford, May 29, 1954.

[44] Letter cited.

[45] Letter to the writer, September 15, 1954.

tended more and more to become a working alliance with various European groups, including labor unions, groups working for European unification and various anti-Communist elements. More and more its propaganda technique was indirect, and more and more its objectives were to change basic political, social, and economic attitudes in Europe rather than merely to advertise or explain American policy.[46]

Three aspects of the European information program are especially noteworthy. First, the ECA became a prolific source of ideas in such specialized activities as documentary film making, radio production, news photography, local exhibits, and traveling exhibitions. With ECA assistance, documentary moving pictures were issued by European producers using local facilities for dubbing films in different languages; these were frequently distributed through commercial channels to reach mass audiences. Arrangements were made with local standard-wave broadcasting chains instead of relying on shortwave broadcasts as did the Voice of America before 1948. Mobile exhibition units were found to be most effective in countries such as Greece, Turkey, and southern Italy where other media were not highly developed.[47]

Second, ECA information specialists took part in the conduct of technical assistance and productivity programs through the development and use of audio-visual aids, assistance in the conduct of demonstrations and training programs, and the transmission of skills in the use of these techniques. "Many millions of farmers, foremen and workers," stated Andrew Berding,[48] "learned more about their own line of work through the efforts conducted by the ECA information people." An outstanding example was the German agricultural information program. Information staffs thus had a training function quite distinct from their normally recognized field of work.

Third, a special ECA division was created with regional and mission staff members to deal with labor information. The division was made up of American trade union people who had entree to European non-Communist unions. They undertook to extend among working groups an understanding of the purposes of the Marshall Plan and to show the benefits that could be achieved through greater productivity and free trade unions. In contrast with earlier American information programs addressed to the intelligentsia and the economically privileged—with

[46] Letter to the writer, September 16, 1954.
[47] Nielsen, memorandum cited.
[48] ECA information officer in Europe, subsequently MSA director of information. Letter to Thomas K. Ford, June 8, 1954.

reading rooms, for example, usually located on fashionable shopping streets—this part of the ECA's informational activity was intended for and channeled through working class groups. "This did not represent a new idea," Nielsen affirmed, "but in terms of emphasis, persistence, and technique it has no real precedent in the history of U.S. overseas propaganda." [49]

The ECA public information program in Europe, as in the United States, is difficult to evaluate. Drawing upon the earlier postwar experience of the American High Commissioner's office in surveying German public opinion, the ECA fostered inquiries with multinational studies, investigating the effect of single programs or single media and the total effect of United States policies and programs on public opinion in Europe. This research was done chiefly through contracts with European commercial research organizations whose formation and activities the ECA helped to promote.[50] These polls furnished useful data on public opinion trends to which ECA informational activity had to be adapted, but they did not justify any general conclusions about the effect of ECA informational efforts. Other means of assessing the effectiveness of ECA informational work in Europe are necessarily more subjective, but a number of general observations may be ventured.

As John Hutchison remarked:

The Marshall Plan information program in Europe was a rather free-wheeling, large-spending operation conducted by persons who, in the main, had very little bureaucratic experience. They were greenhorns in the field of foreign propaganda, but they brought to a rather rigid and unimaginative program . . . fresh, invigorating and oftentimes wonderfully effective techniques.[51]

These techniques were used to support the Marshall Plan operation and contributed to the enormous impression it made upon attitudes and hopes in Europe.

[49] Memorandum cited.

[50] For example, enough business was provided by the ECA to enable Eric Stern, a former Roper executive, to take an active role in organizing a number of European public opinion survey companies; the American Advertising Council cooperated in this effort. The Gallup and Roper-Wilson firms were also active, and the ECA contracted for the services of a number of such commercial organizations. Findings from the polls conducted under contract with the ECA were made available to news organs and other private European and American agencies, including the Committee for a Free Europe. Interview, Robert R. Mullen, Washington, May 31, 1954; Nielson, memorandum cited.

[51] Memorandum to Thomas K. Ford, June 7, 1954.

The information program helped minimize the effect of adverse influences. Considerable pressure, for example, came from the United States for greater publicity on the source of the aid and for eliciting more expressions of gratitude for American assistance. The ECA staff in Europe knew that too great an emphasis on American labels might boomerang and succeeded in playing it down. During the last two years of the program, when the mood in Europe became more grim and enthusiasm for American leadership was dampened by the apprehensions and burdens associated with rearmament, a special effort was made to help counteract this negative trend.

A further observation, supported by Americans and Europeans alike, is that when local initiative was lacking and American staffs felt that they had to assume directly the major burden for informational programs, the programs were less successful and more mistakes were made. Unwitting affronts to local sentiments and attitudes were more likely, as were attempts to inform and persuade peoples through symbols having little relevance to their cultures. Said Donald Mallett, for instance: "American publicity has been vigorous. At times it has given more appearance of American intervention, to which Europeans are sensitive, than seemed desirable." [52] The information programs which netted the best results, in the opinion of Europeans consulted, were those based upon an intimate awareness of local attitudes, habits of thought, problems, and needs. Programs conducted with, through, and whenever possible, by nationals of a country representing different social groups, were at once more acceptable and less productive of negative reactions than those initiated entirely by even the most energetic and resourceful Americans.[53]

ECA informational work abroad had important effects on subsequent United States activities in this field. For about four years State Department and ECA informational programs were conducted side by side. There was some overlapping but their spheres of attention were generally different. The personnel in the two organizations was markedly

[52] Interview, Paris, November 18, 1952.

[53] A further lesson was drawn by Allan L. Swim, ECA regional information officer, when he said: "I personally think that propaganda is no good unless it's tied to something—what I call functional propaganda. At the same time there are dangers in getting too far ahead of what can be accomplished, thus raising false expectations. There are times of real emergency when you have to go ahead and work for quick results, forgetting everything else. But such times are risky when you think in terms of over-all consequences." Interview, Paris, November 4, 1952.

different—the one group more conservative in approach, the other more willing to risk making mistakes as a price of vigorous action.[54] Some friction was to be expected, but the parallel efforts afforded a yardstick and competitive stimulus for each other.

In 1952 the two programs began to merge, by organization of joint staffs in the field and by closer cooperation in Washington. As integration progressed, it was seen that many of the innovations and emphases introduced in connection with the Marshall Plan could be preserved. Many ECA specialists were given key posts in a new combined information agency.[55] The merger found numerous former "greenhorns" in international information activity working quite effectively with "striped pants" colleagues, bringing to the combined effort experience, attitudes, and techniques which, in the opinion of many, energized and notably improved American informational activities overseas. John Hutchison, as an executive of the new agency, expressed the view that "from the standpoint of both competition and contribution, ECA moved the whole U.S. information development ahead several years." [56]

THE SEPARATE-AGENCY ISSUE

The foregoing discussion may provide background for a consideration of the question whether the decision to establish a separate agency was well conceived or whether it would have been better if the program had been conducted by an existing government department. The issue never developed into a real contest. Sentiment in Congress, as we have seen, favored the creation of a new organization designed specifically

[54] Attempting to view such differences objectively, Nielsen wrote: "ECA information officers were characterized by bureaucratic naïveté, high morale and great enthusiasm, superior competence in their respective professional fields, interest in but lack of knowledge about the people and cultures they were dealing with. Most of these qualities proved double-edged. Ignorance of and indifference to red tape, for example, produced momentum and speed in the early days and led to imaginative projects and inventiveness; but it also produced some foolish projects as well as interagency frictions and unnecessary alarm on the part of regular foreign service officers. Openhandedness and absence of guile sometimes won friends in unexpected places, but sometimes backfired. . . . I would not deny that exaggerated loyalties developed in the two groups, including a free exchange of critical comments. . . . But this inevitable and essentially superficial sniping hardly defines the real relationship. . . . The two groups complemented each other at least as much as they duplicated." Memorandum cited.

[55] The U.S. Information Service (USIS) under the Department of State, was given separate status in 1953 as the United States Information Agency (USIA), and most of the information work of the MSA was transferred to it.

[56] Memorandum cited.

to accomplish an emergency operation with maximum efficiency. Some key officials in the executive branch, including Marshall, Lovett, and Harriman, personally favored this course, whereas others, including James E. Webb and Donald Stone of the Bureau of the Budget, were opposed.[57]

The hypothetical question of whether it would have been wiser to launch the operation under State Department auspices has often been informally debated. It has been contended, in favor of such a course, that there would have been smoother continuity in United States foreign policy and relations, with no necessity for other governments to adjust to "another" American agency; that the government would have spoken more clearly with one voice in its foreign affairs; and that the bargaining advantages afforded by such large American aid could have been used to better effect in relation to the country's over-all economic, commercial, diplomatic, and security interests. Against this view some have maintained that the interests, functions, and procedures of the State Department or any other long-established agency were diffused and ill adapted to such a concentration on a massive program as was envisaged. What was involved, they held, was not the conduct of continuing, long-term relationships, but the management under pressure of a huge emergency enterprise. This task, they asserted, required leadership skilled in practical economic operations; it needed to be freed from the braking effect of irrelevant procedures.

Operational Efficiency

Within the ECA, as one might expect, the consensus was that a special agency made for operational efficiency. "As a spot rush operation," said Finletter, for example, "it would never have been as effectively done had the job been given to an established department. For one thing, they couldn't have gotten the men—like Hoffman, Harriman, Foster, and the chiefs of mission. Imagine trying to get men of the caliber we did secure for some of the missions to come in as economic counselors within the embassies."[58] "There was no need," remarked Glenn Craig, industry division chief, "to answer for everything to a bureaucracy.

[57] A Gallup poll indicated that among the people of the country with opinions on the subject, a slight majority favored control and supervision by the State Department. *Public Opinion Quarterly*, Spring 1948.

[58] Interview cited. The ECA's special advantage in recruiting was reduced in the later phases of the operation when it became more difficult to obtain, for an uncertain and probably short future period, personnel of the caliber of those secured earlier for key posts.

Things could be done fast." [59] Frank Dennis, a regional information officer, recalled: "The time was short. The attitude was: Let's get ahead with the job and see what's the best we can do in a limited period of time, being willing to risk mistakes in order to get the job done. This was in contrast to the prevailing attitude in other agencies where there was more of a tendency to protect permanent careers by playing it safe." [60]

Dissenting opinions were to be found in some of the established departments. A vigorous new agency with such important functions was bound to be disruptive and, some felt, detrimental to efficiency. At the same time, it was generally recognized that given the political situation in the United States there was no alternative to a separate agency. And it was generally conceded that the ECA established an outstanding record of performance.

Cooperation with Other Agencies

Much depended upon interagency cooperation. The responsibilities of the ECA, though well defined by law, impinged upon those of the State, Treasury, and Defense Departments and to a less extent the Export-Import Bank and the Departments of Commerce, Agriculture, and the Interior. The most important relationship was with the State Department. Referring to the first two years, Hoffman said, "We never had any friction at the higher levels with State in those earlier days— with Marshall, Lovett, and Acheson." [61] The qualifying words "higher levels" and "earlier days" are noteworthy. "In the first year," commented a former special assistant in the ECA, "we had endless difficulties in clearances and discussions with State and Treasury. In the second year, they were much less interested." "The reason," answered a former division director, "is that we were way ahead; the operation was becoming professionalized." [62]

Although concord was much more frequent than discord,[63] there were numerous instances of friction, mostly relating to procedures and prerogatives rather than to principle.[64] Occasionally, divergent judg-

[59] Group interview, July 16, 1953.   [60] Interview, Paris, November 17, 1952.
[61] Interview cited.

[62] Samuel Van Hyning and Glenn Craig, group interview cited.

[63] One evidence is an almost complete lack of news stories on controversies between the State Department and the ECA.

[64] One substantive issue, discussed elsewhere, involved an emphasis by the ECA upon a "regional" approach to the problem of currency convertibility in Europe as opposed to a "universalist" approach favored by some officials in the State and Treasury Departments.

ments arose from the application of economic and political criteria to decisions on aid allotments. Yet a provision in the Economic Coopera-tion Act for the settlement of differences by referral to the President was never employed.

Certain of the difficulties were attributable to the vigor and drive with which the recovery operation was conducted. "In some countries," remarked Foster, "ECA took the play away from State." [65] During the formative period of planning and programing, when the ECA was espe-cially active in the formulation of government policy in the economic field, joint interests were extensive and the State Department was not always as fully consulted as it felt it should be. After Foster became ECA Administrator, he and Under-Secretary of State James E. Webb held weekly luncheon meetings to discuss questions of concern to both agencies. Foster maintained later that no specific cases developed in which the ECA had in fact taken actions contrary to State Department policy.[66]

Relations between American embassies and ECA missions, after initial adjustments had been made, were for the most part amicable; a decisive factor was the caliber of ambassadors and mission chiefs. The statutory provision that ECA mission chiefs should rank next to ambassadors appears to have been galling to some career foreign service officers. On the other hand, some mission chiefs felt that their status and scope of responsibility were not sufficiently recognized by the em-bassies. "I held out," said Foster, "for a general as against a complete and detailed control by the ambassador. The latter might have been ac-ceptable if the ambassadors had been able to spend the time needed to provide detailed supervision. But it didn't work out that way." [67]

Disagreements on important issues between embassies and missions were infrequent, but when they occurred, for example in Belgium, Italy, or Indonesia, the influence of the American government was impaired. Cooperation was most satisfactory when all United States representatives in an area were able to work as a "country team" under the broad super-vision of a resourceful ambassador. Where this was done, many dual assignments were worked out which enabled one man, from either the State Department or the ECA, to serve as economic counselor, agricul-tural officer, or labor advisor in both embassy and mission.

A viewpoint not uncommon among United States diplomatic person-nel overseas was expressed by Winthrop Brown, economic counselor of the embassy in London: "Certainly one needs new infusion of blood in

[65] Interview cited.   [66] Interview cited.   [67] Interview cited.

government from time to time, especially as old-line agencies grow tired or conservative. But, on the United States side, the new agencies may lead to conflict and friction and lack of clarity in our policies and dealings. It is very important to get greater unity in the United States position than was the case during the handling of the ECA program. Though I don't know the answers, I do know that at times the business of the body politic was hindered by the diffusion of authority. There are operating problems which State can't and shouldn't handle. What is needed, I think, is a little guidance—not too much. If and where there is no such guidance, there is a tendency for new people to go their own ways and to bring about confusion in our councils." [68]

A widely held ECA viewpoint was voiced by Harry Fite, administrative director in the OSR: "The real question is whether old-line agencies can graft on really big new functions, or whether they may not be just too big and unwieldy to do so. Complaints with respect to the problems developed when a new agency goes into operation provide a good checklist as to what an agency should look out for, rather than a valid argument against new agencies." [69] Expressed in these terms, the two points of view do not appear to be irreconcilable.

As previously noted, the interagency problems of the ECA and its successor, the MSA, grew more complicated after their functions became closely intertwined with those of other governmental bodies concerned with the defense program. The adjustments then needed were exceptionally difficult and involved; [70] delay in achieving effective integration was a real deterrent to operational efficiency.

Reactions Abroad

The ECA greatly increased the contacts between Americans and governmental and private agencies in Europe. Some Americans felt that the adjustments required were upsetting. Winthrop Brown, for example, held that "new people coming in and talking more freely creates at first a period of turmoil. It is painful to the governments with which we deal to have to go through fundamentals again and again with new agencies." [71] Harriman, on the other hand, felt that the widening of contacts

[68] Interview, London, November 12, 1952.

[69] Interview, Paris, November 17, 1952.

[70] For a detailed discussion, see MSA, *First Report to Congress,* pp. 44–48. Efforts toward more satisfactory coordination continued beyond the period of our study. President Eisenhower's Reorganization Plan No. 7, sent to Congress on June 1, 1953, culminated in the establishment of a single Foreign Operations Administration (FOA). See *New York Times,* June 2, 1953.

[71] Interview cited.

was beneficial from the outset and that in the participating countries "there was frequently a preference for not dealing through diplomatic channels; they didn't want to appear to be under political pressures." [72] Vincent Barnett, deputy chief of the ECA mission in Italy, believed that through separate-agency dealings it was "possible to work, not always formally, through people whom experience has taught you can get the job done." [73]

Among the Europeans consulted on this question, there was a clear consensus that the extended relationships provided through the ECA were highly advantageous to the recovery program and to mutual understanding generally. Some statements to this effect were qualified, however, by the observation that overstaffing and overzealous advocacy of policies without adequate appreciation of a country's internal problems tended to lessen the net gain. Among the flaws detected in the operation of the ECA as an independent agency was a tendency to cover too much ground. One official,[74] for example, emphasized what he called "maintenance of the objective. This is pretty hard in war," he said, "but it is doubly so in a peacetime activity because of the difficulty of defining the objective. It never really can be simple. We always need to seek three or four things at least, at the same time, since if we achieve one only and miss the rest the taste will be bitter and not sweet as we expected. But just because our objectives in peacetime are complicated it is absolutely vital that we continually seek to simplify them. I think it can fairly be maintained that energy was wasted and direction lost because the ECA, in particular, allowed too many minor activities to be encouraged under the shelter of its major interests. No doubt all of them were important and no doubt there were pretty important reasons to induce the ECA to accept so many strange bedfellows, but it was unquestionably a source of friction in Paris and doubtless in the national capitals as well."

Alternatives for the Future

Experience with the ECA as a separate agency should throw some light on the alternatives for the future in administering American economic operations abroad. While debates about the character and extent of those operations will continue, there is little ground for expectation that they can be terminated or long suspended in the foreseeable future. What would otherwise have been a large dollar gap has been bridged by a substantial rise in the "offshore procurement" of defense items and

---

[72] Interview cited.   [73] Interview, Rome, December 19, 1952.
[74] Unnamed by request.

other American military expenditures in Europe, thus compensating for the reduction in direct economic aid to Europe. As these outlays taper off, and unless trade is considerably increased, the shortage of dollar foreign exchange may reassert itself. Even after Europe reaches full economic self-reliance, many questions of relationship and cooperation in the Atlantic community will remain, and problems of economic policy and development in other parts of the world are sure to persist into an indefinite future.

In his message to Congress on reorganization for the conduct of foreign operations, President Eisenhower pointed out that the history of recent decades had brought a "profound and irrevocable change" in the role of the United States in world affairs. It seems evident that this change involves our economic as well as our political and defense relationships and that unless the United States assumes a leading role for many years to come there is little hope that a steady course can be charted for safeguarding economic stability and progress among free nations.

This being so, the question of how best to organize United States economic operations abroad becomes important for the long term. It becomes necessary to consider such operations not merely as a succession of short-range emergency programs, but rather as a major instrument in the continuing pursuit of American and free-world objectives.

Since the ECA was a temporary agency for an emergency operation, and since its effectiveness depended in part on its ability to enlist outstanding leadership for a short period, the relevance of its administrative experience to the long-range conduct of American foreign economic relations might be questioned. Yet the four-year experience of the ECA was substantial, and its achievement, if the analysis in this chapter is correct, was attributable to many factors, among which its emergency character was only one. Looked at as a whole, it is suggested, the ECA experience lends support to the following tentative conclusions.

First, that if measures are devised to assure proper over-all integration of policies and relationships, American foreign economic operations can be conducted by a well-managed separate agency with a degree of initiative, cohesion, flexibility, economy, and efficiency difficult to attain —individually or collectively—in the existing permanent agencies of the government, each of which has a wide range of other responsibilities.

Second, that continuity in the work of such an agency is essential. Continuity is especially important for long-range planning, for stability in relations with other agencies and governments, and for preservation of experience and momentum. The extent to which American economic operations abroad have become an important continuing activity, distinct from traditional diplomatic, commercial, military, and informational interests of the United States, warrants serious consideration of the establishment of a permanent agency—at a Cabinet level, as the ECA was. Its establishment would imply a recognition that the American government's economic relations abroad are interdependent and coordinate with, not subordinate to, the diplomatic, military, and psychological goals of United States foreign relations. The responsibilities of such an agency should be defined in relation to secular trends and the longer-range objectives of American economic policy, as well as in relation to more immediate emergency situations. The agency would need a full complement of "tools" or methods, sanctioned by law, for the versatile conduct of foreign economic activities. And provision should be made to assure adaptability in expanding or contracting operations in any area or region.

Third, that although funds for emergency operations must be controlled through annual reviews, longer-term programs, including those for technical assistance and new economic development, if they are to be well planned and productive, need to be assured of essential working reserves for much longer periods of time. Without such reserves, it is more difficult to give effective encouragement abroad to courageous, appropriate measures for the solution of long-run problems of economic policy and development.

Fourth, that all official American economic, financial, and commercial relationships with any country or region should be coordinated. The relationships established with such international bodies as the United Nations specialized agencies, its Social and Economic Council, and the OEEC should have as much continuity as possible, whether these relationships are conducted by a separate agency responsible for foreign economic operations or by other parts of the American government.

Finally, that in view of the enormous impact abroad of American economic policies and programs and the need for vigilance in safeguarding the domestic economy, it would be difficult to overemphasize the importance of bringing to the sustained study and administration of the nation's foreign economic affairs the finest talent that can be found.

CHAPTER 12

Conceptions and Goals
of European Recovery

"ONE of the subjects that has interested me," remarked James Reston,[1] "is how the necessities of politics may produce very imaginative things. The Marshall Plan idea I regard as the most positive and hopeful produced in the postwar years. The exigencies of the time forced people into new fields of inquiry."

The aim of this chapter is to analyze briefly the development which occurred between 1947 and 1952 in the conceptions and goals of economic recovery in Europe. Until 1947 it had been generally assumed that the massive relief and rehabilitation program conducted through UNRRA, supplemented by measures to facilitate international loans, payments and trade—through the International Bank for Reconstruction and Development, the Export-Import Bank, the International Monetary Fund, the International Trade Organization, and the General Agreement on Trade and Tariffs—would enable Europe to get on its feet again. But the crisis of 1947 destroyed these assumptions. Clearly, a bold new approach was needed.

The Marshall Plan was intended to provide such an approach. The new element was that the aid provided was to be employed for fundamental economic recovery rather than for temporary relief and rehabilitation. The Marshall Plan still involved an emergency approach,

---

[1] Washington correspondent, *New York Times.* Interview, March 17, 1953.

but the major aim was to help the participating countries attain a degree of economic self-reliance that would render them independent of extraordinary external aid after 1952. Although the projected aid would amount to less than 5 percent of the total national product of the participating countries, it was to consist in large part of equipment and commodities which Europe could not produce and which therefore were much more important than such a low percentage might suggest. The goods and services required were often essential for the enlargement or linking together of complex production processes.

Impetus from Aid Programing

To be effective, aid had to be adjusted to the resources, needs, and policies of the participating countries; within this context, each country would justify to the OEEC and the ECA its requests for assistance. Similarly, local currency counterpart funds had to be used in conjunction with other financial resources. Thus the programing of aid and counterpart gave impetus to general mobilization of national resources for recovery. This effect was enhanced by the consultations in the OEEC, during which each country's economic and financial situation was reviewed and opinions were given on recovery measures being taken. "When working in an organization like the OEEC," said Dagfin Juel of Norway [2] for example, "you learn a lot about economic problems and how different countries are dealing with them; some of these problems are very important to the Norwegian economy."

Aid programing also stimulated a consideration of European resources as a whole. "When we took up the total aid to be requested and the amount for each country," said Sacha Gueronik of the OEEC Secretariat,[3] "we had to consider existing production and export and import programs of the individual countries. The requests for United States aid had to be kept to essentials. This enabled us to ask countries with surpluses to help others, in order to lessen the requests for American aid. Thus there were switches to make better use of total resources."

Evolution in Economic Analysis

From early discussions of the division and use of aid, a definite progression was traceable in thinking about European recovery, in the

---

[2] Chief, International Cooperation Division, Ministry of Commerce. Interview, Oslo, November 25, 1952.

[3] Head of the Directorate of Technical Services and Programmes. Interview, Paris, November 15, 1952.

techniques of analysis employed, and in the goals on which agreement was reached. Thinking about the administration of aid for each country generally began with the preparation of "shopping lists" of needed supplies and equipment. It soon advanced to a broader consideration of aid in relation to the country's balance-of-payments position, and it proceeded toward a national-accounts approach, a more sophisticated type of analysis which provided a framework within which essential data could be intelligibly interrelated.[4] This progression may be traced in the succession of problems tackled by the OEEC and the ECA and the institutional means developed for dealing with them.

THE COUNTRY APPROACH

A full comparative study of the conceptions and emphases developed by the participating countries in their recovery programs would be highly instructive; a good starting point exists in the national reports made periodically to the OEEC. Such an analysis, which would have to take account of wide differences among the economies involved, would be more elaborate than the limits of this volume permit. An effort will be made therefore simply to illustrate succinctly, with no pretension of comprehensiveness, some of the variations in the problems faced, and in the thinking, actions, and policies which emerged.

Each country tried to pursue simultaneously four objectives, which frequently counteracted each other: first, a substantial increase in production, which put emphasis on investments; second, restoration of internal financial stability in countries suffering from or threatened by inflation, which necessitated limitations on investment; third, greater integration with the rest of the European economy for the sake of expanding markets and trade, which sometimes required major internal adjustments; and fourth, dollar savings and increased exports to acquire dollar exchange, which sometimes deprived Europe of goods needed there. When in some countries the benefits of economic improvement did not automatically "trickle down" to all economic groups, a fifth objective was added: better distribution of income to bolster markets, incentives, and social stability.

The interplay of these aims may be briefly illustrated. One problem running through all the country programs was the achievement of a balance between inflationary and deflationary influences. This was at times referred to in ECA jargon as reaching a position of "flation."

[4] See Richard and Nancy Ruggles, *European National Accounts* (ECA, Washington, 1951).

In some economies tight financial controls had to be relaxed to encourage investments; in others, it was feared that high rates of investment might generate uncontrollable inflationary pressures. The factors affecting capacity for economic growth, on the one hand, and financial stability along with such growth, on the other, were complex; they differed greatly between countries.

The way in which each country approached its recovery effort was conditioned, furthermore, by political attitudes and administrative practices. Differences appeared between the approaches favored in economies which were extensively "planned" and those which were not. There were discrepancies, too, between countries in which economic life was highly tradition-bound and those more open to economic change. These and other distinctions will be illustrated as we review the various programs briefly.[5]

We begin with three small nations—the Netherlands, Belgium, and Luxemburg—in which there was a strong emphasis upon both regaining financial stability and broadening the bases of production. Then, we consider West Germany, Norway, Sweden, Denmark, Austria, Iceland, Ireland, and Turkey, in which stress was predominantly on expanding investment and production. Then Italy, Switzerland, and Portugal—widely differing economies in which financial considerations were relatively more decisive in shaping recovery efforts. Finally, we shall consider two countries in eastern Europe, Greece and Yugoslavia, and the two leading powers in western Europe, France and the United Kingdom, in each of which recovery efforts were affected by an unusual range of special conditions.

The Netherlands

Like most countries in Europe, the Netherlands faced a severe shortage of goods, capital, and equipment and an excessive accumulated purchasing power in the hands of its people.[6] The government decided —as had Belgium and Luxemburg—on drastic monetary surgery, temporarily blocking all money in circulation, then gradually releasing a "normal" amount and eliminating the excess by taxation and by forced consolidation in bonded indebtedness; a huge floating national debt was

[5] An effort is made to avoid needless repetition of information on individual country programs appearing elsewhere in this volume. See Index.

[6] For an illuminating discussion of the Netherlands program by competent authorities, see Ministry of Foreign Affairs, the Netherlands, *Road to Recovery: The Marshall Plan—Its Importance for the Netherlands and European Cooperation* (The Hague, 1954).

refunded. Described later by Dr. M. W. Holtrop, president of De Nederlandsche Bank, as "the Benelux solution," this drastic approach was designed to prevent inflation and to permit a quick return to a free internal economy. In contrast with the situation in Belgium, however, financial control was subsequently relaxed and investments expanded so markedly that some inflationary pressure was again generated.

There was much more emphasis on "planning" than in Belgium, and on investment for future production, including large land reclamation projects. The level of investment in relation to the national product came to be one of the highest in Europe. According to Minister for Economic Affairs J. R. M. van den Brink, this was "essential as a means of preventing heavy structural unemployment in a steadily growing population."[7] Full employment was looked upon as a "touchstone of an advanced society."[8]

The Dutch were among the first to see the need for greater unity in Europe after the war and the significance of Germany in any new western European system.[9] "We cannot live," said Van den Brink, "without Germany, our important market." The Netherlands government staunchly supported the OEEC and the change it sponsored in Western policy which enabled Germany to progress in four years from a low-level to a high-level economy.[10] The gains in trade which resulted helped to offset the severe economic shock occasioned by the loss of Indonesia. When the "federal approach" to European unity, as represented by the Schuman Plan, was proposed in 1950, it won more prompt and widespread acceptance in the Netherlands than in any other country.

Belgium and Luxemburg

These countries, which formed the Belgium-Luxemburg Economic Union, spearheaded the "Benelux solution" to the problem of internal financial stability. The benefits of stability were to some extent offset by a lower rate of investment and greater unemployment in Belgium

[7] Interview, The Hague, November 24, 1952.

[8] I. Tinbergen, director, Central Planning Bureau. Interview, The Hague, November 22, 1952.

[9] The importance of German recovery and Germany's place in the framework of European cooperation was stressed as early as January 14, 1947, in a memorandum from the Netherlands government to the Big Four Council of Deputies in London. Interview, H. M. Hirschfeld, Government Commissioner for Economic Aid, The Hague, November 21, 1952.

[10] See J. R. M. van den Brink, "European Integration," in Bank of Amsterdam, *Quarterly Review*, no. 98 (Third Quarter 1952), pp. 1–13.

than in the other countries of northern Europe. The lag in investments left Belgium a high-cost producer, more vulnerable to competition when the era of shortages had passed.

With its own current production enhanced by that of the Congo, however, Belgium's trade and payments position was relatively strong. More than for most other countries, therefore, ECA assistance to Belgium and Luxemburg took the form of "conditional aid" rather than grants; that is, dollar allotments were made as reimbursement for exports to other parts of Europe. This served the double purpose of stimulating needed investments, production, and exports and of relieving shortages elsewhere.

This marginal dollar assistance helped in expanding productive capacity in Belgium and especially in developing the rich resources of the Belgian Congo. "A 10 percent increment in working capital made much more than a 10 percent difference," said Louis Camu, head of the Banque de Bruxelles, "since the particular items thus financed were vital." [11]

The Belgians also attached high importance to the steps taken toward European economic integration; one authority stressed particularly the way in which the "drawing rights" and EPU mechanisms developed by the OEEC had facilitated an expansion in Belgian exports.[12] Convictions also matured on a broader plane. "I don't believe," said Baron Snoy, a leading figure in the OEEC Council, "that we will ever solve the dollar problem without development of the full European market, or that there is any future for Europe except as a cooperative system." [13]

West Germany

The recovery effort in West Germany, regarded by many as the key to the economic health of Europe, was fraught with problems. Long dependent on outside sources for food and raw materials, Germany emerged from the war with cities laid waste, resources depleted, foreign assets gone, heavy new obligations, currency virtually worthless, administration overthrown, and occupying military governments in control. When the nation was split by the Iron Curtain, West Germany was cut off from large producing areas. Problems of food and employ-

[11] Interview, Brussels, November 19, 1952.
[12] Conte Hadelin de Meeus d'Argenteuil, chief, Economic Studies, Federation Industrielle Belgique. Interview, Brussels, November 19, 1952.
[13] Interview, Brussels, November 19, 1952.

ment were aggravated by a large influx of refugees from the east, which eventually reached a total of approximately ten million.[14]

The transition from emergency relief and rehabilitation to recovery effort began with the currency reform of June 20, 1948, carried out under the military government. This reform, by helping restore stability and inducing a spurt in production, was of immense advantage to the Marshall Plan operation.[15]

To the new task of recovery, especially in productive capacity, the German people applied themselves with customary determination and vigor. They were supported by a provision of the United States Economic Cooperation Act of 1948[16] which paved the way for Allied decisions to end the dismantling of plants whose retention would help the European Recovery Program.

Early recovery planning in western Germany was conducted under the supervision of ECA officials attached to the High Commissioner's office. Needs were such that, according to Dr. Karl Albrecht, chief of the Economic Division of the German Federal Ministry for the Marshall Plan, "investment in any sector contributed toward employment and normalizing of the economy."[17] Counterpart funds went exclusively into investments, which were widely dispersed at first but were later concentrated in six or seven selected industries.[18] Although ECA people believed that local financing was often too conservative, the investment program was pressed with vigor and was a major cause of Germany's remarkable recovery. The inclusion of West Berlin in the program late in 1949 increased employment and bolstered morale in that "island in the Soviet sea."[19]

Vice-Chancellor Blücher, of the Free Democratic Party, who headed the Ministry for the Marshall Plan in Bonn, tended to favor *laissez faire* economic policies, as did the dominant Christian Democratic Party, whereas the Social Democrats favored extensive planning. The ECA

[14] For graphic representation, see Ministry for Expellees, *Some Facts about Expellees in Germany* (Bonn, 1952).

[15] Interview, General Lucius D. Clay, former U.S. High Commissioner in Germany, New York, February 25, 1953. The reform provided for revaluation of old currency and bank deposits and the introduction of a new currency with one Deutschemark replacing about 16 Reichmarks. Taxes were reduced and preparations made to remove many price and other economic controls.

[16] Sec. 115(f).   [17] Interview, Bonn, December 3, 1952.

[18] See published summary report through November 30, 1951, by the ECA mission to Germany (Michael Harris, chief), entitled *Utilization of ECA Counterpart Funds in Western Germany and Berlin* (Bonn, 1952).

[19] See Hubert G. Schmidt, *Economic Assistance to West Berlin* (Bonn, 1952).

mission agreed to the lifting of excessive restrictions but considered standby controls over investment desirable; these were maintained until the government, in 1951, adopted laws enabling Germany to cooperate in international controls. At the end of the program, despite considerable opposition from the Social Democrats, plans were being made for a more dynamic competitive system within Germany, a system in which, as Carl R. Mahder, productivity chief in the ECA mission, pointed out, "the producer can't relax because he's in a stream that he cannot avoid through fixed prices and fixed production quotas. The tradition here," he added, "has been that of producing for defined markets at high prices—with the idea of stabilized wages and of everything having its place and everything being in its place. But a shirt-maker with a stable market and stable prices doesn't produce enough shirts; what is needed is for him to be obligated to produce more or go out of business. The aim must be more goods at lower cost, available to the whole population, and a greater sharing out of the returns from increased production." [20]

The status and incentives of workers raised difficult problems. Virtually all labor groups became affiliated in a German Trade Union Federation (DGB).[21] The unions, of diverse political and religious views but generally anti-Communist, wished to raise labor from the status of an economic commodity (*Objekt*) to that of a conscious policy-making group; ultimately, they sought "co-determination" and equal "partnership" for labor in all important decisions affecting the economy as a whole. These political and economic goals were antithetical to those of the Soviet-controlled Free German Trade Union Federation (FDGB) in East Germany. They evinced, at the same time, a much stronger political emphasis than that of American "business-unionism."

In providing incentives for greater output the attempt was made, as Dr. Hans Büttner, economist in the DGB, remarked, "to convince workers that they had to produce more to improve their standard of living. This was not easy when it seemed to them that all that was needed was to raise their wages. They saw that a small number of people had high profits, while their own wages were below prewar and unemployment was around 1,700,000. The rational aspects could be stated. But the economic problems which many unions faced were

[20] Interview, December 3, 1952.

[21] For an analysis of contrasting roles under free and totalitarian systems, see Theodore Lit, "Unions in Democratic and Soviet Germany," *Monthly Labor Review*, January 1953, pp. 1–7.

difficult. For example, the miners and metal workers would not agree to the idea of keeping quiet regarding their demands, and continuing to work for the same wages. The tradition for bargaining was often greater than that for productivity." [22]

In external economic relations the West German regime appeared less restrictionist than the occupying authorities during the period of military government; competition and freer trade within Europe were welcomed. "We never forgot," said Dr. Albrecht, "that the increased density of population made us very dependent on imports and exports. We were most interested, therefore, in seeing our neighbors economically sound. We considered OEEC cooperation not only as our duty but also to our own interest; we participated in it by deep conviction. As regards the liberalization of trade, we were among the first proponents—without special reservations." [23] In 1952 Germany's trading position within Europe was strong and its deficit with the dollar area was being rapidly reduced.

Norway

No other country built more for the future than Norway. Scorched-earth destruction during the war had been exceedingly severe, living standards had plunged, rehabilitation was incomplete, and the foreign exchange earned in wartime shipping had been drained off in a period of falling world prices for Norwegian exports. Consumer needs were pressing. But the idea that lean years should be accepted in the interest of the future had gained support before the Marshall Plan began, and consumption was deliberately held to a minimum. Even Cabinet members were not above riding bicycles to work.

Taxation was used to accumulate capital and prevent inflation. Private earnings were plowed back into industrial expansion. So much of internal resources and United States aid was channeled into investment —in shipping, hydroelectric power, and industries producing for export—that the ECA considered cutting down the level of assistance. But the government, with able lawyer-economist Erik Brofoss, Minister of Commerce, as spokesman, made a case for its program which won support from the ECA Oslo mission and Paris office. As it turned out, there had been an underestimate, in ECA/Washington, of the will and capacity of the Norwegian government and people to hold down inflationary pressures during a period of exceedingly rapid economic expansion.

[22] Interview, December 4, 1952.   [23] Interview cited.

With investments equalling one-third of the gross national product—the highest ratio in Europe—substantial risks were involved. A world depression or new foreign trade barriers could have played havoc with the economy. "But we have to take chances," said Foreign Trade Director Knut Getz Wold; "if not, it would mean a sure road to poverty." [24] And the risk was justified. At the end of the four-year span Norway had achieved economic self-reliance and expanded foundations for progress scarcely matched elsewhere in Europe.

As a country with substantial but unbalanced and largely undeveloped resources, Norway depended on imports for about 40 percent of its needs. Earning foreign exchange through exports and shipping services was therefore a prime objective. At the end of the ECA period, according to Juel, commodity exports had climbed to about 15 percent above prewar and the merchant marine to approximately 25 percent.[25] The country had a slight surplus in its dollar trade but a substantial payments deficit within Europe.

Although Norway had a natural interest in the liberalization of trade and strongly supported it as a goal, it did not favor anything approaching federal union or complete freedom of trade with full currency convertibility. "Ours," said Getz Wold, "is a planned economy. The main arguments regarding the need for larger markets are fully accepted. But we . . . have some fear that pressure toward convertibility may lead to a situation in which there will be a spread of deflation and unemployment." [26] This apprehension did not arise from misgivings about regional specialization in Europe or about competitive efficiency in production; these were accepted as desirable. It stemmed rather from mistrust of a kind of free commercial competition in which depressed wages or deflationary policies in other countries might precipitate a general cycle of falling prices, increased unemployment, and declining production. "Multilateral trade and payments," declared Brofoss, "are good objectives, but not as ends in themselves; they could easily be roads toward spreading depression and economic shrinkage. The most important effect of the Marshall Plan for us is that it led to an expansion of the European economy." [27]

A minority view was expressed by Sjur Lindebraekke, a younger conservative member of the Storting: "The labor attack says that economic 'liberalism' cannot protect full employment. The conservative attack is that if international crisis develops, we cannot maintain full

[24] Interview, Oslo, November 25, 1952. [25] Interview cited.
[26] Interview cited. [27] Interview, Oslo, November 26, 1952.

employment. To give you frankly my personal view, I believe that both are meaningless in national terms alone, and that all these problems should be approached from the international viewpoint. It is paradoxical to develop such strict internal economic regulation while aiming toward external liberalization of trade. There must be essential protections —yes. But these should be regarded as temporary, and we should try to maintain flexibility in developing our international relations." [28]

Sweden

As a neutral, Sweden was far less affected by the war. Direct United States aid for recovery was small and entirely in loans. It was used principally to broaden the range of industries producing for export. Greater significance was attached to indirect benefits from the recovery program. "The economic revival of countries with which Sweden does business has been important to us," said Walter Åmen, head of the influential professional workers' organization. "Our interdependence with these countries is extensive." [29]

Denmark

Denmark had a socialist government at the beginning of the program and a conservative government at the end. The transition was accompanied by a partial shift in emphasis from new investment to the safeguarding of financial stability.

"The Marshall Plan," declared S. Hartogsohn, director of the Central Bank, "made possible the regeneration of the productive apparatus." [30] "Under the recovery program," said O. Muller, who at the end of the period was chairman of a national productivity board, "it was above all important for Denmark to be able to obtain from abroad all necessary raw materials to start production and utilize the productive potential of agriculture and industry. The idea was to increase Danish exports as promptly as possible and thus earn foreign currency, which in its turn should make it possible to import further raw materials and eventually recover and develop the production apparatus after the destruction during the German occupation. Once the machinery had been set going in this way, it was possible in the later stages of the recovery program to put more emphasis on the direct import of investment goods for agriculture and industry. The mechanizing of agriculture was given

[28] Interview, Oslo, November 26, 1952.
[29] Interview, Stockholm, November 28, 1952.
[30] Interview, Copenhagen, December 1, 1952.

high priority; the number of tractors, for instance, which before the war was 4,000, reached 30,000 during the Marshall Plan period. A nationwide electric power development program was commenced, in considerable part for use in agriculture. Success in our efforts to boost agricultural productivity, or production per man-hour, led not only to greater total output but also to a decrease in the number of farm workers.

"At the same time, we have been developing toward higher industrialization, and this is of vital importance with our increasing population and with the shifting of people no longer needed in agriculture. The gains in industry have not been so fast as in agriculture. However, industrial productivity has improved year by year and is now above the prewar level. We would like to follow as natural a line as possible toward developing an industrial setup that is able to supply the Danish population with many needed items and, simultaneously, to compete in high-grade exports. Industrial exports are now substantially higher, proportionately, than before the war." [31]

The controversy which developed over internal financial stability was interesting. Jorgen Paldam, an economist representing the labor viewpoint, put the issue thus: "The former [Socialist] Danish government time and again said that it was all right to push trade, but that it was more important for every country to follow high production and stable employment policies. We emphasized more the long-range considerations. It is risky for our economy to be dependent on a very few' products going to such limited markets. I believe we could have done more, during the latter part of the program, toward diversification of production. This means taking more risks and going beyond the good old investors." [32]

Hartogsohn, expressing the more conservative viewpoint, maintained that "a stable monetary system is essential to confidence. You can increase production by full employment, but you can't go beyond that; it would mean cheap money—with too much started and not enough finished. For example, housing construction, which before the war took nine to thirteen months, required, when these evils were at their highest, two to three years. The effect of our conservative economic policy was beneficial to production rather than the reverse. We do not want to obstruct wise investment, but neither do we want the kind of overemployment which leads to balance of payments difficulties or wrong influences in internal financing. We have said: You should have prior-

[31] Interview, Copenhagen, December 1, 1952.
[32] Interview, Copenhagen, December 1, 1952.

ities—first, activities which contribute to our export trade and earnings; second, housing, etc.; and last, luxuries. The monetary supply is now normal; it would cause damage if we pushed it up further." [33]

As to European economic integration, Hartogsohn said: "EPU and the intra-European trade provisions are of the greatest importance to Denmark. They have meant a transfer from a bilateral to a multilateral system, making it possible for us to sell goods in all directions and reducing our export frustration to a minimum. Our dream is always the triangular approach, giving us a part in providing what is needed." But John Lindeman, one-time deputy chief of the ECA mission to Denmark, noted that while the Danes were quick to realize the benefit to their export trade of a reduction of trade barriers by other countries, they were slow in exposing their own domestic industries to outside competition. "By catering to short-run protectionist interests," he said, "they denied to themselves the stimulus to increased efficiency which would come from having to compete with producers in other countries." [34] This stricture was applicable in varying degree to a number of other countries on both sides of the Atlantic as well as to Denmark.

Austria

In Austria, as in Denmark, there was a shift in emphasis during the latter part of the program from investments, which were a major factor in recovery but which also contributed to an inflation in 1951, to fiscal controls designed to re-establish financial stability.[35]

Initial investments were heavy, with major concentration in basic industries which had been severely damaged during the war: iron, steel, and coal. Later there was some shift to processing industries and to the development of hydroelectric resources.[36] "When rationalization reaches a certain point," said Dr. Hellmuth Boller of the Chamber of Commerce in Vienna,[37] "it is necessary to look out for supplementary pos-

---

[33] Interview cited.   [34] Interview, Washington, December 1, 1954.

[35] For a condensed treatment of the Austrian program, see Central Bureau for ERP Affairs, *Austria and the ERP: Summary Report, April 1948–April 1951* (Vienna, 1951).

[36] An extensive presentation appears in *The Austrian Investment Program: 1950–52*, published by the Central Bureau for ERP Affairs (Vienna, 1951). See also *Austria's Hydro-Power Resources and Their Utilization for European Power Supply*, published by the Federal Ministry of Transport (Vienna, n.d.). In 1952 hydroelectric power, to be available in part to neighboring countries, was becoming increasingly prominent in Austrian investment planning.

[37] Head of the economic department, Austrian Chamber of Commerce. Interview, Vienna, December 8, 1952.

sibilities of employment in other sectors of the economy. Austria has a lot of small-scale business and handicraft which received only half of one percent of the counterpart generated by Marshall aid—not enough. In such industry, now technically behind, our market has shifted to the west, where we meet stiffer competition than we used to find in eastern Europe. This means a need for greater specialization and for adequate investments which can lead to high returns in employment." There was considerable agricultural investment, and later some opposition to its decline with the shift toward more conservative financing. "I think," remarked Robert Baier, coordinator of divisions in the government's ERP Central Bureau, "that agriculture could become our biggest consumer of industrial goods and that a decline in farm labor increases the reasons for rationalization in agriculture, and this calls for continuing investments." [38]

The major aim of the investment program as a whole was to cut down Austria's balance-of-payments deficit. It dropped, as Wilhelm Taucher, head of the ERP Central Bureau, pointed out, from 300 million dollars (equivalent) in 1948–1949 to 120 million in 1951–1952, and to a projected 60 million in 1952–1953. [39]

Financial stabilization was accomplished, in 1951–1952, by credit controls, wage-price agreements, and budget balancing. The impetus to capital formation and to foreign exchange earnings reinforced the wish of some Austrian economists that greater emphasis had been placed, earlier in the program, upon internal financial stability.

American personnel in Austria were much concerned over the extent to which economic competition in Austria was frustrated by concentrations of economic power, abetted by restrictions on trade entry (through trade regulations and government licensing), and by cartel arrangements between producers and distributors. [40]

Despite the political and economic stresses occasioned by four-power occupation and Communist maneuvers, the attitude of the Austrian government toward greater economic integration with the rest of western Europe was strongly affirmative. [41] "All Austrian questions," said Boller, "are European; therefore, the sooner Europe is integrated, the better."

[38] Interview, Vienna, December 8, 1952.

[39] Interview, Vienna, December 8, 1952.

[40] See Harry W. Johnstone, *The Restraint of Competition in the Austrian Economy* issued (unclassified) by the Office of the U.S. High Commissioner (Vienna, December 1, 1951).

[41] See Von Günther Gruber and Von Harro Koch-Loepringen, *Die wirtschaftliche Integration Europas* (Verlag für Geschichte und Politik, Wien, 1951).

"The mere existence of OEEC," commented Taucher, "hinders restrictive commercial practices which otherwise would have taken place, including dozens of trade quotas and other restrictions. But no one can risk it now with OEEC in the picture. And the importance of EPU can't be overrated. Multilateral as against bilateral dealings are of incredible value."

Iceland

Before World War II, Iceland depended largely on the export of fish; during the war physical losses were negligible and there was some increase in agriculture and industry. Investments under the recovery program were directed chiefly to improvement and enlargement of the fishing fleet and to the development of hydroelectric power, fish processing industries, fertilizer and cement production, and agriculture. American military expenditures in Iceland helped to offset the costs of imports for the investment program. At considerable cost in persistent inflationary pressures, a needed start was made in economic diversification.

Ireland

Ireland, principally an agricultural country, suffered during the war a decline in such essential imports as feedstuffs, fertilizers, and machinery. The limited dollar aid provided was chiefly to generate local currency counterpart funds for internal investments. The recovery effort was devoted mainly to raising agricultural production and exports, and to the development and expansion, with technical assistance, of a number of small and medium-size industries. In 1952 exports were expanding, and agricultural production, after a period of stagnation, was showing moderate gains.

Turkey

Turkey entered upon the recovery program as an underdeveloped country. A quarter-century of revolutionary ferment and widening contacts with the West, under Ataturk and Inönü, had made the people far more receptive to new ideas and social changes, but the economy, largely isolated during World War II, was still static and backward in technology; communications were poor and living standards extremely low. Foreign exchange earnings were heavily dependent upon a few agricultural "luxury" items.

In the aspirations of its political leaders two themes predominated: security from external encroachment and more rapid modernization, with the latter seen as a necessary condition for the former. "As a natural consequence of our history," said Foreign Minister Fuat Koprulu, "we put first, freedom; easy life and wealth come next. The reason we have been so eager for rapid economic recovery and growth is to provide the strong military power essential to the protection and maintenance of our freedom and sovereignty." [42]

Untapped resources, particularly in arable land, far exceeded expectations; wise development of them could enable the economy of Turkey to complement that of western Europe. With these conditions and a strategic use of Marshall aid, there occurred in Turkey one of the most striking chapters in the European Recovery Program. The hinterland was rapidly opened up; agricultural output expanded remarkably, savings rose, industrial and commercial expansion quickened, and the national income increased some 40 percent—all this in an economy moving from statism toward a relatively free-enterprise structure.

The most dramatic gains were in agriculture. In 1948–1949, 14 million dollars' worth of wheat imports were needed to supplement local production; in 1952–1953 more than 600,000 tons of wheat, valued at 59 million dollars, were exported.[43] Before these developments occurred, said Ahmed Emin Yalman, publisher in Istanbul, "there had been the idea that agriculture is backward so why bother with it? Why not go directly into industrialization? But agricultural development led to increased purchasing power among the farm populace and thus to a market for industrial products. Steel mills, for example, which previously had not been of much use except for military production, began to produce farm implements and, even with doubled output, could not keep up with the demand." [44]

The extraordinarily rapid increase in agricultural production caused severe growing pains. Many types of tractors were imported for which servicing facilities were lacking. Wheat production far outstripped road and railway transport as well as handling equipment in the ports. Provision for storage was wholly inadequate. High prices paid to farmers as an incentive to greater output were retained after world prices declined, entailing heavy financial losses to the government. A post-

[42] Interview, Ankara, December 10, 1952.

[43] The production of grains increased from about 6 million metric tons in 1947 to 12 million in 1952; cotton output tripled in the same period. Wheat and cotton became the leading exports, outstripping tobacco, dried fruits, and nuts.

[44] Interview, Istanbul, December 11, 1952.

Korea cotton boom was followed by a depression. Inflation reduced the benefits of the tremendous surge in agricultural output.

A hindrance to industrial development was a gulf between government and business leaders. "Businessmen were against government restrictions," said Bulent Yazici, Istanbul banker, "and government officials took the view that business could not be trusted. In consultations with the ECA mission, the idea developed that if an institution with the confidence of both parties could be established, and the necessary financing made available, a rapproachement could be achieved. The matter was put to the World Bank, which assisted with expert advice and with a proposed loan to be matched by our Central Bank and a consortium of foreign banks. The government accepted the proposal, and there was established the Industrial Development Bank, within which was set up later, out of Marshall Plan counterpart, an additional private investment loan fund. This bank began operating in March 1952, with carefully established criteria to prevent its loan operations from becoming speculative handouts, and developed rapidly a growing volume of business aiming toward a balanced investment program. Our major industrial problem now is a lack of experienced management and experienced technicians." [45]

The full aftereffects of the extensive new activities stimulated by American aid and forwarded by bold leadership within the country would not become fully apparent, it appeared, for many years. Continuing adjustments would be needed to achieve balance within the economy and a stable course in future development. How well they would be made depended in considerable part upon the capacity of the bureaucracy to carry through the necessary changes.

Italy

The postwar government of Italy inherited an exceptionally deep-rooted, obstinate set of problems. A long period of autarchy and militarism culminating in the waste and destruction of World War II had left the country prostrate. Rehabilitation through UNRRA was only partial, and basic problems remained unsolved. A growing population, chiefly

[45] Interview, Istanbul, December 11, 1952. In an address delivered in Istanbul on September 9, 1952, U.S. Ambassador George McGhee attested to "widespread evidence that the Turkish government recognizes the contribution that the spirit of private initiative can make toward the development of Turkey's great natural resources." A new petroleum law and a "foreign investment encouragement law" both reflected the government's favorable attitude toward free enterprise and toward foreign investments in Turkey.

agrarian, pressed heavily against insufficient resources in cultivable land. Unemployment was a tough structural problem. Poverty was widespread, especially in the south, where 40 percent of the people lived. Communists were entrenched among labor and farm groups. The economy was heavily dependent upon imports. "In the autumn of 1947," recalled Donato Menichella, governor of Banca Italiana, "the situation was grave. We had galloping inflation. Our foreign exchange resources were exhausted. The agricultural crop was unfavorable, and we had need for big importations of wheat, coal, and raw materials.

"Stabilization," he continued, "was made possible by interim aid. The Communists and associated parties were strong. Interim aid and the prospect of the Marshall Plan made it possible to maintain stability in prices and, therefore, confidence in the lira. These conditions helped to produce the heaviest defeat of the Communists after the war." [46]

The strong emphasis on financial stability reflected in these remarks was common in ruling circles. "The mission and ECA generally," stated another distinguished financier, not for attribution, "have often insisted that we were too much preoccupied with financial stability and not aggressive enough in expanding our productive capacity. This was predicated on the need to raise employment and living standards. But there was in this approach a mistake. In Italy the reestablishment of financial stability was prerequisite to other progress. It has not been realized how difficult it is, at best, to maintain such stability in Italy, where, in addition to normal difficulties, we have enormous pressure of population upon resources. Also, it was not sufficiently realized that the real problem was not total expenditures, but the quality of expenditures. The country is so poor that it cannot afford to spend money on everything. Therefore we must concentrate on the breaking of certain bottlenecks. There is no adequate machinery in Italy for such an approach; this is, of course, primarily our responsibility." [47]

In the ECA mission there was indeed a continuing concern with the fundamental objective of increasing production to the point where Italy, long impoverished, could become self-supporting. Economic development in the Italian south, which presented great difficulties, was regarded as particularly urgent. Vincent Barnett, deputy chief, phrased the problem in these terms: "To what extent should investment go toward building up the basic economy, at the risk of disastrous inflation? What can Italy do, and how much burden can it carry, without in-

[46] Interview, Rome, December 19, 1952.
[47] Interview, Rome, December 19, 1952.

flation? Would a more vigorous investment program lead to more production, more employment, more defense capacity? Most economists think yes. With the Italians, there is the psychological aspect—with a real experience of loss of faith in the currency—and with them, this is compelling." [48]

"It is a matter of judgment," commented Bartlett Harvey, mission programing chief, "as to where you draw the line. The government is more conservative than we, and is likely to operate on the quantity theory of money. They feel that the only way to expand investment is to expand credit—that the seams aren't tight enough to handle suppressed inflation, as the British and Norwegians have been able to do. We have felt that unused resources should be used, and have questioned whether increased demand accompanying investment would not stimulate more production which, in turn, would have an anti-inflationary effect." [49]

"They are in the habit," observed the late Chauncey Parker, who succeeded Zellerbach as chief of the ECA mission, "of .thinking of a fixed pie, and are not easily convinced that the size of the pie is flexible." [50] "So far," said Henry J. Costanzo, finance officer, "we have never been able to get them to thinking in terms of the availability and use of resources, investment, consumption, and the interrelation between all of these. Every year this has led to some kind of impasse. Fortunately, it has been possible to get a fairly considerable investment program going; the effects are just coming in. Now, there is a decided basic change—with defense. Now they are closer to the margin where increased investment would, in fact, imperil financial stability." [51]

At the end of the Marshall Plan period the question was being studied in a more and more detailed way. "The basic development needs to be carried forward," Barnett said, "with emphasis on lighter industries and specialties, using scientific advances. Italy is poor in raw materials, not in human resources. Underutilization or ineffective use of available economic resources, relative to the size of the population, is the way I like to put the population problem. There is needed here the kind of economy in which you have more trade in goods wherein there is a maximum addition of value by skills."

[48] Interview, Rome, December 18, 1952.

[49] Interview, Rome, December 19, 1952.

[50] Interview, Rome, December 19, 1952. Italy did not take as much aid as the ECA was prepared to provide for assistance in expanding the productive base of the economy.

[51] Interview, Rome, December 19, 1952.

Population pressure, with two million unemployed throughout the program, caused the Italian government to lay continuing stress on efforts to facilitate emigration. The desire of the ECA to improve general living standards in Italy—a major factor in social unrest—was reflected in efforts to encourage the growth of a dynamic non-Communist labor movement and a more equitable distribution of recovery gains; these endeavors, however, began to gain headway late in the program, and their effects were far from commensurate with the need. Italy's dependence on external resources and markets, and the advantages of a multilateral trade system to her, were important factors in the strong, consistent support given by Italy to measures looking toward economic integration in Europe.[52]

Switzerland

In Switzerland, which as a neutral emerged from the war intact and required no direct recovery aid, internal financial stability was regarded as "the factor which determines the results to be obtained in the fields of production and the balance of payments." [53] Productivity, it was believed, could be sustained by "specially developed and constantly fostered vocational training; by the application of scientific discoveries to industry; by a high standard of living; and by a relatively high legal number of working hours."

Portugal

Portugal had a tightly controlled economy. Memories of severe inflation before 1928 were still vivid, and government leaders were preoccupied with financial stability. Aid was provided largely through loans, which did not generate counterpart. The ECA did not participate as directly as in most of the other ERP countries in the planning of limited investment programs, which in Portugal were directed principally to hydroelectric development, irrigation, the opening up of mines, and the expansion of industries, including fishing, metallurgy, cement, chemicals, and textiles. There was concern in the ECA over the slow pace of economic development, especially of extensive natural resources in the overseas territories Angola and Mozambique, and over

---

[52] See *The Development of Italy's Economic System within the Framework of European Recovery and Cooperation,* Pt. IV, issued by the Interministerial Reconstruction Committee (Rome, 1952), and translated into English by the MSA mission to Italy.

[53] OEEC, *Interim Report on the European Recovery Program,* p. 172.

the inequitable distribution of income as some lines of production gradually increased.

Greece

In Greece special conditions made for a unique pattern in recovery programing. The economic situation, even before 1940, was far from healthy. During the war, when the country was ravaged and then occupied for nearly four years by German, Italian, and Bulgarian forces, local Communists made their way into key positions in the resistance movement. When peace came, the nucleus for a civil government had been greatly weakened and the country was provoked by stages into an immensely destructive civil war, which began with Communist-directed guerrilla activities in 1944 and continued until 1949. For about three years, the "recovery program" in Greece was, in fact, a continuation and extension of the earlier emergency effort to "put out the fire" and then to produce maximum economic results in a minimum period of time.

The new government, with strong support from the ECA mission, strove to improve land and water resources, to increase the efficiency of the farmers, and to foster an equitable distribution of agricultural products. As pointed out by Brice M. Mace, Jr., chief of the mission's Food and Agriculture Division,[54] the first was essential in a country where the arable base was only about one acre per capita.[55] The second, based on research and an extension service which became a model for trainees from other countries, contributed to gains not only in total output but also in production per man-day. The third, always difficult in an underdeveloped country, could not be dealt with overnight, but real improvements were made in the diets of villagers.

Vigorous programs were also carried out in social welfare, public health, transportation, industry, mining, labor and manpower, civil government administration and finance, and tourism. But the concepts guiding the earlier programs were criticized by later participants and observers, American and Greek, on three main counts. Too much was

[54] Interview, Athens, December 13, 1952, and letter to the writer, September 15, 1954. Valuable groundwork in planning and operations had been laid by the U.N. Food and Agriculture Organization (FAO) and by the predecessor mission for American Aid to Greece (AMAG).

[55] Yield per stremma (1/4 acre) in kilograms (2.2 lbs.) rose, between 1948–1949 and 1952–1953, from 95 to 105 for wheat, 105 to 110 for barley, 93 to 100 for corn, 76 to 93 for oats, 243 to 325 for unmilled rice, 1,117 to 1,216 for potatoes, 592 to 720 for citrus fruit, 262 to 310 for wine, 78 to 100 for cotton, and 51 to 68 for tobacco. U.S. Operations Mission, *The American Aid Programs for Greece from 1947 to the Spring of 1954* (Athens, 1954).

attempted too fast, they believed, with resulting waste, economic imbalance, and inflation. Second, it was felt that more responsibility should have been handed back earlier in the program to the Greeks themselves. And they held that the program should have been guided more clearly by a fundamental analysis of the resources and capacities of the Greek economy, looking to the time when aid would be drastically curtailed.

This last point underlies a major shift in emphasis in the later stages of the program. "The reorientation," commented Edward A. Tenenbaum, an economic advisor in the ECA mission, "was a bit rough. We applied some basic rules. We looked at the balance of payments. We looked at the deficit. Investments were overexpanded. Credit was expanding rapidly. We cut down the credit through Treasury representations. We succeeded in reducing investments and, more important, in helping the government to really deal with its budget. The result has been a basic improvement in the balance-of-payments position before the longer-range investments came into production. And the level of aid has been sharply reduced." [56] The rapidity with which the aid was reduced, however, left a number of enterprises short of capital, delaying the time when they would become productive. Living standards were still low and the country faced a difficult choice between further capital expansion to accelerate economic growth, and a low rate of investments as a safeguard to balanced external payments and internal financial stability.

Yugoslavia

Political considerations bulked large in the economic aid programs which followed discussions between the United States, the United Kingdom, and France. Part of the assistance provided was out of ECA resources. As first projected, the aid was to consist of common-use items, such as cotton, to keep the economy running. Indirectly such help made it possible for the Yugoslavs to continue the most essential parts of the huge investment program they had undertaken as a means of elevating their low-level economy. Investment plans, as projected, seemed to the ECA mission to be too grandiose. In the environs of Belgrade, skeletons of new structures on which work had stopped gave evidence of an overextended effort. But the economy was not bankrupted, and gradually the scope of investments was narrowed, gains were registered in agriculture and industry, and living standards rose somewhat.

[56] Interview, Athens, December 15, 1952.

Of special interest to Western observers, of course, was Yugoslavia's economic and political reorientation after its exit from the Soviet bloc and the rupture of its eastward trade. Through frank exchanges, efforts were made to convince the government that doctrinaire procedures weakened incentive, and that a rigid economic system would not fit into the development of relations with the West. James S. Killen and Edgar A. J. Johnson, chief and deputy chief of the United States economic mission, were convinced in late 1952 that there was a genuine trend toward economic liberalization.[57] More managerial functions came to be exercised by "enterprises," greater reliance was placed on market forces, and more attention was given to the place of incentives within the economy.[58] "There is," observed Edward Rawson, United States economic attaché, "a more reasonable attitude toward the West than there was three years ago; aid has helped in taking off blinders." [59]

"Our official position," said Ljuba Babic, head of the government's Economic Planning Commission, "is that there should be one world market. We know that the existence of this market has been neglected by the Russians and they are trying to destroy it. However, we judge this attitude as most reactionary. We are deeply convinced that we are not moving toward economic autarchy. We see our economy as an interested and able member of the world economy, and we are seeking to develop industries which will promote this end. If you ask whether we are moving toward the French or British system, the answer is no. If it is a question of relation to a world market, then the answer is yes. Naturally, this is not our only goal. We are also interested in the internal economy; otherwise, it would be a one-track development." [60]

France

France, which took a leading part in the efforts toward European integration, was impeded in its own recovery effort not only by wartime losses and depreciation, but also by inertias and divisions at home, the costly war in Indochina, and social unrest in Morocco and Tunisia.

The outlook at first was in some ways encouraging. The large investment program known as the Monnet Plan was conceived and elaborated before the beginning of the ERP; it gave France a head start in its recovery effort. The plan encompassed not only metropolitan

[57] Interview, Belgrade, December 16, 1952.
[58] Letter from Johnson to the writer, September 20, 1954.
[59] Interview, Belgrade, December 16, 1952.
[60] Group conference, Belgrade, December 16, 1952.

France but also North Africa and the overseas territories under French control.[61]

Under the Marshall Plan investments came chiefly from public funds, including counterpart, and from undistributed earnings; capital outlays from private sources were comparatively meager. As Robert J. Myers, director of the ECA mission's Office of Production, pointed out, "this meant a diversion of potential resources, including American aid, from two segments in the economy, both highly important: private industry, which stood in need of re-equipment and modernization and from which was required the types of goods, such as textiles, that would lower prices and living costs, and agriculture, where production has not nearly caught up to either needs or actual demands." [62]

Private industry and agriculture suffered from other disabilities than a shortage of capital. A tradition-bound owning and managerial class, many observers believed, clung to small units and antiquated methods; they resisted the removal of restrictions to competition; they opposed the development of a free labor movement which could provide constructive outlets for the economic aspirations of non-Communist workers. Agriculture was also relatively immobile. The government had only a limited interest in agriculture; it provided few funds for basic improvements. Extension services were weak, and scientific workers were more interested in pure research than in practical applications. A comparable handicap to fundamental recovery, some felt, was the unwillingness or inability of governing circles to sponsor freer competition and more equitable taxation.

Mention has been made of the highly disruptive efforts of the Communists in France, especially through trade unions under their control. They capitalized upon grievances and obstructed both political and economic measures essential to recovery.

The French people as a whole seemed to be striving for two irreconcilable worlds: one, a world of individualism organized in comfortably small groups, each enjoying adequate means of sustenance, considerable leisure, and maximum social security with a minimum of taxation and government controls; the other, a world in which France could again be a major power with no need for extraordinary outside support. The first of these aims could not be assured without the second,

[61] See Commissariat Général du Plan de Modernisation et d'Equipement, *Cinq Ans d'Exécution du Plan de Modernisation et d'Equipement de l'Union Française* (Paris, 1952).

[62] Interview, November 5, 1952.

and the second could not be achieved without a greater degree of collective effort than the first would permit. The conflict in aspirations was a disintegrating influence. The people, conscious of their past and potential greatness as a free nation, were frustrated, unsure, and abnormally sensitive to external criticism or suggestion. "France," remarked a friendly European statesman, "has no confidence in itself."

The dragging effect of these inertias was widely observed. One astute comment was made by Raymond Aron, eminent French writer: "The real obstacle to productivity is resistance to change. It is crystallization of structure. Closing one factory in order to open a more efficient one is unpleasant. If you resist change in a country, it means that you are resisting the hardships of mobility." [63]

The problem of financial instability in France was of long standing. Inflation characterized much of the period after World War I. Inflationary pressures mounted during and after World War II; they continued in the recovery period, with demands on the budget to modernize the economy, develop the overseas territories, carry the rearmament burden, and meet the extremely heavy costs of the war in Indochina. The franc was gravely threatened. Much attention was given to the problem during the first two years of the recovery program. [64] With American aid, an upsurge in basic production, and a determined response to the emergency by fiscal authorities, remarkable progress was made. [65] In spite of many difficulties, prewar living standards were regained and production levels surpassed. But France did not achieve economic viability or financial equilibruim during the Marshall Plan period.

United Kingdom

The United Kingdom's competitive position in world trade, first shaken during the latter part of the nineteenth century by the rise of other industrial powers, received a severe setback from World War I, after which Britain entered a period of chronic economic difficulties featured by fluctuating unemployment. During World War II the country was spared the ravages of land conflict, but it suffered great industrial damage and incurred heavy losses in foreign assets and exchange

[63] Interview, Paris, November 6, 1952.

[64] "Inflation," stated William M. Tomlinson, "was threatening to get out of hand. There was a great deficit with other European countries—some 300 million dollars. This was part of a total deficit of about 1.4 billion." Interview, Paris, November 13, 1952.

[65] See discussion in Chapter 6 under the heading "Role of the ECA."

reserves. Reconstruction was tackled with characteristic determination. Assistance was provided through American loans in 1946 and 1947. A partial recovery had been achieved when the Marshall Plan began.

The British faced, in effect, four sets of closely interconnected economic problems: how to cope with material shortages and financial instability at home; how to revive the health and functioning of the Commonwealth; how to approach the question of European economic cooperation; and how to attain a better balance in economic relations with the rest of the free world, especially the United States. The British were naturally influenced by their own complex position and, to a secondary extent, by the economic philosophies of succeeding labor and conservative governments.

To deal with shortages and financial instability, Britain retained wartime commodity or "physical" controls until the worst deficiencies were made up by internal production and United States aid; then financial controls were substituted. In order to increase incentives for production, ECA administrators favored modification of those control policies which tended to restrict competition.

The British accepted an austerity regime which curtailed consumption of many items. Of the increase in real resources which became available from 1948 to 1950, only about one-quarter was allowed to go into consumption; half went into exports, and the remaining quarter was devoted to capital formation.[66]

The sterling counterpart of the aid to Britain, except for the 5 percent transferred to the American government, was used almost exclusively for retirement of the United Kingdom public debt, despite initial ECA sentiment for a larger use of it for investment.[67]

Although there is financial integration within the sterling area, it was not fully realized when the recovery program began that dollar aid would in effect become part of the resources of the sterling area as a

[66] *The Sterling Area: An American Analysis* (London, 1951), p. 69. This is an exceptionally comprehensive volume prepared under the direction of John M. Cassels, ECA special mission to the U.K.

[67] An analysis of the process whereby the U.S. government decided to concur in British proposals to use these funds for debt retirement is contained in a report prepared by the Treasury Department in 1953 for the International Operations Subcommittee of the House Committee on Government Operations; the report is entitled *The Use of the Sterling Counterpart of ECA-Grant Assistance to the U.K. for the Purpose of Debt Retirement.* The British government did not receive grant aid under fiscal 1951 appropriations. Counterpart arising from fiscal 1952 and later appropriations was used primarily for the support of British defense production.

whole.[68] What actually happened was not that ECA-financed commodities and equipment were extensively distributed throughout the Empire (though some were sent to Britain's dependent overseas territories), but that such aid to the United Kingdom freed for other urgent uses the dollars earned through sterling area exports and services. These earnings were pooled. In drawing upon them and upon local resources and other foreign exchange earnings, the British thought in sterling area as well as national terms.

The linkage between Marshall Plan aid to free Europe and the sterling area as a whole acquired a special significance with the emergence of a new European payments system. The dollars used to support this system in effect put intra-European trade in a favored position as compared with trade between Europe and the United States. This was a departure from earlier American policy, which had aimed at non-discriminatory trade and currency convertibility on a more "universal" basis. The British welcomed the change not only because of direct advantages in the link between the pound sterling and the favored system of multilateral payments in Europe, but also because it was accompanied by some relaxation in American pressure for abandonment of preferential trade within the British Commonwealth.

These adjustments in American policy signified, as noted by Sir Robert Hall, "a tacit acceptance of the fact that ultimate goals are still far off. It seemed to me," he added, "to be looking at problems of a chaotic world situation in a real way—in such a manner as to build toward free world strength and survival—rather than by a more doctrinaire approach." [69]

The sterling area's "dollar gap," estimated at about 4.1 billion dollars in 1947 and 1.7 billion in 1948, dropped to 350 million in 1949–1950.[70] From the fall of 1949, when the pound was devalued, until June 1951, there was a steady increase in the dollar reserves of the sterling area as a whole, and American grant aid was therefore suspended.

[68] The sterling area included—in addition to the U.K.—Iceland, Ireland, Burma, Ceylon, India, Pakistan, Iraq, Australia, New Zealand, Southern Rhodesia, the Union of South Africa, and more than twoscore dependencies in the Western Hemisphere, Africa, Asia, and the oceans; it did not include Canada, whose currency is more closely linked with that of the U.S.

[69] Interview cited. That longer-range goals were not being abandoned had been evidenced by the British devaluation decision of September 1949, which indicated their adherence to an ultimate aim of achieving full sterling convertibility; and by limited but recurrent joint efforts to achieve some reductions in tariffs under the General Agreement on Trade and Tariffs.

[70] *The Sterling Area*, pp. 66–67, 131.

Notwithstanding this impressive record, certain American criticisms of the British recovery effort, heavily buttressed as it was by United States aid, were quietly but persistently pressed. It was felt, for example, that a more determined attempt to break down resistance to overdue technological and organizational changes in industry would lead to greater productivity; that dollar earnings could be increased by more energetic and resourceful marketing; and that an even more vigorous investment program was desirable. A further criticism, applicable to American as well as to British and continental programing, was that in planning for increase in production more attention should have been given to the availability of raw materials and to market analysis. One ECA executive said: "We ended up in England with the engineering industries chockablock with orders for rearmament and other needs, but with Lancashire languishing."

Many Europeans in the OEEC, more concerned with Britain's continental relations than with its Commonwealth ties, wanted more British participation in the efforts to build cooperation within free Europe. This desire was shared by American leaders. "The OEEC," said Harriman, "was set up as rather a looser organization than we wanted. For one thing, the British didn't want to be treated as 'another European country.' We had endless arguments with Bevin and others, trying to convince them that their job was to help build a strong Europe, and that this did not alter the close relationship between the United Kingdom and the United States." [71]

The British took a leading part in the establishment of the OEEC and participated vigorously in its joint discussions. [72] After resisting at first the idea of a European Payments Union, they joined wholeheartedly and contributed importantly to its success. Throughout the recovery period, they looked upon the OEEC as essentially an economic conference in permanent session. On this point Britain's Sir Hugh Ellis-Rees, chairman of the Council in 1952–1953, said: "Expressing personal views, I do not believe that complete political integration is going to be attainable or provide us with a solution to our problems in the foreseeable future. But I do believe in the efficacy of the system we have adopted in OEEC, namely the staging of a perpetual international conference where we are made aware of each other's problems and discuss them

[71] Interview cited.

[72] Evidence of the extent of British participation is contained in *European Co-operation: Memoranda Submitted to the Organization for European Economic Co-operation Relating to Economic Affairs in the Period 1949 to 1953* (H.M. Stationery Office, London, 1953).

together and submit our policies to critical examination. I do believe that this brings some influence to bear on national policies and leads to some harmonization of all member countries' policies without requiring member countries to abandon their sovereignty. I think we have succeeded where other organizations have failed primarily because we are an organization which constantly keeps in touch with the representatives of member governments by obliging their representatives to take part in our day-to-day work; by this constant interchange of views we avoid isolating ourselves from current problems." [73]

In their wider economic relations the British were particularly concerned with adjustments in the geographic pattern of trade which might reduce the world's—and especially the sterling area's—deficits with the United States. With advances in general recovery the sterling area was able to produce and to procure from nondollar areas larger proportions of its requirements, and thereby to cut drastically its dollar outlays. Without raising the level of dollar imports, dollar earnings were upped by increasing exports, especially to the United States.[74] Since these exports consisted mainly of basic materials, they were greatly affected by shifts in the terms of trade between raw and manufactured products, by the level of economic activity in the United States, and by American tariffs and customs administration. These factors and a strong desire to bring to an end the donor-client relationship between the United States and the United Kingdom were largely responsible for the concern shown by the British in 1952 over the possibilities of an economic recession in the United States and for the emphasis which they placed upon the issue of "trade versus aid."

THE REGIONAL APPROACH

The steps actually taken in Europe to increase production, stabilize finances, increase exports to dollar areas, and disseminate more widely the fruits of economic progress were taken largely by the governments and peoples of individual countries. There was little ground for confidence, however, that through national action alone western Europe would be able to recover in full the dynamism which two world wars

[73] Interview, Paris, November 18, 1952.

[74] From 1949 through 1953, U.K. sales to the U.S. advanced from 205 million dollars to 444 million annually, an increase of about 117 percent. During the same period sales to all dollar areas (including Canada) increased from 636 million dollars to approximately 1,130 million, a rise of 78 percent. Letter from Edwin R. Dibrell (trade development officer in the U.K. mission) to the writer, September 28, 1954.

had weakened. Even without those wars, a Europe burdened with internal economic barriers would have found growing difficulty in maintaining its position in the face of mounting competition from other increasingly productive areas around the earth and especially on the North American continent. The wars hastened the loss of Europe's initial advantages through early industrialization, by cutting off or reducing its markets and by multiplying its difficulties in finding alternative outlets—domestic or foreign. Though not strong enough to counterbalance nationalistic pressures, these harsh realities were the source of a strong urge among some Europeans, long before the Marshall Plan, for a freeing of intra-European trade from its shackles.

American Interest

Strong encouragement for greater European integration came from the United States. There were several reasons for this. Experience after both world wars had seemed to indicate that piecemeal aid to individual countries was inadequate without greater cooperation among them. The United States' own historic experience had shown enormous advantages in a single, large free-market area. And the idea had taken root that integration could end Europe's recurring crises and chronic dependence on outside help.

American interest in the "European idea" grew stronger with each year of the recovery effort. There were those who felt, however, that this interest was not "thought through." One American consulted, for example, attributed much of the concern of the American Congress and people in European union to a naïve assumption that, since the United States was an economic success, all that was needed to make Europe successful economically was to create a United States of Europe.

"Was the idea," asked a government official in Europe,[75] "that there should be one European government taking in the whole area from Ireland and Norway to Portugal and Turkey—literally a United States of Europe? Or was the concept one of getting back to the relatively unrestricted international economic intercourse of fifty years ago?" "There was a conflict again," he added, "between the concept of European unity and the concept of international economic unity embodied in the International Monetary Fund and the General Agreement on Trade and Tariffs. These concepts were never really resolved, and it was never really clear what the United States was trying to bring about.

[75] Unnamed, by request.

I always thought it odd that the descendants of the writers of *The Federalist* were content to be misty on the essentials of policy."

In defense of the American position, which was felt in each European capital, it might be said that an affirmative interest in the potential advantages of greater European integration did not carry with it an obligation to map out specifically the course that should be followed. The ECA did take an active part *with* European leaders in helping to devise, and in supporting, the steps toward integration achieved through the OEEC; encouragement was given to the Schuman Plan. To have gone much further in attempting to define the forms that further integration should take, however, would have been to assume initiative which could only lie properly with the Europeans themselves.

But this is only a partial answer. The number of Americans giving serious thought to the longer objectives was limited, and among these there were many differences in concept and emphasis. Much popular thinking on the subject was hazy, except, perhaps, for the single-market argument, which, in view of the American background, had a wide appeal. A growing sentiment in favor of greater European "integration" or "unification" was accompanied by an increasing readiness to see American aid used in support of this positive, if indistinct, goal, with the expectation that thereby Europe's internal frictions might be reduced and its strength and capacity for self-support greatly enhanced.

Among those who were in direct contact with the actual problems that had to be faced, however, there was an active ferment of thinking on the subject which found expression in ECA policies and actions. Necessary adaptations were made to the thinking of the British, French, Germans, and others. As members of Congress talked increasingly about European "unification," ECA technicians, meshing their efforts with those of European economists, grappled with more immediate problems of progressive "integration."

With the end of the recovery program there appeared to be little change in American sentiment on this question, but the active role that the ECA had taken in relation to it was not perpetuated. A supporting impetus had been given, however, especially to greater integration of trade and payments.

Rationale

As is usual, those closest to the problem were the ones most likely to see its complications. Among Europeans there were great differences in opinion about the relative importance which should be given to national and regional approaches, and about the merits of alternative paths to greater economic coordination.[76] The deeper one got into the problem, the more complicated it became.

The basic arguments in the case for economic integration have been summarized many times.[77] Briefly stated, with some oversimplification, they are: that the economic problems of European countries can be greatly ameliorated, but not solved, on a national scale; that if these countries remain separated by high economic barriers they cannot achieve their full potentialities in economic expansion or compete successfully with economies enjoying great free market areas and higher productivity, such as the United States and the USSR; that the best hope for a more rapidly expanding western European economy is in freeing its own great internal market of 270 million people; that the creation of such a single market in place of divided and protected national markets would permit the economies of mass production and greater efficiency in the international division of labor; and that from this would come greater opportunities, higher output, rising standards of living, and a stronger competitive position in the world for western Europe as a whole.

The less sanguine present counterarguments and warn against accepting half-truths. Some who favor greater integration warn against exaggerating the benefits that may accrue from it. Even Marjolin, a leader in the development of cooperative action, remarked: "There is one paramount question on which I happen to disagree with some American friends, and that is as to the relative importance of integration and national action." [78] Fully recognizing the "indisputable arguments" in behalf of greater integration, he pointed to two considerations which weighed against regarding economic-political organization leading toward a single European state as the "sole solution." These considerations were: first, that European unification, with the abolition of trade quotas, tariffs, and so forth, would take a long time; and, second, that many European problems could be solved largely by national action if the countries had the strength, courage, and will to take such action. Others, more skeptical of the potentialities of integration, argue that the western

[76] The impetus and steps toward European integration are discussed more fully in Chapter 16.

[77] See, for example, Marjolin, *op. cit.*, pp. 41–42; or Ellis, *op. cit.*, pp. 390–394.

[78] Interview, Paris, November 14, 1952. Sir Hugh Gaitskell felt that the ECA overemphasized European integration as compared with dollar solvency and that the latter was allowed to drop into the background in too many countries (not the U.K.), especially those that did not use controls. Note to writer, October 7, 1954.

European economies are competitive rather than complementary, and that they must therefore look overseas for the greatest gains from trade. They believe that the specialization of national economies resulting from greater integration would not benefit all countries equally, that some might be worse off than they are now. They consider unlikely in the foreseeable future a free movement of labor. A removal of all protective barriers, it is argued, would result in exporting depression from economies with unemployment and low production to others with full employment and higher production. And it is said that a large numerical market does not necessarily mean a large market in terms of purchasing power.

These arguments are mentioned not because they invalidate the case for progressive European economic integration, but because they inject a note of realism in assessing the obstacles to its full and rapid realization. It will not come by fiat—European or American. The steps toward integration during the Marshall Plan years [79] gave solid ground for believing that extensive benefits would result from further progress in the same direction.

The Way Ahead

There are many possible roads and byroads to further integration. The two approaches that have received the most attention are represented by the OEEC, which owes its origin to the Marshall Plan, and the Coal and Steel Community arising from the Schuman Plan. There is, perhaps, too much tendency for advocates of each type to underrate the other.

The first relies on voluntary cooperation among sovereign states. It has an extraordinary record of achievement in influencing governments, in reversing the trend toward economic nationalism, and in devising specific methods of cooperation, notably in trade and payments.[80] Even this record fell short of the hopes of some in both Europe and the United States. But the harmonization of European economic interests, after centuries of intrenched nationalism, was enormously complicated. Effective pursuit of this goal required a spirit as well as a method. In injecting such a spirit, the OEEC was a pioneering institution. "In my opinion," commented John Lindeman, "one of the most important 'integrating' forces that actually developed and bore fruit in Europe was the habit of consultation, which required responsible ministers to view their own national problems in light of the larger group interests

[79] See Chapters 6 and 7.   [80] See Chapters 2, 4, 13, and 16.

and which at the same time gave them sympathetic insight into the purely national problems of others. This habit first developed in the OEEC, and it was later carried over into the NATO councils. It probably would have contributed considerably to Western cohesiveness if the United States, along with the Europeans, had become firmly addicted to this habit of consultation; it is not yet too late." [81]

The Schuman Plan approach relied on significant transfers of national sovereignty to a supranational authority having control over important sectors of the economies of the six member countries. There had not been time during the period of our study for the Plan to demonstrate what could be done through such federalization—to increase production and trade, to improve working and living conditions in the industries concerned, to overcome national inertias, and to break down political as well as economic barriers. In 1952 many problems had still to be faced. But advocates of the Plan believed that its potentialities, both in direct accomplishment and as a model for further steps toward greater unity in Europe, were immense.

The two types of approach may be considered as complementary rather than competitive or mutually exclusive. They were so considered by the United States government, which gave encouragement and support to both. When the Marshall Plan program ended, the problem of developing a continuously expanding western European economy without the support of external aid or the pressure of war or rearmament was still unsolved, although notable progress had been made. Maximum effort was still needed, by individual nations and through every promising channel of cooperation.

[81] Interview cited.

CHAPTER 13

European Initiative

WHEN Secretary Marshall said "the initiative, I think, must come from Europe," when Administrator-to-be Hoffman declared that "only Europe can save Europe," and when Congress voted American support for "a joint recovery program based upon self-help and mutual cooperation," they were all placing responsibility where it belonged. American aid was intended to buttress a major effort by Europe, not to take its place.

Many Americans are much more aware of the magnitude of American aid than of what the Europeans did in their own behalf. The Marshall Plan was frequently discussed as though it were something being done *to* Europe rather than *with* Europe. Even ECA people at times exaggerated the importance of the agency's activities as compared to those of the peoples with whom they worked. One American ambassador,[1] speaking of the "phenomenal progress" in the country to which he was assigned, expressed bluntly the view that "it would have come anyway. The ECA gave impetus to local efforts. However, we need to avoid exaggeration in talking about the contributions of our experts."

What were the facts? Was the emphasis on European initiative as strong in the thinking of European leaders as it was in the minds of

[1] George McGhee. Interview, Ankara, December 11, 1952.

those who launched and administered the Marshall Plan? To what extent did they exercise initiative in planning and carrying out recovery measures? Let us consider these questions from the standpoint, first, of collective action.

THE EVIDENCE

The reader will recall the first European response to the Marshall speech: the immediate reaction of Bevin and Bidault, the Big Three conference in Paris, the sixteen-power conference, the formation of the CEEC, and the work of that body which set the basic pattern for the European recovery effort. Then the Organization for European Economic Cooperation (OEEC) was established as a continuing European institution, with two main functions: to coordinate the recovery programing activities of member countries and to initiate and carry out cooperative action designed to speed and facilitate the recovery effort. What were the strengths and the weaknesses of the OEEC?

OEEC Strengths

The first task of the delegates from sixteen nations was to set up a constitution. The OEEC Convention was hammered out under the chairmanship of Sir Oliver Franks. It provided for a European organization, with the participation of Americans as observers, which held without alteration throughout the recovery program.

More important than this legal basis, however, was the spirit of cooperation which developed. Underneath all the differences, which were many and often heated, lay the realization that vigorous combined effort was needed to avert economic disaster and that pressure was necessary if results were to be achieved in four years. The delegates sensed that the OEEC was in the forefront of the effort to build new foundations for cooperation in place of constant dissension in Europe.

This required, as Ambassador Eric Berthoud of the United Kingdom put it, "a lot of give and take." [2] Sir Leslie Rowan observed: "In order to justify aid, each country had to make its case to OEEC, where it was closely examined, with Americans sitting in. There was thus built up something quite intangible—beyond the measurable elements of the recovery program. A lot of people were brought together and developed similar thinking about their problems." [3] Many others who took part in the early work of the OEEC had similar things to say. Vice- Chancellor

[2] Interview, Copenhagen, November 22, 1952.
[3] Interview, London, November 10, 1952.

Blücher of Germany commented: "The OEEC had at least one great element. European men came together, knew each other, and were ready for cooperation."[4] Albrecht of Germany declared: "We considered it a token of European solidarity that 120 million dollars [equivalent] in credits were granted to Germany, without United States participation in the decision. This encouraged us to intensify our efforts toward European cooperation."[5] Frank Figgures of the OEEC recalled: "It is remarkable how much the delegates became denationalized. To win the confidence of the group, people had to demonstrate that they were not cheating in favor of their own countries or showing undue partiality. There developed within the OEEC a crusading spirit which was, I believe, quite without parallel in international organization."

Dag Hammarskjold[6] of Sweden remarked: "On the part of the small group at work there appeared to be less interest in aid as such than in getting ahead with the European approach. There were national interests, of course. But there was also faith in the European approach." Gueronik of the OEEC Secretariat noted: "Aside from the money to divide, an important factor has been the development among participating countries of a corps of workers with a common outlook. This has led to a tendency, when facing problems, to try to find a solution which not only satisfies a delegate's own country but also goes at least half way to meet the problems of other countries."[7] "Looking back," said H. M. Hirschfeld of Holland, "one can say that there is not precedent for the degree of cooperation that developed, despite the flaws and difficulties."[8]

Mutual criticism between the OEEC and the ECA was not lacking. Yet Henry Tasca of the ECA's European offices expressed a view shared by many of his colleagues when he said: "The OEEC was an amazing institution. NATO has nothing like it. The understanding that was developed there, the real breaking down of national barriers, was unique."[9]

The OEEC was able, especially in its earlier years, to develop innovations and experimental approaches. "The OEEC experience shows," said Eric Roll of the United Kingdom, "that you can start out with new

---

[4] Interview, Bonn, December 3, 1952.

[5] Interview, Bonn, December 3, 1952.

[6] Later elected Secretary-General of the U.N. Interview, Stockholm, November 28, 1952.

[7] Interview, Paris, November 15, 1952.

[8] Interview, The Hague, November 15, 1952.

[9] Interview, Paris, November 17, 1952.

conceptions and mechanisms. This holds an important lesson for the future. We shouldn't regard the present organization as fixed." [10] Among the many innovations already cited, for example, was joint aid programing. "The something new that was added," observed Olivier Wormser of France, "was the plan that commodity experts together should undertake the task of working on European requirements." [11]

The OEEC's methods of work were down to earth. "One important thing about the organization," said Rowan, "is that it took a practical rather than a legalistic approach to its problems. For example, in connection with Germany, we asked the question: 'What can we do to make this right?' We didn't go to Germany with Article C-4 of the OEEC regulations as our starting point. Thus we went at the real problems of countries in deficit and of countries in surplus. The OEEC has attempted to get at such problems in their totality; if this is done, then special problems of shock to an economy can be dealt with." [12] The technical performance of the agency was massive, highly competent and sober. By and large, the committees and Secretariat eschewed presentations designed to please any particular group—European or American—in favor of realistic analyses and forecasts.

The OEEC was uniquely effective in considering intra-European economic problems—including the internal economic policies of participating countries as well as trade and payments—all as a unity in which interrelationships were carefully analyzed and actions or recommendations proposed. This aspect of the OEEC experience may be applicable to the work of wider international economic institutions.

There is no way of measuring the extent of the OEEC's influence on individual governments. The organization's penetrating annual review of each member country's economic situation, problems, and policies unquestionably had a significant impact. And there were many instances in which countries which at first opposed a line of cooperative action were persuaded to adopt the majority view. Delegates, when convinced that a course of action favored in the OEEC was right, were often able to change or modify the views of their own governments. The Managing Board of the European Payments Union and the Steering

[10] Interview, Paris, November 18, 1952.

[11] Interview, Paris, November 13, 1952.

[12] Interview, Paris, November 17, 1952. One OEEC official asserted: "Provided the work itself is important enough, so that the right people are made available, there seems almost no limit to what can be accomplished in a new organization and it is infinitely better for it to start under enormous pressure than to build up slowly."

Board for Trade, while governed by the unanimous decisions of the OEEC council, carried weight with all members of the OEEC. While the participating countries retained their full formal sovereignty, they accepted fairly strict rules of conduct. A kind of code, written and unwritten, of European solidarity developed in the OEEC. Any country wishing to receive help from the others was honor-bound to observe that code. Particularly important was the obligation of each government to explain to the OEEC any action which might adversely affect its fellow members.

OEEC Weaknesses

One general criticism of the OEEC administration, expressed by a senior delegate, was that as time went on and delegations grew larger there was more and more routine and less and less freedom to innovate. "For the big decisions," said Hirschfeld, "we don't need so much detail. We need an equilibrium between the wisdom of the statesmen and the knowledge of the experts. Sometimes people felt that the figures represented the wisdom. For example, gross-national-product figures do give some important guidance, but they do not give automatically solutions to the problems we have to face. I don't think this was always realized, and the demands for piles of papers tend to produce irritation." [13]

There were times when the OEEC and its committees seemed excessively cautious and slow.

The extent to which the technical committees and working parties were prepared to go beyond factual analysis to the development of constructive recommendations for cooperative action varied greatly from group to group and, of course, with the types of problems under consideration. It was natural—given the newness of the relationship being established between sixteen governments and the unique supporting role of the United States—that there should have been, especially in the OEEC's earlier phases, considerable reliance on the ECA for stimulus. But as time went on, the OEEC built up its own strength and momentum. With the termination of the ECA, it remained as a significant European institution.

Areas of Accomplishment

The actual work of the OEEC has already been reviewed. Where was it most successful, and where least?

[13] Interview cited.

There was significant accomplishment in coordinating country programs, exchanging information previously guarded by national governments, developing analyses of the European economic scene far surpassing previous efforts, exploring national and common problems, recommending divisions of aid, attacking restrictions on intra-European trade, developing a multilateral system of payments, and establishing strong cooperative institutions, notably the European Payments Union and the Steering Board for Trade.

The OEEC was not successful in devising an approach to European investment that would eliminate needless duplication and facilitate more efficient use of resources. Active interest in a coordinated effort for greater productivity per worker developed late. A short struggle with the problem of tariffs was unsuccessful. The OEEC did not consider that it should conduct an active public information program, nor was it prepared to take responsibility for end-use checking to ensure efficient use of aid supplies. There was little coordinated action on overseas territories.

The appraisal of the OEEC's performance during its first four years depends partly upon whether its accomplishment is viewed in relation to total need and an ideal conception of what might have been done, or whether it is looked at in relation to the previous history (or lack of history) of intra-European cooperation and to the many obstacles which had to be dealt with. In any event the performance of the OEEC, on balance, brought it high prestige in Europe and elsewhere.

The OEEC kept alive and strengthened the "European idea" and, in so doing, helped pave the way for such further developments as the Schuman Plan and NATO. Through the Marshall Plan and the OEEC, western Germany was for the first time after the war brought into a cooperative European endeavor on a basis of full equality.

In the words of one ECA executive, the work being carried forward by the OEEC when the Marshall Plan came to an end was "much too important to be junked." Its continuing activities were not dramatic, but they were important. Notable among them were annual economic reviews of country programs, an extensive exchange of information between governments, the development and issuance of informative studies and reports, continuous consultation and action on many common problems, the operations of the EPU, and persisting efforts toward full convertibility of currencies.

Dag Hammarskjold expressed a widely held view when he said:

"OEEC has knowledge and authority gained in many countries, and teamwork. Now—with all the discussion about NATO, the Council of Europe and the Schuman Plan—it would be a great mistake to cut away support from the general approach that has been developed, and from what has been built up through the OEEC. The OEEC is the child of the Marshall Plan experiment. It is the kind of political cooperation that involves international teamwork, dragging governments along, developing new and varied economic links. It has established a new direction in international cooperation. The results are sufficiently important so that Europeans regard it as having proved its value. Apart from economic results as such, then, I believe this is of interest from both the European and United States standpoints, and from the standpoint of principle. Setbacks are unavoidable. I believe that the main effort will survive." [14]

Performance by Individual Governments

The initiative developed by individual governments took many forms and varied greatly according to their capacities and the problems with which they had to contend. All had to deal with inertia and resistance to change. Some were unable or unwilling to face up to tough problems such as tax reform or the curtailment of unnecessary imports. ECA missions were at times impatient over delays in taking actions which were agreed to be desirable. But as one European remarked: "In a poor country, it is difficult to get even a small appropriation through the government. There are many formalities. There are certain expenses which we reasonably should incur, but sometimes budgets are so formal that it is difficult to get the funds without great delays. You have your formalities for five or six months [referring to ECA presentations to Congress, committee deliberations, etc.] then we have ours after that."

There were wide discrepancies in the efficiency of political institutions. A national of one country said candidly: "A big problem here is that the government's administrative machinery is flat. We have needed to set up, for example, a machinery to help deal with housing—an adequate machinery. But it has been largely a restoration of previous machinery, with many of the same people. There are too many state and parastatal agencies competing jurisdictionally instead of collaborating. There is a good deal of vested interest, with groups safeguarding their own interests and not enough concerned with the main job to be

[14] Interview cited.

done. There is need for a national agency, with enough authority to coordinate."

Many other difficulties and shortcomings might be mentioned. But a simple statistic worth repeating is that even in the first year of the operation, American aid came to less than 5 percent of the aggregate national product of the participating countries in Europe. The aid was crucial, providing essential goods which Europe could not purchase due to dollar shortages. But the resources mobilized were overwhelmingly European resources. A few illustrations may indicate the extent and variety of initiative shown.

Denmark and Turkey displayed extraordinary enterprise in dealing with problems of agriculture. Denmark, long dependent on dairy exports for foreign exchange, was faced with a serious payments problem which threatened to cut imports of animal fodder. Ministry of Agriculture officials described what was done to meet this situation.[15] "We have had big endeavors," said one, "to increase our own fodder production—especially of crops richer in protein than those which we ourselves produced before the war. Particularly important were clover, alfalfa, and beet tops. We developed a systematic campaign to develop these in a rational way and to convert them, by modern methods, into silage for use in winter." "Our cattle," another said, "have to be in barns seven months of the year. We started during the war, of necessity, to build fodder storage facilities and had already had some success when the Marshall aid began. In 1945 there were silos on 45,000 farms, whereas before the war we had only a few thousand. The effort was continued, and in 1952 there were silos on 93,000 out of a total of a little more than 200,000 farms."

In Turkey the ECA helped survey rich but inaccessible land, plan a better road system, and provide tractors for cultivation. These activities were enthusiastically expanded by the Turkish government and its farm population—to a point where ECA officials were justly fearful that the economy might be thrown off balance.

In industrial production, German initiative was outstanding. With rich experience and unusual reserves of competent management and skilled labor, Germany accomplished a near miracle in industrial recovery. The attainment might have been even greater if labor-management relations and incentives to the workers had kept pace with investment, technology, and employment.

Many countries made outstanding records in investment, and the

[15] Group conference, Copenhagen, December 1, 1952.

general level was extraordinary. The Monnet Plan in France has been mentioned, and the extensive investment program carried out by Britain. In the latter, as in Norway and Sweden, self-disciplined populations accepted austere living conditions in order to devote as much of their resources as possible to building for the future. Britain succeeded in restoring its balance of payments through a greatly expanded volume of exports without any corresponding increase in the volume of imports. Said Getz Wold of Norway: "We have considerable opportunity for development, but a limiting factor is the extent to which we can continue to import capital. We therefore adopted controls which reduce the level of consumption and we are holding imports to a minimum in order to save on our capital accumulation. We have kept up our rationing on clothes, refrigerators, cars, and other commodities longer than other countries." [16] When another Norwegian official was asked for an explanation of the willingness of the people to accept these sacrifices, he replied: "I believe that important factors have been our wartime traditions, the lack of any strong Communist element and consequent pressures from such a group, and the degree of public interest in, and understanding of, political matters—which has made policy along this rational line easier to pursue."

Many countries took politically difficult measures to stabilize their finances. Mention has been made of the "Benelux solution" to this problem. Steps taken later in the Netherlands to deal with fiscal crisis were described by Richard P. Aiken, deputy chief of the ECA mission: "When things turned down after Korea, the government adopted a program to cope with the situation. At the beginning of 1951 reserves were below one billion guilders, and Holland was faced, at the same time, with the necessity of superimposing an armament program. The measures adopted by the government included a reduction in housing—which was touchy—reductions in public investment, reduction in subsidies on food, an increase of the discount rate, and a cut of 5 percent in real wages voluntarily taken by labor. It was an orthodox approach, supported by the people, and was extremely successful. Reserves are now over 3.5 million guilders, and the Dutch payments position in EPU is greatly improved." [17] Austria and Greece, once thought to be hopelessly bankrupt, greatly strengthened their financial positions before the end of the recovery period by the introduction of sound internal financial policies.

A unique example of informational activity relating to the recovery

[16] Interview, Oslo, November 25, 1952.
[17] Interview, The Hague, November 21, 1952.

program was cited by Ambassador Arne Skaug of Norway. "In our country," he said, "considerable work has been done to bring the OEEC work up for discussion by our Parliament. For example, the first and second OEEC Annual Reports were translated into Norwegian and were presented to the Parliament for purposes of information and discussion. We can have such discussions in our Parliament based on reports submitted by the Government and unrelated to actual pending bills." [18]

ELEMENTS IN INITIATIVE

Individual Men

"The individual man has been most important in this whole development," said former Netherlands Foreign Minister Dirk Stikker, who had served for two years as chairman of the OEEC Council. "Past cooperation between such men as Hoffman, Harriman, Hall-Patch—a complete international servant—and others was very vital to the success of the undertaking. Individual men and close cooperation made success possible." [19] The list might have been extended to include Stikker himself, Spaak and Snoy of Belgium, Hirschfeld of the Netherlands, Monnet, Marjolin and Schweitzer of France, Rowan and Figgures of the United Kingdom, Blücher and Albrecht of Germany, Cattani and Malagodi of Italy, Brofoss of Norway, Hammarskjold of Sweden, and many others.

In 1952 Hammarskjold observed: "The basic experience in Paris was, I think, that the best result in an international effort of this kind can be obtained if the people appointed are not only of high intellectual quality and good experience, but if they also carry such weight with their own governments that they have adequate influence. If such people are working as a team, they are likely to get compromises and agreement beyond what any government would do itself. Then, going back to their governments they can say: 'this is the only thing that could be done—the best that could be done.'" [20] Such men sometimes became, as one ECA executive put it, "prophets in their own countries in the cause of European cooperation."

Snoy of Belgium, among many acute observers, paid tribute to the quality of the OEEC's staff of international civil servants and their contribution to a "great standard of efficiency in efforts looking toward

[18] Interview, Paris, November 18, 1952.
[19] Interview, London, December 22, 1952.
[20] Interview cited.

the development of a European market." [21] It is the writer's impression that among the influences making for solid progress in the OEEC's work, none was more significant than the quality of performance maintained in the Secretariat.

Many who contributed significantly to the ERP were little known outside the immediate circles in which they worked. Take the case, for example, of Paul Hertz of Berlin, a former refugee from Hitlerism who after the war gave up American citizenship to return to Germany and work for his own people. He was elected to the Berlin Senate. Understanding Germans and Americans alike, he was an invaluable bridge to mutual understanding. Asked to account for his acknowledged influence with both groups, he quoted simply a sentence which he had spoken on his return to Germany: "You can only take a task in which you can believe." [22]

Those who in fact participated in the Marshall Plan extended far beyond the limits of the administering agencies in national capitals. Among the many private citizens in Europe who gave it strong support was Ahmed Emin Yalman, a Turkish editor whose outspokenness won him the deep enmity of those who wished the Plan to fail. Sitting in a room overlooking the Bosporus, on his first day out after recovering from five bullet wounds, he said unpretentiously: "I was the victim eighteen days ago of an assassination attempt. I am very happy that it happened, because it has led to an awakening to the dangers of camouflaged communism." [23]

A Job to Do

"If you want to keep an organization like the OEEC really strong and vital," said one participant, "you've got to keep giving it really important things to do. The best men are sent by governments to the most important jobs." The working of this principle was illustrated by Attilio Cattani: [24] "From a psychological more than a practical point of view, it was most important to have the division of aid—that is, recommendations regarding the division of aid—through the OEEC. It gave to the organization both a responsibility and a test. It gave to the problem not the aspect of each trying to get all that he could—as when meat is thrown to a pack of wolves—but more the aspect of trying to reach

---

[21] Interview, Brussels, November 19, 1952.

[22] Interview, Bonn, December 4, 1952.   [23] Interview cited.

[24] Italian Ambassador to the OEEC; chairman of the Council, 1952–1953. Interview, Paris, November 18, 1952.

compromise and eventual agreement among friends. This was a very wise move by the Americans. Despite the initial reluctance of some, the results were good. We came to understand better each other and the need of each other. And we were all fighting for our reasonable and consistent share in the shaping of Europe. We came to see important issues not yet solved—monetary and fiscal issues, and coordination between political economies. Though no final solutions were possible in so short a time, we began understanding that we must move toward decisions." Perhaps, paraphrasing Emerson, we can say that not only men but institutions and societies do not grow tired so long as they can see where they are going.

Administrative Factors

Although the "rule of unanimity" [25] was not easy to operate under, the OEEC convention simplified the task in some measure by specifying the procedures under which the OEEC would function. But there was no agreement, in Europe or the United States, on the meaning and character of the economic and political unity to be sought. "The constitution of the OEEC has rather fluffed that issue," commented a British official.[26] "In the United States, there has certainly been one school of thought favoring unity of a sort that the United Kingdom and the Scandinavian countries, for example, haven't agreed to at all." The rule of unanimity often slowed action, but it had a compensating advantage. "It gives solidity," said Cattani, "with the backing of all participating countries, which may be lacking when cooperation is imposed." [27]

Under the rule of unanimity, expeditious action depended on the extent to which delegates were empowered to speak for their respective countries without continual briefing from their own capitals. The practices of the several governments varied widely here. The United Kingdom, for example, looking upon the OEEC as an "international conference in permanent session," operated on a basis of formal consideration and approval by London of virtually all actions by its delegates. For Sweden, with the Secretary-General of the Foreign Office (Hammarskjold) heading the country's OEEC delegation, briefing was unnecessary and telephone clearances were enough.

"There has been some criticism of the unanimity rule in the OEEC," remarked Marjolin. "There is something to it; there have been occasions when we couldn't agree. But I believe that the argument is overdone.

[25] See Chapter 4.   [26] Unnamed, by request.   [27] Interview cited.

Whenever it was found that an important body of opinion was in favor of a solution, pressure was usually strong enough to bring about agreement. On the other hand, the possibility of countries putting up opposition to particular proposals has had advantages in making it necessary for larger countries to make their cases better and not to neglect the problems of smaller countries." [28]

With unanimity among affected countries as a prerequisite to all OEEC decisions, the resolution of minority opposition to significant proposals was of course crucial. For sharp differences inevitably developed on many issues. In numerous cases when deadlocks could not be breached in ordinary conference, recourse was had to what Stikker dryly called "the torture chamber of the chairman," in which discussion with the minority delegate or delegates would proceed—"all night if necessary" —in order to arrive at the agreement needed. Individual countries generally proved loathe to assume the responsibility for blocking cooperative measures genuinely desired by a substantial majority. A conviction among the members that agreement must somehow be reached on important issues became a part of the tradition of the OEEC.

Opposition and Support

The most direct and vociferous opposition to the European Recovery Program came of course from the Communist camp. The most important support came from the people of the participating countries. There was stimulus to initiative and confidence in the knowledge that neighboring nations were moving in the same direction as one's own. Active American support and participation constituted a further influence, to which we turn in the following chapter.

[28] Interview cited.

CHAPTER 14

Aims and Techniques of

American Participation

SIR Robert Hall of the British Cabinet Planning Office, reflecting on the situation in 1947, remarked: "We now realize more clearly than then that the United States was going to have to get the economies of the free world going again before we could stand up to Russia. It was a great political judgment."[1]

What was behind the American decision to act? What techniques were used to give maximum effect to the aid provided, and how fruitful were they? What impact did American participation have? What conditions affected the influence exerted by the United States?

American Aims and Role

A succinct statement of the political, economic, and humanitarian interests of the United States in European recovery was given in the Harriman committee report.[2] The first and most important interest,

though it may for simplicity be called political, it is in fact very much broader. It stems from the realization that a European recovery program is an investment in the continued survival of a world economically stabilized and peace-

[1] Interview, London, November 2, 1952.
[2] President's Committee on Foreign Aid, *European Recovery and American Aid* (Washington, 1947), pp. 17–22. See Chapter 3.

fully conducted, in which governments based upon fundamental democratic principles can prosper, in which right, not might, prevails and in which religious freedom, economic opportunity, and individual liberties are maintained and respected. . . . Any program for the democratic rehabilitation of Western Europe must overcome not only the complex economic problems resulting from the ravages of war, but also the deliberate sabotage by the Communists who see in the continuance of misery and chaos their best chance for an ultimate victory.

America's economic interest was described in these words:

Our economic self-interest is closely related to the fate of Europe. American trade with Europe has always been a factor of paramount importance to the American economy. A progressive decline in the producing and buying power of 270,000,000 people in Western and Central Europe would have a powerful impact upon American prosperity. . . . The deterioration of the European economy for lack of means to obtain essential imports would force European countries to resort to trade by government monopoly—not only for economic but for political ends. The United States would almost inevitably have to follow suit. The resulting system of state controls, at first relating to foreign trade, would soon have to be extended into the domestic economy to an extent that would endanger the survival of the American system of free enterprise.

As to the humanitarian impulse, the report declared:

There is deeply rooted in the hearts of most Americans . . . a will and a wish to give whatever is possible to those who are in dire need of help. . . . We as a nation, who are enjoying comparative luxury, cannot in good conscience do otherwise. To withhold our aid would be to violate every moral precept associated with our free government and free institutions.

This was not the whole picture. In the fibers of popular sentiment and inclination which fed into the main roots of support for the Marshall Plan were many lesser interests not so readily detectable—such as desire for the good will or gratitude of those to whom aid was being proffered or the hope of some that large-scale help over a four-year period would make possible a withdrawal from involvement in Europe. The latter sentiment may have accounted in part for support given to the Plan from sources previously regarded as "isolationist."

The basic political aim was to strengthen independence, liberty, and democratic institutions in western and southern Europe. As the Marshall speech and the Economic Assistance Act of 1948 made clear, there was no aggressive design against the Russian people or their government.

Communism was to be parried instead by a constructive program which would produce strength rather than weakness in western and southern Europe. The original economic objective was to help provide a cure rather than a mere palliative in Europe's ills, by developing self-reliant economies capable of maintaining reasonable standards of living without indefinite assistance.

The swing from predominantly economic to predominantly security aims, which began in the summer of 1950, occurred more rapidly than did changes in the capacity of some of the European countries to effect the transition which Communist military action had imposed. In the struggle with such problems as how much defense could be planned in Europe without jeopardizing existing economic gains and political stability, the forward economic aims of the recovery program receded for a time, then, to a limited extent—particularly as regards productivity—came to the fore once more.[3] Perhaps the economic objective did not go far enough. As John Hulley remarked in 1953, "The initial idea was too simple: that we would work with these people, give them of our substance, help them to get on their feet, and then retire."[4] Or as H. Van Buren Cleveland put it: "The economic and political conception of what ailed Europe and what had to be done to restore its economic health and political strength was, it developed, far from adequate."[5]

But if the Marshall Plan operation did not yield a full vision of what was needed to give effect to the great hopes which it inspired, it did represent an extraordinary step forward in both European and American thinking. It signalized a further departure from America's relative isolationism to a position which, as one observer put it, "riveted us into a more dynamic relationship with Europe and the rest of the free world." The national interest was never lost sight of, but neither was it portrayed as the exclusive foundation for national policy, apart from the realities of international interdependence and responsibility.

If American aims lacked long-range perspective, they had a compensating strength. The recovery program was conceived and developed as a joint concern. It reflected no desire to impose conditions contrary to the interest of the European peoples, much less to subordinate their economies to that of the United States. Whatever else may be said about the objectives of the Marshall Plan, they were ethically sound. This was of incalculable importance in establishing the moral position of the United States and in evoking, among its own people and those of co-

[3] See Chapter 8.   [4] Interview, Washington, May 8, 1953.
[5] Interview, Washington, June 23, 1953.

operating countries, confidence and energetic action in behalf of mutually advantageous aims. A course was being staked out in the direction of democratic world leadership as contrasted with imperialism.

The precise role which the American government—or, more specifically, the ECA—would play in the joint effort was by no means clear at the start. Congress gave the agency broad responsibilities but left to the Administrator wide latitude in determining how to carry them out. It was soon seen that recovery depended more on the way OEEC member nations used their resources as a whole than on the precise uses to which the ECA aid was put. Thus, it came about that ECA activity was increasingly directed toward influencing governments to adopt sound recovery policies, in which the use of aid was but one of several important elements.

TECHNIQUES EMPLOYED

It was one thing for the ECA to be given a role to play in relation to significant interests and goals. It was another to act effectively. There was no blueprint or any standard "kit of tools" with which to work. Some of the working techniques, concepts, and practices adopted by the ECA had been tested during the war and through a variety of postwar agencies. Others were new departures. Our interest in this chapter is the whole range of techniques employed rather than on their genealogy. Let us consider first the means adopted in laying the groundwork for cooperation.

Invitation to Action

The initial approach was established by the Marshall speech of June 1947 when he stated that "it would be neither fitting nor efficacious for this Government to undertake to draw up unilaterally a program designed to place Europe on its feet economically. That is the business of the Europeans. . . . The program should be a joint one, agreed to by a number, if not all, European nations." [6] The extraordinary response in

[6] Illustrating his conception of this approach, Hoffman said later: "If for example in Studebaker I believed that our body department was not as efficient as, say, that of Oldsmobile, I wouldn't go to the Oldsmobile company, study what they are doing, and then give an order to the head of our body department. Instead, I would talk to our man, saying that they seem to be doing some interesting things in connection with bodywork at Oldsmobile, and I would suggest that he go and take a look. When he comes back, and if he is any good, he will have ideas. He will say that Oldsmobile has developed this or that which is desirable, but of course it needs modification and improvement; he takes the initiative for suggesting improvements, and he accepts the responsibility. In a larger way, we were successful in getting this done in Europe. There was development by each country

Europe, which provided the basic framework and rationale of the recovery program, has been described.

Consultation

No single technique employed in the course of the recovery program was more basic or productive than the close consultations at policy and technical levels, to which frequent reference has been made. They made it possible to iron out differing preconceptions and to avoid misunderstandings which might have led to serious difficulties. They paved the way to every significant cooperative measure undertaken.

Later, mutual understanding was to some extent reduced with changes in personnel, in goals, and in organizational relationships—all reflecting the new, unavoidable pressures and urgencies of defense programing. Commenting on this transitional phase, an experienced but harassed United States official in Paris said in 1952: "There is a partial failure to learn how to work with these people. The number of Americans running around today and telling everybody what to do is very large. We don't come in as equals, but always on a platform. There is quite a difference between this and the development in 1948 of the OEEC Convention— the point of which was that we agreed on broad goals, without rigid mechanisms for living up to those goals." The multiplication of frictions and the growth of anti-Americanism in Europe during 1951 and 1952 was attributable, in the view of many consulted, not only to nervousness over the international situation but also, in part, to this variation in approach from the American side, involving not necessarily greater firmness, but more "toughness," less understanding and less tact.

It is perhaps not too much to infer, from the ECA experience, that when there is heavy pressure to achieve results quickly, informal consultation is even more important than under more leisurely circumstances. The broader and more genuine the understandings initially reached, the greater possibility there is of seeing problems as a whole rather than in a fragmentary way, of avoiding ill-considered actions, and of anticipating and trying to forestall difficulties rather than waiting until they become real issues.

Technical Collaboration

Consultations at the policy level paved the way for an unprecedented degree of collaboration between European and American technicians. In Italy, for example, some fifteen Italian-American joint committees, in

of its own plans and proposals. It was their initiative and enthusiasm, and they took the responsibility for the plans." Interview, New York, January 28, 1953.

which technicians played an important role, worked on many detailed questions.

Collaboration among specialists, especially in economic programing, was an arduous process in which many divergencies in viewpoint and opinion had to be reconciled. Yet special advantages accrued from the practice. Many problems could be better approached from a technical than from a political point of view. When men speaking the same technical language were given responsibility for developing analyses and recommendations on specific questions, they were often able to get results which could never have been achieved through diplomatic negotiations alone. Referring to the EPU [7] as "one of the most important things in this century in Europe," Ambassador Cattani of Italy said: "Its economic effects were very significant, but more important was the discussion of financial questions and the fact that a small number of technical minds were allowed to work upon and discuss these questions. These common discussions, leading toward advice to particular governments, were not meaningful to the man in the street. But to governments they were tremendously important. Previously governments had not been allowed to discuss these questions—even bilaterally." [8]

Joint Responsibility

The American request that the European governments should take the responsibility for recommending the division of aid between countries also helped lay the groundwork for cooperation. Interestingly enough, the Europeans attached more significance to this proposal than did most Americans. "In practice," said one ECA staff member stationed in Washington, "the division-of-aid effort was too much of a burden to put on any international committee."

A very different view was found in Europe. Gueronik of the OEEC said, for example: "I believe the decision was fundamental to the success of the Marshall Plan. For it gave us the means for asking countries to cooperate in a number of ways. And the countries accepted things, for the sake of such cooperation, which they wouldn't have if American aid hadn't been at the end of the process. And so the lines of work developed." [9] Said Robert Hall of the United Kingdom: "I believe that by far the most important thing in the early Paris operation was the decision on the division of aid by cooperative action of the participating countries, although legally the United States retained the final voice. It

[7] See Chapters 6, 7, and 12.   [8] Interview cited.
[9] Interview cited.

meant that the approach was: How does it look to you? What do you think? It showed a spirit of cooperation and gave to the participating countries something practical to do and decisions that they had to take." [10]

There were significant advantages from the American standpoint. The United States government was freed from the delicate obligation of making unilateral decisions. And the fact that the participating governments were carrying the primary responsibility demonstrated that the program was being administered, not in behalf of any hidden United States interest, but in full support of the declared and jointly accepted objectives of the Marshall Plan.

National Accounts Analysis

Although OEEC recommendations on the division of aid were generally followed, the final decisions had to be made by the ECA, and the latter had the responsibility of administering the aid after allotments had been made. In doing so, the agency developed programing procedures which were, necessarily, quite technical in character. Certain of these merit mention.

Since the 1930's economists had been interested in the use of such aggregate measures of economic activity as gross national product, national income, consumption, and capital formation. Because various countries prepared data for their own uses, there were inevitably differences in the statistical methods employed. It was felt that a greater degree of comparability could be secured. The ECA was interested in the intrinsic value of national accounts data and the information they would yield on the relative progress of recovery in the participating countries.[11]

[10] Interview cited. These statements, and many like them, were made in spite of the inherent difficulty of the division-of-aid exercise, especially after it became apparent that it would be necessary to take into account not only estimated balance-of-payments deficits but also "drawing rights" under the first intra-European payments agreements. Aid during the first year was divided mainly on the basis of estimated balance-of-payments deficits. For the second year the OEEC adopted a revised approach known as the "Snoy-Marjolin formula," which involved an across-the-board percentage reduction in the apportionment of aid. As previously indicated, this had the advantage of giving added incentive to individual countries to reduce their payments deficits and to "make do" with less aid. After the first two years, the bases on which a reduced volume of aid was divided were modified and the U.S. government assumed the major responsibility, taking into account, however, the Snoy-Marjolin formula.

[11] See Richard Ruggles, *National Income Accounting and Its Relation to Economic Policy* (ECA [OSR]; Paris, 1949).

Two American experts engaged by the ECA, Richard and Nancy Ruggles, cooperated with the OEEC in making plans for setting up the National Accounts Research Unit in Cambridge, England, referred to in Chapter 5.[12] Meanwhile the OEEC fostered and made use of the work of member governments in the field of national accounts.[13]

National accounts data, by indicating the sources of income by major economic sectors and the uses to which these funds are put, make it possible to assess the factors contributing to a change in national income and to predict the effects of specific policies.[14] Comparative study of the national accounts of different countries makes it possible to estimate their relative levels of consumption or investment and to analyze the relative performance of their economies in response to particular stimuli.

Although the programing of economic aid was based primarily on balance-of-payments estimates for each participating country, national accounts analyses provided a useful auxiliary tool for assessing recovery plans and policies and their effects in individual countries.

Other Analytical Approaches

Another analytical device used to check the consistency of assumptions and projections relating to European recovery was the "world trade and payments model," prepared by the ECA Trade Analysis Staff.[15] The model provided historical data and projections on the trade and payments of the world, broken down according to areas. Previous analyses had been made of world trading patterns,[16] and the usefulness of projecting a world trade matrix had been pointed out in economic literature,[17] but

[12] In April 1950, the unit published *A Simplified System of National Accounts*, which provided the basis for comparable systems of reporting national accounts data in OEEC countries. This was followed in 1951 by the first of a series of studies of the national accounts of the participating countries, presented according to the recommended accounting methods. In 1952 *A Standardized System of National Accounts* was issued providing a more complete accounting procedure for the presentation of national income data.

[13] This was initiated by questionnaires to the participating governments.

[14] For a lucid treatment of the rationale and techniques of national accounts analysis, see Richard and Nancy Ruggles, *European National Accounts* (Washington, 1951).

[15] See Chapter 6.

[16] E.g., League of Nations, *The Network of World Trade* (New York and London, 1942).

[17] See Ragnar Frisch, "On the Need for Forecasting a Multilateral Balance of Payments," *American Economic Review*, September 1947, pp. 535–551.

there seems to be no evidence of the preparation and *use* of such projections before the one developed in the ECA.

The European Program Division of the ECA prepared more limited projections of the trade and payments of the participating countries with the other areas of the world. The world trade model provided an indication of whether the projections for individual countries were consistent with what was known of the economies of the non-OEEC countries.

Initially, foreign trade information for some of the participating countries was unsatisfactory for analytical purposes for a number of reasons. Commodity classifications were not comparable in most cases; it was therefore impossible to combine trade data for the various countries and obtain a figure on European imports or exports of a single commodity. And in some instances it took as much as nine months for foreign trade data by geographical area to be made available. In the spring of 1948 the ECA published a "commodity code" which, though admittedly inadequate as a permanent system of reporting commodity trade, made it possible for the ECA to gather comparable statistics from the different countries. In the fall of 1950 the ECA agreed to accept commodity reporting by OEEC countries according to a code newly developed by the United Nations Statistical Office,[18] thereby furthering the widespread adoption of a permanent system of classification by the participating countries. The time required for standard reporting on foreign trade was reduced to approximately one month.

Such detailed information, while highly useful to trade and commodity specialists, was too voluminous for extensive use in general economic planning. "I have advocated," said J. Tinbergen [19] of the Netherlands, "planning on a macroeconomic basis, with full information on major aspects as against the enormous mass of figures relating to commodities and so forth which do not lead to so clear a general picture. I am glad that, with United States support, the national accounts approach gained ground."

Persuasion

These are some of the techniques adopted to ensure cooperation and efficiency in aid programing. The ECA also undertook, sometimes with

[18] U.N., *The Standard International Trade Classification* (New York, 1950).

[19] Director, Central Planning Bureau. Interview, The Hague, November 22, 1952.

the collaboration of other United States agencies, to exert a positive influence upon European governments. The matter was put quite simply in a study of the ECA's internal workings by a group of its administrative officers:

ECA is in two businesses: (1) the influencing of European recovery along lines favorable to both Europe and the United States and, to the extent desirable, attempting to bring about changes in the plans, policies and actions of the participating countries and OEEC; and (2) administering aid to the participating countries. Although both of these businesses are essential and interrelated, one with the other, influencing European policy in the direction of recovery of a character that would be most beneficial to Europe is really ECA's main purpose.[20]

The justification of this emphasis was the need of the United States to ensure the most efficient use of the limited aid resources at its disposal. The "most" was defined in terms of jointly agreed objectives, and this was of utmost importance; the aid had to be used in a manner that would promote mutual interests. The participating governments, though resentful at times on specific issues, generally recognized the bona fide character of ECA aims and the need for active American participation if recovery goals were to be approached in four years. The word "participation" conveys more acurately the spirit and conduct of the ECA's role than does "intervention," with its baleful connotations.

Influence was most frequently exerted through direct discussion and suasion. Although the ECA Administrator was empowered to curtail or terminate aid in the event of nonfulfillment of agreed obligations, care was taken not to give the impression that the ECA wished to resort to sanctions. As it turned out, questions involving compliance with agreements were resolved through negotiations; in no case was aid terminated as a penalty.

The ECA's efforts to influence internal policies varied greatly, as might be expected, from country to country. It was great in Greece, which had been almost without a government during the early postwar years, quite extensive in Italy, considerably less so in France, and relatively limited in the United Kingdom. Nowhere were the ECA's contacts more extended, or more significant, than with the OEEC—through special conferences, or meetings of the committees of the Council which ECA representatives attended as observers, or at technical levels, or through informal out-of-hours discussions. On two occasions Hoffman delivered

[20] Fite *et al.*, *Survey of Relationships of the Parts of ECA*, p. 9.

formal addresses to the OEEC Council, on the urgent need for efforts in behalf of increased production and for the removal of trade barriers.

Control of Dollar Aid

The control which the ECA exercised over the use of dollar assistance was another means through which American influence could be exerted. This "leverage" in negotiations was not abused; it was employed solely in support of mutually agreed principles and objectives. Control over dollar assistance was also used, specifically, for the establishment of incentive funds. The ECA established, for example, a special overseas development fund which could be drawn upon by governments responsible for the administration of overseas territories only when projects conforming to established criteria were presented. This fostered an acceleration of basic development in the territories.

Probably the most significant example of the use of dollar assistance to influence policy was in the development of "conditional aid" for freeing intra-European payments and in the support given to the European Payments Union.[21]

ECA administration of the funds appropriated by Congress carried with it the responsibility of ensuring that the materials and equipment procured were put to effective use in the recipient countries.[22] The procedure developed for this purpose was called "end-use checking"; in recipient countries it was increasingly referred to as "program accountability," reflecting a broadened approach. For as time went on, the ECA Controller's Office came to view the procedure less as a "watchdog" operation and more as a means of working with governments and businesses to maximize the effect of the aid. This made it possible, without relinquishing responsibility for spot checks on the use of aid supplies, to develop this function into a joint effort, sometimes accompanied by technical advice on the use of newer types of equipment.

Voice in Use of Counterpart Funds

It will be recalled that, according to the ECA enabling legislation and the bilateral agreements which followed, each government was to deposit

[21] See Chapters 5 to 7.

[22] It was thought at first that the arrangements needed for end-use checking might be worked out through the OEEC, but its representatives were reluctant to undertake the responsibility. This was a disappointment to some in the ECA, who felt that it would have given the operation a more international flavor.

into an account, jointly controlled by it and the United States, local currency funds equal to the amount of grant aid received.[23]

The extent to which this joint control actually provided a means for influencing government policy was at times exaggerated, even by members of the ECA staff. For the governments could usually find other funds for purposes which the ECA might not approve for counterpart financing. Or where inflationary pressures made it appear desirable, the counterpart could simply be frozen.

Counterpart funds were important to the economies of the participating countries, however, permitting larger allocations of internal resources to urgent purposes other than dollar-earning exports. In practice counterpart had in some countries a wide variety of uses for recovery purposes. They were particularly important in the shaping of investment programs in Austria, Italy, Greece, West Germany, France, and Turkey.

Project Procedure

A supplementary technique designed to bring ECA influence to bear on the selection and conduct of key enterprises involving substantial American aid came to be known as the "project procedure." A portion of the aid funds was utilized for specific, carefully developed projects conforming to established criteria and subject to detailed review by industrial or other technical specialists in the ECA. The ECA adopted here an approach somewhat comparable to that of the investment banker. ECA personnel (or engineering firms paid out of ECA funds) also participated in the preparation of the project proposals and at times assisted in the selection and installation of equipment and the launching of operations. An illustration of the project procedure was given by Oscar B. Bransky [24] of the European regional office: "Beginning with almost nothing at the end of the war, oil refining in Europe has expanded remarkably since. This was done mainly with European capital and enterprise, but ECA help was provided at critical places—both as regards equipment and technical work. It was not the volume of aid, but the items and the technical help that were important. The first projects required more ECA help. The prewar refineries were generally small and new refining processes had not been much developed except in the case of two larger companies. Help was therefore needed

---

[23] The 5 percent of these funds which reverted by agreement to the U.S. reduced by that percentage, in effect, the total grant aid made available.

[24] Chief, Petroleum Branch; subsequently deputy director, Industrial Resources Division, OSR. Interview, Paris, November 3, 1952.

on the part of American engineering firms of repute to design new modern plants and to construct them. The procedure was that the company that wanted the job done would work with a United States engineering firm in developing a blueprint, plans for installation, lists of equipment etc.; the Europeans concerned would choose the American firm, sometimes from a list of reputable firms provided by ECA. The work provided the basis for an industrial project. The application would be submitted by the participating government through the regular procedure for such projects. The oil branch in ECA/Washington would then consult refiners and together consider and analyze the project—mainly from the standpoint of its technical and its economic justification in terms of future returns."

The project procedure afforded scope for engineers, power technicians, and agricultural, conservation, and commodity specialists to contribute to the quality and productivity of Europe's industrial plant.

Technical Assistance

Technical assistance, sometimes linked with the project procedure, provided one of the most important means of stimulating advances in production methods and productive efficiency. This technique is discussed in the following chapter.

EFFECTS OF AMERICAN PARTICIPATION

There is no way of measuring the influence actually exerted through these techniques of participation. The channels were diverse, the results not subject to computation. Effects on patterns of thought were often more important than immediate changes in practice.

Illustrations

In the United Kingdom, American cooperation affected considerably industrial practices and Britain's role in liberalization of intra-European trade and payments.[25] But, broadly speaking, the British were well abreast of Americans in economic sophistication, and American influence upon British economic thought and practice was less than in most of the other participating countries.

A very different situation developed in Turkey. Here was a country economically poor but passionately independent, in which decades of revolutionary ferment had created a strong desire for change. Fear of

[25] See Chapter 6.

Russian encroachment had produced a strong emphasis on military strength. These influences seem to have been stronger than sensitivity to the participation of foreign personnel in internal recovery measures. The Turkish government indeed consciously desired close ties with a great power. Hence in the Turkish program, American participation and influence were outstanding, in agricultural and industrial development and in various aspects of public administration. During a small group conference in Ankara, in December 1952, Leon Dayton, United States economic mission chief in Turkey, remarked: "The acceptance of another country into the intimate affairs of a country is even more unprecedented than the Marshall Plan itself." To which Heyder Bey, director of the recovery program, replied: "True. Countries are not used to this sort of thing. It is quite a new experience to have such intimate relations—entering into all aspects of public life."

Some of the effects of American participation in the European recovery effort were contradictory. Attempts were made by the ECA to break down restrictions upon free private enterprise (e.g., by trade associations) and to encourage competition throughout the European market.[26] Yet administration of the aid program influenced governments in many cases to increase economic planning and controls. To demonstrate their economic needs and how they proposed to bring about recovery, they expanded the apparatus for central supervision of their economies. "It was quite impossible," remarked one Britisher, "for a government confronted by keen cross-questioning from OEEC and ECA over the whole range of the economy to say 'We do not know; we rely upon getting the incentives right; the forces of the market will then look after our economy and steer it in the right direction.'"

American influence on the European economy as a whole showed great variations. It was more significant in intra-European trade liberalization and multilateral payments than in the coordination of investments or in the field of public information. It was greater in petroleum production than in power. The effect on agricultural development was much greater in Denmark and Holland than it was in France.

Too Much or Too Little?

The question naturally arises whether there was too much or too little American participation. Opinions vary greatly. An adequate analysis of

[26] See Chapter 15.

the question would require a book, but a few typical reactions may be cited.

In the case of Greece, where extensive intervention was unquestionably necessary in order to prevent political and economic collapse, many in the ECA as well as in the Greek government felt that too much was attempted during the earlier part of the program, entailing a loss of initiative on the part of Greek officials and too much dependence on the Americans. Said Leland Barrows, ECA mission chief in 1952: "Now we have the job of pulling out. It's under way. We no longer claim responsibility for the use of all resources. We expect by stages to give up controls." Yet, with the program nearing termination, Constantine D. Tsatsos, Minister of Coordination during the heyday of the program, was apprehensive lest the Americans pull out too quickly. "My chief worry now," he said, "is not too much United States interference, but too little. There is no danger of American domination, but rather the contrary." [27] He emphasized the need for continuing cooperation, especially in technical assistance.

Certainly there was the feeling in some countries that American influence, though well intentioned, was at times misguided. Officials consulted in the Italian and Austrian governments, for example, felt that American pressure toward greater investments, involving some increase in the risk of financial instability, was a mistake. In Norway, on the other hand, governmental leaders believed that ECA headquarters in Washington showed excessive concern lest their investment program be too large. Such differences in judgment were bound to occur and tended on the whole to advance more balanced development. In very few instances did they lead to real friction. A greater source of irritation was the "protective clauses" or other conditions attached to ECA's enabling legislation, such as the stipulation that 50 percent of all assistance goods must be transported in American ships. Many in the ECA felt that as the program advanced these conditions became too numerous and too restrictive and that the measures which the ECA had to take to ensure compliance increased difficulties in the participating countries, chiefly where the conditions were not clearly related to the agreed objectives of the program.

There were some, on the other hand, who felt that in some cases not enough American influence was exerted. Donato Menichella of Italy,

[27] Interview, Athens, December 15, 1952.

for example, held that "if there is going to be continuation of any form of aid to Europe, it should be used very firmly to put pressure on European countries to achieve greater unification. Europe should not go back—especially as regards the EPU and similar developments." [28]

Dagfin Juel of Norway commented: "Some countries were somewhat fearful at first of receiving United States aid. The Communists argued vigorously that such aid would lead to a relationship of dependence on the United States. Many non-communists were also apprehensive. There was much discussion about this—some saying, 'let's take less before the aid provided places us in a dependent relationship.' After a while—approximately the first year—this discussion disappeared. American political interference did not take place. The existence of OEEC was also a quieting fact." [29] Said Eric Virgin of Sweden, where the aid program had been terminated: "I really think it's a pity now that we don't work together the same way as we used to with members of the ECA mission. Nothing brings people together so much as having a common problem." [30] After talking with more than a hundred well-informed nationals in thirteen countries, the writer gained the impression that these views were widely representative of opinion among Europeans who participated actively in the Marshall Plan.

CONDITIONS AFFECTING AMERICAN INFLUENCE

Future historians may see in the Marshall Plan and other developments in American foreign policy during this period evidences of a search for an effective alternative to imperialism as a means of stabilizing the world situation in a time of upheaval and danger. It is appropriate, therefore, to ask the question: What were the features of American policy and conduct, in connection with the Marshall Plan, that most affected the influence of the United States in Europe, for better or worse? At the risk of some oversimplification, let us consider this question briefly.

Affirmative Goals

The Marshall Plan's affirmative goals gave it an immediate appeal. In the confusion, division, and discouragement which marked the scene in Europe in 1947, the clear and simple statement of a policy directed "against hunger, poverty, desperation and chaos" proved, as Senator Vandenberg said, to be "a shot heard 'round the world." The general objective was translated into more specific aims upon which there could

[28] Interview cited.   [29] Interview cited.
[30] Interview, Stockholm, November 28, 1952.

be virtually unanimous agreement among freedom-loving peoples. These practical, affirmative goals provided a new sense of direction [31] and new confidence in the possibilities of cooperative action.

Clarity in Administration

Affirmative aims could have been quickly dissipated, however, without clarity in administration. Large purposes had to be transformed into immediate concrete objectives; ends had to be translated into means.

The work of the CEEC and the bilateral agreements between each country and the United States laid an indispensable groundwork of mutually accepted principles. National and international consultations provided further bases of agreement. Major potential sources of misunderstanding and disagreement were to a large extent identified and dealt with at an early stage. Even so, there were weaknesses which should be recognized, the most important of which, perhaps, was a decline in the clarity of both policy and administration after the advent of the defense program.[32]

Mutual Understanding and Respect

One of the most important conditions of American influence was the degree to which mutual understanding and respect were actually developed. Economic and political as well as ordinary human understanding were needed. None of these came easily.

The problem was identified by Brofoss, in speaking of European unification: "It is well to bear in mind that small countries have a long tradition of hard struggle for survival as national units and have put all their strength into that fight. One can still arouse feelings regarding the Germans. How long did it take the United States to overcome the repercussions of the Civil War? It is even astonishing that the Scandinavian peoples welcomed the Germans for the Olympic games. The Germans in north Norway conducted the most complete scorched earth policy. The Russians came and, after one day of disorders, behaved very well. It is hard to say to the people that the Germans are now our friends but the Russians are now our enemies. We shouldn't press this too hard, but give time to forget." [33] The importance of understanding in personal, human terms was emphasized by Michael H. B. Adler of the ECA mission to Greece: "It is necessary to know the people with whom you work. The Greeks, for example, are proud and nationalistic. If you can

---

[31] See Chapter 12.   [32] See Chapter 12, also Chapters 8 and 18.
[33] Interview cited.

really appeal to something in them and to their own initiative, you will stand a chance of getting results." [34]

Much depended on the attitudes of American officials and staff members toward other cultural patterns and values, and the ways in which those attitudes were modified as a result of experience in the program. After making a number of criticisms of the conduct of the program, Robert Buron, an influential younger member of the French Parliament, said: "Yet Americans are full of good will. That is the best quality of American representatives abroad." [35] Of basic importance, too, were integrity and tact. "Although there was a considerable measure of real confidence in United States motives from the outset," commented Cemal Bark in Turkey, "the meticulous care which ECA showed in approaching budgetary questions and especially the use of appropriated funds led to deepening confidence in the disinterestedness of the American approach; our experience in this regard was the same at that of other participating countries." [36]

But when pressure was exerted without a sufficient knowledge of conditions within the country, negative results were apt to follow. On this point Adler remarked: "Some who came in had ideas of great American aid as obligating the Greeks to do many things at once. They tended to point to what the Greeks hadn't done and to take the attitude: why in the world don't you do thus and so? The effect on Greeks as individuals, with their national pride, was disastrous." [37] Constantin B. Tsatsos made the same point: "Our people have suffered greatly themselves and don't have the feeling that too much has been given to them. There is a feeling that the Americans have at times injured the sensibilities of the Greeks here. They would not want the Americans to leave. Yet they don't like to be told constantly what they must do. Public statements of a critical, demanding nature are especially resented; when these have been made on economic problems, some have had political repercussions." [38]

Following Korea there was a difficult turning point and, as one American remarked, "We weren't very graceful about it. We lost ground politically in the transition from a giving program to one involving sacrifices." In the same vein, John Lindeman said: "A basic error was the tone of the approach which we made to our Allies in about July of

---

[34] Interview, Athens, December 15, 1952.
[35] Interview, Paris, November 15, 1952.
[36] Interview, Ankara, December 11, 1952.
[37] Interview cited.   [38] Interview cited.

1950, calling for significantly greater military effort on their part. The approach was peremptory in tone as we requested immediate estimates of the military expenditures that each country would make in the light of new world conditions. It took no account of internal politics or of the legislative and parliamentary processes necesary in European countries. It gave them only a few days in which to reply and was widely regarded as an ultimatum. We didn't get any more defense effort as a direct result of this particular effort." [39]

A number of Europeans consulted were no less articulate on this general point. Hirschfeld of the Netherlands stated: "I said in a speech at a dinner given by the ECA mission chief that the United States had developed a first experience in the giving of large aid in peacetime, since the war, with no *quid pro quo*. This was important in that it was building toward a new world policy. But against this relationship is the fact that, as in the case of assistance to individuals, those receiving aid are touchy when their behavior is criticized. It is therefore best, I said, not to give the impression of one-sided aid, but to convey more a sharing-of-the-burden idea. Although the attempt to do this in connection with the military was a failure, finding something of the sort, I said, was of great importance." [40]

Of course, understanding had to be a two-way street; it was important that American aims be understood. "One thing that has impressed me," commented Huntington Gilchrist, chief of the ECA mission to Belgium, "has been the extent and character of misconceptions about the Marshall Plan in both Europe and the United States.[41] In Paris, a thoughtful observer [42] remarked upon the extraordinary degree of misunderstanding among French workers about the condition of the working population in the United States, the degree to which the American economy was controlled by Wall Street, and the purposes of American aid. While in most of the European countries the aims of the Marshall Plan came to be well understood by the people, this was not true in all, especially where Communist propaganda was effective.

Political and Economic Dependability

The degree to which United States leadership was accepted was based in large measure also on the dependability of American foreign policy and the stability of the American economy. In her book *The West at Bay* (1948), Barbara Ward commented on how the prophets

[39] Interview, Washington, January 22, 1953. [40] Interview cited.
[41] Interview, Brussels, November 20, 1952. [42] Unnamed, by request.

of doom warned Europe, when the Marshall Plan was launched, against adjustments which depended on the consistency and stability of the United States. They argued that America was still fundamentally isolationist, that the American economy was unstable and threatened by depression, that American policy was likely to become increasingly imperialistic and aggressive, and that the United States elective system prevented continuity in the conduct of foreign affairs. The Marshall Plan did much to dispel such fears, since, as Miss Ward emphasized, it was designed to restore their strength and was not based on any disadvantageous concessions on their part to the United States.

As late as 1952, however, many Europeans continued to question the steadiness of American leadership. In general, there was a greater sense of assurance when American policies were directed toward joint economic goals than when they were directed toward military defense against Russia. It was not primarily a question of the decline in economic aid, for few responsible European leaders wished to continue a donor-client relationship longer than necessary. Nor was it primarily a question of reluctance to make sacrifices for the common defense, although that was a factor in some instances. It was, for many, a question whether the United States, in leading the defense effort, would chart a wise course politically, and whether it might lose interest in continuing to lead also toward a workable economic system for the free world, in which America itself would be an active, responsible participant.

Along with uncertainties about American foreign policies there was considerable apprehension lest deflation and an economic recession within the United States undo many of the gains achieved with Marshall aid.

These concerns were not limited to Europeans. In 1952 an American trade expert in Paris remarked sadly: "Washington interest in trade matters is not now very strong. We have no response to our reports. I heard one Washington official say recently that trade liberalization was bad!" This was a straw in a wind. American interest in developing a single European market was not being steadily sustained.

Consistency between Principles and Action

In its effect on the willingness of Europeans to accept American leadership the adherence of the United States government and people to the principles they proclaimed was crucial. Consider, for example, the principles of mutual assistance and trade liberalization. In the first, American action was fully consistent with the principle it espoused. But in the second it was not. American influence in behalf of European economic integration was seriously impaired by our unwillingness to cut down our own restrictions on trade and immigration. The moral effect of this was probably more important than the economic. Our position seemed to be that the countries of Europe should move toward greater economic integration, but that for the United States it was another matter.

Many Europeans consulted were outspoken on this point. For example, Jahn Halvorsen, a Norwegian economist,[43] speaking of the changing structure of the world economy since 1900, said: "One major factor is the development of the U.S. from a capital importer before the year 1900 to by far the greatest capital exporter in the world. This development, however, has not been accompanied by a corresponding change in its trade policy. There is, undeniably, something paradoxical in the fact that the greatest creditor in the world is at the same time an extreme protectionist."

On the other hand, the consistency with which the United States government practiced the principle of noninfringement upon the basic rights of other governments was a decisive factor in winning confidence in even an independent Communist country, Yugoslavia, where Ambassador Stanislav Kopcok said: "There was a propaganda around the world that the United States in giving aid wanted to take away the independence of other countries. I wouldn't like to go into the matter of how far we credited this. True, the United States did attach certain conditions to this aid. But true, also, the United States did not attach conditions which could not be accepted. I believe this should be underlined. And I would like to emphasize that this principle, practiced in the first aid made available, encouraged our highest people to enter into further relationships." [44]

Discrimination in Exerting Pressure

"We must always be pressed in Europe," said Cattani, "but not too much." [45] "Just this year," asserted Taucher of Austria toward the end of 1952, "we have been overloaded with an inflation of interventions. Intervening once or twice a year is O.K. But if there is an intervention every week, it depreciates in value and doesn't mean anything." [46] It

[43] Chief of Division, Ministry of Foreign Affairs. Letter to the writer, September 30, 1954.
[44] Interview, Belgrade, December 16, 1952.   [45] Interview cited.
[46] Interview, Vienna, December 8, 1952.

was very difficult," remarked E. Delville of Belgium, "to impose internal policies upon a country. Maybe it could be done infrequently, but not as a continuing thing." [47]

Were there any useful guide lines, growing out of ECA experience, as to the ways in which American pressure, when considered to be important, could be most discriminatingly exerted? One, certainly, was that careful preparation paid dividends. The issue involved needed in each case to be carefully analyzed, from all relevant standpoints, and a mature judgment reached before specific action was taken. It was important, too, that the line taken be clear and not shifting. The constitutional structure and processes of the governments being dealt with had to be kept in mind. "In my opinion," stated E. H. van der Beugel of the Netherlands,[48] "one of the fundamental reasons for difficulties between the States and Europe may be explained by the totally different relationship between executive and parliamentary powers in Europe and in the United States."

Many Europeans and Americans consulted felt that influence quietly exerted was usually more effective in the end than public pressure. "You just don't tell a proud sovereign people what they've got to do," said C. Tyler Wood [49] on one occasion.

There was a tendency in 1952 to make economic "defense support" assistance more exclusively dependent in various ways upon levels of performance in individual countries. "I have been worried," remarked Paul Porter in 1952, "by the recent tendency to relate an increasing number of special objectives to decreasing amounts of aid. We have been trying to lift too many things with a short lever. The concept of leverage in that sense has, I think, been a rather cheapening thing. The way to get dependable alliances is to establish mutual confidence—not to put a price tag on so many men in the army, etc. We'll get better results that way. What I'm trying to say is: Let's build real alliances on a partnership basis." [50]

One of the clearest lessons of the Marshall Plan was that much can be done through multilateral channels that could not be done as well bilaterally. When the multilateral agency is an effective body, it can

[47] Interview, Vienna, December 8, 1952.

[48] Director (1948–1952), Office of the Government Commissioner for ERP, responsible for economic and military aid program. See his article on "Co-operation with Americans," in Ministry of Foreign Affairs, The Hague, *Road to Recovery.*

[49] Assistant administrator for operations, ECA headquarters; later deputy special representative in Europe.

[50] Interview, Paris, November 15, 1952.

often exert an appreciable influence on countries which for one reason or another might otherwise be reluctant to take an action which the majority favor. Reaching agreement through such group suasion was much to be preferred, when feasible, to unilateral pressure exerted by a single country.

Commitment

When Henry L. Stimson wrote in 1947 of the illusion that we could be "partly in the world and partly irresponsible" and of "the withering effect of limited commitments" and "the regenerative power of full action," [51] he was pleading for public support of the Marshall Plan. But he was also pointing to a key to effective American leadership in the present era. After the Marshall Plan had ended and its record was open to all, Attilio Cattani, one of the Europeans most closely associated with it, said quietly, "It is association in a partnership that we need and welcome." [52]

[51] "The Challenge to Americans," *Foreign Affairs,* October 1947, pp. 4–14.
[52] Interview cited.

CHAPTER 15

Production and Productivity

A FIRST premise of the European Recovery Program was that production was the key to economic revival. There was a strong desire in Europe to surpass prewar production levels as rapidly as possible. In no area of activity was the United States better equipped to help. Fifty years earlier, the product of an American industrial worker had been roughly equal to that of his opposite number in Britain, France or Germany. But since then, his productivity, or output per man-day, had tripled. Between world wars it rose about 3 percent annually, as compared with less than 1.5 percent in western Europe. The contrast in the productivity of American and European agricultural workers was equally striking. In 1949, the United States industrial laborer had the help of nonhuman energy equivalent to nearly seven horsepower. The European had about two and one-half horsepower. In 1951 the American worker, turning out nearly 40 percent more than before the war, was producing from two to five times as much per day as his European counterpart. Having drawn from Europe much of the knowledge and capital needed for its own earlier industrialization, the United States was now in a position to give back some of the benefits of its greatly enlarged productive capacity.

PRODUCTION

Phases

It is possible to distinguish three main stages in the European production effort. First came the massive operation to meet critical shortages in food, raw materials, and replacement items. The second phase was featured by an essentially new investment program with aid taking, to a larger extent, the form of "recovery goods" or "multipliers" such as machine tools and other modern industrial and power equipment. Special attention was paid to items that would facilitate an expansion in indigenous investment. On the heels of this emphasis came, third, a direct approach to the many-sided problem of productivity—which proved to be one of the most creative aspects of the entire recovery program.

Investment

It has already been pointed out that many Europeans and Americans viewed the recovery effort as primarily an investment program, on a scale designed to put Europe "on its feet." The effect of American-financed equipment for production could be observed in every participating country. In Britain, which received the largest apportionments, an official publication stated:

These supplies have provided a general support to the whole U.K. economy, and without them it would have been impossible either to achieve the steady expansion of industrial production which took place in 1949 or to sustain so large a programme of capital investment. . . . There is not a single industry or district in the country which has not benefited in some way from American aid.[1]

There as elsewhere it was demonstrated that a given amount of external aid, filling important gaps in the investment field, can step up enormously the rate of economic recovery. A corollary lesson was that, if adequate measures are taken to avoid inflation, a massive investment program can be carried out rapidly without undue shock to the economy.

The most important source of domestic investment funds, in every participating country, consisted of government savings supplemented, in most countries, by substantial counterpart funds.

Private capital in most of Europe consisted much more of auto-

[1] *Economic Survey for 1950* (Command Paper 7915, in a series of reports to Parliament by the Secretary of State for Foreign Affairs and the Chancellor of the Exchequer; London, 1950), p. 9.

investment, or a ploughing back of surplus earnings of individual companies, than of investments out of individual savings. Taxation, the leveling of income during the thirties and World War II, and the widespread exhaustion of personal savings, had largely dried up this source of investment capital.

With a scarcity of capital, investments had to be made with special care. Power was of course crucial,[2] as were coal, petroleum, steel, and a variety of manufacturing industries. Substantial investments were made in hydroelectric facilities, but the time required to complete such projects delayed their contribution to production. Agricultural investments were heaviest for machinery and for reclamation; the former were financed out of both aid and counterpart funds, the latter mainly from counterpart and other domestic resources. Large investments were made for production of raw materials needed for both industrial and strategic use. By far the greater part of these investments went into the overseas territories of the United Kingdom, France, and Belgium. From the end of the war to 1951, the equivalent of 19 billion dollars was spent by the Europeans themselves (in addition to aid provided) to rehabilitate their transport systems. In 1952, despite an unprecedented four-year record, several governments were still acutely conscious of unfilled investment needs.[3]

PRODUCTIVITY

The recovery program might have developed differently if it had been as clear at the beginning as it was at the end that the most significant indicator of increasing productive capacity was not so much gross production (important as that was) as output or yield per man-day. This concept is defined in an illuminating volume by Graham Hutton, *We Too Can Prosper.*[4] In this book, based upon the experience of indus-

[2] "Power," said Hoffman, "was a key to other factors, therefore we put a lot of stress on it. The relation of nonhuman energy per factory worker to standards of living is a real index." Interview, New York, August 10, 1954.

[3] In the U.K., Gaitskell commented that investments were not yet maintained at "a proper level, which means that we are not building up our future as we should. I believe that the engineering industries especially must be built up more in terms of investment leading to greater productivity." Interview, London, November 12, 1952.

[4] George Allen & Unwin, Ltd. (for the British Productivity Council; London, copyright 1953), pp. 13ff. Quotations in this chapter are reproduced by permission of George Allen & Unwin and the Macmillan Company, New York. The Anglo-American Council on Productivity (see pp. 107–108) was succeeded in 1952 by the British Productivity Council.

trialists and workers who visited the United States under the auspices of the Anglo-American Council on Productivity, Hutton said:

Productivity is not production. Production is mere volume of output; it may be falling while productivity is rising; and vice versa. Productivity is the efficiency, the economy, the best organization of production. You can increase *production* easily by not counting the costs; by taking on more labour, buying more materials and fuel and power, and machines. But you only increase *productivity* if you turn out more output from the same quantity or less, of the ingredients of production. . . . In all industrial countries manpower is so much in demand and so costly and important that productivity has popularly come to be understood as the fruitfulness or efficiency of human work. Productivity is the relation of output to man-hours of effort expended.

The Ingredients of Productivity

The "fruitfulness or efficiency of human work" depends not on one or two or three influences, but on a whole series. A single change—for example, adding an hour to everyone's working day—might produce a sudden spurt in total production. But if the result desired is a steady rise in the output per man-hour of a whole industry or a whole nation, the multiple ingredients of productivity must be considered.

What are they—besides investment? There is no single authoritative list; the following are selected, somewhat arbitrarily, as those which came to be regarded as particularly important as the European Recovery Program advanced.

Technology and technical training	Full employment
Attitudes and incentives	Markets
Managerial competence and training	Diversification
Human relations	Competition
Labor efficiency	Governmental action

These components were not of course new in themselves. What was new was an increasing appreciation of the potentialities of each and of their interdependence in a dynamic economy.

Technology and Technical Training

Modern industrial technology involves not only mechanization, but also standardization, simplification, specialization, and a variety of techniques having to do with plant layout, materials handling, and assembly-line processing, as well as continuous scientific and technical research.

Mechanization had developed much farther in America than in Europe.[5] The contrast was striking enough for "basic mechanical operators" on factory floors; it was much more marked with respect to such equipment as mechanical aids and tools, and lifting, moving, handling, and packaging machines.

Economical mechanization depends, to a large degree, on simplification, standardization, and specialization.[6] The three are interdependent; in combination, they may lead to extraordinary increases in productivity. This was found to be true when they were consciously applied in medium-sized and even small industrial units in Europe. A complementary group of technical developments which gained headway related to plant layout, work flow, and material handling. European plant layouts often followed theories long discarded in modern manufacturing practice. Scientific and technical research was recognized as another major influence in increasing productivity. Research in Europe and the United States had yielded much information which could be used in expanding the output of European industries; here the problem was primarily one of appropriate dissemination. But many problems remained which could be resolved only by additional research. Here the need was not so much for more scientific talent as for a greater interest in applied science. Since constant research would be needed to keep European industries abreast of technological progress, greater financial support was also needed.

The projects aided through the ECA special project procedure frequently served as demonstration or pilot plants, which could be used to disseminate knowledge of recent progress in industrial techniques.

[5] In the U.S. rated horsepower capacity of prime movers more than doubled between 1899 and 1939, while that of motors run by purchased energy increased more than 160-fold. The electric power per production worker in American manufacturing industry rose from 8,608 kwh in 1939 to 14,384 in 1950. The actual gross input of new industrial capital in equipment ran somewhat ahead of that in plant between 1910 and 1932, after which it spurted ahead until, in 1951, it reached approximately 27.4 billion dollars for equipment (at 1950 prices) as compared with 6.9 billion dollars for plant. See Hutton, *op. cit.*, pp. 74–83; data are drawn from U.S. *Census of Manufactures*, U.S. Department of Commerce, *Business Statistics*, *Monthly Labor Review*, National Industrial Conference Board, Federal Reserve Board Bulletin, and Machinery and Allied Products Institute publications.

[6] These three terms, often loosely used, were defined by Hutton as follows: "Simplification is the deliberate reduction of variety of manufacture, whether of component or end product. Specialization denotes the concentration of factory or production-unit on a very narrow range of products—the consequence of simplification pressed to the limit. Standardization, a term often used as an alternative to simplification, is here taken to mean organized agreement upon and definition of performance, quality, composition, dimensions, method of manufacture or testing of a product." *Op. cit.*, pp. 96–97.

Technological cooperation found its principal expression, however, in the ECA-sponsored technical assistance program, which later came to be called the "productivity and technical assistance program." As related earlier, an auspicious beginning was made in the Anglo-American Council on Productivity;[7] on the continent the technical assistance program was slower in getting under way. During the latter stages of the Marshall Plan, with specialists in increasing number crossing the Atlantic both ways,[8] the potentialities of technological advancement came to be looked upon with increasing enthusiasm in European circles. The technical assistance program, costing less than one-half of one percent of total ECA aid, was beginning to make a significant contribution to growing productivity.

Although agriculture received, by and large, less attention than industry in the European recovery program, technological advances and technical assistance were no less significant in the agricultural sphere. Disseminated through extension programs and selected projects, they covered nearly every aspect of farming, including mechanical equipment; soil analysis, reclamation, and irrigation; seed selection; and improvements in storing, processing, and packaging foodstuffs.

There is no way of measuring quantitatively the contributions of the technical assistance programs to increased productivity in Europe. But it seems probable that no activity conducted under the Marshall Plan program yielded higher or more sustained dividends.

Attitudes and Incentives

Neither investments nor technology could suffice, however, without the will to produce. Discussing productivity as a major objective, an OEEC report asserted:

Unless the whole community is convinced that benefits, rather than increased unemployment, will ensue from efforts to raise productivity, the effort will be in vain. Success cannot be achieved unless both labour and management can be wholeheartedly interested in the problems of increased economic efficiency. And this can be brought about only through an increased understanding of the benefits that improved productivity may confer on all those concerned in the effort.[9]

But why was there any need to explain the benefits of productivity? Many Americans were mystified at the reluctance of Europeans to

[7] See Chapter 5. [8] See Chapters 6 to 8.
[9] *Europe: The Way Ahead*, p. 194.

adopt techniques which seemed so obviously to their own advantage. Broadly speaking, a different "climate" in relation to productivity existed in Europe. Said E. Carstens [10] of Denmark: "In the United States there is more push, whatever the cause, toward increased production and standard of living. It is not the same in Europe, where there are smaller markets, more emphasis on bargaining, and more past internal protectionism and restriction." Europeans were by no means convinced by the acknowledged productive capacity of the United States that they should become undiscriminating imitators. Hutton wrote of the longstanding anxiety—not only of the direct workers of machinery but also of philosophers, sociologists, psychologists, artists, and others —over the effect on the individual and society of faster and farther mechanization of life. And he noted that there was more than a little feeling in Europe that the United States had reached the stage where "the machines run the men," with loss of individuality and cultural values.

Thus the problem of attitudes and incentives was not simple. As the program developed, more and more Europeans and Americans came to view it as the most crucial problem in the effort to make European economic life more dynamic. The fourth OEEC report declared:

With regard to both productivity and required changes in the structure of production, it is apparent that progress will be adequate only if there is sufficient inducement in terms of financial incentive. The incentive of appropriate price relations has already been stressed. In addition, however, incentives that directly affect the earnings of labour and enterprise must be emphasized, including wage incentives and the incentives that can be given through adjustment in taxation. [11]

High taxes on corporate profits had lowered the incentive to expand and improve industry in many countries. [12] Owners and managers often resisted technological changes which might disrupt employment. The ECA therefore emphasized the lowering of all kinds of production costs, without undue emphasis upon labor saving alone. [13]

European workers were afraid of technological unemployment and underemployment. They had what one observer called "a psychological abhorrence of the man with a stopwatch." There was less tradition of

[10] Onetime chairman of the machine committee in the OEEC. Interview, December 2, 1952.
[11] *Europe: The Way Ahead*, p. 23.   [12] Cf. Hutton, *op. cit.*, p. 86.
[13] Interview, George Knutson, August 22, 1952.

greater individual output leading to larger individual income. Where wages were fixed, with little differential among workers, a man could not expect to augment his real wages very much no matter how efficiently he worked. The benefits of expanded productivity naturally appeared remote. In a good many kinds of production, moreover, there was a pride in craft which was endangered by mechanization.

In recognition of these conditions, more attention was given to better distribution of the gains from greater productivity. Efforts were also made to demonstrate that mechanization, while reducing the individual worker's share in making the completed product, need not eliminate pride in craft, since it required additional skills and, in many instances, highly specialized skills at that.

Incentives to agricultural output were sought through measures to increase the stability of prices for farm products; to assure markets for larger production; to show how higher productivity could raise farm incomes; and to make available more consumer or "incentive" goods for farmers to buy with their expanded earnings.

Among consumers, it was important to emphasize not only that increased productivity would yield a higher volume of goods for all to share, at lower cost per unit, but also that with standardization in production the total variety of goods offered could still be as great or greater than before.

While the changes in thinking needed to develop a new climate for productivity in Europe would obviously require many years, real progress was observable. Louis Camu noted that "the most important effect of technical assistance has been its indirect effect—in that it has generated new attitudes toward production and productivity and toward social problems. One can say that it is not so applicable when there are different customs and habits. Yet, three to six months later, we find people getting ideas and making changes—as a result of the stimulus of contacts and experiences within the technical assistance program."[14]

Managerial Competence and Training

Management requires many aptitudes and skills. The larger the enterprise, the more management tends to become a profession, divorced from ownership. A growing recognition of the importance of management was emphasized to the writer in country after country. In Turkey it was referred to as "our most urgent problem." In Norway, "managerial

[14] Interview, November 19, 1952.

inertia" was mentioned as "a difficult problem due to stratification" and to trade associations which reduce competition. "We have been trying," it was noted in the United Kingdom, "to get industries to plan more." "It is possible," said an Austrian, "to increase productivity here through better equipment and a better organizing of production and movement within a plant—what they call, in the United Kingdom, 'redeployment'—and in these ways to raise productivity without real cost."

The British productivity teams which visited the United States were ungrudging in their estimates of the role and competence of industrial management in the United States.[15] Visiting industrialists and workers from other countries were similarly impressed. Many were surprised at the living standards of American workers and the extent to which they often participated as partners with management in efforts to increase productivity.

As previously noted, the provision of stimulus and training for industrial managers took several forms, including observation and study tours in the United States by joint labor-management teams, the provision of technical assistance in European industries and special projects, and conduct in the participating countries of management seminars which, on occasion, were international in scope.

The task of European producers in increasing the effectiveness of management was much wider than a simple taking over of American practices. In every country, as in the United States, the development of management was necessarily an evolutionary process in a given social setting, involving a combination of initiative, resourcefulness, and the exchange of ideas. Technical assistance tours and management seminars helped accelerate this process.

Human Relations

The most technically skilled management may founder, of course, if its human relations are bad. Simplification, standardization, specialization, and all of the other techniques used to increase production and productivity, as Hutton pointed out,

incur the risk of worsening the human relationships in industry, of having a de-humanizing effect on work people, of causing a loss of their pride and in-

---

[15] Hutton, *op. cit.*, chs. ii and v; also reports of the Anglo-American Council on Productivity, on *Education for Management, Universities and Industry, Training of Supervisors, Plant Maintenance, Management Accounting,* and others listed in *Final Report of the Anglo-American Council on Productivity* (London, 1952).

terest in work, a consequent deficiency in their self-respect and their sense of "social significance" and therefore a perilous intensification of frustration and pent-up dislikes. Such evils are apt to multiply unless closer attention and greater skill in application are given to *all* human relationships involved in the firm.[16]

American progress in this field enabled the United States to make a great contribution to European productivity. Of course fully comparable developments had been occurring in some European countries. Hutton believed that industrial relations in Britain were on the whole as good as in America—perhaps better. Jorgen Paldam said of Denmark: "I have the impression that workers here, in relation to management, have a greater interest in increasing production than in the United States. That is, there is opposition to management which does not push hard toward the most efficient production. There seems in this to be a contrast with what you have had in New England." [17] But many European economies exhibited social and political rigidities which obstructed progress in labor-management relations. Hutton commented:

American society is new. It has never "jelled" into historical classes, castes, "estates," and class-mentalities organized in political parties. It has not the task of emancipating itself from tradition, custom, and socially inherited attitudes—the most formative elements of the climate of opinion. . . . We have to recognize the greater rigidity of British and European institutions.[18]

In a similar vein, Norbert Thumb, speaking as an Austrian participant in the management seminar or Productivity Conference at Fregence, Italy, noted that

there are certain factors in human nature which will offer opposition to our activity in the plants. First of all, there is the inner security of an individual whose set patterns are threatened by a new task in a new environment. Then there is the factor which has been described as "conservatism as an economic principle," i.e., every change of attitude, every new adjustment means an additional effort for the person undergoing the change.[19]

Resistance to change in industrial relations was extreme in some countries. In France, for example, one observer consulted put the problem in these blunt terms: "Business leaders and others don't want a rise of labor." Referring to such situations, Thumb observed:

[16] *Op. cit.,* p. 136.   [17] Interview, December 1, 1952.
[18] *Op. cit.,* p. 139, 141, 142.
[19] *Produttività* (Rome), Special Suppl. to no. 6, 1952, p. 17.

We know that man judges all things in the light of his own experience. The experience of both management and labor has been such as to engender between them a feeling of mutual distrust, and this distrust is evident in the conviction that the two parties have that any new development brought about by one would be exploited by the other solely for his own benefit. We must now try to persuade both parties that it would be to their mutual advantage to change this attitude to a more cooperative one.[20]

It is perhaps worth repeating that changes in industrial relations cannot be arbitrarily imposed in a free society. As Hutton pointed out:

The reforms, improvements, and changes needed—in principles and practices, in manners and methods, in activities and attitudes—are far-going. They represent a break with the accumulated rigidities and encumbrances of many decades. For this reason they are unlikely to be applied on the scale needed unless they are both devised and applied cooperatively by both sides of industry.[21]

Labor Efficiency

The efficiency of labor is of course crucial to productivity. Divergencies in the productivity of individual workers result from differences in aptitudes, intelligence, habits, vocational and in-work training, health, and working and living conditions.

A method of increasing efficiency which was comparatively new to European industrialists and workers was the work study, or the analysis of individual functions with a view to improving performance. This involved not only time and motion studies and the like by management, but suggestions by the workers themselves. On this aspect, the comment of Stephen Greene, a precision equipment manufacturer, is particularly pertinent: "It is precisely that person who is immediately responsible for the performance of any task who is by far the best qualified to stream-line the accomplishment of that particular task." [22]

The training of foremen was given considerable attention in the productivity program. This had expanded in American industry when "training within industry" (TWI) was organized by government, industry, and labor experts during World War II. The method spread from the United States to Canada, then to England, where over 250,000 were trained during and after the war by government and private organizations. Later it was applied in Belgium, Holland, Denmark, Sweden, Norway, France, Austria, Germany, and, to a lesser extent, in Italy.

[20] *Ibid.*   [21] *Op. cit.*, p. 181.   [22] *Produttività, op. cit.*, p. 21.

Full Employment

The relationship between full employment and the willingness of both management and labor to work toward higher productivity is fairly obvious. A tight labor market is an incentive for management to increase its efficiency. Ample employment opportunities, by the same token, lower the workers' resistance to the introduction of techniques which might result in transitional unemployment.

In his own discussions with Europeans, Paul Hoffman used to tell this story: An American was watching a group of workers dig a ditch with shovels. After a while he asked the supervisor whether the job could not be done more rapidly and economically with machinery. "Perhaps," replied the supervisor, "but this way we can give a lot more employment." Whereupon the interrogator asked whether still more employment might not be provided if tablespoons were used instead of shovels.

The story expresses a point of view more widely held among Americans than among Europeans, for understandable reasons. For one thing, unemployment has been more chronic in most European economies than in the United States; during the Marshall Plan there was substantial unemployment in Italy, Greece, West Germany, and, to a less extent, Belgium. In several other countries fear of unemployment was a potent influence behind "planned" economies which put greater emphasis on measures to ensure employment than on measures to increase productivity. In any case, as Hutton said,

unemployment—whatever its cause—exercises a powerful inhibiting, deterrent, and disincentive effect on the readiness of organized labour, everywhere, to adopt methods for raising the productivity of labour. . . . In Britain (and Western Europe) there has always been a strong undercurrent in labour organizations—industrial and political—of distrust for machines, of fear of "technological unemployment." [23]

Such apprehensions among European workers constituted perhaps the most important single obstacle to increased productivity. The fears could not be allayed by abstract argument. They could only be overcome by actual experience and demonstration. Such an illustration was provided by Kurt Brandes, a Berlin industrialist, one of the leading machine tool producers of western Europe,[24] who increased the

[23] *Op. cit.*, pp. 176–177.
[24] Chm., Board of Directors, Fritz Werner, Inc. Interview, Bonn, Dec. 4, 1952.

number of employees in one plant from 800 to 3,100 and in another from 700 to over 2,000, as a result of investment and increased productivity.

Markets

The "most powerful incentive to increased productivity," declares the fourth OEEC report,[25] "must come through the action of competitive forces and the opportunity of developing production for a wider market." "Productivity," said Snoy of Belgium, "means a large market." [26] "In the Marshall Plan," said Vincent Barnett of the ECA mission to Italy, "we have emphasized production. But to the individual producer, production follows outlets—and we didn't worry enough about the distribution side." [27] Hutton pointed out that while productivity of manpower, materials, machines, etc., is almost universally measured as a procedure in production, "distribution is almost universally kept out of the discussion. But it ought not to be kept out of it." [28]

These remarks are applicable, of course, to both internal and external markets. Internal markets are affected not only by the distribution of income and purchasing power, producing a mass-consumption base for mass-produced items, but also by the rate of growth of the economy and the marketing facilities and methods employed. Reference has been made to the extraordinary stimulus afforded by an expanding agricultural economy to the steel industry in Turkey.[29] The deterrent effect of restrictive and inefficient marketing on incentives for productivity was cited by Paul A. Jenkins, discussing the situation in Greece: "One of our failures, in agriculture, was the field of cooperative marketing. Individual fruit growers are victimized by merchants— with fixed prices—giving the farmers only a fraction of what they should get." [30]

External markets and the stimulus which they can provide to productivity fluctuate with transport costs and the oscillations of demand and price, and are blocked by trade restrictions.[31] "We saw the necessity of increased production," said P. A. Blaisse; [32] "this in turn made more clear the necessity for multilateral trade. And we saw that this had to go hand in hand with multilateral financial arrangements."

Market expansion was also sought in improvements in transport, re-

[25] *Europe: The Way Ahead*, p. 24.				[26] Interview cited.
[27] Interview, Rome, November 18, 1952.			[28] *Op. cit.*, p. 117.
[29] Interview, Yalman, cited.				[30] Interview, November 14, 1952.
[31] See Chapter 16.
[32] A member of the Netherlands Parliament. Interview, November 24, 1952.

finements in marketing research, and new techniques in advertising and merchandising.

Diversification

As a factor in productivity, diversification in industry may be important in countries where unemployment and underemployment prevent a full use of available skills and manpower, or where resources and potential markets permit an expansion in the range or quality of goods produced. Discussing the problem of diversification in Denmark, Carstens said: "We are largely limited in agriculture to a few commodities. But industrial exports are now up to 40 percent of our total exports—and in this field we have spread more through the world. We can't in a small country go in for mass production, but we can produce more items for export. What is called for is individuals and groups who have a will to develop specific types of production over a number of years; among the items developed, some will grow up and contribute quite a bit to exports in the long run. Of course we can't know whether all these items will stay, surviving competition. It may take ten years or so to find out." [33]

Opportunities for diversification were greater in some countries than were actually realized during the recovery period. The emphasis given to basic industries in the French investment programs of this period, for example, worked against diversification, with the result that the impetus to productivity in France was not as evenly spread as it might have been.

Competition

The European productivity teams which visited the United States were impressed with the extent and keenness of competition in American economic life and the spur which this provided to "high efficiency for survival." Some who had heard much talk of American "monopolies" were surprised to learn how much the American legal and institutional framework was devised to maintain and foster competition in business, and how vigorously antitrust laws were actually enforced. In many European countries restrictive agreements to fix prices, allocate output, and fence off exclusive markets were common.[34]

Thierry de Clermont-Tonnère of France,[35] discussing the broader question of international competition in Europe, expressed the opinion

[33] Interview, Copenhagen, December 2, 1952. [34] See Baum, *op. cit.*, p. 393.
[35] Secretary-General, Prime Minister's Committee on Economic Cooperation, France. Interview, Paris, November 5, 1952.

that "there is need for the restoration of competition. We have lost ground in this since the defense crisis; in both the United Kingdom and France, there has been an increase in restriction. The problem needs to be fully recognized in Europe and the United States. We need a new battle to defeat the protectionists. We nearly won such a battle two years ago and we must take up the fight again."

But there were also wide and deep-seated resistances to the idea of free enterprise. This was apparent among many intellectuals [36] and was prevalent in European labor circles, notably in France and Italy but also in segments of labor opinion in other countries, including the Bevan group in the United Kingdom. Another source of resistance was the trade associations. These, as Everett Bellows [37] said, "are not like our trade associations; they are much more restrictive. They are also extremely powerful—for example, in Austria." And another sort of resistance was encountered in countries with Socialist or Labor governments, where belief in government planning and controls, as well as in government operation of basic industries, was widespread.

The ECA approach to the problem of competition was pragmatic rather than doctrinaire. Its efforts were economic rather than political or philosophical and varied from country to country. In Germany an effort to promote investment under official free market policies met with some success, especially in the use of counterpart funds. Bringing industrialists to the United States had as part of its purpose frank discussions with American industrialists about ways in which private enterprise and competition may invigorate a country's productive system. A similar purpose, as we have seen, underlay the contacts arranged

[36] "For most European intellectuals," wrote Raymond Aron in an article on "Transatlantic Relations," "anti-capitalism is much more than a mere economic theory; it is an article of faith. It pervades Catholic and Protestant circles to some extent, as well as anti-clerical Socialist circles. For those intellectuals to agree to debate the merits of free enterprise versus nationalized enterprise, the free market versus national planning, in the light of their respective achievements, would be to agree to surrender both the emotional and philosophical bases of their belief. They will not look at what has happened to capitalism in your country [the U.S.], and thus learn what can be done with it socially. They have shut their eyes and have swallowed wholesale the Marxist argument that the sole cause of man's exploitation of man is private ownership of the means of production. . . . Their basic assumption is that capitalism is evil; . . . therefore they refuse peremptorily to debate it." In a symposium, *America and the Mind of Europe*, ed. by Lewis Galantière, Hamish Hamilton (London, 1951), pp. 22–23. Quoted by permission of Hamish Hamilton, Ltd.

[37] Onetime chief, ECA Technical Assistance Division. Interview, Paris, November 16, 1952.

between European and American labor leaders. Part of the purpose of the Benton and Moody amendments, cited earlier, was to encourage private enterprise and competition in Europe. Liberalization of trade and payments fostered competition by encouraging each OEEC country to buy more from the best producer. These efforts produced no miracles. But in spite of the increased government controls which accompanied aid programing,[38] they helped widen the area of competition.

Governmental Action

The final ingredient affecting productivity is governmental action. Governments, as we have seen, played a major part in running technical assistance programs, in developing productivity centers, and in launching productivity drives. Farm extension programs were developed under government auspices. Technical education, in-work training, and industrial and agricultural research were given impetus by government appropriations and encouragement. Statistics of industrial and agricultural output and other technical data published by governments not only provided the basis for estimating progress in productivity, but also furnished information of interest and value to individual enterprises.

The fourth OEEC report emphasizes the incentive to productivity which governments may provide through adjustments in taxation. "The success of the United States and Canada," it stated, "in directing investment to priority fields during the past two years, through the provision for selective rapid amortisation of new investment, is an illustration of the power of appropriate tax incentives."[39] With less current wealth to tax, the European countries did not have as much leeway as the United States or Canada. And, as John Williams pointed out in 1949:

Taxes, always essentially restrictive, have been raised so high on both individual and business incomes, as to dry up saving and destroy incentives among workers, producers, and investors. This is a process by which any gains in productivity . . . are put in constant danger of being swallowed up in expenditures that do not contribute to productive effort.[40]

As recovery advanced, however, some countries were able to lower taxes on earnings and thus make new investment more attractive. Adjustments in taxation sometimes favored the working class, pro-

---

[38] See Chapter 14. [39] *Europe: The Way Ahead*, pp. 23–24.
[40] *Economic Stability in a Changing World*, p. 135.

viding a double benefit—more incentive to workers and larger markets.

Governments also exercised significant influence on the pattern of investment through control of national budgets, aid programs, and counterpart funds, and through regulation of financial institutions. Measures to stabilize or regulate prices and interest rates also had an important bearing on investment and productivity.

Joint governmental action through the OEEC to foster greater interest in productivity began modestly with a Committee for Scientific Research which evolved into a Committee for Productivity and Applied Research. The work of these committees paved the way for the establishment in May 1953 of the European Productivity Agency (EPA) as a special organ of the OEEC.

The Problem of Momentum

To what extent was a new dynamic, a durable new momentum, achieved in Europe's productivity? Granted that the short-term gains were, all things considered, extraordinary, justifying the resources and energies expended, did they forecast a steady long-term improvement?

The evidence in 1952 provided little ground for complacency. During the decade 1940–1950, as Knut Getz Wold of Norway pointed out, "the United States increased its level of production by roughly 100 percent, the USSR about 75 percent, but the rest of Europe only about 40 percent." [41] The rate of increase was greatly accelerated during 1947–1952, when industrial production in western Europe went up more than 50 percent. Yet "despite this progress and evidence of strength," declared the OEEC in late 1952, "the present economic situation of Western Europe is far from satisfactory. . . . Production in the various countries is either not rising or rising at a relatively modest rate." [42]

"We have succeeded in restoring the physical basis of production in Europe," said Marjolin. "But we haven't wiped out all of the effects of the war, nor have we eliminated difficulties from which Europe suffered even before the war. The Marshall Plan has raised productivity during four years. But it hasn't created a basis for permanent increase in productivity; we still have to make constant new efforts toward such increase. We have not yet created a system in which production is naturally expanding." [43]

But the picture was not wholly discouraging. There was a clearer understanding of the "more" that was needed. The number of leaders

[41] Interview, November 25, 1952.   [42] *Europe: The Way Ahead*, p. 15.
[43] Interview, November 14, 1952.

in European industry, labor, and agriculture who were developing a new enthusiasm about the possibilities of productivity was steadily increasing. "The productivity idea," remarked Robert J. Myers, "is certainly taking hold. During the past two years there has been much greater understanding of the concept. Productivity has become a household word, is the subject of many articles and is discussed in public meetings quite widely." [44] Influences were at work which, given adequate opportunity, reasonably favorable conditions, and increased confidence in the future, might in time restore Europe to its position as one of the dynamic economic areas of the world.

Among the conditions most important for such a development was greater integration and expansion of the economy of free Europe as a whole. We turn now to a special consideration of this problem.

[44] Interview, Paris, November 5, 1952.

CHAPTER 16

Impetus and Steps toward

European Integration

PREVIOUS chapters have sketched the course of European cooperation through the OEEC and touched upon the rationale of the regional
approach to recovery which that body fostered. The present chapter is
concerned with the significance of that record in relation to the wider
movement toward European integration.

The European Idea

The idea of European unity can be traced back, of course, to the
Roman Empire. In the late twelfth century, Frederick I (Barbarossa)
of Germany dreamed of establishing a new Holy Roman Empire. Pierre
Dubois of France, in the early fourteenth century, envisaged the formation of a European league to enforce peace through combined military action and economic boycott. Napoleon followed another road.

In the present era, thinking about peaceful steps toward unity began
after World War I and was given expression in a proposal submitted to
the League of Nations on May 1, 1930, by Aristide Briand. His proposal envisaged not a "United States of Europe," as is often supposed,
but an intergovernmental organization which preserved the sovereignty
of the members and aimed at "solidarity" through "moral unity" and
collaboration among governments. He looked upon European consoli-

dation as primarily a political matter requiring a political approach. But the international organization he proposed would have had a variety of advisory functions in the field of economic and social welfare. Although Briand's proposal was not acted upon, the European idea lived on.

New Impetus

The fresh impetus to serious thinking about European unity given by the Marshall Plan was portrayed by Ambassador Cattani in the following manner: "The most important effect of the Marshall Plan and the whole European operation has been, I think, the feeling in Europe that unity is fundamental. There was no idea, then, that drastic changes were needed. The thought was that we needed a breathing space, during which more resources provided by an export surplus would help us to rebuild our economies. This was the crude idea of the Marshall Plan itself.

"There was some glimmer of an idea that more was needed, but it was vague. The idea of close cooperation was probably clearer in the mind of Americans than of Europeans. There was the idea, implicit, of aid being contingent upon some undertaking to do something jointly. Probably the commitments in that direction were gladly taken because no one really understood what was involved.

"Most important was the United States emphasis on the need of having a joint European organization which could develop a common approach and stronger ties within Europe. I don't think that it was clear to the Europeans what path they were starting upon. Some had the attitude: well, the Americans want it; let's do it, therefore, in order to get the aid needed for recovery. With others, there was more enthusiasm regarding the real political prospects involved. As the discussions developed, it became clearer that we were doing something new in both the political and economic sense.

"I am sure that this made possible the movement toward something deeper in other fields. In my mind it's absolutely sure that the Schuman Plan and the EDC proposal couldn't have developed without the ground being prepared and fertilized by the Marshall Plan endeavors.

"To sum up, there have been successive stories. There was the American urging toward European cooperation. In Europe there was a gradual increase in understanding of the necessity—with or without American aid—for association to build up common efforts toward economic welfare and toward political development through whatever

manifestations they might come to take. With United States cooperation we have been preparing the ground in all respects." [1]

Other strands of thought also quickened the interest of many thoughtful Europeans in the possibilities of any realistic approach to greater
unity. Faith in the ability of small, divided states to keep peace with each
other and to safeguard the independence, security, and well-being of
their peoples had been deeply shaken.[2] The heat of an external danger,
historically a condition for the internal welding of social groups, was
present in the Soviet threat. In the United States there was a growing
belief that without substantial increases in cooperation and integration
Europe would never find its way out of an economic and political
wilderness. Through the Marshall Plan, that belief was linked with the
proffer of aid.

But if there were supporting influences, there were also many obstacles. Wars and rivalries, especially between France and Germany,
had left deep wounds which could not be quickly healed. Each step
toward integration meant adjustments and sacrifices. Protected industries, protected farming, protected trade, and protected employment
within each country would have to be modified with the freeing of
intra-European trade and payments. Any meaningful growth of European cooperation would also mean some progressive limitations
upon the complete sovereignty of individual states. There were wide
variations in economic and political systems, each with separate traditions and momentum. "It is hard," said a Norwegian, "to see Norway
as closer to Portugal than to the United States." Britain was both in
and out of Europe; only about a fifth of its trade was with the continent, its political ties were similarly divided, and a position of relative detachment and freedom of action was strong in British tradition.
The special problem of Germany, if unsolved, would block any effective
integration of the continent.

Testing of the OEEC

When the OEEC came into being, therefore, it was subject to
severe testing. For meeting this test, it possessed an exceptional asset
in its central core of delegates and professional staff. "What you had,"

---

[1] Interview, Paris, November 18, 1952.

[2] Illustrative of numerous problems that "cannot be solved on a national basis,"
according to S. L. Mansholt, Netherlands Minister of Agriculture, was the chronically depressed situation in southern Italy, where a large proportion of the agricultural labor force remained unemployed. Letter to the writer, September 28, 1954.

said Frank Figgures of the OEEC, "was a kind of trade union of a group who had worked together until they had acquired enough confidence in each other to talk frankly—with no necessity to pretend—each coming to understand the others' diplomatic language and what it really meant. There was a good deal of candid discussion of this kind, though you couldn't talk the same way publicly." [3]

A first challenge to the OEEC's operating capacity was whether it could function under the self-imposed rule of unanimity for decisions of the Council. A second was whether it could carry through without rupture the initial division-of-aid exercise.[4] When these had been met, the OEEC moved on with greater assurance.

The development of effective collaboration between larger and smaller nations provided another test. The full participation of the stronger powers was of course essential to a vigorous cooperative effort. Said Stikker of the Netherlands: "My view, when I was chairman of the OEEC, was that the great problem there was how to bring Germany and Great Britain into the proposed payments union. I was more afraid then about Britain than about Germany. Our calculation was that it would be difficult for Britain to join EPU due to its extensive commonwealth relations." "Sometimes," he added later, "the influence of small countries may be helpful in bringing about effective cooperation, provided you find men with a broader view." [5] One of the OEEC's most significant accomplishments, so gradual and undramatic that it attracted little public attention, was bringing Germany into a cooperative European system on a basis of full equality, thereby helping to forestall a trend in Germany's external relations comparable to that which developed after World War I.

But for the competence of the technical people assigned to the OEEC by member governments the organization would have foundered amid the complexities of its task. The work of this staff, in turn, would have been crippled but for extensive and unprecedented exchanges of information.[6]

One measure of the vitality of an organization is, of course, to be found in the extent to which original and practicable ideas emerge from its work. Many were developed and tested in the course of OEEC deliberations; some found expression in new intra-European institutions, notably the European Payments Union, the Steering Board for Trade, and later the European Productivity Agency.

[3] Interview cited.   [4] See Chapters 4 and 13.
[5] Interview, London, December 22, 1952.   [6] See Chapters 4 to 6.

Of these the most significant was the EPU, widely regarded as one of the most important economic developments in Europe of the postwar period, perhaps even of the century, since it marked a reversal of the previous disastrous trend toward economic nationalism. Despite its success, some concern about its functioning was expressed in 1952. Getz Wold of Oslo, for example, said: "I am a bit worried with the way the system is now working. It seems to be approaching the gold standard type system. Now there are two big debtor countries and seven substantial creditor countries, with only the Scandinavian countries on a normal basis. The desire of the United Kingdom and France to regain their gold (or dollar) balances and the desire of the big creditor countries to continue earning gold (or dollars) from the other European countries may lead to mutually incompatible policies, with dangers of resultant inflation and greater import restriction. Some countries feel that the movement toward a gold standard type relationship is an improvement, since it would lead toward wider convertibility, but I do not believe that conditions are now present for universal convertibility." [7] Stikker of the Netherlands feared that the United States, having contributed so largely to the establishment and early work of the EPU, might not continue to take full advantage of it, but might return to bilateral dealings on financial questions which would reduce the EPU's effectiveness. [8]

Commenting in 1952 on the work of the OEEC for trade liberalization, Ethel Dietrich [9] said: "Without exception I do not believe any member country would want to return to bilateralism for trading arrangements, although all countries have retained some import quotas on 'hard core' items either for bargaining or for outright protection."

The OEEC was not in itself, except in an extremely limited sense, a supranational organization. "The driving force for cooperation," observed Marjolin, "is located in London, Paris, Brussels, Bonn, and other capitals—and, of course, Washington." [10] Instead of acting for, or in place of, national governments, the OEEC sought to promote understanding between governments, to coordinate their policies and actions, to foster mutual aid, and, frequently, to influence their decisions by bringing to bear the thinking and judgment of delegates and technicians from other countries.

[7] Interview, November 25, 1952.   [8] Interview cited.

[9] Director, Trade Division, MSA regional office in Europe, interview, Paris, November 3, 1952.

[10] Interview, Paris, November 17, 1952.

Relation to Other European Developments

While the OEEC, the first of the important European regional organizations after the war, was developing and fulfilling its role, other regional organizations, with different scope and features, were also taking shape and serving different purposes. Even before the creation of the OEEC, limited customs unions had been discussed. The CEEC considered the establishment of an inclusive customs union among ERP nations. This approach was favored by United States representatives, provided nothing was done that might obstruct a wider freeing of trade. It was also well received by some in Europe who believed, with Count Sforza, that European union could only be built "piece by piece." [11]

In September 1947 a Study Group for a European Customs Union was set up to explore such a plan; the group reached pessimistic conclusions, but the idea was not abandoned. In the same year Belgium, Holland, and Luxemburg concluded a Customs Convention which abolished duties on goods exchanged among them and provided for uniform tariffs on goods imported from other countries. During the same year a conference was held at Copenhagen to examine a plan for economic union among the United Kingdom, Denmark, Iceland, Norway, and Sweden. This led to an agreement—known as Uniscan—providing in general terms for cooperation, and a follow-up commission was established.

A conference to study the question of a Franco-Italian customs union completed its work with less than enthusiastic endorsement.[12]

The most ambitious project of this type was variously called Finebel or Benefit or Fritalux. It was an attempt to extend the proposal for a Franco-Italian customs union to include Benelux, and called for the removal of certain trade quota controls, increased convertibility, and adjustments in exchange rates to minimize balance-of-payments disequilibria. Before agreement had been reached on how to implement it or whether to include West Germany, OEEC negotiations on the EPU and trade liberalization were so far advanced that the project was dropped.

[11] *Le Monde,* December 23, 1948, quoted by Diebold, *op. cit.,* p. 389.

[12] A draft treaty produced was never submitted to the French and Italian Parliaments for ratification. The voluminous commission reports outlining the obstacles to union between the two countries remains the only lasting monument to this effort.

Consideration of the proposals discussed above indicated ways in which the formation of subregional groupings within Europe, for the reduction of tariffs, would not necessarily advance the goal of wider European economic integration. In a guarded endorsement of them, Hoffman cautioned that they should contribute toward, and not be turned against, the greater integration of the whole of western Europe and its overseas territories.

The Schuman Plan was advanced mainly on political rather than economic grounds.[13] Unlike the OEEC which operated under the rule of unanimity and had no power to impose sanctions on member nations, or the Council of Europe which was a deliberative body with neither legislative nor executive powers, the Schuman Plan involved the establishment of a genuine supranational authority. On April 12, 1951, the foreign ministers of six continental countries—Britain having decided against participation—signed the treaty in Paris. As already noted, this instrument and its annexed documents described the mission of the Coal and Steel Community as that of promoting economic expansion, developing employment, and improving the standard of living of the participating countries through the creation of a single market. All trade barriers (tariffs, subsidies, import quotas, etc.) for the iron and steel industries were to be abolished, and such practices as discrimination or subsidization, incompatible with the aims of the treaty, were prohibited. A transition period of five years would allow adaptations by the more vulnerable industries, especially Belgian coal and Italian steel; by a special system of compensations the more favored industries and governments would share with the less favored ones temporary losses arising from unification.

A preliminary review of the Schuman Plan in the ECA raised some questions, but the ECA, wishing to lend prompt support to a constructive proposal developed entirely on European initiative, gave it strong moral backing. In August 1951 the United States announced that it would establish close working relations with the High Authority. In the Mutual Security Act of 1951, Congress backed the new organization by authorizing the transfer of funds directly to the Coal and Steel Community.

To many observers the political implications of the coal and steel pool seemed even more important and far-reaching than its economic consequences. The establishment of a genuine supranational authority in two limited but important economic sectors might, some believed,

[13] See Chapter 8.

pave the way to further delegations of sovereignty and eventually to some kind of political union in Europe.

Meanwhile proposals were emerging for greater integration in the military sphere. These are outside the scope of our study and are mentioned here as part of the general "European Movement" during the Marshall Plan period. The two main developments, of course, were the North Atlantic Treaty alliance and the proposal for a European Defense Community (EDC). But before either of these took shape, two other significant developments occurred. The Dunkirk Treaty allying a demobilized France and a demobilized Britain was signed in March 1947. The Brussels Treaty, ratified in March 1948, bound Britain, France, Belgium, Holland, and Luxemburg to give military and other assistance in the event that any one of them should be the object of an armed attack. The Brussels Treaty powers were instrumental in drawing up a draft treaty (completed in April 1949) for the North Atlantic powers. The North Atlantic Treaty, as finally developed, provided that an armed attack against any signatory in Europe or North America would be considered an armed attack against all members of the pact. In addition, it obligated all signatories to self-help and mutual aid in order to increase their collective capacity to resist attack. And it established the North Atlantic Treaty Organization.

NATO was set up as essentially an organization of national states. The Supreme Headquarters of the Allied Powers in Europe (SHAPE), set up by the North Atlantic Treaty countries, was not subject to any supranational political or legislative body, nor did it provide for a full integration of national forces. But the placing of national forces under an international command was an extraordinary move in the delegation of executive responsibility.

On October 24, 1950, René Pleven proposed a further major step, namely, the creation of a unified European army under a single ministry. This contemplated a much more complete integration, through federalized political control, than did NATO. During the next year and a half, the EDC proposal was actively debated in both Europe and the United States while work progressed on a draft treaty.[14] In May 1952 the treaty

[14] The draft treaty and annexed protocols provided for the integration of military contingents of the member countries under a joint body to be composed of nine members serving for six years. As in the Schuman Plan, the decisions of this supranational body were to be binding on all members, and sanctions were provided to ensure their enforcement. In addition, provision was made for an Assembly (the same as that for the Coal and Steel Community); a Council of Ministers, whose function would be to instruct the joint body on major policy issues and to harmonize

was signed, subject to parliamentary ratifications, by France, Germany, Italy, and the Benelux countries. The necessary ratifications, however, were far from assured.

In the political sphere the Council of Europe was the most advanced attempt during the Marshall Plan period toward a general intra-European organ. Like NATO, it originated with the Brussel Pact powers. From the outset, discussion of a European political authority was marked by disagreement between the "intergovernmentalists," such as Britain and Scandinavia, and the "federalists," who wished to set up a full-fledged European political federation. Early in 1949 work on the project bogged down in this disagreement, but eventually the Preparatory Conference for the Creation of a Council of Europe worked out a compromise emphasizing the intergovernmental approach. On May 5, 1949, delegates from France, the United Kingdom, the Benelux countries, Italy, Denmark, Norway, Sweden, and Ireland signed the agreement setting up a bicameral Council.

The Council consisted of a Committee of Ministers, composed of the foreign secretaries of the participating countries, and a Consultative Assembly composed of representatives appointed by the member governments.[15] The Council's aim as defined in the treaty was "to achieve greater unity between its members for the purpose of safeguarding and realizing the ideals and principles which are their common heritage and facilitating their economic and social progress." Unity was to be attained by "discussions of questions of common concern and by agreements and common action in economic, social, cultural, scientific, legal and administrative matters." [16] The purpose and functions of the organization were thus quite general, and it remained, in 1952, a purely consultative body with no real powers of its own. It furnished, however, a useful channel for continuing intergovernmental deliberations on further measures in the direction of political integration. Its chambers served as a forum for the discussion and clarification of the Schuman Plan.

Mention should be made, finally, of the United Nations Economic Council for Europe (ECE) which, like the parent body, included in its membership not only the countries of western and southern Europe,

---

its acts with those of the member governments; and a Court, with functions parallel to those of the Coal and Steel Community.

[15] In the Assembly, France, Italy, and the U.K. were accorded 18 seats each; Belgium, the Netherlands and Sweden 6 seats each; Denmark, Ireland, and Norway 4 seats each; and Luxemburg 3.

[16] Article I(d).

but other nations as well, including the USSR and the satellite states. This organization served as a vehicle for research, discussion, and publications [17] on a variety of European economic questions.

During the early postwar years, the Marshall Plan precipitated the establishment of the first major body within the total "European movement," the Organization for European Economic Cooperation. The OEEC, in turn, did much to prepare the ground not only for its own offshoot, the European Payments Union, but also for NATO and the Schuman Plan. Within the economic sphere the OEEC, embracing the free countries of western and southern Europe, may be contrasted with such subregional groupings, involving a further measure of consolidation, as the Coal and Steel Community generated by the Schuman Plan.[18] The latter type of organization seemed to point to an acceleration of integration among a limited group of states within Europe or, as some would express it, toward the greater consolidation of a "little Europe" within the larger area of free Europe.

The OEEC may also be contrasted with the more "universalist" approach represented in the immediate postwar era by the International Monetary Fund (IMF) and the General Agreement on Trade and Tariffs (GATT). Space precludes any attempt to review here the complex arguments advanced in favor of the "regional" and "universalist" approaches to the problems of international economic cooperation and coordination of policies. The latter, in simplest terms, has the great merit of including all countries ready and willing to cooperate in working toward agreed objectives. It does not encourage rival groupings of states or such possible undesirable developments as a consolidation of soft currency blocs. But it also has the weaknesses inherent in attempts to achieve unity in principles, policies, and actions among nations around the world having widely disparate cultures and economic traditions. Progress is inevitably more gradual. It is doubtful whether anything comparable to the energetic cooperation achieved through the European Recovery Program could have been accomplished through one or more "universal" agencies. The progress attained in four years, through ERP, may have brought much closer the realization of wider aims which should never be lost sight of—such as currency convertibility and increased cooperation in fostering the development of economically retarded areas.

[17] Especially useful as a general source is the ECE's *Annual Economic Survey*, published in Geneva.
[18] See Chapter 12.

As the period of the Marshall Plan was drawing to a close, proposals looking toward further economic integration within western and southern Europe were submitted to the OEEC.[19] Numerous other suggestions, not officially submitted to the OEEC, were also being put forward for consideration. All were indicative of a continuing ferment of ideas on the subject of European economic integration.

The OEEC stood out as the first organization through which the disintegration of western Europe into autarkic islands had been checked and a reverse trend established. During the transition both immediate economic necessity and temporary American aid were important contributing factors. With advancing recovery these factors receded in importance. That the trend did not then collapse seems to have been due chiefly to the successful demonstration given by the OEEC and other emergent European institutions that positive benefits of distinct value to all members could be achieved by closer economic cooperation. The disastrous effects of intensified economic nationalism and conflict were avoided. A heightened realization of the damage that one nation could bring to others by selfish and shortsighted economic practices was accompanied by the growth of a joint sense of "European" responsibility. Through consultations of unprecedented scope, continuity, and intimacy, and through the establishment and effective use of new cooperative institutions, undramatic but solid foundations were laid for further progress. Integration as a goal synonymous with unification—economic or political—was still far from realization. But integration as a continuing dynamic process of joint effort to deal with common problems through reason and consent had become a new reality on the European scene.

[19] See p. 142.

CHAPTER 17

Economic Strength

and Military Security

WHEN THE Communists attacked in Korea, they tipped their hand and forced upon the free world a tardy realization that a great increase in military strength was essential to its security. In his penetrating analysis of Europe in mid-century, Theodore H. White asserts:

The Korean War changed everything, and all the Western world turned to one new objective—defense and rearmament. The original Marshall Plan had stipulated that not one penny of its largesse might be used by a European government for military purposes or to support such non-productive enterprises as the war in Indo-China. Eight months after the Korean War broke out, the United States government informed the Europeans that every penny of Marshall Plan aid would be allotted on a basis of how much it contributed to the Western defense effort. Originally, American aid had had as its sole purpose the reshaping of Europe's peaceful life by making a more fruitful community of men. From 1950 its overriding purpose was to arm Europe. By 1952, eighty percent of American aid was given in military weapons and the other twenty percent in defense support.[1]

REARMAMENT

The transition in emphasis from "economic cooperation" to "mutual security" took time. The law under which the ECA operated in 1950–

[1] *Fire in the Ashes* (Sloane, New York), pp. 70–71. Copyright 1953 by Theodore H. White. Quoted by permission of William Sloane Associates.

1951 was little different from that of 1949–1950; until the end of 1951 the ECA continued to function as the agency responsible for the administration of United States foreign economic aid. The momentum of the recovery program continued almost unabated for nearly a year. But when Congress convened in early January 1951 it was clear that preoccupation with the savage conflict in Korea, increased by the entry of Communist China in November 1950, had profoundly affected the temper and outlook of the American people and Congress. With a war in progress and the free world's military needs in arrears, economic objectives receded in favor of a tremendous new emphasis on rearmament.

Differences of opinion soon developed over such questions as the relative emphasis to be placed on American efforts in the Far East and Europe; the extent to which Europe had recovered its economic health and should now be expected to contribute to the common defense; and the priorities which should be given to military and economic aid. But there was little disagreement about the urgency of rearmament at home and the need to encourage a vigorous defense effort among allies abroad.

Some European Views

Across the Atlantic, where total war was still an all-too-vivid memory, widespread apprehension existed lest the Russians take rearmament as a provocation, and lest western Europe's military strength not be built up in time to offer an effective deterrent to the Soviet Union.[2] Yet there was every reason to understand and fear the threat from the east and to build up their military strength. As early as 1948, Great Britain, France, and the Benelux countries, as we have seen, had entered into a pact for mutual protection. With the rise of NATO in 1949 other countries had begun looking to their defenses.

The short-range outlook, however, was not reassuring. Denis de Rougement, director of the European Cultural Center in Geneva wrote: "Europe has become a handful of dependent states not one of which

---

[2] The Soviet Army, with a peacetime strength of more than 4 million men and some 25 million reserves, had an estimated 265 divisions (170 infantry, 35 armored and 60 artillery) with first-class weapons of Russian manufacture. Military forces in satellite countries had been organized on the Russian pattern, and in Germany's Eastern Zone preparations were being made for a universal draft which would result in a "people's army" of 400,000 men. "Memorandum on the Russian Military Power," by a group of German generals, *United Nations World*, June 1950, pp. 14–17.

can for an instant claim to be strong enough to cope by itself with the realities of the contemporary situation." [3] In some areas, neutralism was strong. Commenting on one neutralist group, Raymond Aron, a forthright French intellectual, said: "From any practical point of view the neutral position taken . . . is clearly untenable. As Frenchmen they must be aware that their Government, like all others, is forced to choose between the Russian camp and the American camp. As intellectuals they must know that Communism makes no room for neutral nations or opposition parties; it recognizes only partisans and enemies." [4] Another source of uncertainty in Europe lay in the fears of some that American leadership might be unstable. The heartening effect of the firm stand taken in Korea was followed by some concern over the possibility of precipitate action that might increase the chances of a third world war.

The importance of these attitudes should not be exaggerated in importance, but they contributed to the reluctance of Europeans to see their dependence upon the United States, which they had hoped was approaching its end in the economic sphere, now suddenly extended again in the military sphere.

There were of course many who took strongly a more affirmative view, as Aron when he wrote:

The United States is probably the first nation in history to dominate a whole area of civilization without having sought that privilege and while continuing to detest it. This American leadership, this product of historic forces rather than of human will, is something which the people and the governors of Western Europe are forced to recognize whether they like it or not. . . . If they [the Americans] do not lead there is no free nation that can replace them; and if the post of leader remains vacant a vacuum is created which the Soviet power must rush in to fill. [5]

Interdependence of Military and Economic Strength

In presenting a 1951–1952 budget to develop the strength of the United States, President Truman emphasized that a "defense program of the size now being undertaken must be supported by a strong and expanding economic base." A Brookings Institution report asserted that, except at the cost of storing up the need for future economic assistance, there was "no escape from the problem of providing the economic base that is necessary to sustain military strength." [6] The relationship

---

[3] In *America and the Mind of Europe*, p. 30.   [4] *Ibid.*, p. 22.
[5] *Ibid.*, p. 26.   [6] *Current Issues in Foreign Economic Assistance*, pp. 83, 87.

was simply expressed by Foreign Minister Koprulu of Turkey in 1952: "Our economic strength has been gaining from day to day. Therefore our capacity to resist aggression is growing each year." [7]

Without the degree of recovery achieved between 1948 and 1950, a rearmament effort on the scale contemplated would have been impossible. But more was needed. Only if the European economy continued its growth could a rearmament effort of the magnitude required be mounted and sustained over an indefinite period.

Where could Europe find the additional resources required for rearmament? Output could be expanded to some extent through a better utilization of existing resources. But the necessary European contribution to the rebuilding of Western military power could not be derived wholly from such an increase, even on the most favorable assumptions. There was much less leeway for belt tightening in Europe than in the United States, with its enormous productive capacity. Unless wisely conducted, rapid rearmament could gravely impair Europe's economic stability and strength.[8] The immediate dangers were inflation and shortages in basic materials, as Bissell wrote in the spring of 1951:

The alignment of free nations must now begin to spend collectively at the rate of something like 70 billion dollars a year for rearmament. It is scarcely surprising that inflation is again the great internal problem. Nor is it surprising that the great external problem is how to maintain a sufficient supply of foods and raw materials on not too exorbitant terms. . . . If inflation is not controlled, it can undo everything that has been accomplished in the last three years.[9]

Problems for the United States Government

Presentation to Congress of the proposed aid program for 1951–1952 posed a difficult problem for the executive branch of the government. The record of European recovery as set forth in previous ECA testimony had stressed comparisons with prewar conditions, without corresponding emphasis upon the structural weaknesses which still prevented the realization of a fully dynamic, self-reliant economy in Europe. An impression had been created that the original Marshall Plan objectives had been largely attained, but this impression was justified in only a limited sense. The margin available for purposes of rearmament in Europe was severely limited. It was urgent that the momentum

[7] Interview, Ankara, December 10, 1952.
[8] See CED, *Economic Aspects of North Atlantic Security*, pp. 14–19.
[9] *Op. cit.*, p. 84.

generated in the direction of an expanding European economy should not be lost; otherwise, defense itself would become progressively more burdensome.

Until Europe was in a position to absorb the additional load imposed by rearmament, both military and economic assistance were needed. But there was no easy way to distinguish between the two. Who was to say, for example, whether food, which would enable a recipient country to devote more of its own manpower and resources to defense, should be regarded as economic or defense aid? Obviously it was both. In the face of this dilemma differences in emphasis developed in the thinking of the ECA and other executive agencies. Some officials favored a progressive merging of military and economic aid. Others, including Hoffman, viewed with some misgiving the idea of putting both "into the same pot," or of having the ECA assume the new and in many respects different task of fostering military production in Europe. They foresaw that the coordination of military and economic programing would present substantial organizational problems. There was, therefore, in spite of contrary pressures within the ECA, considerable sentiment for separate handling of the two programs, with the ECA adhering largely to its initial objectives.[10]

There were many other transitional problems. Priorities had to be established in granting American assistance, the conditions to be attached to such assistance had to be worked out, and the manner in which aid negotiations were to be conducted had to be defined.[11] The size of the defense budgets to which the European governments were prepared to commit themselves became an increasingly important consideration in the planning of aid.

THE NEW ORIENTATION

The Soviet record, Soviet policies, and Soviet power had left no alternative to the free world but to rearm swiftly and on a massive scale. The stake of the United States in a joint system of defense was clear. As the Mutual Security Agency stated in its *First Report to Congress:*

---

[10] The need to continue an avowedly balanced program—of increasing military assistance without sacrificing the longer-range objectives for which continued economic aid would be needed—was emphasized by the Gray and Rockefeller reports and by such private organizations as the National Planning Association, the Brookings Institution, and the Committee for Economic Development.

[11] See Brown and Opie, *op. cit.,* pp. 554–555, 559–560.

Our reliance on our allies is just as great as their reliance on us. Western Europe's industrial might, for example, stands as a critical margin of power on our side. Combined, we outproduce the Soviets by at least four to one. But should the entire industrial production of Europe ever be joined with that of the Soviets, the ratio between the free world and the slave world would be nearer one to one. Similar calculations reveal our dependence on the resources of the Near East, Africa, Asia and Latin America. . . . Our Defense Mobilization Program would be wasteful and ineffective if it did not carry with it a program of support to the defense effort of our allies.[12]

Shift versus Expansion

An attempt was made to maintain a balanced emphasis between military and economic goals. The MSA report referred to the Mutual Security Program as a fourfold investment, with military, economic, political, and moral objectives. The Gray report held that "the provision of military equipment is not by itself enough to enable Western Europe to expand its own military production and forces with sufficient rapidity. What is needed, therefore, is a reassessment of the outlook of Western European countries in the light of their revised requirements and their capabilities under the joint defense effort."[13] The Committee for Economic Development maintained: "It is clearly the task of the western powers to organize a comprehensive and balanced security program. . . . Next to the failure to rearm, perhaps the costliest error that the United States and its allies could make in the next few years would be to act as though rearmament and security were synonymous."[14]

But popular attitudes and political pressures did not display so measured a balance. Defense aims tended to push into the background other aspects of foreign policy as assistance for rearmament was stepped up in Europe and extended to Spain and Yugoslavia and parts of the Far East and Latin America, and as greater emphasis was placed upon the expansion of strategic materials production in the overseas territories and elsewhere.[15]

In adjusting to these changes, the ECA and the Department of State followed perhaps the only politically feasible line, and called for support to military rearmament without continuing a strong stress upon economic growth as a coordinate objective. This emphasis was reflected in the ECA's *Tenth Report to Congress:* "If internal financial

[12] P. 5. [13] *Report to the President on Foreign Economic Policies,* p. 37.
[14] CED, *Economic Aspects of North Atlantic Security,* pp. 6–7.
[15] See MSA, *First Report to Congress,* pp. 18–34.

stability is to be maintained, national economic policies will have to be adjusted and this will generally involve the subordination or postponement of previous objectives." [16] The reorientation was apparent throughout the ECA and MSA programs, at home and abroad. "The question now," Bart Harvey, a member of the mission to Italy, commented, "is what defense the economy can support, and what aid is needed to support a given defense effort." [17]

Gains and Losses in New Orientation

With the doubling of defense budgets in two years came larger imports of high-cost raw materials. Prices and living costs rose. Western Europe's trade gap with the rest of the world increased and its foreign exchange reserves dropped. During the first half of 1952 western Europe's adverse trade balance with other parts of the world averaged 507 million dollars monthly, as compared with an average deficit of only 280 million a month in the final quarter of 1950. A sharp decline in gold and dollar earnings during the first three months of 1952 was only partially offset by a slow recovery between March and June.[18] The gold and short-term dollar assets of the participating countries fell from nearly 8 billion dollars in mid-1951 to something over 6 billion by June 1952. Industrial production, which toward the end of 1951 reached a level 40 percent above prewar, declined during the first half of 1952 to about 37 percent above the 1938 level. Agricultural output leveled off. Although investments in the overseas territories continued, the problems of these areas remained formidable.

In 1952 some compensating factors were coming into play. United States "offshore procurement" of military items in Europe—including materials for the construction of bases there, American outlays for support and training of its own forces in Europe, and American contributions to NATO—were beginning to help restore the dollar resources of some countries. Certain of these expenditures, including aid given to industries under the Military Defense Assistance Program, bolstered nonmilitary areas of economic activity as well. But these gains were gradual and did not offset the rising internal costs of defense. Furthermore, the economic posture required for defense was not always consistent with the requirements of economic growth. As Vincent Barnett

[16] P. 3.   [17] Interview, Rome, December 19, 1952.
[18] The losses in reserves stemmed principally from a shrinkage in the U.K.'s hard currency holdings, which dropped 2.2 billion dollars between June 1951 and June 1952.

remarked: "Rearmament leads to types of industrial development where there is a discarding of economic measuring sticks. It means continuing or expanding or reinstituting noneconomic industries. Even such dollar assistance as that provided through offshore procurement, while it is a shot in the arm, means a postponement of the basic problem." [19] Thus, after the rapid economic growth experienced during the heyday of the recovery program, the European economy seemed to be entering at least a transitional phase of much more gradual growth.

As relations with the United States took on increasingly the aspect of a military alliance, moreover, new strains in relationship were added. One of these was occasioned by the increase in American concern over East-West trade. The will of European allies to cooperate in imposing specifically defined controls over this trade was not helped by the fact that the restrictions proposed often gave the appearance of being not the combined judgments of partners but measures initiated by the United States Congress and linked with the threat of economic sanctions. The resentments that resulted were detrimental to relations. But the American government avoided a bludgeon approach in administering the legislation adopted, as it sought cooperation in remedying numerous weaknesses in existing controls.[20]

Robert Hall of the United Kingdom noted that "the United States is not only the head of a new military alliance but the leader toward imposing new burdens. Recovery has been set back by rearmament, and therefore relations have moved into a less constructive setting." [21] Although the Mutual Security Program, as President Truman emphasized in transmitting the MSA's *First Report to Congress*, was undoubt-

[19] Interview, Rome, December 18, 1952.

[20] This was attested later by several leading British publications. The *Manchester Guardian* of September 28, 1953, said, for example: "The Battle Act, passed by Congress in 1951, looked like being one of America's most hurtful measures towards its allies. . . . But, as is liable to happen with American policy, ferocious gesticulations gave way to sound common sense in practice. The administrators of the Act have moved prudently and have taken great care to consult with other countries about the reasons for their trade with the Soviet bloc." Similarly, the *Economist* of October 3, 1953, after commenting on an American "genius" for investing awkward and unworkable laws, of which "an outstanding example was the Battle Act with its termination-of-aid provision," stated: "How fortunate it is that under the discreet and sensible direction of Mr. Harold Stassen (and his predecessor, Mr. Harriman) there has never been occasion to wield this crude weapon." The *Financial Times* declared that no part of U.S. economic policy had caused more ill will and misunderstanding than the Battle Act, but added that it "has not been administered unreasonably."

[21] Interview cited.

edly a "program for peace," there was insufficient general recognition that the military program needed to be accompanied by continuing, unabated vigor in other aspects of our foreign relations. Something of the "more" that was needed was suggested in an article by Howard K. Smith, which maintained that more equitable distribution in European economies, further progress toward a single market for western Europe, and the establishment of more mutually beneficial relationships with Asia and other backward areas were among the issues not being adequately met.[22]

The Limitations of Containment

To some Europeans it seemed that America was not only occupying a new and unaccustomed role, but that its foreign policy, evolving in a context of debates over appropriations required for immediate and urgent defense tasks, was formulated and administered too much on a year-to-year basis. American preoccupation with the weight and complexity of the defense burden could be explained, but this did not remove uneasiness over an apparent diminution in the wholeness of outlook evident during the early Marshall Plan period.

General H. G. Martin argued, in a composite volume on *Western Defenses*,[23] that a "purely defensive policy of containment is suicidal. Military strength, to be sustained, requires a concurrent maintenance and growth of economic, political and psychological strength." Jean Allary asserted in the same volume: "We can only defend a reality." Far from weakening the military effort, the continued fostering of economic strength and a community of understanding and affirmative purpose serve to buttress the political solidarity without which military might alone could prove to be of little avail. The importance of such a broad approach was underscored by President Eisenhower in his address of April 16, 1953, to the American Society of Newspaper Editors. After listing essential steps toward peace, including the achievement of just political settlements and closer unity of the nations of western Europe, he said:

The fruit of success in all these tasks would present the world with the greatest task—and the greatest opportunity—of all. It is this: The dedication of the energies, the resources, and the imaginations of all peaceful nations to a new kind of war. This would be a declared, total war, not upon any human enemy,

[22] "An American Looks at Europe," *International Affairs*, October 1950, pp. 470–476.

[23] Ed. by Brig. J. G. Smyth (Allen Wingate, London, 1951).

but upon the brute forces of poverty and need. The peace we seek, founded upon a decent trust and cooperative effort among nations, can be fortified—not by weapons of war—but by wheat and by cotton, by milk and by wool; by meat, timber and rice. These are words that translate into every language on earth. These are the needs that challenge this world in arms.

The Balance Needed

Could a better balance have been maintained? Or can it be recovered? The question is not one, essentially, of too much concern with military strength, but too little concern with the other elements needed to hold firm and strengthen the Western alliance. If there had been, after the Korea attack, a clear public determination not to allow the Communists to impair the Marshall Plan halfway, great emphasis could still have been given to rearmament without attendant uncertainty as to whether there would be a weakening in other directions. The multiple Communist attack—military, economic, political, and social—might have been met more effectively by a multiple response. The common goal would have been seen more clearly as balanced security.[24]

When the military outlook altered, a great new emphasis on rearmament was essential, but with it was a complementary necessity for a growing economic base capable of supporting the defense effort without a retreat from long-range objectives. What was needed was public support for a raising of sights all along the line in order that a new plateau in defense might be achieved and sustained over a long period, if necessary, without jeopardizing other aspects of free world strength and unity.

Rephrasing a Clausewitz dictum: If policy is great and powerful, so also will be peace. The security of the free world required that all the components of national and international strength should be fortified. To neglect military strength would be suicidal; to neglect non-military strength would play into the hands of the Communist conspiracy.

---

[24] Article 2 of the North Atlantic Treaty affirmed a continuing interest in political, economic, and cultural bonds, but the efforts of NATO were centered largely upon the problem of defense.

CHAPTER 18

Development in Asia and Africa

THE years 1948–1952 witnessed an extraordinary growth of interest in underdeveloped areas. One reason for this was the shock produced by the Communist bid for power in China and the fear that all of Asia might be swept into the Soviet orbit. The Western powers had been moving toward an altogether different pattern of relationships in the Far East. To the intensified nationalism of the period, they had responded by relinquishing unequal treaty rights in China and granting independence to the Philippines, India, Pakistan, Burma, and Ceylon. Freedom had been pledged for Korea, and similar action was being weighed for Indonesia and Indochina. Aid had been extended to these countries and to Japan, betokening a desire to see their peoples freed from the fetters which had held them back and to assure cooperative relations with them.

The interdependence of the free world and the vast, largely uncommitted areas outside the Soviet sphere was becoming increasingly manifest. The peace and security of the one was bound up with that of the other. Europe and North America relied heavily on the products and markets of Asia and Africa just as those continents depended on the products and markets of the West. Was the era of growing independence and voluntary cooperation, for which the Western powers hoped, to be stillborn as a result of Communist expansion?

The ECA and Other Programs

The programs linked legislatively with the Marshall Plan and administered by ECA represented only a part, albeit an important part, of the expanding activity which soon developed. Point Four assistance, administered by the State Department, went to other economically retarded areas—the Middle East, independent countries in Africa and, after a merger of previous programs, Latin America. Several European countries were engaged in similar activities. The United Kingdom, France, and Belgium, with marginal ECA subsidies, undertook large investment programs in Africa and elsewhere. Britain took the lead in projecting the Colombo Plan for assistance in India, Pakistan, and neighboring areas. The World Bank sponsored a broad range of developmental loans. Specialized agencies of the United Nations—notably the World Health Organization, the Food and Agriculture Organization, and the Economic Commission for Asia and the Far East—provided surveys and research, advisory aid, and technical services on a significant scale. Private agencies, notably the Rockefeller and Ford Foundations, sponsored a wide range of experimental and pilot projects.[1] Two major types of activity were involved, apart from emergency relief—investment and technical assistance. The latter, designed to help people help themselves, grew into what Eugene Black[2] called "the greatest technological education campaign ever undertaken."[3]

The aim of this chapter is to treat succinctly, without pretension

[1] On the problem of coordination, see section below on "Formulation and Integration of Programs."

[2] President, World Bank, in an address to the U.N. Economic and Social Council, April 14, 1954, quoted in the *New York Times,* April 15, 1954.

[3] Concurrent with these far-ranging efforts was a rapid growth in the study of underdeveloped areas and their problems. The literature on economic development alone has been characterized by Jacob Viner as having an immensity in the last decade and a scarcity earlier that were "almost beyond belief" (in "America's Aims," a chapter in *The Progress of Underdeveloped Areas,* ed. by Bert F. Hoselitz [University of Chicago Press, 1952], p. 185). One recent volume based on a discriminating selection of sources (Eugene Staley's *The Future of Underdeveloped Countries* [Harper & Bros., for the Council on Foreign Relations, New York, 1954]) lists at the end 172 authors and works cited. For a more comprehensive annotated bibliography see *The Economics of Underdeveloped Areas,* compiled by Arthur Hazlewood (Oxford University Press, London, 1954).

Yet, as Raymond T. Moyer noted in late 1953: "No one has yet done for the Point Four idea, clearly and convincingly, what was done for the ideas of Secretary Marshall when they were given flesh and blood in the Marshall Plan and built into a concrete program under the Economic Cooperation Administration." Memorandum, "Relook at Point Four in Asia," 1953.

of comprehensiveness or finality, the deepening awareness of the problem of the underdeveloped areas which emerged partly as a by-product of ECA experience and to indicate some of the insights which developed in the course of actual operations.

AWARENESS OF THE PROBLEM

Any illusion that dollars and technical "know-how" were endowed with mystic qualities that could make economic deserts bloom like the rose was quickly dispelled in the face of hard realities in Asia. Difficulties read and talked about in abstract terms took on a wholly different appearance when encountered at first hand by ECA men. The indistinct pictures that had been brought to mind by books, memoranda, or orientation lectures were suddenly translated into vivid settings filled with struggling human beings speaking strange languages. Each country was unique, complex, full of seeming paradoxes. Each problem had to be looked at anew. American experience, it soon appeared, was far less relevant than had been supposed. Advice from foreigners was not awaited with bated breath. Pat solutions toppled like tenpins, and the truth dawned that a great deal of learn-how was essential before know-how could be put to effective use. Workers in the field began to have an awareness, difficult to convey to people at home, that the bold new effort to bring help and encouragement, on a scale never before envisaged, to depressed economies around the world meant opening a vast but little known frontier in human affairs, one that could absorb the energies of people for generations to come. Gradually they acquired greater insight into the problems that had to be faced.

Communism versus Democracy

What was the explanation for communism's powerful appeal among the people of Asia and other depressed parts of the world? It seemed obvious at the outset that it was hunger and want so severe and widespread that people were ready to grasp at any new hope, any utopian promise. What was there to lose? But it was ironical that the Communists should be the ones to demonstrate anew that men—even hungry men—do not live by bread alone. Into postwar China (before 1948) the United States and its allies poured hundreds of millions of dollars' worth of relief and rehabilitation supplies, not to mention other aid. The Communists poured in propaganda and won the support that enabled them to take over the country. It was a hard lesson. And it was of little avail to say later that the case presented by the Communists was built on a fraud, although much of it was; [4] by then their grip upon that vast nation was secured.

It was clear that to prevent a repetition of the China experience in other parts of Asia the United States should offer as an alternative to Communist blandishments assistance designed explicitly to help the peoples still free to realize progressively their own legitimate aspirations. Experience quickly brought home the lesson that no program, however well conceived, could bring a quick release from present sufferings or a speedy realization of hopes and desires for the future. Resources, organization, technology, and leadership far beyond the levels of existing capacity were required. The answer, it was then assumed, lay in giving technical help which might enable the countries to develop more efficient methods of production, better transport, improved facilities for health and education, and more modern political and economic institutions. Surely the United States could outstrip the Communists in these areas. Efforts along these lines began immediately, however, to cut across established customs and vested interests.

To overcome such obstacles, some thought that it would be well to "get a little tough," perhaps curtailing aid if reforms were not forthcoming. But such an approach, it was found, could boomerang in unexpected ways. Colonialism and semicolonialism had produced a state of mind, cultivated and reinforced by Communist propaganda, distrustful of the motives of the Western powers, a distrust from which the United States was by no means exempt. Efforts to induce reforms, especially when accompanied by public criticism, did not alleviate such distrust.

In the face of a seemingly interminable cycle of difficulties and frustration, there was an understandable temptation, reflected in Congress, to give the whole thing up or to cut down on economic assistance and to rely predominantly on military means to check Communist expansion in Asia. From the Communist standpoint such a course could have been highly desirable. It could have been, in effect, a passive acknowledgment of defeat. It could have contributed to further confusion, grievances, bafflement, and loss of confidence in the West, upon all of which Communist propaganda could capitalize. It could have given the Communists further opportunities to disrupt the economies of the Far East. As Adlai Stevenson said:

---

[4] To assume that the entire case was fraudulent is to underestimate seriously the strength and appeal of communism. Although broad promises were illusory, evidence could be cited of notable economic development projects in Russia and, to a much less extent, in China.

The Communists may well believe that in the aspirations and the grievances of the East they now have the key to world power. They hope, and perhaps even expect, that the West cannot rise to the challenge in the East. Furthermore, they may not feel the same need for quick and tidy solutions that is felt in certain quarters in our own country. They may believe that they can afford to have a patience equal to the stakes involved. And the stakes are nothing less than an overwhelming preponderance of power—for with Asia under control, they could turn with new energy and vast new resources in an effort to win a bloodless victory in a weakened, frightened Europe.[5]

If the answer to so deep a peril was not to be found either in withdrawal or in dependence on military strength alone, where did a solution lie? Where but in recognizing the dimensions of the problem and the extent of the intelligence, determination, and patience that would be required to meet it?

It was essential to realize that communism was only one aspect of the dilemma confronting the underdeveloped areas. Their fundamental problem lay in the conditions that made communism possible and that would be a potential source of danger whether communism existed or not. Moreover, the revolutionary, nationalistic ferment which the West had helped generate in Asia had become deep and pervasive, and the Communists had turned it skillfully to their own advantage. Revolution meant change and the demand for more change, and the course it took would depend on whether Communist or democratic leadership could appeal most effectively to the aspirations of the people and mobilize their energies.

Communist propaganda made much of Western cultural, as well as political and economic, "imperialism"; American culture was constantly described as "money-mad, pleasure-mad, and sex-mad." Point Four aid was pictured as a steppingstone to American domination and a stifling of national "liberation" movements. The democracies, dealing in facts instead of deception, seeking solid advancement by peaceful consent instead of more radical revolution through dictatorship, were at an initial tactical disadvantage. But they also had a far more valuable article to sponsor—an approach geared to gradual but *genuine* fulfillment of the aspirations of the people, not to their ultimate enslavement.

In any case, the battle was joined. Communism had become a dynamic "competing civilization" in Asia.[6] Behind the military struggle

[5] San Francisco speech, reported in the *New York Times*, September 10, 1952.
[6] W. W. Rostow, *The Prospects for Communist China* (Technology Press and Wiley, New York, 1954), contains a highly informative analysis of the sequence

was a deeper contest for loyalties. The purpose of any Western military action, in Korea or elsewhere, could easily be thwarted if the time gained at so heavy a cost was not used to open new paths to development in Asia. The International Development Advisory Board said in 1951: "Our strategy must be a positive one, based on constructive progress and a genuine sense of humanity's needs for common effort toward the future. It must be both global, embracing every part of the world, and total, with political, psychological, economic, and military considerations integrated into one whole." [7]

The programs undertaken in the underdeveloped areas through the ECA, while primarily economic in content, were also political, psychological, and strategic in their purpose and impact. What additional light did they throw upon the nature of the vast problems to be faced in these areas?

Economic Problems

Many basic facts, of course, were already widely known. Whereas dire poverty was an occasional problem in the United States and western Europe, it was a chronic problem in the underdeveloped areas, especially in Asia. Approximately half the people of the world received, in 1939, average per capita incomes equivalent to less than 45 dollars a year, as compared with an average of about 460 dollars per year among the 13 percent of the world's population living in the fifteen most economically advanced countries.[8] In many economically depressed areas, agrarian problems were deep-rooted.[9]

Several new and practical emphases developed out of the ECA and concurrent programs. It was found, for example, that opportunities to adopt improved practices in agriculture were likely to elicit a lukewarm response unless farmers had some assurance that increased production would bring better incomes. There was little incentive to produce more if the gains were to be lost in higher rentals, interest rates, and taxes. Thus the problem of distribution of income was seen to have, in un-

and implications of Communist policies and actions in China since 1949. See also Paul M. A. Linebarger in *Southeast Asia in the Coming World,* ed. by Philip W. Thayer (Johns Hopkins Press, Baltimore, 1953), pp. 180–188.

[7] International Development Advisory Board (Rockefeller Report), *op. cit.,* p. 4.

[8] See *Economic Development and Cultural Change,* II (1953), 5–6; and Point Four publication 3719 (January 1950), App. C, pp. 103–124.

[9] See *Land Reform—A World Challenge,* Dept. of State Pub. 4445 (Washington, D.C., 1952).

derdeveloped areas no less than in advanced economic societies, a fundamental bearing upon the problem of production.

As in Europe, it was found that much could be done to augment productivity in both agriculture and industry without large new capitalization. The high cost of installing and using imported capital equipment and the lack of trained managers and workers made it imperative to use great care in determining priorites for investment programs.

Shortage of private savings, the frequent nonproductive use of such savings, and lack of experience in modern industrial enterprise all tended to require government to play a larger role in the early stages of development. This was particularly true in the provision of such basic services as transport and power and in the training of personnel.

Seen as a whole, the postwar economic problem in the underdeveloped areas was vastly different from that of western Europe. The latter was primarily one of restoring and improving an existing economic structure. In economically retarded areas it was principally one of developing the unused physical resources and the latent skills and energies of the people.

Population

One grim economic fact stood out. An impressive body of evidence indicated that population growth in some densely crowded countries, if it continued unchecked, would probably keep pace with or exceed for some time the increases that seemed possible, with currently known technology, in agricultural and industrial production. So long as this occurred, no basic improvement in general living standards appeared attainable even with maximum developmental effort.

The 1953 edition of the *Demographic Yearbook,* published by the Statistical Office of the United Nations, estimated that the world's population in the middle of 1952 was 2,469,000,000—an increase of approximately thirty million since the middle of 1951.[10] This is an average of 82,000 more people per day. The rate of increase, moreover, was greatest in the underdeveloped areas, with birth rates averaging over 35 per thousand per year (as compared with less than 25 per thousand in the most economically advanced countries) and with death rates generally declining. A report to the MSA by its Advisory Committee

[10] According to U.N. estimates, total world population, from 1920 to 1950, increased from 1,834 million to 2,406 million, and that of Asia (excluding Russia) from 997 to 1,272 million. U.N., *The Determinants and Consequences of Population Trends* (New York, 1953), p. 10.

on Underdeveloped Areas, in discussing "the dilemma of population and resources," stated bluntly:

We do ourselves and our friends in the less developed countries a disservice if we pretend that the poverty in those countries reflects only the inadequacy of resources or their ineffective utilization. . . . A massive attack on the production problem, including an emphasis on those health measures that will most directly benefit production, combined with real steps in the direction of conscious promotion of population limitations, both seem to be required.[11]

To persons concerned with this problem came the disconcerting realization that assistance in public health and food production might well contribute to increased population pressures and hence to even more widespread poverty. An effort was made on a minute scale, through the JCRR program in China, to disseminate birth control information through simple charts and pamphlets adapted to the knowledge and economic status of poorer sections of the population. The response gave some ground for the view that the problem might not be wholly insoluble. But much greater efforts backed by research and with open governmental indorsement—such as that given by Prime Minister Jawaharlal Nehru in India—would be required over a period of many years before any appreciable results could be expected.[12]

Colonialism

Aid programs in south and southeast Asia brought the United States government into closer contact than before with the vestiges and aftermath of colonialism in that region. The vestiges were to be found in Indochina, Malaya, and Indonesia, which had not yet received full independence. The aftermath of passionate antipathy to colonialism was everywhere.

Since by 1948 the Western powers, with the possible exception of France, were in fact liquidating their empires in Asia, the understandable feelings of most of the peoples concerned would not have presented a political problem but for intensive Communist propaganda which discounted Western intentions and played constantly on the theme of Western imperialism. It portrayed the Communist regimes of Soviet Russia and China as the true champions of liberation. To the West,

[11] *Economic Strength for the Free World* (Washington, 1953), pp. 17–18.
[12] See *The Interrelations of Demographic, Economic, and Social Problems in Selected Underdeveloped Areas,* Proceedings of the 1953 Annual Conference, Milbank Memorial Fund (New York, 1953); especially paper by Irene B. Taeuber on "Demographic Transition in Japan: Omens for the Future of Asian Populations."

such a propaganda line appeared so fantastic that it could not be taken seriously. It did not seem fantastic, however, to Asians who had never experienced at first hand the realities of Communist "liberation."

This raised some difficult problems in providing technical and economic assistance to non-Communist Asia. Attachment of "strings" to the aid, however justified in the interest of the peoples concerned, was likely to be seized upon as evidence of a new American or Western encroachment. Any attempt to align the recently freed countries of the region with the West in a general defense against communism encountered strong neutralist sentiments in such countries as Indonesia and Burma. This problem was particularly acute in Indochina, where it was difficult to provide assistance in consultation with the French without seeming to align the United States with an effort to perpetuate French colonialism. The same problem arose in French North Africa. To a less degree it was present in other colonial areas which were not moving toward self-government as rapidly as their inhabitants desired.

The ECA experience dramatized the need for a more fundamental rapport than had ever been sought among the democratic powers on the whole question of Western policy toward underdeveloped areas. Only the periphery of that problem was reached.

Nationalism

Colonialism and the "unequal treaties" by which Western powers had in the past imposed their wills on weaker nations were undoubtedly a major factor in the rise of intense nationalism throughout much of Asia and in other parts of the world. The empire building of earlier centuries had produced what one writer has called a "glaring disparity between the possibilities of ethnic equality and the actualities of Western arrogance and discrimination." [13] Certainly colonialism had violated the conceptions of personal and racial dignity to which the peoples concerned were deeply attached. Paradoxically, the better impulses of the colonial powers also stimulated nationalistic feeling. Education and the widening cultural contacts fostered by the colonial powers spread ideas of individual and national freedom. Thus nationalism and the desire for independence may be traced to intense aversion to colonialism, on the one hand, and strong attraction toward new concepts of freedom and independence, on the other. These divergent origins tended to give nationalism in Asia both negative and positive aspects.

On the negative side, nationalism was frequently expressed in antiforeignism, anti-Westernism or anti-white-raceism, and a continuing

[13] Morris Watnick, in Hoselitz, *op. cit.*, p. 156.

revulsion against external influences upon internal political and economic affairs. There were instances, in both the ECA and Point Four programs, of resistance to improved technology merely because it was foreign in origin or because a foreigner suggested its adoption. Such attitudes restricted the possibilities of cooperative action for economic development because advice was proffered by a country whose motives might appear to be suspect, or because the very process of accepting such advice might seem to imply that one party was inferior to the other.[14] There were instances in Indonesia, for example, where leaders wished to attract foreign capital, but the necessary legislation to facilitate such investment was prevented by nationalistic sentiment.[15]

But nationalism also had its more positive aspects. To many Asians it meant the right to govern themselves, to stand on their own feet, to organize their economies as they thought best, and to walk with equality and self-respect among the peoples of the world. It meant spirit and pride and an end to legal and other symbols of inferiority. It meant the beginning of a new sense of responsibility in national and international affairs. Political leaders who did not reflect such aspirations were likely to find their tenures of office abbreviated.

The question was how to encourage constructive nationalism as a rallying force for internal cooperation and against subversion without impairing mutually beneficial relations with other nations. Understanding, magnanimity, and avoidance of giving needless offense through ill-considered public statements, were vital to the success of any cooperative effort. As the International Development Advisory Board said in 1951: "The problem of constructing a lasting peace is not one of *preserving* an existing order in the world but of building a new structure in which all nations can work together, exchanging their skills, labor, and capital to mutual benefit." [16]

Cultural Factors in Economic Development

In the burgeoning literature on underdeveloped areas, considerable attention had been paid by anthropologists and sociologists to cultural factors.[17] The day-to-day experience of ECA workers did not add significantly to the sum total of formalized knowledge on the question of

[14] See Samuel P. Hayes, Jr., "Personality and Culture Problems of Point Four," in Hoselitz, *op. cit.*, p. 228.

[15] See the *New York Times*, International Financial Review, January 6, 1953, p. 85.

[16] International Development Advisory Board (Rockefeller Report), *op. cit.*, p. 11.

[17] For example, a series of lectures at the University of Chicago, published in

relations between divergent cultures, but it did in many cases extend the limits of individual understanding. Conclusions drawn from such experience are illustrated in a booklet subsequently issued by the MSA:

Concern for the customs, institutions, underlying values and attitudes of other people must take into account (a) the sensitivity of other peoples about external interference, (b) the difficulty we often experience in making clear to the less developed areas the mutuality of our interests and theirs, and (c) the severe limits on our own understanding of the values and attitudes, customs and institutions most conducive to economic development of the kind serving our mutually agreed objectives.[18]

In economically retarded areas, especially in Asia, centuries of deprivation and insecurity had given rise to an intense attachment to the protection of personal dignity or "face," even at the cost of unfavorable consequences. Witness the Chinese proverb: "Better to be a broken jade than a whole tile." Somewhat related were the attitudes of workers toward production and productivity when the benefits of increased output were not reflected in their own incomes. This helped explain an otherwise puzzling indifference to measures for improving economic conditions generally. Increasing the worker's share in the product of his labors (e.g., through land rent reduction) proved to be an effective incentive to greater productivity. It did not eliminate suddenly, however, the more leisurely pace of work or the less hurried conception of time which characterize the economic life of relatively static societies.

The attitudes of educated persons toward manual work were often adversely affected by the relatively low status of artisans and laborers in the social system and by the customary exemption of privileged classes from such work. Another factor in the detachment of intellectuals from the practical problems of economic life was to be found in school curricula, in which scientific as well as cultural studies tended to be dissociated from the workaday world. The result was a shortage not only of managers and technicians, but also of sufficiently educated intermediate workers, such as foremen.

Hoselitz, *op. cit.*, included the following: "Cultural and Personal Factors Affecting Economic Growth," by Ralph Linton; "The Problem of Adapting Societies to New Tasks," by Melville J. Herskovits; "The Problem of Selective Culture Change," by Morris E. Opler; "The Interrelations between Cultural Factors and the Acquisition of New Technical Skills," by Walter R. Goldschmidt; and "Personality and Culture Problems of Point Four," by Samuel P. Hayes, Jr.

[18] *Economic Strength for the Free World*, pp. iv–v.

Many social and cultural influences retarded capital formation and investment. One was the extent to which economic life was rooted in personal relationships and small, custom-bound social units such as the family, the guild, or the tribe. People were unwilling to trust personal or family savings to institutions—such as impersonal corporations —outside the orbit of such habitual relationships. As a result, corporate forms of organization, even on a small scale, were slow to take root. Acceleration of investment was further impeded by a want of experience in the organization and development of medium and large productive enterprises. Still another common deterrent was the possibility of augmenting personal fortunes by speculation, or by moneylending at high interest rates, instead of by productive investment.

Finally, the conception of government as actively responsible and responsive to the needs of the people was by no means an automatic accompaniment of nationalism. Gradually increasing awareness of such influences as these enabled ECA personnel in economically retarded areas to approach their work more realistically.

Lack of Modern Institutions

A general lack of political and economic institutions capable of initiating and supervising substantial development programs also constituted a serious handicap to economic growth. In almost every area there was a dearth of effective governmental services for agriculture, education, health, conservancy, scientific and statistical surveys, and the like, and of modern credit institutions and business organizations. Standards of governmental performance were generally inadequate for the competent handling of major economic functions. Trained personnel were few and there was seldom a vigorous "middle class" on which to draw for political and technical leadership.

Under such conditions, the ECA came to attach increasing importance to "institution building"—by assisting local leaders to improve and expand, step by step, the political and economic organizations and practices through which urgently needed measures for economic growth could be carried forward.

The Time Dilemma

ECA personnel working in the underdeveloped areas had a strong sense of urgency. Added to distressing conditions and the need for demonstrable results as a counterpoise to Communist propaganda was the fact that ECA programs were short-term, emergency efforts. If these programs were to be justified and to win continuing Congressional support, they had to show evidences of positive achievement. But while some projects might be developed in a short period of time, fundamental change was another matter. Rapid economic progress had never before come to densely populated regions with high illiteracy and a low level of technical skills. In fact, only a few countries in the world had ever experienced speedy economic growth.[19] Moreover, local peoples did not usually have the sense of hurry and impatience widely regarded as particularly characteristic of Americans. They were not habituated to rapid social changes. And there were penalties for making mistakes, or violating local customs, or offending one or another individual or group.

Repeated frustrations reconciled ECA personnel to the view that gradualness was inevitable. With experience, many field workers came to attach greater importance to fundamental meetings of minds with local leaders and local peoples than to quick agreement on specific measures, recognizing that without such basic rapprochement any forward momentum generated through aid programs would soon be dissipated. To give up all sense of urgency would have been fatal; not to modify it would have been stupid. The need was always to strike a balance, taking into account the circumstances of each particular situation.

ACTION AND INSIGHTS

Increasing comprehension of the conditions affecting economic growth in the underdeveloped areas was accompanied by insights into some of the requisites of effective economic assistance to such areas.

Choice and Training of Personnel

After preliminary agreement on the scope of the effort to be undertaken and the terms under which aid would be provided, the first of these requisites was a wise choice of personnel. In general, individual resourcefulness, adaptability, friendliness, enthusiasm, willingness to listen and learn, perceptiveness and skill in human relations, and broad competence and capacity for unobtrusive but effective leadership

[19] See Jacob Viner in Hoselitz, *op. cit.*, p. 199. Even Japan's rapid industrial development over several decades was not accompanied by a corresponding rise in living standards for the country as a whole.

were found to be more important than a highly specialized background. Caution against the flaunting of prejudices or of disparities in living standards was found to be of utmost importance.[20]

The most valuable training was found to be that acquired on the job. Some orientation before departure for the area was desirable, however, especially when conducted by persons of wide and recent experience in the country or region. Although a series of orientation lectures formed part of a brief preliminary indoctrination for ECA personnel awaiting departure to the field, the full potentialities of such preliminary training were by no means realized under the ECA program.[21]

Formulation and Integration of Programs

Owing to wide variations in local economic, political, and social conditions, greater diversity in methods, as well as more ingenuity and flexibility in administration, was needed to aid underdeveloped areas than to deal with advanced economies. Planning—or program formulation—proved in fact to be a continuing process, changing in detail, perhaps even in direction. As one problem was dealt with, others emerged or other facets of the same problem came to light. On this question, Moyer declared:

The proper development of a program is a difficult task, and the way to approach it deserves the most careful thinking and planning. A creative effort is called for, carried out in close consultation with the leaders and people of the host country. This effort will seek to identify the major problems of the country to which attention should be directed; to follow with formulation of the broad programs that might be undertaken in getting at the solution of these problems; and finally to select for assistance those specific projects which will best advance step by step the development of those programs. This effort requires leadership of a high order, possessed of a sound sense of what it is hoped to accomplish, an imagination able to spot the small beginnings out of which significant endeavors can be developed, and the wise judgment to select for encouragement those endeavors which will transform useful ideas into practical and substantial accomplishment.[22]

In some areas, the ECA was not the only agency offering assistance. Duplication and confusion threatened unless effective coordination

---

[20] See Moyer, memorandum cited, p. 5.

[21] See Chapter 11; also Wallace S. Sayre and Clarence E. Thurber, *op. cit.*, ch. vi.

[22] Memorandum cited, p. 29.

could be achieved with other United States government activities and with similar or parallel efforts conducted under United Nations or other auspices. It was important also to distinguish between the aims and organization of temporary emergency assistance, through food, fertilizer, cotton, and other commodities; the provision of equipment and supplies for productive investment; and the furnishing of technical assistance for longer-range developments. The coordination of economic assistance with other United States government activities, relating, for example, to mutual security or commercial policy, needed especially to be clarified, both administratively and in public statements. Otherwise, experience showed, there was risk of misunderstanding and misinterpretation of United States policies as a whole.

A consensus growing out of ECA experience was that coordination of aid efforts in behalf of any area could be most effectively achieved at the country or local level.[23]

Balanced Economic Development

The obstacles to development—such as limited capital resources, shortage of trained personnel, cultural patterns resistant to change, scarcity of capital, inexperienced governments—made it especially important that available resources be apportioned in such a manner as to foster, as far as practicable, a balanced economic development in each area. In common with other national and international agencies, the ECA looked upon economic aid, particularly its use for investment, primarily as a means of inducing economic growth for the benefit of all concerned rather than as a means of generating financial returns to the dispensers of loan or grant assistance. This removed the likelihood of a repetition of previous errors of promoting, through international investments, distorted "colonial" patterns of economic development emphasizing too exclusively agricultural and raw material production beneficial to the investing countries rather than a more durable de-

[23] This view was set forth in a letter of October 30, 1950, from R. Allan Griffin, then director of the Far East Program Division, to the chiefs of ECA missions in Asia. Citing the President and the Act for International Development in support, Griffin further stated that it was American policy to move as conditions permitted in the direction of increased reliance on U.N. agencies, and the STEM missions were instructed to make use of the facilities afforded by such agencies for the performance of tasks when this was in conformity with ECA legislation, when action would not be unduly delayed thereby, and when security would not be jeopardized or the integrity and reputation of the agencies concerned weakened by acceptance of funds or other facilities that might be made available through ECA channels.

velopment geared to the total resources, potentialities, and needs of the underdeveloped areas themselves internally and as partners in international trade. The more inclusive approach gave rise to a number of fundamental problems, three of which appear particularly significant.

The first was that of the relative emphasis to be given to agricultural and industrial development. It was one thing to discount the myth of unrealistically rapid industrialization. It was another to underestimate the possibilities of industrial growth as an evolutionary process which could be accelerated by wise planning, analysis of available resources, and the provision of essential services in transport, power, education, and health; by the fostering of rural and semirural as well as urban industries; by the encouragement of private and public savings and their channeling into the most promising productive enterprises.

Industrial and agricultural development were seen to be not so much competing areas for investment—though with limited resources choices had to be made—but complementary and interdependent parts of a total economic picture. And for agricultural development, discrimination in choosing the objectives of investment (seeds and tools, fertilizers and pest control, extension services, research, land reclamation and irrigation, etc.) was no less imperative than in the industrial sphere. Commenting on this problem in general terms, Jacob Viner has said:

> The one correct general principle, or so at least it seems to me, is to make decisions in terms of projects or related groups of projects rather than of wholesale groups of categories and to base these decisions on careful estimating of prospective long-run returns to what is to be invested, always with reference to what types of resources, material and human, are needed for different types of development and what types of resources are relatively abundant in the country in question.[24]

The second problem, to which we have already alluded, is that of land reform as an integral feature of agrarian development. In mainland China, Formosa, Korea, and the Philippines, the fundamental importance of land reform, broadly conceived, was repeatedly demonstrated. This problem, as we have seen, was many-sided, with important political as well as economic implications. Progress in dealing with it depended on circumstances peculiar to each area, on a versatile rather than a dogmatic approach, and on the measure of understanding and common purpose achieved by and between local governments and the agricultural populace.

The third problem was the degree to which emphasis should be

[24] In "America's Aims," a chapter in Hoselitz, *op. cit.*, pp. 193–194.

placed upon "social" investments—in schools, public health, housing, and other facilities. Here difficult choices had to be made by each government concerned. To what extent should it aid and supplement severely limited private initiative in each of these fields? The needs were beyond all possibility of fulfillment in any foreseeable future. An effort to meet them adequately would have drained away resources urgently needed in expanding the bases for economic growth. No hard and fixed rule could be adopted. The question was one of seeking a rational balance and of attempting to use to maximum effect the resources and techniques available.

The achievement of fundamental economic progress in each of the underdeveloped areas in which the ECA provided assistance was at best a difficult task. Within each area, it called for clear goals, educational programs to provide needed leadership and skills, social discipline, diversions of income from current consumption to capital formation, greater incentive to enterprise and to productive effort, equitable tax systems, good government. Externally, it called for a helping hand through technical assistance in many forms, and through commercial policies that would enable the underdeveloped areas—in lieu of long-continuing grant aid on a substantial scale—to sell abroad the products of their labor and thereby acquire the capacity to import essentials which they themselves could not produce.

Cooperation in African Development

The ECA faced a different situation in the European dependencies, lying principally in Africa, where the parent countries and their colonial regimes were responsible for over-all sponsorship and supervision of development. As of 1951 the colonies, protectorates, trusteeships, and mandates of countries in western Europe had in all approximately 170 million inhabitants and covered a total area of more than 9 million square miles—about three times the area of the United States. European dependencies in Africa covered roughly three-fourths of the continent. Although most of them were still in a relatively early stage of development, they were already large producers of raw materials, including many strategic items of vital importance to the free world. Western Europe was heavily dependent upon them for basic commodities, and they in turn were heavily dependent on Europe for capital and for technical aid.

As the ECA undertook to encourage more rapid development in these territories, it was confronted with a sensitive area in its relations with the European powers concerned.[25] The essential problem was how the United States could help to induce the acceleration needed for short-term gains in production and for long-term development without arousing suspicion as to its aims and objectives. Commenting on this question, Bissell, in a letter dated March 3, 1950, to Assistant Secretary of State George McGhee, said:

There is, of course, a characteristic difference in outlook between ourselves and many Europeans as regards the time required to effect economic improvement in underdeveloped areas. A recent editorial in the *London Economist*, commenting on the way in which the "possibility of bigger and better developments in Africa has caught the imagination of the State Department and of ECA officials" states: "The development of Africa, however, is not as simple as some think. The stirring political consciousness of the Africans, the lack of food and the lack of labour make it essential for the European powers to move slowly and cautiously with their plans." Curiously, these very reasons cited in support of an emphasis on gradualness are the ones apt to engender in Americans a sense of urgency. Stung by our reverses in China and the manner in which the cold war seems to be turning against us in some of the other economically backward areas, we tend to emphasize increasingly the need for greater resourcefulness and energy in considering the problems of underdeveloped territories generally.

This is, I submit, a natural, healthy difference in viewpoint which can be frankly recognized. We need, as a check against impracticality and impetuosity in our thinking with respect to Africa, the benefit of the longer experience and greater sophistication of our European friends. Perhaps they need no less—particularly among colonial office personnel—the contribution that we can make to an invigorated approach to the problems of economic advancement in colonial areas. These differences can be an asset rather than a liability unless they are accompanied and undergirded by deeper suspicions and misunderstandings.

As related in earlier chapters, the ECA's contribution to the invigoration of development in these areas (aside from the fact that regular program funds could be employed for this purpose—and were, extensively, by the French) took three forms: (1) assistance, through grants and loans, for road and railway construction, river and port improvements, reclamation and irrigation, power plants, and other projects designed to help accelerate basic economic development; (2) assistance for strategic materials development through loans—repayable in materials—and through a long-term procurement program; and (3) technical assistance, on a limited scale, for a variety of purposes,

[25] See pp. 149–150.

including resource surveys, soil analysis, transport, agricultural and health programs, and locust control. The total amounts expended under the European Recovery Program for these three purposes during 1948–1952 totaled, respectively: (1) about 61.5 million dollars; (2) the equivalent, in dollars and United States-owned local currency, of 47.6 million dollars; and (3) 1.04 million dollars.[26] The negotiations pertaining to aid for the overseas territories were conducted with the European governments concerned. The economic results achieved and the momentum given to further development have been cited in earlier chapters.

Teamwork in the Area

In the other undeveloped areas where the ECA was operating more directly, it was not always easy to make clear the aims of an aid program. As an MSA publication said, "If we explain our objectives in terms of our own short-run interests, we may be accused of exploitation; if in vague terms of altruism, we arouse suspicion of hidden motives." [27] There was need, therefore, to focus upon questions on which there could be a clear and frank recognition of mutuality of interest; emphasis could at times be placed upon broader free world interests which were none the less both local and United States interests as well.

Negotiation of bilateral agreements was a useful means of giving formal expression to mutually accepted aims, but this was only a first step. Perceptive citizens in the underdeveloped areas were well aware that significant signs of American attitudes could be found in statements made in the United States. Mission personnel at times found themselves handicapped by press accounts of impetuous or tactless public statements back home. One such statement, for example, referred to the "common dignity" of French, British, and American soldiers killed in Indochina, Malaya, and Korea, but it contained no reference to the Indochinese, Malayan, and Korean lives sacrificed; this was interpreted by some in the East as indicating that the United States was concerned only with the support of colonial regimes.

It was found to be highly important for field personnel to become aware of political and social imponderables in the country to which they were assigned. ECA personnel learned (as others had learned before them) about the ineptness of a patronizing approach on the one

[26] *Postwar Economic Aid to Africa by the US, IBRD and UN* (Dept. of State, IR Report No. 5970, 1952), Table I.

[27] *Economic Strength for the Free World*, p. 7.

hand or excessive humility on the other; about the importance of the distinction to be made between what is done *with* a people and what is done *for* them; about the need for care in the use of such terms as "native"; about the importance of not causing individuals to lose face before their associates; about the desirability of giving credit wherever possible to the local government or local leaders; about the altogether different effects of candid criticism offered in private on a basis of mutual confidence and friendship, and public condemnation; about the importance of personal friendships and the contribution to rapport of genuine interest in, and appreciation of, local history, achievements, culture, and folklore. They learned that among a proud and sensitive people the success of an undertaking might depend fully as much on *how* it was carried out as on *what* it was. For no condition of success was more indispensable than fostering local enthusiasm, initiative, and responsibility; this was a key to the development of an internal dynamic.

Undertakings developed through such an approach were far less apt to be resented as alien. They might be slow in getting under way, but they had an indispensable foundation. When a genuine meeting of minds was achieved on fundamental aims and ideas as well as on specific measures or projects, such touchy problems as probity and efficiency in government or the need for greater local initiative and responsibility could be discussed, and the best means of making progress in dealing with such questions could be inquired into without a constant risk of misunderstanding and provocation.

The Principle of Jointness

Among the methods for bringing together local initiative and leadership, on the one hand, and Western technological and administrative experience, on the other, none was found to be more rewarding, during the period of ECA operations, than that of combining local officers and American personnel into a single planning or administering unit. As indicated earlier, this was done in various ways, through joint planning units, or joint governmental commissions, or local business enterprises utilizing the services of American engineering consultants. The pioneering example was that of the Joint Commission for Rural Reconstruction (JCRR) in China and Formosa.[28] The experience of this commission was on the whole a happy one, and the results which it was able to achieve in a limited period of time and at relatively small cost made it a subject of lively interest not only within the American government but in many parts of Asia as well.

[28] See Chapter 9.

The JCRR could not have attained the degree of success that it did without a fulfillment at the outset of a number of essential conditions. There was full agreement between the American and Chinese Nationalist governments on the general character of the program to be undertaken. The sovereignty and prestige of the Chinese government were protected by local chairmanship of, and majority membership in, the commission. Both governments exercised care in selecting commissioners and staff. The group began its work in an atmosphere of mutual confidence and was equipped to approach each problem on its merits. It was not surprising, therefore, that the differences which developed within the commission—and there were many—did not in any case involve a split along purely national lines. There was no formal rule of unanimity, yet unanimity was in fact achieved through full and adequate discussion before major decisions were reached. Special group and sectional pressures within the country were effectively resisted.

At the same time, certain limitations in the joint-commission approach were frankly recognized. The JCRR could act only on matters of real interest to both countries; what was of interest to only one could not successfully be made part of a jointly administered program. The commissioners of each nation had to function within the terms laid down by their own government and to recognize corresponding restrictions placed upon the other members. With a further necessity of harmonizing ideas within the group, initial delays were inevitable.

But these limitations were more than offset by compensating advantages. Plans, procedures, and operations were evolved with the benefit of both the intimate knowledge of local conditions possessed by the Chinese and the administrative and technical experience of the Americans. The Chinese were more able to detect, at an early stage, any attempts to defraud the agency. The very fact of participation in a joint undertaking gave each government an added incentive to appoint personnel of proven ability and stature. The dual composition of the JCRR made it easier to establish appropriate relations with officials and agencies of both countries. Particularly advantageous were the sense of teamwork and the greater ease with which, under joint sponsorship, innovations could be given a real test.

Joint commissions are not immune, of course, to the dangers and pitfalls of other agencies; the JCRR was no exception. There were pressures from special interests to give undue attention to specific projects or areas, or to employ personnel without proper regard to qualifications. Pet ideas of questionable merit were sometimes urged on the commission with embarrassing vigor. Representations were made for the construction of impressive buildings and installations which, in the commission's view, should be given low priority or none at all. But early resistance to these and like pressures enhanced the commission's prestige within the country.

Many practical lessons emerged from the JCRR experience. Three, on "what to do," were stressed in a letter sent by the chairman, Dr. Chiang Mon-lin,[29] to ECA headquarters in Washington:

To learn from the farmers and the local people what they want . . . we do not know better than they what they themselves need.

To keep in mind the idea of social justice when striving for the increase of production. . . . Keep in mind first—a fair distribution.

To find a sponsoring agency to take up our work. If there is no sponsoring agency it is better not to go into a program.

Farmers' organizations, if well developed and coordinated, might well become, in Chiang's opinion, the "overall agency to carry on rural services and protect their own rights," serving as "a forceful weapon for democracy." But it was not possible, he held, to foresee with certainty the pattern of organization or program that would ultimately emerge; full allowance had to be made for diversity, for adaptions according to local needs and opportunities.

Other lessons drawn by the commissioners from the JCRR experience pointed to the importance of extended visits to rural centers for detailed observation and discussion, the need for comparative evaluations of programs in different districts, and the desirability of emphasizing projects which would receive maximum local support and which could produce appreciable results in a limited period of time.

These techniques produced no miracles, unless it be considered a miracle that, as the Nationalist government was rapidly disintegrating on the China mainland, hundreds of local projects, large and small, were initiated and carried forward with enthusiasm—projects relating to land reform, the expansion of farmers' organizations, the extension of rural credit facilities, irrigation, better use of fertilizers, seed multiplication, animal breeding, plant and animal disease control, public health, and audio-visual education.

The JCRR demonstrated that, when the essential ingredients of spontaneous local interest and sincere support by local authorities were present, much could be accomplished in a relatively short period of time without large amounts of external aid. The funds devoted to these

[29] Dated December 3, 1949.

efforts represented only a fraction of those allotted to commodity assistance and military aid. Perhaps the most fundamental lessons were that miracles are not to be expected, that "crash programs" are unsuited to the promotion of basic changes, but that with patience, a desire to understand, and determination, external aid can be effectively linked with local initiative.

The type of intergovernmental commission represented by the JCRR was not reproduced, during the ECA period, in other parts of Asia. It was approximated to a degree by the exceptionally close cooperation achieved at times between the Philippine Council for United States Aid (PhilCUSA) and the ECA mission in Manila. Working partnerships of a different type were developed through ECA-supported contracts between local governments and American engineering firms providing advisory and technical services in many fields of development. Still another type of joint effort came with the engaging and assignment of American specialists, upon request, to assist either governmental or private agencies in the training of personnel and in the planning and carrying out of many types of constructive programs and projects.

Rudiments of a Rationale

It would have been unrealistic to suppose that the ECA, operating on a year-to-year basis in a short-term emergency program affecting seven widely differing economies in Asia and more than a score of European dependencies, would evolve a matured rationale for the development of economically retarded areas. Nor did any such definitive doctrine emerge from the Point Four program or the other national and international efforts referred to earlier. But among thoughtful participants in the ECA there was a good deal of searching for answers to questions of wider import than immediate projects and programs in specific areas. It may not be amiss, in concluding this chapter, to indicate some of the lines of thinking that were beginning to take shape.

At the outset not enough was known, even by people of the area, about how they could best be helped. The factual bases for intelligent national and international policy—including quantitative data on population, health, food, agricultural and industrial production, income, trade, and finance—were still woefully deficient. Much of the expanding literature was either elementary or highly theoretical. More was needed from those who had struggled at first hand with the practical problems that must be faced in Asia, for in their experience and reflections probably lay the most important untapped resource of constructive, realistic thinking on the problem. Although no one had made a realistic assessment of accomplishments or failures in these areas, a few broad principles were beginning to gain acceptance.

Under conditions of utter poverty for the majority of the people, the basic economic need was not for relief, rehabilitation, or reconstruction, but for new development. The view that such development must be excessively costly in monetary terms was seen to be a myth. The capacity of low-level economies to assimilate and support massive investments is severely limited. Development of human capacities and skills is at once more urgent, more needed, more difficult and, in financial terms, less costly. Investments in basic services such as transport and power are essential—but not all at once and in huge amounts. Diversification in production is imperative—but not in spurts. Economic growth is manysided and, to be sustained, must be firmly rooted in the soil of the country. It must be accompanied by a parallel growth in the capabilities and self-reliance of the people and in their wholehearted support of the objectives of development. Only then can technical assistance fulfill its functions—the transfer of useful knowledge and skills, the development and inspiration of local leadership, and the creation and expansion of institutions upon which economic stability and growth must depend.

One definition of the objective of economic assistance in underdeveloped areas, by former ECA mission chief Raymond T. Moyer, is worth quoting. The aim, he said, is

to give support to the efforts of underdeveloped countries to bring about their own economic, political and social development along lines emphasizing the welfare of their people, the strengthening of free institutions, and cooperation with other nations in working toward a world at peace, up to the point where they have achieved such strength and stability as will enable them thereafter to maintain a continuous growth which they themselves can sustain, aided only by the forms of assistance normally available to other countries.[30]

As indicated above, increasing emphasis was needed upon acquiring a background of comprehensive and balanced economic analysis, based on a widening study of each area, its resources and its problems. Too much emphasis on the rapid dissemination of the benefits of a program to the poorer sectors of the population could lead—as it did in

[30] Memorandum cited. For a full discussion, see Staley, *op. cit.*, pt. I.

Greece, an underdeveloped area in Europe—to underemphasis on financial self-reliance, internal capital formation, and the solid foundations needed for future economic growth.

There was a growing awareness that the underdeveloped areas, especially in Asia, are in an age of revolution, and that the forces making for change would find outlet in one way or another. The aim of the democracies, many felt, should not be to buttress the status quo or to prevent overdue changes from taking place, but to help guide genuine revolutionary aspirations into constructive rather than destructive or retrogressive channels. It was much easier to recognize this imperative, however, than to find effective means of achieving it in the face of intrenched local or colonial interests.

It was also necessary, while recognizing the strengths and values of historic cultures and the inevitable gradualness of cultural change, not to become so enamored of existing traditions as to encourage rigidity in the social structure. There was little risk on this score, however, among the "realists," representing various types of practical competence, who by and large were charged with the conduct of ECA program abroad.

A greater danger lay in ignoring moral and spiritual aspects of social development and of relations between Western peoples and those in the underdeveloped areas. The immediate problems were largely economic and technical, but the people with whom rapport was needed were complex human beings. While the Communists were engaged in painstaking efforts to enlist the loyalties of peoples possessed of minds, ideals, passions, hopes, and prejudices, Americans, though demonstrating good will at every turn, seemed curiously oblivious at times to the desire of peoples in Asia to rise from debasement of the spirit as well as wretchedness of the body. As a consequence they sometimes conveyed, for all their generosity and technological competence, an impression that Americans were superficial and materialistic in their approach to life. In defense it should be said that the terms of reference under which our field personnel worked took into little account the psychological problems involved in American relations with the peoples of economically retarded areas. In any event, the result was at least a partial failure to provide urgently needed—and wanted—moral leadership. This was, perhaps, the greatest single weakness in the programs for assistance to underdeveloped areas during the period of ECA operations. The full explanation for this, and the means whereby it might have been overcome, remained largely unsolved problems not only for the ECA, but also for the whole group of national and international agencies concerned with the inseparably related aspects of advancement in underdeveloped areas.

Great discrimination was needed, it was found, in determining the manner and methods in which influence might best be exerted in these areas. It was most difficult to influence governments and other institutions to set their houses in better order or to adopt policies and practices urgently required in the interests of their own people. Frequently more could be accomplished by wise and skillful consultation and assistance than by economic or political pressure; when such pressure was exerted its power to get results depended in large measure on its moral basis and the extent to which that basis had been honored by the country whose representatives were attempting to influence the local situation. Whenever it appeared to an underdeveloped country that it might be viewed as a "pawn" in a larger struggle, external pressures were apt to boomerang. This was illustrated in Indonesia and Burma [31] when attempts were made under the Mutual Security Program to link economic assistance with military commitments.

Two general points remain to be made. The first is that there was little prospect that strong, mutually beneficial relations between the Western democracies and the underdeveloped areas could be effectively promoted during the next generation without a more enlightened public opinion at home. For we are here concerned with what is still a relatively new area of experience; we are still far from a position in which the problems of the underdeveloped areas are meaningful and vital to the peoples of the West as a whole. Without an informed public opinion, there is little likelihood that the democratic nations will be able to agree on broad principles and policies to be followed in the underdeveloped countries. Yet such agreement is essential as an effective counterpoise to the determined and well-organized Communist effort to subvert those countries. Herein lies one of the most important and most neglected long-range problems now confronting the free world.

Finally, only the United States has the surplus energy and resources to lead a sustained effort in the underdeveloped areas. But that leadership calls for much more than material aid and technical skills. It requires vision, perseverance, and resourcefulness in developing, testing, and retesting practical approaches.

The consensus among those who participated in ECA programs in

[31] See Chapter 10.

underdeveloped areas seems to be that American sights must be set for a long course ahead—not so much in terms of specific financial commitments as in terms of purposes and policy. We cannot escape at least partial responsibility for the results of our experimentation in accelerating economic development. Nor can we ignore, except at our peril, the need for confidence among the governments and peoples of half the world that we will not desert them capriciously when reversals occur or when the novelty of our interest wears off. If a long course can be set, after full public discussion, we can make advances in evaluating our experience; in developing long-range aims and operating policies; in enlisting top-flight personnel whose value would be greatly enhanced by continuous experience; in stimulating needed cooperation on the part of universities and organs of public opinion; and in relating our objectives in the underdeveloped areas to other aspects of international policy. Even more important, we can make steadier progress in fostering self-reliance within the areas themselves.

CHAPTER 19

Seeing Accomplishments

as Beginnings

THE introduction to this book cited some of the underlying influences that have given our age the aspect of continuing and deepening crisis, a crisis so profound that after World War II it could not be escaped by simply returning to previous norms and patterns. The great problem for the United States and for the free world generally, we said, was nothing less than how to build, amid the dangers and uncertainties of our time, a secure and workable free world system.

The Marshall Plan did not, of course, provide a solution. But it went beyond any previous international effort in its attack on the economic aspect of the problem, and the results must be regarded in retrospect as the first steps on a long road. In the face of hopelessness, bewilderment, and inertia, the Marshall Plan undertook to help restore a strong and independent Europe. Through associated efforts it undertook to bring security and opportunity to people in underdeveloped areas, especially the new independent countries of Asia. Implicit in both these endeavors was the broader and less clearly defined aim of consolidating the free world and strengthening it against Communist encroachment.

The Cold War and Long-Range Goals

The East-West rift, which was becoming increasingly evident in the spring of 1947 and which widened steadily thereafter, produced a change in the world outlook to which every major policy and every major action of the United States in the international field was thereafter inescapably related. The Marshall Plan was no exception. The new era of cooperation for which many in the West had hoped had found no place in Communist doctrine. Imbedded there instead was the dogma of inevitable conflict between the "capitalist" and the "socialist" systems, a conflict which, it was held, could be resolved only by the ultimate overthrow of the "capitalist" states. The Communist and democratic systems were thus based on antithetical world views, irreconcilable so long as the goals and methods of the former remained adamantly opposed to any fundamental reconciliation by means other than the capitulation of all who opposed its aims.

Although the Marshall Plan was directed "not against any country or doctrine" but against misery and frustration, it was nevertheless a defense against the Soviet threat. The danger from the Communist camp was by then fully recognized. The Truman Doctrine had been enunciated in March 1947. Discussing the implications of his conference with Stalin in April, Marshall said: "It was my feeling that the Soviets were doing everything possible to achieve a complete breakdown in Europe. That is, they were doing anything they could think of to create greater turbulence. The major problem was how to counter this negative Soviet policy and restore the European economy." [1]

Senator Vandenberg, in the fall of 1947, when the Marshall Plan was under consideration, sent a letter to Senator Taft in which he said: "We now apparently confront the Moscow challenge on every front and on every issue. It is a 'total war of nerves,' at least. . . . At long last we have got to have an integrated foreign policy which is just as comprehensive as that of the Soviets. I am sure that Secretary Marshall is fully alive to this fact." [2]

---

[1] Interview, Washington, February 18, 1953. Referring to the same period, former Secretary of State Acheson stated: "It seemed that, from the political point of view, we were faced with a series of enveloping movements by Russia in which the pressures were very well devised. Any one of these movements was calculated to accomplish their purpose. Success in either Greece or Turkey would bring about the collapse of the other, and then that of the whole east Mediterranean area. At the same time, there were two other movements centered in Italy and France, with efforts to gain political control in these countries; they also had the great merit for Russia that either one if successful carried success over other areas to the east. Thus the Russians had any number of chances—with almost unlimited possibilities for success in each. This became clear as one studied it and lent very great seriousness to the whole situation." Interview, Washington, October 20, 1953.

[2] Vandenberg, *op. cit.*, p. 374.

The impact of the Marshall Plan, even before the first aid shipment started, was notable. A wave of new hope swept across western Europe. Despite veiled threats and a barrage of Communist propaganda against the United States and the recovery program, the cooperating nations attacked with renewed vigor the task of recovery. This surge of effort gave hope that communism might not only be checked but even "rolled back" in western and southern Europe. Poverty appeared to be the great breeder of communism; the cure, it was thought, was to be found in alleviation of misery and in expansion of economic opportunity. In the "battle for minds," it was thought, actions would be much more effective than words. If a real resuscitation of the economies could be achieved, surely the strength of communism in western Europe would be curbed.

These expectations, though not for the most part officially expressed, were quite widely entertained. They contained, as it turned out, elements of both truth and fallacy. Communism and the fear of communism were reduced throughout most of free Europe. In France and Italy, where Communist organization was particularly strong among the working classes, its expansion was halted. But communism, though checked, was not rolled back, and its appeal was not restricted to those who were in poverty. Even among the poor, its attraction was not limited to promises of release from privation. American actions spoke loudly, but so did words skillfully employed to instill doubt and suspicion as to the motives behind the actions.

The contest between democracy and communism was not, then, a simple matter. Beginning with the hope of an economic "solution," the Americans responsible for the administration of aid found themselves drawn into an ever-widening conflict. The contest was especially crucial in France, Italy,[3] and Greece.

Since the Communists have nowhere distinguished themselves in improving the living standards of depressed classes, it is strange that they should be so effective in persuading such groups of their ability to effect such improvements and that they should have gained in the United States and elsewhere a reputation of near-invincibility in capitalizing on misery for political purposes. In any event, they were able in parts of Europe as well as in the Far East to identify themselves with the cause of economically less fortunate workers. From these large elements they drew the main strength of their parties and mass political

---

[3] One survey, for example, indicated that among the most depressed farm laborers in southern Italy, about 34 percent thought that only the Communists could help them raise their standard of living.

followings. In France and Italy they succeeded in gaining a large measure of control over organized labor. The economic improvement which the recovery program brought to western and southern Europe undercut Communist strength most effectively where workers participated most directly in the benefits or where, as in west Germany and Austria, they were sufficiently familiar with the real "benefits" of Communist rule not to be deceived by promises of "liberation." Neither in France nor Italy did these conditions apply among large sectors of the working populace.

If the Communists were unable to "deliver the goods," where did their strength lie among working groups? Chiefly in their propaganda work and in their ability to make Communist ideology and organization a vehicle of protest against all manner of grievances. Their propaganda was related principally to economic, political, and social issues within the country concerned, and to the alleged motives and consequences of American aid and American policies generally. The inception of the recovery program was followed by a wave of good feeling toward the United States throughout much of Europe. But this sentiment was less marked in some areas than others, and it appears to have declined among many European groups during the course of the recovery effort. There is no way of measuring the extent to which Communist "information" was responsible for this change, but many witnesses assert that it was a subtle and potent factor. A survey of French opinion conducted early in the program indicated that approximately 70 percent of the people who had heard of the Marshall Plan considered that it was bad for them.[4]

---

[4] Said a knowledgeable French commentator (not for attribution) in 1952: "I am sure that many French people do an injustice to Americans as regards their goals. For Americans, free enterprise carries a connotation of economic and social progress. In France we don't have such great confidence in capitalism. The great problem here is the social problem. Many people who are not Communists are not satisfied. Business leaders and others don't want a rise of labor. And among labor groups, Americans are widely considered as supporters of the bourgeoisie. The American people don't understand quite well the social problem in Europe. There is a widespread impression here that U.S. aid has been helping the rich. In France there has been virtually no progress in the more equitable distribution of income. The money of the Marshall Plan has led, it appears, to greater profits for the wealthy. This is a feeling of the workers—a very strong feeling."

"Since the war," he continued, "labor legislation in France still exists, but there has been no progress. The beginning of the Marshall Plan coincided with the strengthening of the Right. So workers blamed the U.S. They think the U.S. has made the government turn more and more to the right. They don't realize the social progress that has been achieved in the United States. The U.S. is thought of as pure capitalism, with American financial interests wanting to dominate."

As one shrewd observer has pointed out, "Struggles fought in the field of economics require, in order to be truly won, a transmutation of their economic results into political results; the contest engaged in may be economic, but the points measuring success or failure are tallied on a political 'computing machine.'" [5]

The experience, looked at as a whole, made it clear that the East-West struggle was a total struggle, that weakness on any one front might affect adversely any or all of the others, that democratic strategy would have to gain and hold the initiative on all fronts, and that democratic efforts should be planned and developed with imagination, thoroughness, and a determination strong enough to be maintained over an indefinite number of years ahead. Only then could the democratic faith and hard-earned freedoms of recent centuries give ground for hope that the East-West chasm might ultimately be bridged without loss of security, liberty, and dignity for men of good will.

The Broader View

The threat of communism, however, as Henry L. Stimson emphasized, is but one of the factors in the crisis of our time.

Our central task in dealing with the Kremlin is to demonstrate beyond the possibility of misunderstanding that freedom and prosperity, hand in hand, can be stably sustained in the western democratic world. This would be our greatest task even if no Soviet problem existed. . . . I do not mean to belittle the Communist challenge. I only mean that the essential question is one which we should have to answer if there were not a Communist alive. Can we make freedom and prosperity real in the present world? [6]

The Marshall Plan was, in a sense, a collective response to this question. The central aim of these concluding pages is to restate briefly some of the major contributions and limitations of the Marshall Plan enterprise, to indicate some of the problems that it left unsolved, and to suggest what seem, at this writing, to have been some of the more significant insights gained from this unique episode in American and world history.

Toward a Free, Self-reliant Europe

Any assessment of the results of the Marshall Plan in Europe will hinge upon the questions that are asked and the criteria applied.

[5] A. Rossi, "Soviet Communist Pressures on Western Europe" in *The Threat of Soviet Imperialism,* ed. by C. Grove Haines (Johns Hopkins Press, Baltimore, 1954), p. 236.

[6] *Foreign Affairs,* October 1947, pp. 9–10.

Did the European Recovery Program, for example, actually stave off a collapse of western and southern Europe? Were economic and political conditions so threatening that without such a program the continent would have been exposed, country by country, to the fate of the satellites to the east? The answer to these questions, by many competent observers, is yes. Unable to pay for the food and materials from abroad on which their economies depended, Europeans in the absence of the ERP or its equivalent would certainly have been plunged into deepening chaos and vulnerability. Forestalling that result was a *preventive* accomplishment of incalculable significance, one that is too easily forgotten.

Did the recovery program make possible the completion of postwar reconstruction, repairing the enormous damage of the war years and bringing economic activity back to prewar levels or better? The answer, again, is yes—with some qualifications. Deep physical and psychological scars remained. Some parts of the economy remained depressed. Recovery in some countries was less than in others. Many problems persisted. But in comparison with the rate of reconstruction after World War I, Europe scored a phenomenal success. And the results, "although they would have been inconceivable without Marshall Aid," were also "a sure indication of the vitality with which Western Europe itself . . . faced its economic problems." [7]

Industrial production rose to more than 35 percent above prewar levels, with extensive new investment and striking gains in many lines. Agricultural output climbed to more than 10 percent above prewar, balancing an equivalent rise in population. Europe's gross national product climbed in three years to a new plateau, with a gain equivalent to more than 30 billion dollars at 1949 prices. This was a rise in the annual level of production several times as great as the average annual cost of the Marshall Plan over the same period. Severe inflationary pressures were generally brought under control, and confidence in currencies was restored. The volume of trade between OEEC countries expanded some 70 percent. Between 1947 and 1950 the dollar gap for western Europe and its associated monetary areas was reduced by more than 7 billion dollars, though it rose again by more than a billion in 1951. [8] In human terms, as Hoffman pointed out, Europeans were eating, they had jobs, they were working, and working hard. Gaitskell called it "a great recovery." Marshall described it as "a near miracle." What was important, as Marjolin observed, was what Europe did with the eco-

[7] OEEC, *Europe: The Way Ahead*, p. 15; see also Ellis, *op. cit.*, p. 476.
[8] See OEEC, *Economic Progress and Problems*, pp. 14–16.

nomic assistance given and how quickly that assistance could be reduced without stopping economic progress.[9]

Reconstruction was essentially, however, a continuation and extension of the rehabilitation effort begun soon after the war ended. Was this the full measure of Europe's attainment under the ERP? Or did the recovery program also achieve its larger aim of bringing western Europe to the stage where it could be self-supporting as "a healthy economy independent of extraordinary outside assistance?"[10] To this question, the answer must be a qualified no.

There was little ground for complacency. While recovery gains were most impressive, they were, in a long perspective, the easier gains. In 1951–1952 próduction leveled off, at least temporarily. Private consumption was still only a little above prewar. Imports were held down for lack of adequate exports. Europe's economies were straining, with little slack left for a prolonged defense effort. Economic integration within Europe still had far to go. Social inertias were still pervasive, and incentives to further change and adjustment throughout the economic system were not strong. The continent was far more healthy than in 1948, but it had not yet acquired the dynamism needed for accelerated growth independent of external aid.

The recovery program had, in a word, contributed to an unprecedented surge in economic activity without breaking down some of the longer-range influences making for economic sluggishness. Western Europe had not regained the economic vitality it had enjoyed for nearly a century before World War I. Alongside the expanding economies of the United States, Canada, and Russia, most of the continent remained competitively in a weak position.

The French economy, in 1952, was far from self-sustaining; it was not in balance with other European countries or with the United States; added to internal burdens was the costly, protracted war in Indochina. Politically, the country was divided and unstable. Underlying both economic and political stresses were weaknesses in the social fabric, marked by maldistribution of income, regressive taxation, inadequate housing, insufficient production of consumer goods, and the lack of a strong, healthy free labor movement. Italy was still handicapped by population pressure, inadequate internal resources, chronic unemployment, depressed sectors in the economy, and, like France, by a splintering of political parties and social weaknesses of a structural character.

[9] Robert Marjolin, *op. cit.*, p. 8.
[10] Public Law 472, 80th Congress, 2d Session (1948), Sec. 102.

Germany had experienced a remarkable economic revival but, with the population enlarged by ten million refugees from the east, still suffered from unemployment and depressed wages. Political harmony was difficult to achieve amid seemingly irreconcilable desires for national reunification, on the one hand, and collective security from Russian aggression, on the other.

The European picture as a whole was much more hopeful, however, than it had seemed in 1947. The position of other countries was greatly strengthened. Recovery had brought new confidence. Productivity was taking root. Experience had shown that, given sufficient strong common interests and a well-conceived plan, problems of economic organization and cooperation were not beyond reach. Through the OEEC the possibilities of joint effort had been convincingly demonstrated. And a strong cooperative defense system was emerging.

The advances made within each nation and in cooperation among them were basically European accomplishments. American support was crucial, particularly in the earlier stages; but the recovery program was not carried out for Europe by the United States, nor was it the product of a great charity. Rooted firmly in conceptions of mutual interest, self-help, and voluntary cooperation, it was primarily, as Secretary Marshall had emphasized at the outset that it should be, "the business of the Europeans." But for their own determined efforts it would have failed utterly. When initiative was weak, efforts tended to founder; when it was lacking, efforts were impotent. The function of American aid was not only to provide encouragement, tangible support, and active participation in programing, but also to afford time within which European initiative could be mobilized. By the middle of 1952 great strides had been taken with the recovery and security programs, but a long, difficult road had yet to be traversed before western Europe could assume its full potential role in the world community.

Toward a New Era for Retarded Areas

The efforts associated with the Marshall Plan to assist in the advancement of economically retarded areas commenced some months before President Truman's announcement, in the fourth point of his Inaugural Address of January 1949, of a "bold new plan" for technical help to underdeveloped areas.[11] The Foreign Assistance Act of 1948

[11] See Chapters 7, 9, and 10.

encompassed the overseas dependencies of the European participating countries. The China Aid Act, a part of the same over-all legislation, was later extended to cover economic and technical aid to the countries of southeast Asia, the Philippines, and Korea.

Assistance to the European dependencies, comprising roughly three-fourths of Africa plus a few territories in the Far East and the Western Hemisphere, was derived from regular program funds (especially in the case of France) and from special funds set up for economic development, strategic materials production and procurement, and technical aid. The equipment and materials financed from these sources helped carry out accelerated investment programs, especially in the territories controlled by France, the United Kingdom, and Belgium. All of the aid provided was at the request of, or with the approval of, the European governments directly concerned. There was little disposition on the part of those governments, especially France and Portugal, to solicit or welcome on-the-ground participation by American technicians. And there was only a bare start toward realization of the possibilities of fruitful cooperation among the European countries concerned through joint planning of transport, power, and other territorial projects on a regional basis.

Exports from the overseas territories to western Europe rose from approximately 260 million dollars in value monthly during 1948 to an average well in excess of 350 million in 1951; in the latter year, commodities valued at more than 90 million dollars a month were also exported to the United States. Industrial recovery in Europe and increased demands arising from defense programs were major factors in these increases, as were the investments in production and transport facilities. A more important effect of the investment programs, however, was in the foundations that were laid for continuing economic development.

While assistance to the dependent overseas territories was largely an adjunct of, and subordinate to, the European recovery and defense support programs, the efforts made to assist the countries of eastern Asia and the southwest Pacific involved deeper American participation. Although backed by humanitarian impulses, they were, primarily, politically motivated. The ECA program in China, begun in 1948, was a product of growing American concern and bafflement over the spread of Communist influence and power there. Described as a means of helping to arrest the rate of economic deterioration, it was, in plainer language, part of an eleventh-hour attempt to save China—or at least a part of China—from absorption into the Communist world. The attempt failed, except for Formosa and adjacent islands. But in contrast with earlier aid programs in China, an attempt was made to develop a realistic approach to the deep-seated problem of agrarian reform. The direction of the effort and what was learned from it that could be applied elsewhere than in continental China seem far more important in retrospect than the results achieved on the mainland.

When it became increasingly apparent that the China mainland was going Communist, anxiety with respect to the rest of eastern Asia mounted. Through a series of Congressional acts provision was made for economic and technical assistance to Korea, the Philippines, Indochina, Thailand, Burma, and Indonesia, as well as Formosa. Although Communist infiltration and propaganda had gained a head start in most of these areas, military action did not appear to be imminent except in Indochina and possibly in Korea. There was yet time in which to demonstrate the genuineness of American good will and to develop forms of assistance that would help new, inexperienced moderate governments to win the confidence and support of their peoples.

The aid programs in these areas were initiated in 1949 or 1950. Limitations upon what could be achieved by 1952 were imposed by a legacy of ancient and modern problems in each area. What was accomplished—after the Communist conquest of the China mainland—may perhaps best be characterized as a holding action accompanied by efforts to stimulate and support a broadening of the bases of production and a progressive development of institutions and services responsible and responsive to the needs of the people. Some success was achieved—how much cannot be measured—in convincing the peoples of the area, outside the China mainland, that United States aid in meeting their problems, while in the American interest and that of all free nations, was untarnished by imperialistic designs. Communist propaganda taught otherwise, however, and there was a widespread desire, especially in southeast Asia, to keep out of the cross-fire of rivalry and possible conflict between the United States and the USSR.

The outlook was still far from certain. Whether unremitting Communist maneuvers—especially in Indochina, Burma, Thailand, and Indonesia—would be matched by a sufficient counterweight of resourceful efforts and whether the tide of Communist expansion would, as a result, be turned in Asia remained unanswered questions as the Marshall Plan period drew to a close.

Ends and Beginnings

It would be possible, in deference to sentiment and with considerable validity, to close this account with a peroration hailing the Marshall Plan undertaking as one of the great success stories of all time. It furnished a counterpoise to the forces of aggression. In so doing, it probably forestalled a collapse of western Europe and the Mediterranean area and their unwilling incorporation into the orbit of world communism. It afforded without stint the critical margin of resources and energy needed to make possible an amazingly rapid recuperation of the European economy. Its affiliated programs in the Far East ameliorated desperate conditions there and brought fresh hope to millions. It demonstrated, in unprecedented fashion, the possibility of organizing and carrying out vast international endeavors—not for destruction, but for construction and peace. Belying in performance the charge of imperialism, it gave the United States a new stature in the world as a leader to be trusted. And it set in train a succession of promising developments. Could more be asked of a single enterprise?

Why not stop, then, at this point? Because to do so would be to distort the quality of the Marshall Plan as actually administered and to miss its deeper meaning.

From beginning to end, it was an altogether human struggle against odds, with shortcomings as well as successes. It was limited in concept and its goals were in part illusory. After three years the vision with which it commenced had grown dimmer. Europe's dollar balance was still precarious. There was no sense of finality, of ultimate cure. Some problems had been overcome, but others remained, and new ones were added as free nations were compelled to gird themselves against a vast military threat.

Should we swing then from elation to disillusionment and conclude that it was, after all, of little avail? That having failed to solve everything, it solved nothing?

A more reasonable view is that the more immediate objectives of the Marshall Plan, such as regaining prewar levels of production and trade in Europe, were largely achieved, more quickly and at less cost than anticipated; that important new ground was broken in helping to deal with the intractable problems of economically retarded areas; and that larger aims, such as eliminating trade barriers and freeing Europe from dependence upon external assistance, were partially realized.

The Marshall Plan was a phase, as was the Mutual Security Program which followed, in American acceptance of leadership in the free world.

It induced an historic forward thrust in international understanding and cooperative effort. It was a movement, the most important of the earlier postwar years, toward greater economic strength and political solidarity among free peoples. Without it, or a comparable program, our situation would be infinitely worse than it is today. But it was only a part of the sustained effort needed before the free world could hope to break out of the tangled forest of problems surrounding it.

Elation or disillusionment over each new triumph or setback are luxuries—or escapes—that can be ill afforded. If the Marshall Plan experience is any guide, no objective attained or partially attained can safely be regarded as a resting point. It must be looked upon rather as a starting point for further effort.

The Unfinished Task

When the Marshall Plan came to an end organizationally, communism had been checked at least temporarily in Europe, but it had not been dissipated as a political and military force. In Asia, its Korean assault had been halted; its guerrilla bands in the Philippines and Malaya had been thwarted; but it was still on the march in Indochina and its propaganda was everywhere. The Communist effort to confuse, divide, and weaken the free world continued unabated and contributed its quota to increasing frictions. As the cold war continued, enormous military power on both sides mounted at a rate difficult for the layman to comprehend. There was no sign of abatement in the East-West struggle.

This background gave greater urgency to the problems remaining unsolved when the Marshall Plan ended. The military threat posed by the Soviet bloc was no more real than the peril that the Communist conspiracy might succeed in promoting fatal divisions in the rest of the world, capitalizing in every way it could on current differences as well as "the economic and social ills of centuries." This meant that even as the West built up its defenses it could only at mortal risk abandon the long-range task of constructing an international system so productive of justice and opportunity that it could withstand indefinitely both internal strains and the adamant, infinitely patient efforts of the Communist conspirators to divide and conquer.[12]

This was the unfinished task which confronted the free peoples of

---

[12] For a provocative study of this broad problem, see *The Political Economy of American Foreign Policy: Its Concepts, Strategy and Limits,* Report of a Study Group sponsored by the Woodrow Wilson Foundation & the National Planning Assn. (Henry Holt, New York, 1955).

the earth in 1952. Only the United States possessed the reserves of strength necessary for leadership. It had proven its capacity as the foremost power of the Grand Alliance of 1941–1945. It had projected and supported immense programs for postwar relief and reconstruction, culminating in the Marshall Plan. It had entered upon a program of technical and other assistance to underdeveloped areas around the globe. These were undertakings which drew upon the patriotism of the American people, their capacity for organization and emergency action, their generous impulses and advanced technical skills. But strength is not wisdom. Did the American people also possess other requisites of effective leadership for the longer and, in many ways, more difficult task that now confronted them—requisites of knowledge, sensitivity to other peoples' views and feelings, vision, steadfastness of purpose, discipline, mature judgment? In a hundred forms, this basic question was being asked and discussed by anxious people in other lands.

In Europe, regaining its vitality, there was, as one writer has remarked, all the irritability of the convalescent. Each country still faced its own array of problems. The continental economy was still out of balance with that of the United States, still not strong enough to make its way and defend itself without help. Its dependent territories in Africa and elsewhere were in sore need of economic advancement, and their further development was of crucial importance to Europe. In some of these areas, and in the Middle East, there were deep stirrings of discontent. The situation in eastern Asia remained ominous. Postwar programs there had brought appreciable gains in health, in economic activity, and in the capacities of local governments. But most of the deeper problems remained: general poverty, social rigidities and unrest, population pressure, shortage of leaders and technicians, passionate nationalism unmatched by political experience, and, what proved to be especially portentous, the specter of communism. With China, long regarded as the balance wheel of Asia, in the Communist camp, the outlook was fraught with uncertainties and danger.

A Classic Campaign

The Marshall Plan was launched under circumstances no less forbidding. Its effectiveness in enabling many nations to veer away from the chasms of bankruptcy and subversion has been widely acclaimed. It has not been so generally recognized, perhaps, as the most telling single effort of the postwar years in behalf of a stable, advancing free world system. As such, it might be regarded as a kind of classic campaign.

The fundamental difficulty in attempting to derive useful "lessons" from an experience like that of the Marshall Plan is that methods found suitable under one set of conditions may not be so under another, and principles which appear to have wide or even universal validity may require modification or change in other settings. Realizing that whatever is said must be subject to repeated testing and continuous refinement, let us review briefly what, in the eyes of a variety of acute observers, the Marshall Plan can teach that is of most general relevance for the future.

1. The Plan began with an idea. It was an idea which satisfied a widely felt yearning and fired the imagination and hopes of millions. Its conception and projection was a creative event. Yet the uniqueness of the concept was less extraordinary than its historic timing, the way in which it entered into and became a part of existing currents of thought and feeling. History is not liberally dotted with ideas, like that of the Marshall Plan, leading to wholehearted, energetic cooperation across political boundaries. To usher in a new era in relations between peoples—an era in which the energies released in cooperative enterprises eventually outstrip those dedicated to defense or destruction —not one or two ideas but a whole sequence of new concepts is needed. One of the lessons of the Marshall Plan appears to be that for an idea to be effective in the international sphere, as has been true in the industrial sphere, it must be addressed to a situation that is ripe for it.

2. The idea behind the Marshall Plan was translated into a responsible proposal and a statement of broad purpose. This was an act of statesmanship, carefully conceived yet carrying with it a large element of calculated risk. No one could predict with assurance the reaction which it would meet at home or the response abroad. Marshall's words at Cambridge will bear repeating:

It is logical that the United States should do whatever it is able to do to assist in the return of normal economic health in the world, without which there can be no political stability and no assured peace. Our policy is directed not against any country or doctrine but against hunger, poverty, desperation, and chaos. Its purpose should be the revival of a working economy in the world so as to permit the emergence of political and social conditions in which free institutions can exist. . . . Before the United States can proceed much further, . . . there must be some agreement among the countries of Europe as to the requirements of the situation and the part those countries themselves will take in order to give proper effect to whatever action might be under-

taken by this Government. . . . The initiative, I think, must come from
Europe. . . . The program should be a joint one, agreed to by a number, if
not all, European nations. . . . With foresight, and a willingness on the part
of our people to face up to the vast responsibility which history has clearly
placed upon our country, the difficulties I have outlined can and will be overcome.

The "electric effect" of Secretary Marshall's "few sentences in a quiet
sequence" [13] was produced not only because they were a brave response
to a critical situation, but also because they proposed a course which
appealed profoundly to the dignity, self-respect, and initiative of Europeans, to the realism as well as the responsibility and idealism of Ameri-
icans who were increasingly skeptical of indefinitely continued relief,
and to common hopes for peace. Though the goal envisaged—a cure
rather than a palliative—proved not to be wholly attainable through
an emergency program, it gave the proposal a unifying objective.

3. The proposal, after exhaustive preparation, was translated into a
plan of action. The outlines of the plan were drawn up and agreed to
on the ground—in Europe; the background and specific proposals relating to aid and its use were examined with painstaking care in the
United States. On both sides exceptionally able administrators, legislators, and technicians were engaged; their services were the more needed
since the problem faced was extraordinarily complex and in many ways
new. More attention was focused on the problem itself than on anticipated political pressures in the United States, although the latter were
not ignored. When the plan was presented to the United States legis-
lature for indorsement, Senator Vandenberg was able to say: "It is the
final product of 8 months of more intensive study by more devoted
minds that I have ever known to concentrate upon any one objective
in all my 20 years in Congress." [14] Even though the concepts upon
which the plan was based proved to be inadequate in several respects,
particularly in underestimating the dimensions of the problem, a strong
foundation was laid for the immense cooperative effort that followed.

4. Exceptionally wide public discussion of the proposal took place
while the analytical work was in progress. Unlike other "great debates"
of the period, which were largely concerned with past disasters, that
over the Marshall Plan concerned a constructive enterprise on which
the American people were being summoned to embark and for which, if
they did so, they would pay the bill.

[13] Vandenberg in *Congressional Record*, March 1, 1948.   [14] *Ibid.*

The outcome of public debate was overwhelming popular support which ensured bipartisan backing in Congress and a strong impetus for the program when it was launched. Popular support reflected growing concern with the Soviet menace, previous lessons on the futility of isolationism in a time of danger, historic ties in Europe, economic interests, and humanitarian urges. But there was more. The issue was taken to the people by leaders of both parties and by influential citizens, publications, and organizations across the country. Given a constructive goal for which to work, private organizations, upon whose initiative democratic decision so often depends, went into action. Once the issues were made clear, the opposition, with no effective alternative to offer, weakened steadily.

This wide support, however, was not adequately sustained across the four-year span, despite vigorous efforts exerted through a public information program. The big story tended to become blurred. Yet for those working on the program there was a big story—of European initiative and cooperation, of growing awareness as to what was needed to achieve economic strength in Europe and progress in retarded areas, of America's role in trying to bring a sick world back to health, and of the bearing of the Marshall Plan on the East-West struggle. A gulf tended to develop between the technicians and the American people. Those who were best equipped to help bridge it were overburdened with administrative and legislative responsibilities. Public debate tended to center more and more on the case for and against Congressional appropriations. The reduced breadth of outlook became an increasingly severe handicap.

5. Each participating government and the United States made real commitments before the program was launched. The Plan was not initiated in halfhearted spirit of seeking for cheap solutions. The obligations of the cooperating countries were assumed with full awareness of the responsibilities entailed under the concept of self-help and mutual cooperation. Supporting legislation by the United States Congress was broad and flexible; the scope of the undertaking envisaged was liberal. It recognized the ultimate economy of an adequate effort.

This point, however, should not be overstated. A four-year program was precedent-breaking; it made possible a far more basic approach to the problem of European recovery than would otherwise have been feasible. But it was not a commitment to see a specified job througth to completion. The concept of recovery was not defined nor was there a clear delineation of other goals. Authorizations and appropriations were on a year-to-year basis, and a deviation from this would have meant a further break with precedent. With appropriations finally acted upon weeks or even months after the beginning of a fiscal year, long-range planning by the participating governments was at best uncertain. The American commitment, in short, entailed massive support for a four-year emergency program, with appropriations on an annual basis. It did not envisage the follow-through that might be needed to establish a sound balance between the American and European economies or to promote and ensure the effective functioning of a more closely integrated Atlantic community. It did not obligate the American government to participate in the liberalization of trade and payments that it was urging upon the governments of western and southern Europe.

But the principle of interdependence was never before more clearly recognized or supported in time of peace. The Plan was a recognition that a parochial outlook was inconsistent with the enlarged role and responsibilities of the United States.

6. The successes achieved under the Marshall Plan must be ascribed in significant measure to the choice of men, in Europe and America, to direct and administer the program. One of the abler staff members in the ECA testified that he had joined the agency believing that the role of personalities in a governmental organization was of secondary importance, but that his own experience had convinced him that this was a wholly mistaken view. Those selected for top administrative posts and for staff responsibilities in the recovery program were for the most part men of imagination and character, with high competence in their respective spheres and exceptional dedication to their tasks. Partly, no doubt, because the enterprise was one in which early results were imperative and flexibility essential, younger personnel of talent and judgment were given unusual scope. Working procedures were such that men and women down the line had opportunity to make their contributions to policy formation and the conduct of major operations, and this was a notable factor in morale. According to a number of Europeans consulted, the general quality of American personnel in ECA missions abroad provided one of the most effective answers to Communist propaganda.

7. The central organizations established—the ECA and the OEEC—were specifically adapted to the purposes of the Plan. The ECA was given unusual latitude in carrying out its responsibilities. Coordination between it and other branches of the United States government was not complete, and the demarcation of responsibilities between its central

headquarters in Washington and the regional headquarters in Paris left something to be desired. But the agency's management, policy direction, initiative, morale, and over-all performance were of a high order. The main work was not crippled by administrative shortcomings. Many useful innovations were introduced and new techniques tested.

The OEEC proceeded with understandable caution. With distinguished delegation leaderships, an extraordinarily unified spirit and outstanding economic policy talent, it weathered difficult problems and issues and built, without fanfare, a solid structure of European cooperation. Its pioneering efforts gave the first strong lead in the direction of European integration.

8. Full consultation between the ECA and the participating governments and among those governments through the OEEC was basic. The effort to ensure, as far as possible, a genuine meeting of minds before policy decisions were reached paved the way for the degree of effective cooperation achieved and, incidentally, was a real factor in the prestige of the United States abroad. "Perhaps the enduring lesson of the recovery program, the health-bringing feature," according to one thoughtful ECA participant, "is to be found in the getting together that occurred." He was speaking not only of top-level consultations, but also of day-to-day collaboration among technicians which produced understanding and agreement which never could have been attained through formal negotiations alone.

9. Constant inquiry led to an evolution in the conception of the task and in the tools of analysis. By 1950–1951 the approaches developed in 1948 seemed rudimentary. In individual countries there was a progression from rough balance-of-payments analyses (supplemented by relatively uncoordinated consideration of commodity requirements for different sectors of the economy) to more sophisticated approaches. Especially noteworthy was the development of national accounts analyses. An even more striking evolution occurred in thinking and action on European integration as, step by step, means of practical, attainable cooperation were discovered and explored.

A simultaneous development took place in thinking with respect to economically retarded areas. Experience showed that the best-conceived projects were unlikely to take root without time-consuming consultation and adaptation to local attitudes and interests. To reach a genuine —as contrasted with a polite—meeting of minds was more difficult in Asia than in Europe, but it was no less indispensable. Persistent effort was needed to comprehend local outlooks and aspirations more fully and to plan together the types of projects capable of enlisting maximum enthusiasm and support. Aid programs involving types of knowledge and skill in which the local area was deficient were sometimes found to be more effective if temporary joint organizations could be developed that would give scope and prestige to local leadership while making use of American administrative and technical assistance. This provided a middle course between an aloof and ineffectual advisory relationship, at one extreme, and an attempt, at the other, to assume too large a measure of direct responsibility.

The "principle of jointness" came to be increasingly stressed in connection with efforts to help relatively inexperienced governments to develop modern, efficient institutions and services.

10. The Marshall Plan demonstrated that the free nations can seize the initiative in the East-West struggle if goals are set which exert a wide and potent appeal and if enough intelligence, energy, and resources are devoted to the attainment of those goals. But it also demonstrated that when such purposes become weak or obscure, difficulties mount and the initiative may pass into Communist hands again. Great spurts of effort, like that of the European Recovery Program, may accomplish great results. But if continuity is impaired by sudden changes of emphasis and direction, gains achieved at heavy cost may be sacrificed. It was repeatedly found during the years 1948–1952 that ground lost on any front in the total struggle may imperil the free world's position on the others.

It was when the aims of the Marshall Plan enterprise were most constructive, farsighted, and challenging that the effort was most infused with the dynamic spirit once expressed by Senator Vandenberg in these words: "We are joined together in a crusade for enduring peace. We grip friendly hands across the sea. We have no enemies unless aggressors nominate themselves as such. Our common cause is human rights, fundamental liberties and a free world of free men." [15]

[15] *Private Papers*, pp. xxi–xxii.

Index